Also by Ivor Noël Hume

HERE LIES VIRGINIA

1775

Another Part of the Field

1775

Another Part of the Field

IVOR NOËL HUME

Alfred A. Knopf / NEW YORK

1966

TO THE MEMORY OF

CAPTAIN

CHARLES FORDYCE

A N D

His Brother Officers & Men

O F   T H E

FOURTEENTH REGIMENT

WHO FELL AT THE

BATTLE OF GREAT BRIDGE

DECEMBER 9, 1775

PREFACE

As AN Englishman living and working in the United States I have frequently asked myself where my ultimate loyalties are due: to Virginia my home, or to the England of my birth. It was out of that persisting enigma that the idea for this book emerged.

Like the Virginia colonists of the eighteenth century, I wait eagerly for the belated arrival of English newspapers; I read English magazines and books, import English food and furniture and, more important, have an English wife. Together we look homeward to English families and English friends—who frequently remind us that England is not what it used to be. Every two or three years we go back, and we find that they are right. It is not; at least not as we think we remember it. While there, we soon find ourselves talking of coming home again, home to Virginia. In short, we have become that same hybrid which caused so much trouble in the 1770's: English Americans, or, more correctly, English Virginians. Fortunately this divided allegiance is not now incompatible, and I can but hope that it will never be challenged.

In March of 1775 Patrick Henry declared: "I know no way of judging of the future but by the past." That thought has been repeated down through the years in innumerable forms; but it seemed to me that if Henry thought that history could point the way for him in 1775, then that year might offer some guidance for us as we approach 1975. The study of it has not, unfortunately, solved my own problem of divided loyalty. The dilemma

was the same, but it was no more easily resolved then than it can
be now. It was, and still is, a very personal and private struggle,
the length of whose scars are not to be measured by the
yardstick of history.

Families with roots generations deep in American soil could
more readily defend the land on which they had been raised than
lose it in support of a mother country many had never seen or a
government whose policies they opposed. Similarly there were
great numbers of first-generation immigrants who had come
with nothing and had left nothing behind; now they had
property of their own, and naturally they would favor the place
of their success. On the other hand, there were those who
maintained strong family or business ties with England, and
such people would be more likely to oppose any breach—unless
they also had debts which a war might absolve. Most historians
are agreed that at the outbreak of the Revolution one third of the
colonists openly favored it, one third less openly opposed it, and
the remainder simply wanted to be left alone. One might add, of
course, that the first group contrived (as do all dissenters) to
make the most noise and to attract the greatest public attention,
and as a result they may have given the impression of being
more numerous than they actually were, at least in the months
before the lines were finally drawn.

I think it fair to claim that the role of the Southern colonies
in the Revolution has been minimized by the majority of
historians. It is true that the heaviest thunder emanated from
the North, but we must not forget that the outcome of the war
might have been very different if the South had not played its
part. Virginia was the largest of the thirteen colonies, and it also
possessed the largest population; at the same time, its principal
towns were little more than villages, and it possessed no major
industries. Its economy was based on the plantations and their
tobacco crops, and as that tobacco was marketed in England the
colony's ties with her were strong, forged in gold, silver, and
copper.

The militancy of Massachusetts Bay and its neighbors in

such exploits as the burning of the *Gaspee* and the rather childish handling of the Boston tea affair had brought the wrath of the Crown down upon their allegedly surprised heads. Consequently the New England colonies were subjected to the hated Coercive Acts and the indignity of British troops patrolling their streets and being quartered in their homes. The South, on the other hand, had committed no unpardonable excesses, was subjected to none of the punitive laws—and there was not an oppressive redcoat in sight. Yet it was Virginia that would provide the Revolution's military leader, as well as some of its most eloquent voices. Indeed, it was John Adams who told Thomas Jefferson, "You are a Virginian, and a Virginian ought to be at the head of this business." In the colony's British governor, Lord Dunmore, General Washington saw the makings of "the most formidable enemy America has." Ultimately, of course, it would be in Virginia that the final battle would be fought and won.

This book is not a history, for the historian must evaluate the period he is studying in the context of what happened before and after. But I have created nothing more than the chronicle of a year. My characters are those who made news in 1775; I have laureated no heroes and condemned no villains. I dare to hope that my own rather unusual and special relationship with Virginia has enabled me to look at both sides without bias. To claim that I have not injected my own point of view would be ridiculous. In emphasizing this event, minimizing that, or ignoring the other, one's own interests and attitudes must show through. Nevertheless, my purpose has been nothing more sinister than to include only that which I think you may find interesting.

On July 27, 1775, an elderly Virginia planter, Colonel Landon Carter grumbled into his diary saying: "It is amongst the oddities in Authors whether travellers Essayists or Naturalists, they all write as if every reader knew beforehand what they were writing of as well as themselves; for this reason in hardly any one instance do they give any Particulars." Nevertheless, regardless of this apt admonition, I have assumed that my readers will already know enough about the American Revolution to make it unnecessary to go back over the major events that led up to 1775. In any case, more than half of the happenings that are discussed contributed nothing to the mainstream of '75; they occurred and were forgotten almost at once. They created passing pleasures, satisfactions, fears, distresses, to the persons immediately involved, as well as a degree of titillation to those who read about them in the papers. They were simply scraps of life—and that is what the book is all about. To corset it around with too many of the bones of political history would force it into a most unnatural posture.

It is unfortunate that complicated issues cannot be simplified without the truth incurring some damage along the way, and I know that I have chipped it a little myself in my use of such terms as "patriot" and "loyalist." I must explain therefore that these were, and still are, simply convenient labels. When the year 1775 began it was possible to be both a patriot and a loyalist, a patriot to the cause of American rights and loyal to the King at the same time; but even at its end and when the two had become incompatible, many colonists were still unable to make up their minds as to which they were. Nevertheless, for the sake of brevity, I have used the term "patriot" to describe any colonist who opposed the policies of the British government and "loyalist" to mean any who supported it.

In American eyes loyalists were synonymous with "Tories" on the grounds that Lord North's administration was considered to be Tory. But here again the word was merely a label. The Tory Party, as it had existed in the reign of Queen Anne, did so no longer; Britain did not have a neat, two-party system of Whigs and Tories. On the contrary, government supporters in the House of Commons were generally drawn from a coalition of three groups: the placemen whose careers rested on court and administration favors, the politicians and their power-hungry factions, and the large number of independent country gentlemen who voted as their consciences and personal quirks dictated.

During Lord North's administration this line-up was somewhat knotted by the presence of a political and court group known as the "King's Friends" whose purpose was to rebuild the leadership of the Crown. Because Lord North happened to be the most amicable of the "King's Friends," the widespread American fiction that the colonists' troubles could be blamed on the Ministry and not on the King was wholly invalid.

The word "Ministry" is another which I have used with some frequency, and again it is a label tied round the neck of something much more complex than one might suppose. Colonial affairs were handled largely by the Cabinet, with the Secretary of State for the American Colonies instructing the governors on behalf of the King. The Privy Council reviewed legal disputes, the Treasury handled the revenue, the Admiralty (through the Navy and High Court of Admiralty) looked after maritime affairs, the War Office controlled the army, and the Bishop of London the clergy, while the Board of Trade stood ready to give advice and information upon request—and sometimes without it. Together these officers and agencies formed the American-oriented artery of a dinosaurlike creature whose head often had trouble keeping track of its tail. Nevertheless, this was the package known to the colonists as the Ministry, and those supporting it were Ministerialists and Tories—and so they shall be here.

My aim throughout has been to enable us to live through the year together. Just as we cannot, now, be sure what tomorrow or next week will bring, so I have refrained from discussing the various occurrences in the light of subsequent events. Thus, we end each month of 1775 not knowing what the next will offer, and when the year is over, so is the book. That was the way it was lived.

Wherever possible I have allowed the people of 1775 to speak for themselves, even when they are contradictory and when we now know that they were wrong. Sometimes as the year progresses it becomes apparent just how wrong they were, but in many instances the unfounded rumors and downright fabrications remain unexposed to the end. Thus anyone reading these pages in search of hard facts will begin in confusion and end in frustrated exhaustion. To them I make no apology, for it is my intention to create some, admittedly, frail impression of what it was like to live through the year 1775—and in Virginia there were many who began the year in confusion and ended frustrated and exhausted. However, I hope that many more people will pick up the book in search of nothing more lofty than fireside relaxation. To you I can say only that I enjoyed myself immensely while reading the mass of source material from which *1775* is derived, and I hope that enough of that enjoyment has transferred itself to these pages for you to be able to share it with me. But I must emphasize that whatever amusement or pleasure you find here will not have been of my creation; it comes to you across the years from 1775.

Being an archaeologist whose field happens to be that of colonial America, I am constantly dealing with the minutiae of seventeenth- and eighteenth-century life. Consequently, when a novelist asks me, as a reader, to imagine an eighteenth-century tavern, I do so with aplomb: I see the colors and shapes of the bottles on the shelves, the decoration on the stoneware tankards; I envisage the styles of cutlery, the clay tobacco-pipes, the buttons and buckles on the topers' clothes, the lighting fixtures, and even the hinges on the bar door. So busy am I "seeing" the tavern that I frequently forget the characters whom the author has sent me there to meet. Such reading in depth can therefore become more of a liability than an asset, for had the writer wanted me to dwell upon the buckles on his hero's breeches, he would doubtless have drawn my attention to them. Nevertheless, I did think that this familiarity with the setting of colonial life would be immensely helpful in writing this book. But it turned out to be less so than I had hoped. My ground rules required that I include only those details that are known to have been so, or were said to be so, in 1775. I could not identify the clothes on the backs of my actors unless a description or a picture survived to provide that information. I could not describe a winter's night in Williamsburg as cold, bitter, chill, or damp, unless somebody reported that it was so. It would have been cheating to accept the word of a diarist in the Piedmont when we know that weather conditions in that area often differ drastically from those of lowland Tidewater. I confess that I often found these limitations painfully restrictive, and I admit that every now and again an uncorroborated adjective does slip in. But by and large I have played the game according to the rules.

Having made this claim, I began to review the manuscript and found to my dismay that in the first paragraph of Chapter I. I had expansively described the treble choristers of the Chapel Royal in St. James's Palace as "blooming above their surplices." Choirboys can always be relied upon to bloom; but did they wear surplices? It appears that they did *not* do so in colonial Virginia. Fortunately and to my considerable relief, the Lord Chamberlain's Office at St. James's Palace was able to assure me that the children of the Chapel Royal did wear surplices and produced an order for them dated 1663 as well as a washing bill of 1728. Consequently, when you read the opening paragraph, you can reasonably envisage the trebles not only in surplices, but in clean surplices.

While in some areas information I would have liked to include was not forthcoming, in others I found more than I could use. In discussing attitudes, conditions, and descriptions of places, as opposed to specific events, I have thought it legitimate to use information recorded not only in 1775 but also in the years immediately preceding it. I have also thought it fair to draw on accounts of 1775 that were written some years later, providing that the writers were relying either on their own memories or on those of their contemporaries. My use of John Burk's frequently suspect *History of Virginia* may well produce raised eyebrows in historical circles, yet it was first published in 1805 when its author had access to verbal and documentary sources that are closed to us today. For that reason I have thought it legitimate to use Burk to add touches here and there and to fill gaps left by others.

I know that I have cheated a little by sometimes inserting English events as they happened, instead of waiting until news of them reached Virginia. But I would add in self-defense that each such lapse has been carefully weighed to be sure that I was not detracting from some significant reaction that occurred when the news finally arrived.

My principal sources have been the Virginia newspapers, the Journals of the House of Burgesses, and Governor Dunmore's official correspondence with the Secretary of State for the American Colonies, all cemented together with details and comments from a miscellany of reports, letters, and diaries, both American and British. Throughout the multitude of direct quotations, I have retained the vagaries of the original spelling, capitalization, and punctuation, on the grounds that these are our sole links with the characters of the writers. In one respect only have I deviated from this course, and that is in my adoption of a uniformity of spelling for proper names. To see, for example, Colonel Adam Stephen disguised as "Stevens" or "Stephens" was unnecessarily confusing.

If I have failed to treat my sources with the solemnity that many historians feel they merit, I can only counter that if we are able to use laughter to take the edge off the grimness of the present, I can see no reason for treating the past any differently. An event that occurred yesterday is today part of history; if it was reported in the papers, you have probably already consigned it to the garbage can, and in England it is being used to wrap fish. Time cannot alter that event; it may dim our recollection, cause us to misinterpret, distort, or embellish, but it does not change it nor does it ennoble. To treat the past with awe or glum reverence serves only to drain the last drops of life from it and thus to frighten many people away who might otherwise find pleasure in exploring it.

It is no coincidence that many of the things that were said, written, and done in 1775 have a surprising air of immediacy about them. Yet we should not be surprised, for in the ensuing years neither human graces nor human frailties have changed one iota. We may have grown a little taller, be more uniformly educated, and, if we leave each other alone, we may stand to live rather longer; but emotionally we are much the same as we were in the year 1775, 1475, or 75. When we talk of history repeating itself (a cliché that dies astonishingly hard) we are usually thinking of wide-screen wars and of the rise and fall of empires. It rarely occurs to us that most of history is built out of day-to-day living and from the actions and reactions of individuals. At that level history has been repeating itself ever since Genesis or perhaps *Zinjanthropus boisei.*

Regardless of these similarities, this book really has no nutshell message; but if you must try to crack one out of it, it might be that when factions decide to be unpleasant to each other, two hundred years have wrought very few changes. Revolutions then were no more glorious in their execution than they are today.

Williamsburg, Virginia   **INH**
July 24, 1965

ACKNOWLEDGMENTS

GIVING CREDIT AND THANKS WHERE BOTH ARE DUE IS ONE of an author's more pleasant tasks, but at the same time it is among the most nerve-wracking. Lurking in the back of one's mind there is always the fear that the most important name has been inadvertently left out. It is therefore reassuring to know that that cannot happen here, for I am constantly aware that I owe to my wife the most valuable contribution of all—the time to work. For more than two years she has uncomplainingly shouldered the vast majority of those domestic duties which should be mine, and, in addition, she has spent many long hours preparing the provisional index. Without these contributions this book would probably be still unfinished in 1975.

For wise professional counsel I am deeply indebted to my friends and colleagues on the staff of Colonial Williamsburg, notably to Edward M. Riley, director of research, his associate John Selby, and especially Jane Carson, who so generously agreed to review the manuscript and whose guidance helped me to avoid many a pitfall. I am also appreciative of the help given me by Lester J. Cappon, director of the Institute of Early American History and Culture; to United States National Park Service historian at St. Augustine, Florida, Albert C. Manucy; to John L. Lochhead, librarian at the Mariners' Museum at Newport News, Virginia; to Howard H. Peckham, director of the William L. Clements Library at the University of Michigan; to Anne Freudenberg, acting curator of manuscripts at the University of Virginia Library; to Milton W. Hamilton, acting director of the Division of Archives and History at the University of the State of New York; and to numismatist Eric P. Newman of St. Louis. I am equally grateful for the advice so freely given by Lieutenant Colonel L. H. Yates, O.B.E., librarian of the Prince Consort's Library at Aldershot; A. H. Waite, deputy curator in the Department of Models and Relics at the National Maritime Museum, Greenwich; to Colonel T. P. Butler, resident governor and major of the Tower of London; Peter Townend, editor of *Burke's Peerage;* and lastly, and therefore conspicuously, by John Murray, ninth Earl of Dunmore. All these people, including my long-suffering editor, Angus Cameron, and Diane Olsen, my splendid copy editor, have graciously helped me to avoid mistakes; their contributions are consequently to that which is good in the book, leaving that which is not to be entirely my responsibility.

It is inevitable, of course, that any historian's greatest debt is to those who have labored in the same field before him. While I am not a professional historian, I do have this in common with them. The footnotes leave no doubt as to when and where credit should be given, and on those few occasions that I have quoted from secondary sources, I have said so. In addition, the bibliography includes those works from which I have obtained information but which are not specifically quoted. Beyond these acknowledgments I must single out Percy Burdelle Caley's monumental *Dunmore: Colonial Governor of New York and Virginia*, whose innumerable references provided me with many basic avenues of research. I should mention, too, John Hampden's *Eighteenth-Century Journal, 1774–1776*, which provided me with English newspaper references that were not otherwise available; also David Mays' *Edmund Pendleton*, which best summarizes the uneasy relationships that existed between the Virginia patriot leaders in the summer and fall of 1775.

For permission to quote from manuscript sources I am indebted to Colonial Williamsburg, Inc., for use of the *Journal of Nicholas Cresswell;* to the Trustees of the National Library of Scotland, owners of the Charles Steuart Papers; to the London Library, custodian of the Journal of Augustine Prevost; and to the University of Virginia Library, owner of the Wormeley Family Papers. My largest single debt in this category is to the Controller of H.M. Stationery Office for permission to quote from Crown-copyright Colonial, Audit, Admiralty, and War Office records, in the Public Record Office, London.

For permission to quote from published sources I wish to acknowledge my debt to the following: to Colonial Williamsburg, Inc., for the *Journal of John Harrower, 1773–1776* (Riley, ed.) and for the *Journal and Letters of Philip Vickers Fithian* (Farish, ed.); to Cornell University Press for Burnaby's *Travels through the Middle Plantations in North-America in the years 1759 and 1760;* to Frances Norton Mason for *John Norton & Sons, Merchants of London and Virginia;* to Harvard University Press for David J. Mays's *Edmund Pendleton;* to Macmillan and Co. for John Hampden's *An Eighteenth-Century Journal: 1774–1776;* to the Massachusetts Historical Society for the "Aspinwall Papers" in its *Collections* (4th ser., Vol. X); to the University of North Carolina Press for the Marquis de Chastellux's *Travels in North America in the Years 1780, 1781 and 1782* (Rice, ed.), and for *Baroness von Riedesel and the American Revolution* (Brown, trans.); and to the Virginia Historical Society for *The Diary of Colonel Landon Carter of Sabine Hall, 1752–1778* (Greene, ed.).

For the use of microfilm records and papers in their collections I am indebted to Colonial Williamsburg, Inc., for films of Colonial, Audit, and War Office papers in the Public Record Office, London; and to the Institute of Early American History and Culture for lending me films of the 1774 and 1775 *Virginia Gazettes* of Williamsburg and Norfolk.

For permission to publish pictures, plans, maps, and objects in their collections I wish to express my appreciation to the National Galleries of Scotland (Pl. 1); the Library of Congress (Pl. 2, 3 & 21); Colonial Williamsburg, Inc., (Pl. 4, 6, 14 & 18);

the College of William and Mary (Pl. 5); the Trustees of the
National Maritime Museum for British Admiralty plans (Pl.
7 & 8); The Mariners' Museum at Newport News (Pl. 9); the
Virginia Historical Society (Pl. 11); Washington and Lee Uni-
versity, Lexington (Pl. 12); The William L. Clements Library,
University of Michigan (Pl. 10 & 22); the City Art Museum of
St. Louis (Pl. 15); the Science Museum, London (Pl. 16); Eric
P. Newman (Pl. 17); H.M. Stationery Office (Pl. 19); The
Prince Consort's Library, Aldershot (Pl. 20). The photographs
used in plates 2, 3, 4, 5, 6, 13, 14, & 18 were kindly supplied by
the Public Relations and Audio-Visual Departments of Colonial
Williamsburg, Inc.

In conclusion, and realizing that only those who have been
overlooked will have bothered to read this far, I would like to
offer my apologies to those friends whom I have so churlishly
neglected during these years of apparent hibernation. You have
been most sorely missed.

A Note on the Footnotes

FOOTNOTES ARE OFTEN CONSIDERED TO BE THE OUTWARD and physical manifestations of inner depths of scholarship, and the more there are, the more erudite the author is assumed to be. In deliberately scholarly works footnotes have a valid place as repositories for peripheral research, and many a student mining his way through a mountain of pedantry has discovered larger nuggets in the footnotes than in the body of the text. However, there is much to be said for the point of view that if the content of the note is not worth working into the text it is not worth dangling from the end of the page.

This book is, itself, largely a footnote to history, and I would like to have dispensed with notes altogether. But their presence is inescapable. They are, however, almost entirely bibliographic, enabling the reader to go back to the original sources, avoiding an endless repetition of dates, and permitting me to acknowledge my specific debts to the authors and editors who have trodden this path before me.

For the sake of brevity the most frequently used sources have been reduced to abbreviations, which are explained below. For the same reason, dates have been shortened to days and months, the year being added only when it is something other than 1775.

Abbreviations Used in the Footnotes

AHR	*American Historical Review*
CSP	Charles Steuart Papers
JHB	*Journal of the House of Burgesses, 1773–1776*
LNCVA	*Lower Norfolk County Virginia Antiquary*
MHS	Massachusetts Historical Society
N-YHS	New-York Historical Society
PRO,CO	Public Record Office, London, Colonial Office papers; AO, Audit Office; WO, War Office papers
RCHP	*Richmond College Historical Papers*
VHR	*Virginia Historical Register and Literary Companion*
VMHB	*Virginia Magazine of History and Biography*
WMQ	*William and Mary College Quarterly Historical Magazine*, the title contracted to the *William and Mary Quarterly* in 1944 at the beginning of the third series

CONTENTS

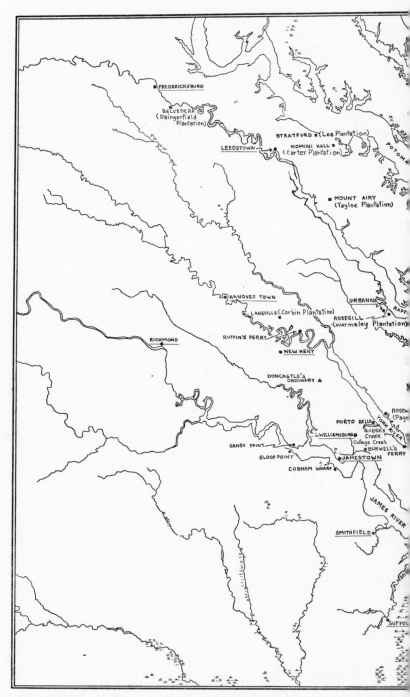

A map of Tidewater, Virginia, showing the principal locations mentioned in the text.

ILLUSTRATIONS

1775

Another Part of the Field

———————————

SEVENTEEN HUNDRED SEVENTY FOUR,
Is now forever past;
Seventeen Hundred Seventy Five
Will fly away as fast.

But, whether Life's uncertain Scene
Shall hold an equal Pace,
Or whether Death shall come between,
And end my mortal Race;

Or whether Sickness, Pain, or Health,
My future Lot shall be;
Or whether Poverty or Wealth,
Is all unknown to me.

One Thing I know, that needful 'tis
To watch with careful Eye;
Since every Season spent amiss
Is registered on High. . . .

(Anon.)
Virginia Gazette (Dixon & Hunter)
January 7, 1775

[*I*]

JANUARY

The first of January was a Sunday, and in London the bells rang out from scores of towers and steeples summoning the godly to beseech their Maker to bring England a prosperous and prestigious 1775. In the little Chapel Royal at St. James's Palace, a golden-throated organ lifted its notes of praise to the painted ceiling as his Majesty, King George III, and his Queen, preceded by the Sword of State, arrived for Divine Service. Standing in their pews were members of the royal family and of the court, all resplendent in their orders; beyond them in the stalls stood the choristers, the basses grey and saintly and the trebles blooming above their surplices, scrubbed, and temporarily angelic. The Reverend Dr. Kaye was muttering to himself as he toyed with his phrases and shuffled his notes to ensure that he would make the most of the soul-stirring sermon that he had so carefully conceived for the occasion.

In Alexandria, Virginia, the soul of Nicholas Cresswell was to be less adequately served. "The Parson is drunk," he wrote in his diary, "and can't perform the duties of his office." [1]

If you have never heard of Nicholas Cresswell, it is hardly surprising; he was quite unimportant. Indeed, were it not for the fact that he wrote a journal which happened to survive, he would have passed into limbo along with hundreds of thousands of others who visited or immigrated into the American colonies

[1] *Cresswell*, 52; Jan. 1.

in the eighteenth century. Cresswell came from a family of what
passed for rural gentility in Derbyshire, and at the age of
twenty-four he decided that he had had enough of it. In 1774 he
took ship for Virginia to see if he liked that better, and, if so, he
planned to return later to settle. But instead of the tranquil life
he had envisaged, he found the colonies seemingly bent on self-
destruction. The spirit of '76 was already in the air, and it was
not to his taste.

On a lower rung of the social ladder sat John Harrower, a
penurious Scots merchant, who, like many of his kind, had
suffered from the economic strictures of the early 1770's.
Having failed to find employment in England, "frendless and
forsaken," and reduced to his last shilling, he was "oblidged to
engage to go to Virginia for four years as a schoolmaster [his
spelling notwithstanding] for Bedd, Board, washing and five
pound during the whole time." [2] Like Cresswell, Harrower
inadvertently slipped between the pages of history as the result
of having kept a diary which has come down to us. It is,
however, not nearly such an important document as the *Journal
of Nicholas Cresswell*, which sheds much light on both the
social and political life of the colonies at the beginning of the
Revolution. Harrower was more concerned with keeping his
place and leaving opinions to his betters. His achievements were
quite small, though none the less satisfying; like growing a
watermelon "2 feet 4 Inches round the one way & 1 foot 9 Ins.
round the other way" [3] and then eating it. If anything earth-
shattering happened on January first, it passed John Harrower
by; he made no entry in his diary that day. It was a quiet day,
too, for Colonel George Washington, who spent it "At home all
day" [4] at Mount Vernon, his estate on the Potomac, which his
family had owned since 1674. Unlike either Cresswell or
Harrower, the Colonel belonged where he was, and conse-

[2] *Harrower*, 17; Jan. 26, 1774.
[3] Ibid., 105; July 30.
[4] Washington, *Diaries*, II, 181.

quently everything around him was so familiar that it did not call for description, thus making him a singularly unhelpful diarist.

Had Washington lived in England his tenants might have brought him a capon or a goose as a New Year gift, the residue of a long tradition of gift giving, which had reached ridiculous heights at the court of Queen Elizabeth and which had subsequently dwindled away. Even the goose giving had been shorn of its ritual:

> Ye used in the former days to fall
> Prostrate to your landlord in his hall,
> When with low legs, and in a humble guise,
> Ye offer'd up a capon-sacrifice
> Unto his worship, at a New Year's tide.[5]

So wrote Abraham Cowley in 1678. But even if the giving of gifts had declined, the superstitions of New Year survived in rural England. If a woman was the first visitor to enter your house the prospects for a happy new year were minimal. No "ashes, or dirty water, or any article, however worthless," [6] should be thrown out on New Year's Day, nor should one take any light out of the house, for this would surely bring a death before the year's end. While the rustic Englishman supposedly spent his day hanging onto his lights, surrounded by his slops and ashes, and beating women away from his door, he would also be wearing at least one new garment—to have failed to do so would have meant a year with little material gain.

I have been unable to discover the kind of weather Virginia enjoyed on January 1, 1775, but according to the *Sheperd's Kalender* of 1709, "if New Year's Day in the morning open with duskey red clouds, it denotes strifes and debates among great ones, and many robberies to happen that year." [7] If Lord

[5] Brand, *Antiquities*, I, 11.
[6] Ibid., 20.
[7] Hone, *Year Book*, 253.

Dunmore, Virginia's royal governor, had looked out of his palace window in Williamsburg that morning, there is a sporting chance that that was the sort of sky he saw.

When the year began, Virginia possessed two leading newspapers, both published in Williamsburg and, rather confusingly, both titled *Virginia Gazette*. One was issued by Messrs. John Dixon and William Hunter at the post office, while the other was "Printed by John Pinkney for the Benefit of Clementina Rind's Children," Mr. Rind having died in 1773 and his widow in '74. Both papers could be relied on to flay the British government whenever the more vociferous Virginians felt it deserved it, yet each was willing to publish letters from correspondents who were clearly out of step with the times. The Pinkney (nee Rind) *Gazette* continued fearlessly to inform its readers, as it had since 1766, that its columns were "Open to ALL PARTIES, but INFLUENCED BY NONE." Dixon and Hunter were a little more specific and announced in their issue of January 7 that "Whatever may be sent us in Favour of LIBERTY, or for the PUBLICK GOOD, shall be published with Cheerfulness. . . ." If anything, the Dixon-Hunter paper was the more conservative, probably because Hunter's undeclared sympathies leaned toward the British cause, though there is considerable doubt as to the strength of his feelings at this stage of the game. Hunter had previously been in partnership with Alexander Purdie—a partnership that, after nine years, had been amicably terminated last December. Purdie was now preparing to launch his own paper, which he too proposed to call the *Virginia Gazette*. The first edition would appear on February 3 under the motto: "Always for LIBERTY and the PUBLICK GOOD." In addition to the Williamsburg papers, another had been established in the port of Norfolk in June 1774. Its publishers, William Duncan and Company, scratched their collective heads for a name and, being somewhat short of imagination, settled on the *Virginia Gazette* and then, in a small effort to avoid confusion, added the subtitle *or, the Norfolk Intelligencer*. It was a middle-of-the-road paper trying to be suitably loyal to Virginia while not losing sight of the fact that it was circulating in a strongly Tory town.

For our purpose, as far as January is concerned, it is quite enough to consider the two Williamsburg *Virginia Gazette*s. Both papers were about the same size and offered four pages, each with three columns of alarmingly small print, the third and fourth pages being devoted predominantly to advertising. Both were sold at an annual subscription rate of twelve shillings and sixpence, or slightly less than threepence a copy. It is virtually useless to draw a purely mathematical comparison between the buying power of money today and that of the colonial period. I shall note only that instead of buying one issue of the *Gazette*, a Virginian of 1775 might have bought himself nine inches of black hair ribbon or half an ounce of brown thread. If he chose to forego his paper for five weeks he could have treated himself to a bottle of West India rum. Pinkney's *Gazette* came out on Thursday and the Dixon-Hunter version on Saturday, and unless something startling happened on Thursday or Friday they contained much the same news. Sometimes, however, they were late going to press and so contained reports of events occurring on or after the date on their mastheads—a peccadillo doubtless designed to unhorse the unwary historian.

Had you been a reasonably literate Virginian you would probably have spent part of Saturday, January 7, reading your paper and if you were also passably sensible you would have tried to do it before the sun went down. Reading that size print by the light of a candle did one's eyes no good at all. We may be forgiven, therefore, for choosing to peer over the shoulder of a *Gazette* reader who happens to be holding it in a good light, seated, perhaps, close to the window of the tap room in Williamsburg's Raleigh Tavern. There would have been few customers to disturb him, as neither the courts nor the assembly was in session.

We who obtain our international news via television, radio, suboceanic telephones, or bounced off satellites in the sky must inevitably find it difficult to comprehend how important a part

time played in the distribution of information in the eighteenth
century. In 1649 a description of Virginia revealed with obvious
satisfaction that "The seamen of late years have found a way,
that now in 5, 6, and 7 weeks they saile to *Virginia* free from all
Rocks, Sands, and Pirats; and that they return home again in 20
dayes sometimes, and 30 at most: the Winds commonly serving
more constantly, being Westerly homeward, the Easterly outward bound." [8] In the ensuing hundred and fifty years ships
were built larger, but not much faster, and in the fall and winter
when storms made the longer southern route appreciably safer
news still took six weeks or so to cross the Atlantic in a westerly
direction. Thus, in the first week of January, the *Gazette*'s
English and foreign news came "By the Tiger, Capt. Hall, in
six weeks from London, arrived in James river." [9] The London
news was dated October 29, 1774, but the European was
naturally even older. The latter provided wide coverage and
included events from Madrid, Paris, Stockholm, Copenhagen,
Vienna, and Petersburg, with each location identified in parentheses as the capital of its respective country. We might be
permitted a small smile of superiority at the thought of the
ignorant readers who needed such geography lessons—but only
if we can instantly identify Bastia as the capital of Corsica. It
was from there that the *Gazette* took its lead story, an account of
a "troop of banditti" who had captured the fort at Aleria. From
Madrid came news of an outbreak of what was probably foot-
and-mouth disease among "horned cattle"; and in Stetin, Germany, "a merchant there having collected a large quantity of
gunpowder, set fire thereto, and blew himself up, with his house
and whole family." The news from Petersburg was that "The
rebellion is now at an end, and the tranquility of this empire

[8] *A Perfect Description of Virginia* . . . c. (no author), (London,
1649), 7; Force, *Tracts*, II.

[9] *Virginia Gazette* (Dixon & Hunter), Jan. 7. This is the issue from
which all the *Gazette* quotations used in this chapter are taken, unless
otherwise stated.

restored by the taking of the rebel Pugachev, who has been so long the disturber of it."

The front-page news from England was hardly more momentous. The Biship of Bangor had expired, leaving vacant "many valuable preferments" in the Church; the cargo of a French slave ship had escaped and murdered the entire crew, sparing only a white woman passenger—who probably wished she had not been spared. The Queen of France was pregnant, a revelation which was apparently received with great joy throughout the country, except perhaps by the Chancellor, who, we discover (seven paragraphs lower down the column), "had his head struck off by command of the King, for speaking disrespectful words of the Queen's honour."

The best-placed story concerned the funeral of a seventy-two-year-old waterman at St. John's Church, Horsleydown, a suburb of London. The *Gazette* described the procession, which began with the parish children singing hymns, next the corpse, followed by six watermen in coats and badges (their traditional uniform), plus the chief mourner, behind whom followed a "porter carrying a pair of sculls painted black; a knot half black half white; and six brushes used for painting the bottoms of boats." Then came the dead man's son wearing his father's wedding clothes, in turn followed by miscellaneous mourners. "Previous to the procession 155 poor children had each a roll and treacle given them. The expenses of this funeral were paid eight years ago, except those for the rolls and treacle, which had been paid for four years."

It is a well-worn truism that nothing interests people like people—particularly, one might add, odd people. The press of the eighteenth century was no different from the tabloids of our own times, and I have little doubt that all these stories occurring today would find their way into print.

Turning to page two of the *Virginia Gazette* we find news of greater pertinence to America, some of it accounts of events in the northern colonies, which had been shipped to England and

then relayed back to Virginia. An unidentified London correspondent loudly called for a better deal for his American
cousins, which was nice of him, even though his reasoning
might have been thought a trifle mercenary:

> The miscreants of power in this once happy kingdom have
> now nearly reduced it, by their arbitrary and scandalous
> proceedings, to a most dangerous and wretched situation. By
> a dispute with America (which they ought to have prevented,
> instead of provoked) we are deprived of the advantages
> resulting from their trade and commerce; an advantage which
> our rivals, the Dutch, are already improving, by lading their
> vessels for America which our wise Councellors have,
> through fear, prohibited. Britons! How long will you remain
> the dupes of pensioned hirelings, and behold yourselves
> robbed and plundered of your trade?

It is doubtful whether the average Virginian would have
been particularly distraught at the prospect of English merchants feeling the pinch of trade embargoes, while the more
militant patriots were bound to have been delighted. The latter
group would certainly have enjoyed the following gem from an
adjacent column:

> History informs us that the Romans, in the decline of their
> empire practiced on each other the civility of kissing and
> embracing: The English, fond of following the examples of
> those people, always pick out their worst for imitation;
> among which is that of the men kissing one another, which is
> certainly odious, and it is feared will be accompanied with the
> same consequences as it was among the Romans,—Decline of
> Empire, &c.

Less inclined to promote levity was the announcement of the
death of "Master William Gage, second son of General Gage,
now at Boston." For all its baldness, this was the same
Lieutenant-General Gage who had fought with Braddock in '55,
had become military governor of Montreal in 1760, and was
now governor of Massachusetts and commander-in-chief of all
the British forces in America. As far as American patriots were
concerned, he was the voice in America of the British prime

minister, Lord North, and for that, if for no other reason, he was roundly despised. Nevertheless, he had spent long enough in America to respect its cause; yet at the same time he too was a patriot in the fullest meaning of the word—one who exerted himself to promote the well-being of his country. The words "patriot" and "traitor" were being batted back and forth like bedraggled shuttlecocks, and they had reverse connotations depending upon which side of the net you were standing—a net which very obviously divided the ocean but which frequently stood between neighbors or straddled a dinner table. To make loyalties even more divided, the same game was being played equally vigorously in England, where similar epithets were tossed between the benches of the House of Commons and flung like gauntlets onto the pages of newspapers. There were those in the Tory government who considered General Gage to be dangerously liberal in his approach to the rebellious colonists of Massachusetts, yet our *Virginia Gazette* of January 7 quotes from a letter from Boston saying that "the populace burn the Commander in Chief in effigy before his door, in the face of the troops, almost every Week." If Gage did have sympathy for the rebel cause, and many people feel that he did, this sort of provocation was hardly designed to strengthen it. But then, of course, mob demonstrations have never been memorable for their ability to distinguish between real and imagined enemies.

Among other pieces of news of Boston relayed back to Virginia from London was an account dated November 7, 1774, describing Gage's blockade of the town and editorially inquiring as to whether or not the general had overstepped his parliamentary mandate, which was only to seal the harbor. "This measure carries a very hostile appearance," declared the London source, "and will certainly be taken by our fellow subjects in America as a manifest intention of subduing and bringing them under a military power; and the consequences of it will very probably be a resistance, and produce the worst of all evils, a CIVIL WAR."

On the same day that *Gazette* subscribers were pondering
London's reaction to the British exhibition of strength at
Boston, London readers of the *Daily Advertiser* were digesting
news from Charlestown, Massachusetts, which told of a British
merchantman, the *Britannia*, which had arrived there at the
beginning of November. Its commander, Captain Bell, had
found a reception committee of none too friendly townspeople
assembled on the quay, having heard that the ship carried a
small cargo of tea. However, in keeping with the now well-
established practice of breaking the cases and tossing them into
the sea, the importers went aboard and did penance by breaking
the chests themselves. The slightly thwarted crowd then went
off round the town towing a mobile scaffold from which hung
effigies of the Pope, Lord North, and the Pretender, the once
legendary "Bonnie Prince Charlie."

The readers of the *Daily Advertiser* could very well assume
that Prince Charles Stuart was as unpopular as Tories and
Popery in America. But if they happened to express such an
opinion to a devotee of the *Morning Chronicle* they would
probably be assured that the opposite was the case. Why, it was
only last November that we heard on the best authority that
"the Pretender, in the character of a private gentleman, is very
busy in America, in spurring the rebellious people to revenge
themselves, and is daily supplying them with materials for that
purpose." [1] The newspaper's added comment, that it could not
believe these whispers to be true, would have been hardly worth
remembering, nor would it have cut much ice to point out that
the dashing hero of the Jacobite Rebellion was now so fat that
he had difficulty getting around, that his face was covered with
carbuncles, or that his principal intrigues were confined to
sustaining an adequate supply of liquor in spite of an alarming
shortage of money.

Thus, on both sides of the Atlantic, rumors both true and
false, and often a little of both, were served to the public on the

---

[1] Hampden, *Journal*, 131; quoting the London *Morning Chronicle*,
Nov. 24, 1774.

pages of their newspapers, and the readers, being then no less gullible than they are today, generally accepted them as facts. For some extraordinary reason the public still possesses the same faith in the printed word that it has exhibited for centuries, being prepared to accept the most outrageous nonsense as the gospel truth, providing it is served on a printed page—and the printed pages of 1775 were full of such fodder.

Following the November news from London, the *Gazette* offered dispatches from Boston dated December 16 which told of the arrival of more British troops; also news from New York dated the fifteenth, most of which concerned donations of supplies from Virginia and elsewhere being sent to aid the citizens of Boston. While both characterize the respective British and American reactions to the Boston Port Bill, my principal reason for drawing attention to them is to stress the ever-present time lapse between events in one place and reactions to them in another. Thus the world could be exploding in Boston and yet the seaborne bang could take up to three weeks to be heard in Williamsburg, and longer still to reach Charleston, South Carolina. Under special circumstances news could be relayed overland from New England to Virginia in ten days. Between England and Williamsburg there was no short cut; the Colony's throat could be slashed in London six weeks before it began to bleed, and a royal governor requesting instructions from his government could expect to wait three months before he would receive an answer, by which time the circumstances that prompted the request could have changed so drastically that the answer would have been quite useless. There was, of course, some advantage to this snail-like system of communication in that it discouraged precipitous action and gave passions time to cool. On the other hand, in cases when the established order of things began to crack there was no time for the governors to delay decisions pending further instructions, and they were forced to make their own, for which they might later be soundly chastised and even relieved of their posts.

When Lord Dunmore had been appointed governor of

Virginia in 1771, Lord Hillsborough, then Secretary of State for the American Colonies, had provided him with the most detailed instructions as to what he could and could not do, any deviation from which would be followed by recall and dismissal. In the halcyon days of colonial America the governor's best course was to play it safe and make as few decisions as possible, and above all to secure the confidence and friendship of the members of his council, for it was only through their acquiescence that directives issued in London could be implemented in Virginia. This worked very well as long as the assemblies were made up of reasonably contented gentlemen who were not inclined to rock the boat; indeed, some of Virginia's governors never even bothered to cross the Atlantic. As the *Annual Register* [2] pointed out, the turnover in colonial American governorships had been so great that there were now living in England three ex-governors of Boston, three of New York, four of New Jersey, four of South Carolina and three of Virginia. Those of Virginia were listed as Lord Loudoun, Lord Pownal, and Lord Amhurst, none of whom ever set foot in the colony. Lord Dunmore would have preferred to have stayed away too, not because he aspired to being an absentee governor but simply because he did not fancy the job at all.

In January 1775 few Virginians could have been without some sort of opinion as to the quality of their governor. The citizens of Williamsburg were constantly reminded of his authority and allegiance by the stone-faced lion and unicorn standing sentinel at the gates of his red-brick palace—and in the current issue of their *Gazette* they would find that he had other, more vocal supporters. At a time when the British government and its colonial officers were being assailed on all sides, it was odd to hear voices from the center, the Norfolk and Williamsburg city fathers, praising their governor and wishing him all kinds of well. But there were the words in black and white, enough to make a reader pause and review what he knew of

[2] *Annual Register*, 1775, "Chronicle," 122.

Lord Dunmore. It may even have occurred to him that in doing so he might find some inkling of what to expect in the future.

John Murray, the fourth Earl of Dunmore and Viscount Fincastle, was born in 1730 and was elevated to the peerage on the death of his Jacobite father in 1750. At the age of twenty-five he had completed his military education and emerged from the army as a lieutenant in the 3rd Foot Guards. In 1759 he married Charlotte Stuart, the third daughter of the Earl of Galloway, who bore him his ninth child in Williamsburg in December, 1774. In the House of Lords Dunmore supported the Whigs and perhaps gave some inkling of a sympathy toward the rights of the American colonists by saying that he believed "the Americans would soon be quiet, if they were only left to themselves." [3] This was neither profound nor, under the circumstances, very practical; but it did suggest a tolerance that either vanished after four years of colonial service or which was ignored by most of the contemporary writers whose comments about him have survived.

The only extant description of Lord Dunmore's physical appearance was written in October 1770 shortly after his arrival in America. He was then thought "to be Six or Seven & thirty, Short, Strong built, well shaped with a most frank and open countenance, easy and affable in his manners, very temperate, and a great lover of field Sports, indefatigable and constant in pursuit of them. In Short," wrote this admirer, "he seems Very likely to secure the affections of the Gentlemen of this Country." [4] Fortunately the portrait of this estimable peer painted five years earlier by Sir Joshua Reynolds is preserved among the treasures of the National Galleries of Scotland. In it he strikes a somewhat martial pose, the effect of which is slightly marred by the fact that the face is a little too podgy to be firm, and by his being shown facing into the wind while wearing the kilt and

[3] Caley, *Dunmore*, 7; quoting from the *Pennsylvania Magazine of History* (Philadelphia), XI (1887), 244.

[4] James Rivington to Sir William Johnson, Oct. 22, 1770; *Johnson Papers*, VII, 945.

bonnet of the Highlander. To the irritatingly irreverent Sassenachs, the combination of wind and kilt has always been thought wildly amusing; consequently any Virginian who saw the picture would probably have found it more funny than fierce.

His Lordship was appointed governor of New York in 1770, a post which he enjoyed and which he filled with reasonable efficiency. He did, however, contrive to fall foul of his lieutenant governor, Cadwallader Colden, who described him as a "capricious ignorant Lord." [5] But Colden was then a man of eighty-two who had lived in America most of his life and who had been acting governor before Dunmore's arrival. It was he who had steered the colony through the storms generated by the Stamp Act of 1765 and who had subsequently obtained the suspension of the assembly through Act of Parliament. Having borne the brunt of those years of turmoil it would have been surprising indeed if he had not resented the appointment over him of an inexperienced man half his age. But Colden was not the only person to express an opinion of Lord Dunmore. Soon after his arrival in New York one Charles Inglis made a cryptic but possibly significant comment on his politics and his religion, saying: "The Whigs had great Expectation from him, thinking he was a Presbytarian. But they are intirely mistaken." Then he added: "No Certain Judgment can yet be found of his Character. He appears to be affable, polite and good natured." Another observer remarked that he was "a very active Man Loves walking, & riding, & is a Sportsman." [6] All in all, his Lordship gave every indication of being a pretty creditable Englishman—providing one could forget that he was a "Scotchman." His years at the English court had irradicated the tang of the heather, though the present earl has provided evidence that his

[5] Caley, *Dunmore*, 71; quoting Cadwallader Colden to Dr. W. S. Johnson, May 8, 1771; N-YHS, *Collections*, X, 323. See list of abbreviations in A Note on the Footnotes.

[6] Charles Inglis to Sir William Johnson, Oct. 25, 1770; *Johnson Papers*, VII, 966; and Benjamin Roberts to Sir William Johnson, Feb. 19, 1770; ibid., 400.

ancestor knew Gaelic even if he rarely spoke it. But Lord Dunmore's origins seemed to bother no one at this stage of his career, and after he was transferred to Virginia an admirer recalled, "He was realy a verry honest good Man & I think would have made us all very happy." [7]

Although the governorship of Virginia was actually a promotion from that of New York and worth more money, Dunmore had no wish to leave. He had found himself some congenial friends (too congenial, others thought), and he was in the process of acquiring a considerable estate. He had not requested the transfer; it had apparently been arranged entirely without his knowledge. When he first received news of it, Dunmore wrote to influential friends in England to try to have the honor withdrawn; but they were not influential enough. In a letter bemoaning his good fortune, he wrote of Virginia that its "Climate is such, that it will oblige me to live without my Family, which makes my residence in that Country, where there is little or no Society, so tiresome, that I cannot be certain I should be able to stay there any time." [8] An acquaintance writing to Sir William Johnson, the fur trader, in February 1771 reported that Lord Dunmore "says he will not go to Virginia, as he prefers Health & good Society to a greater Salary." [9] However, it was James Rivington, the Tory publisher of the *New-York Gazetteer*, who explained his Lordship's enigma most succinctly, explaining that: "He is a Chearfull free liver & an Anguish Climate will ill suit his convivial Disposition." [1]

It was talk of Lord Dunmore's convivial disposition which most loudly preceded his arrival in Virginia. Particularly

[7] Hugh Wallace to Sir William Johnson, Sept. 19, 1771; ibid., VIII, 263.

[8] Caley, *Dunmore*, 82; quoting Dunmore to Hillsborough, July 2, 1771; PRO,CO 5/154.

[9] Hugh Wallace to Sir William Johnson, Feb. 17, 1771; *Johnson Papers*, VII, 1145.

[1] Rivington to Sir William Johnson, Feb. 25, 1771; ibid., 1157.

savored was the story of how "his Lordship with a set of his Drunken companions, sallied about midnight from his Palace, and attacked Chief Justice Horsemanden's coach & horses. The coach was destroyed and the poor horses lost their tails." [2] Dunmore's predecessor had been the gentle and amiable Lord Botetourt, who had died in office in 1770, a man so popular in the colony that it was in the process of obtaining a statue to be erected in his honor and on whose base would be carved eulogies to his "prudent and wise administration," and to the "many public and social virtues, which so eminently adorn's his illustrious character." The prospect of his being succeeded by a drunken rake was enough to cause a heavy drain on the supplies of smelling salts among the ladies of Virginia, while their husbands, who were often more constant to their horses than their wives, knew instinctively that any man who tampered with a horse could not possibly be any good. Dunmore did not improve his image when he wrote to the president of the Virginia council explaining that he liked "his situation at New York so well, that he hath wrote the Minister to desire leave to Remain." [3] Consequently even before he arrived in Williamsburg it was being said both that he would be unwelcome in Virginia and that he, himself, did not welcome the prospect of coming there—and both, of course, were true.

When Lord Dunmore was transferred to Virginia, the governorship of New York was bestowed upon William Tryon, then governor of North Carolina. But when the latter arrived to take up his new post he found Dunmore still in residence and offering to trade jobs. However, in August Dunmore sent his dogs and some of his baggage to Virginia, though he, himself, did not appear until late September, giving plenty of time for rumors and speculation to ferment into a quite damnable brew.

[2] Richard Bland to Thomas Adams, Aug. 1, 1771; *WMQ*, 1st series, V, No. 3 (Jan. 1897), 156.

[3] William Nelson to Samuel Athawes, May 16, 1771; *WMQ*, 1st series, VII, No. 1 (July 1898), 27.

If the Virginians expected their new governor to come reeling off the ship with a wench under one arm and a case of gin under the other, they were disappointed. He did, in fact, make very little initial impression one way or another, and nearly three months later a correspondent would say only that "The knowledge we have of him at present is negative, he bears no simlitude to his Predecessor." [4] It was inevitable that Lord Dunmore would be compared to the immensely popular Governor Botetourt and equally inevitable that the comparison would be odious. Baron de Botetourt had died in office at the height of his popularity and so had left an emotional scar on the colony that would be slow to heal. In addition to his personal appeal he had served during two years in which there were signs that colonial grievances would be redressed. It would not be so easy for his successor.

Lord Dunmore was not in the least like Botetourt, nor was he the roistering tosspot that many Virginians expected. Years later Judge St. George Tucker would recall that "Lord Dunmore was Governor when I first arrived at Wmsburg. He was not a man of parade: his predecessor I believe was." [5] The English have two adjectives with which they traditionally label the Scots: dour and canny. Before long there would be many who considered that Dunmore merited both. Curiously, however, the most open attack would be publicly voiced, not in Virginia, but in South Carolina, whose *Gazette* let fly at him only a year after his arrival.

In *Virginia* their new *Scotch* Governor began his Government with Negligence and Disregard to the Duties of his Office. His Lordship was hardly ever visited, very difficult of Access and frequently could not be spoken with, when the most urgent Business of the Public called for his Attendance. These spirited Colonists could not bear these haughty Airs,

[4] Jerman Baker to Thomas Adams, Dec. 24, 1771; *VMHB*, XXIII, No. 4 (Oct. 1915), 366.

[5] Tucker to William Wirt, re the latter's biography of Patrick Henry, Sept. 25, 1815; *WMQ*, 1st series, XII, No. 4 (April 1914), 252.

but deputed one of their Lawyers to remonstrate against this supercilious Behavior, so inconsistent with the service of the great Prince whom he represented. At first he stormed, but at last he agreed to name Office-Hours, when every Person concerned might attend on Business. Since which time all things have gone on very peaceably, and his Lordship has become much more tractable, to the Honour of his Master, and the great Advantage of the important Colony he presides over. Thanks to the true *American* Spirit of Liberty.[6]

Knowing Lord Dunmore's feelings about coming to Virginia at all, it is likely that he had indeed been difficult when he first arrived and also that he mellowed as he found that Virginia and Virginians were not as unattractive as he had expected. After an initially shaky start, it would seem that the new governor settled down to serve both his King and the colony to the best of his ability. In a letter to George Washington in August 1773 the frontier land prospector John Connolly wrote: "I flatter myself I shall not widely differ from your sentiments if I conclude him to be a Gentleman of benevolence & universal Charity, & not unacquainted with either Man or the world." [7] Washington's writings do not recall whether he shared Connolly's opinion, though we do know that he dined at the palace in Williamsburg from time to time, and that he had intended to accompany the governor on a trip to the disputed western boundary of Virginia in the summer of 1773, until sickness prevented him from doing so.

It was late in November of that year that Lady Charlotte Dunmore and her children set sail from Cowes aboard the ship *Duchess of Gordon*, accompanied by his Lordship's secretary Captain Edward Foy and his wife, the former having been sent

[6] Goodwin, *Williamsburg*, 68; quoting the *South-Carolina Gazette*, Charleston, Sept. 10, 1772, in turn quoting a London source of June 19, 1772.

[7] *Correspondence of the American Revolution: Being Letters of Eminent Men to George Washington*, edited by Jared Sparks (Boston, 1853), 253; Aug. 29, 1773.

to England to escort the Dunmore family to its new home. They were bound first for New York, a voyage which took them forty-four uncomfortable days. After a short stay there the party continued by sea to Virginia and arrived at Yorktown on February 26, 1774, on which date Dunmore was reunited with his wife for the first time in three and a half years. When he had last seen her she had been pregnant with her eighth child, a son who was born in December 1770 and who was now still too young to have made the voyage to Virginia. Another son, William, had died in 1773. However, the rest of the family was there: George Murray, Lord Fincastle, the eldest son; Alexander and John Murray; and daughters Catherine, Augusta, and Susan Murray. Declared the *Virginia Gazette* on March 3, 1774, the arrival was "to the great Joy of his Excellency the Governour, and the inexpressible Pleasure and Satisfaction of the Inhabitants, who made a general Illumination upon this happy Occasion, and with repeated Acclamations welcomed her Ladyship and Family to Virginia." [8]

Although there is little evidence that Lord Dunmore had made himself particularly unpopular in Virginia up to that time, there can be no denying that his wife made a more palpable and immediate hit than he had. Dr. Philip Mazzei, a Swiss doctor with no obligations to or affection for the British crown, noted in his memoirs that "At first sight, it seemed to me that she deserved a better husband, and I soon learned that I was not mistaken. There were two daughters—one seventeen and the other fifteen and a half years old—as charming as their mother, both in personality and in appearance; and one son, who seemed disposed to imitate his father." [9] It is, of course, much easier to be a historian than a journalist, and Mazzei was writing some years after the events of 1775 had settled themselves comfortably and permanently into the lap of history. But even so, his

[8] Purdie and Dixon.
[9] Philip Mazzei, "Memoirs," *WMQ*, 2nd Series, IX, No. 3 (July 1929), 166.

memory was not of the best, as Lord Dunmore's family in Virginia comprised three daughters and three sons—not two daughters and one son.

Another visitor remarked on the qualities of Lady Dunmore and her family; in his diary, written immediately after dining at the palace, Lieutenant Augustine Prevost added that "his Lordship is I believe a Consumate Rake & does not pay that attention to his Lady that she seems to deserve, She is extremely jealous I am told, (I almost discovered it my self) of a young Lady, whom it was reported was very Dear to him previous to her Ladyship arrival & the scandalous Chronicle says his Lordship is very Great there still." [1] The words in parentheses were heavily crossed out in the manuscript, and they may be quite meaningless. On the other hand they do give us a titillating hint of a scene stolen from a Restoration comedy.

The arrival of Lord Dunmore's family naturally created a good deal of interest and comment, most of which never found its way onto paper. This interest was not confined only to the family; the gentlemen of Virginia took a long hard look at his excellency's secretary too (not, of course, in the way that one might today), perhaps seeking a key to the door of gubernatorial favors or a stopcock that could be readily turned to emit classified information. Colonel Landon Carter of "Sabine Hall," son of the great early-eighteenth-century landowner Robert "King" Carter, considered himself one of the lords of Virginia and was prone to making somewhat testy and waspish comments about nearly everyone; after meeting the new arrivals he duly scratched his opinions into his diary. "Capt. Foy is rather more Cunning than sensible," he concluded. "I observed he talked but on few things and was always cautious of saying anything about the present dispute with the ministry of whom I fear he is too justly suspected of being a devotee." Such comment might be simply translated as meaning that Foy was likely to do his duty and would not be easily subverted. Then,

[1] Prevost, "Journal," July 4, 1774.

with what smacks of an old man's envy, Carter concluded: "His Lady really agreeable & more fond of her husband Perhaps than the politeness of the day allows of." [2]

Early in 1774 the Shawnee Indians had become increasingly belligerent as a result of ever-increasing pressures by frontier land-grabbers, who were relentlessly pushing westward, regardless of existing treaties and specific directives from London to hold the line. The situation was made the more volatile by a festering animosity between Virginia and Pennsylvania over their mutual borders. Dunmore's agent and admirer, John Connolly, had taken possession of Fort Pitt at Pittsburgh, from which the British garrison had been withdrawn two years earlier. Connolly renamed the outpost Fort Dunmore and there made pugnacious noises, which irritated both the Indians and the Pennsylvanians. In the summer of 1774 Lord Dunmore had taken leave of his wife and family and set out at the head of a force of militia, ostensibly to chasten the Indians. However, a number of historians have since dismissed "Dunmore's War" as a simple land grab to enrich himself and his friends. But the fact remains that, with the aid of the militia of southwest Virginia under the able command of General Andrew Lewis, the campaign resulted in a major victory on the Kanawha river at Point Pleasant, after which a new and useful treaty was signed, one that held every promise of peace on the Ohio. George Washington, who in June had written with grave concern of the threat of "a cruel and blood thirsty Enemy upon our Backs, the Indians, between whom and our Frontier Inhabitants many Skirmishes have happnd, and with whom a general War is inevitable," [3] subsequently declared "that we look upon the Peace, which Lord Dunmore made with the Indians to be conclusive and certain, and I dare say it will be of lasting duration." [4]

[2] Landon Carter, *Diary*, June 27, 1774; *WMQ*, XIV, No. 4 (April 1906), 248. N.B.: The Greene edition (II, 837) is not used here owing to the fact that it is somewhat at odds with the original MS in its use of the word "entertaining" instead of "Cunning."

[3] Washington, *Writings*, III, 224.

[4] Ibid., 266.

Just how much of the victory was won through Dunmore's own military strategy or prowess is distinctly open to debate. Prevost, who visited his camp during the campaign, observed: "Methinks his L - - p schemes & Plans of Operations are very like those of a Novice, & of a Man that is ignorant of the Matter he is upon. . . ." [5] The decisive battle at Point Pleasant was started by the Indians and ended before Dunmore's troops from Fort Pitt linked up with those of General Lewis. Nevertheless, the fact remained that the Royal Governor had trekked across the Allegheny Mountains to the very edge of English America in the middle of summer, waged war on the Indians, and personally extracted a workable treaty from them, backed up with hostages and the release of the prisoners in their hands. There could be no denying that the governor was a man of fortitude and personal courage and that he possessed what seemed to be a head for diplomacy—though there were some who interpreted the last as merely a talent for intrigue. But regardless of those Virginians whose breaths smelled a little of sour grapes, Lord Dunmore and his militia marched bravely back to Williamsburg amid the public demonstrations of affection and gratitude always bestowed upon a winner.

Returning to the columns of our *Virginia Gazette* of January 7, we find the published address of the mayor, recorder, aldermen, and common council of the city of Norfolk, who were officially

impressed with a deep and grateful Sense of the important Services rendered to this Colony by your Excellency's seasonable and vigorous Exertiton in the late Expedition against a deceitful and treacherous enemy, conducted under your Auspices to so fortunate an Issue. . . . While we applaud your Lordship's Moderation, in giving Peace to a merciless Foe, we cannot but exult in the Happiness of our Fellow Subjects on the Frontiers, who, by your unremitted Zeal and spirited Conduct, have acquired the Blessings of Ease, Security, and domestick Enjoyment.

[5] Prevost, "Journal," Sept. 11, 1774.

With an obsequious tug at the corporate forelock the address continued: "As we sincerely participate in every Circumstance of your Publick Glory, neither can we be insensible to your private Happiness in the Birth of a Daughter, and the recovery of Lady Dunmore; on which joyful Occasion we beg Leave also to add our most cordial Congratulations." The child, presumably conceived within days after Lady Dunmore's arrival in Virginia, was born on December 3, the day before the governor came marching home from the war. No doubt her Ladyship had a few unladylike thoughts regarding the King's Service, which had caused the absence of her husband through two successive childbearings. Dunmore, on the other hand, was able to return when all the fussing and fearing was over, riding into a welcoming Williamsburg to the plaudits of the crowd, and to receive his new baby signed, sealed, and delivered, as it were, into the colony. It was all very fitting, and in case anyone failed to grasp the symbolism he declared that the infant should be named Virginia. For a moment the persistent rumbling of approaching storms was banished amid the cheering, the cracking fireworks, and the roar of saluting cannon.

Words of praise and congratulation flowed in from all sides; the council of Virginia in terms of "heart-felt Joy, and unfeigned Pleasure" applauded Lord Dunmore for his statesmanlike leniency toward the Indians, saying: "You have taught them a lesson, which the savage Breast was a Stranger to, that Clemency and Mercy are not incompatable with Power, and that Havock and Bloodshed are not the inseparable Concomitants of Success and Victory." [6] The president and professors of the College of William and Mary were also moved by "an impulse of unfeigned Joy," saying: "And may you always feel the enlivening Pleasure of reading in the countenances around you, wherever you turn your Eyes, such expressions of Affection as can be derived only from applauding and grateful Hearts!" [7]

[6] Enclosed with Dunmore to Dartmouth, Dec. 24, 1774; PRO,CO 5/1353.
[7] Ibid.

The mayor, aldermen, and common council of Williamsburg were a little less effusive and derived only "pleasure" from Dunmore's successes, though they concluded by asserting that "we wish to your Lordship every degree of Felicity, and we shall contribute towards its attainment, as far as lies in our Power, during your residence amongst us." [8]

Unfortunately there was one very sour apple in the governor's barrel of happiness in the shape of a series of letters from the Secretary of State, Lord Dartmouth, which were awaiting him on his return. The Earl of Dartmouth had succeeded Lord Hillsborough in August 1772, and, as Dunmore had not been home since his appointment to the governorship of New York in 1770, neither had met since they had been in office. Indeed, one of Dunmore's first contacts with Lord Dartmouth had been his request to return home to recover from a long illness which had laid him low during his first summer in Williamsburg—to which the new Secretary replied that if his Lordship decided to come home he should be sure to report immediately on arrival so that a replacement could be appointed. In effect, the ailing governor was told to stay at his post or resign. It was not a very auspicious start for a relationship between the two instruments of the King's policy in Virginia, one which may thenceforth have become a little more distant than mere miles dictated.

All Lord Dartmouth's letters related to the deteriorating situation on the western frontier, to the disputed Pennsylvania-Virginia boundary toward the Ohio, and to Dunmore's willingness to grant land patents in Indian territory. Admittedly he had been slow to absorb the drift of previous instructions and he may even have deliberately misread them, but the Secretary's epistle of September 8 was a little excessive and was delivered with all the force that the language of diplomacy permitted. It asserted that the King's sacred word stood pledged to maintain existing treaties with the Indians and that "every attempt on the part of The King's Subjects to acquire title to and take possession

[8] Ibid.

of Lands beyond the line fixed by His Majesty's authority, and every encouragement given to such attempt, can be considered in no other light than that of a gross indignity and dishonour to the Crown, and an act of equal inhumanity and injustice to the Indians that cannot fail to be attended with fatal consequences."

Lest Dunmore should feel that it was the settlers and not he who had been instrumental in bringing indignity and dishonour to the Crown, Lord Dartmouth went on to explain precisely where the royal displeasure should rest.

I am commanded by The King to signify to your Lordship His Majesty's just Displeasure that such a proceeding as that to which your letter refers, should have received any degree of Countenance or encouragement from you; and it is not without real concern that I find myself obliged to observe to your Lordship, that if His Majesty had not been graciously pleased out of His great tenderness and lenity, to suppose that your conduct upon this occasion has proceeded from inadvertency to the facts above stated, it must have been followed by other marks of the royal Displeasure, which I mention to your Lordship with a wish of putting you more upon your guard for the future. . . .[9]

Lord Dunmore's Indian summer had not lasted until the season of good will, and on Christmas Eve he sat down to answer the charges made against him and to give an account of the events of the past months. He began with a long justification of his own actions which amounted to the claim that he was doing the best he could under very trying circumstances—which was certainly close to the truth. He assured his superior that he had not been deriving personal gain from the land grants that had been issued and that, furthermore, the western boundary of the colony was in such dispute that he was not sure where certain sections of it ran.

Reading Dunmore's letter today, nearly two centuries later, we can still clearly see the man creeping out from behind the

[9] Dartmouth to Dunmore, Sept. 8, 1774; PRO,CO 5/1375.

mantle of the King's governor, first answering each charge that
had been leveled against him, becoming increasingly irritated
that he should be forced to give such an account, and finally
exploding into a roar of exasperation and frustration. He was, he
said,

> incapable of intentionally encouraging any attempt against
> the Dignity and Honour of the Crown. But if His Majesty
> thinks otherwise, or has any other person in view, whose zeal
> and fidelity he has a better opinion of, than he has of mine,
> and he thinks would Serve him to better effect than I can, I
> shall only be sorry that I have been continued in my
> Government any time after such an Idea has been entertained
> of me; and I have no desire to remain longer in it than his
> Majesty approves of my conduct.[1]

Most of the long letter concerned the problems of the
frontier, to assaults by the Indians, retaliatory atrocities by the
settlers, and to an account of the militia's recent expedition and
the resulting treaty. These matters are not strictly relevant and
need not be related here; my purpose is only to illustrate
something of Lord Dunmore's relationship with his superiors in
England and to learn from his own mouth what the problems
and prospects of 1775 might be.

On Tuesday, May 24, 1774, the Virginia House of Burgesses had declared itself to be deeply disturbed by what it
called "the hostile Invasion of the City of Boston . . . Whose
Commerce and Harbour are on the first Day of June next, to be
stopped by an armed Force . . . ," and it ordered that the
same day should be set aside by the members as a "Day of
Fasting, Humiliation, and Prayer" to call on divine aid to avert
a civil war and to give them the strength to oppose "by all just
and proper Means, every Injury to American Rights. . . ."[2]
So obvious an act of defiance left the governor no alternative but
to dissolve the legislature—which he accordingly did on May
26. On the following day the burgesses transferred their

---

[1] Dunmore to Dartmouth, Dec. 24, 1774; PRO,CO 5/1353.
[2] Goodwin, *Williamsburg*, 250; quoting *JHB*, 1773–76, 124.

deliberations to the Apollo Room of Williamsburg's Raleigh Tavern, where they called for a congress of representatives from all the colonies to meet in Philadelphia in September. They also agreed to meet in a convention of their own on the first of August, which would be attended by delegates chosen by all the counties of Virginia.

When the convention met in Williamsburg the governor had already departed for the frontier, an absence that undoubtedly saved him considerable embarrassment as well as the necessity to voice his objections and thus further aggravate the situation. The delegates dutifully professed loyalty to the mother country and proceeded to pass a series of twelve resolutions designed to kick her hard in her economy. The first required that after November 1 there should be a total embargo on all British imports other than medicines; others banned the further importation of slaves and tea, called for an end to tea drinking, and ordained that if all grievances had not been redressed within a year all exports to Britain would be stopped.

In his report to the Secretary of State, Lord Dunmore expressed the opinion that the convention's resolutions would defeat their own ends.

Their non importation, non exportation &c. cannot fail in a Short time to produce a Scarcity, which will ruin thousands of Families: the people, indeed, of fortune Supply themselves and their Negroes for two or three years, but the middling and poorer Sort, who live from hand to mouth, have not the means of doing so; and the produce of their lands will not purchase those Necessaries without which themselves and Negroes Starve. . . . As to Manufacturing for themselves; the people of Virginia are very far from being Naturally industrious, and it is not by taking away the principal, if not the only encouragement to industry that it can be excited. . . . The lower class of People too will discover, that they have been duped by the richer Sort, who for their part, elude the whole effects of the Association, by which their poor neighbours perish. What then is to deter those from taking the Shortest mode of Supplying themselves? and, unrestrained as they are by laws, from taking what ever they want from where ever they can find it? [3]

The Continental Congress had adopted most of the measures proposed by the Virginia convention; committees of safety were established in every county to see that its resolutions were carried out and were given the power to seize merchants' books, to investigate their political beliefs, and to haul suspected miscreants before them for interrogation. No doubt the Congress took comfort in the old saw that the end would justify the means, even though the means opened the door for the exploitation of private hatreds, personal aggrandizement, the evasion of debts, and the destruction of the dignity of men. The spying or lying servant could turn informer and destroy his master and be called a patriot for having done it. If that did not satisfy him, a stop at the nearest tavern would rustle up a fine band of bully boys with a bucket of tar and a sack of feathers. Though the local committees publicly frowned on such unseemly methods of avenging themselves on those who did not agree with them, they were nevertheless zealous in their pursuit and destruction of their neighbor's good name, and public penance (with whatever consequences it might provoke) was generally the fate of the disaffected. Thus on January 7, 1775, the readers of the *Virginia Gazette* learned of the disloyalty of John Morris of Caroline County:

To the PRINTERS

GENTLEMEN,
The Committee of Caroline desire you will publish, without any correction whatever, the enclosed apology, made before a numerous assembly of people at a meeting of the Committee, by John Morris, merchant in the said county.

SAMUEL HAWS, jun. Clk. Com.

It Having been proved by the Deposition of Several Witnesses that I have made use of Certain expressions foreign from the Good of this Country. I do therefore Confess myself

---

[3] Dunmore to Dartmouth, Dec. 24, 1774, PRO,CO 5/1353.

Heartily Sorry for it and Concurring in the Association Hopes that this will Prove Sufficiently satisfactory to the Gentlemen of this Country who have had so Just a Cause of Complaint and Confessing my Error hopes that my futture Behaviour Will be a means of my again Regaining their Esteem.

JOHN MORRIS.

The case of John Morris and, for that matter, all the others who were examined by the county committees in 1774 and early '75, possessed one remarkable feature in that whereas such investigations are commonly the aftermath of revolution, here they were occurring when no revolution had been declared. The committees did not consider themselves illegal, nor were they, for no existing law condemned them. In promoting such committees the congress was allegedly doing nothing more improper than working toward the peaceful redress of just grievances, and the issue at the county level was simply local control of local institutions; at least that was the rationale at the beginning of the year. The committees were avowedly loyal to the King, the King's officer still governed the colony, and its economy was still directed through the Board of Trade. Officially all was as it had been for the best part of a century—yet John Morris had only to express himself as being satisfied with the established order of things to find himself hauled before a committee of his peers and forced to make a public denial of his beliefs. All was very obviously *not* as it had been.

Lord Dunmore's little parcel of letters from the Secretary of State had included one urging him to use his authority to restore the status quo, though it omitted to explain how this could be achieved. The Virginia governor had no army to enforce his directives; after all this was a British colony peopled almost entirely by British subjects, and in theory the only dangers to it would come from without, from the Indians (who were now without, and had been for some time) or perhaps from Spain or France. The defense of the colonies could therefore be left to the colonists themselves, to the militia companies. But even as

Dunmore marched back from his successful Indian war, his officers were thinking of new commissions. In their absence the counties had agreed to establish independent companies, which, as Dunmore explained to the Secretary of State, were raised "for the avowed purpose of protecting their committees, and to be employed against Government if occasion require." [4] Thus the soldiers who had fought beside Dunmore against the Indian enemy now found a new allegiance.

"As to the Power of Government," wrote Dunmore to Lord Dartmouth, "which your Lordship in your Letter No. 11 directs should be exerted to counteract the dangerous Measures pursuing here, I can assure your Lordship, that it is entirely disregarded, if not wholly overturned." [5] He went on to assert that there was not a single justice of the peace left in Virginia who was not a "Committee Man"; the local courts had been abolished, and although the general court, presided over by the governor and his council, was still officially scheduled, cases were not tried because the lawyers would not attend. In short, the governor had become a toothless lion, a role which he did not relish in the least. His only hope was to obtain physical support from home, but he knew that he had little chance of averting attention from the more obviously explosive problems in Massachusetts.

"These undutifull People," he wrote, "should be made to feel the distress and Misery, of which they have themselves laid the foundation, as soon as possible, and before they can have time to find out ways and means of Supplying themselves. Their own Schemes should be turned against them, and they should not be permitted to procure under hand, what they refuse to admit openly; and, above all, they should not be permitted to go to foreign Ports to Seek the things they want. Their Ports should be blocked up, and their Communication Cut off by Water even with their Neighbouring Colonies." [6] Dunmore

[4] Ibid.
[5] Ibid.
[6] Ibid.

believed that this could be achieved with no more than a single man-of-war, one frigate, and a couple of tenders stationed off the Chesapeake Bay. He would later demonstrate that this was a pretty fair estimate, though he was wrong in assuming that the tree of revolution could be so easily blighted.

There can be no denying the general accuracy of Lord Dunmore's summary of the parlous state in which Virginia found itself at the close of 1774. The more vociferous patriots might have contended that the cool fresh wind of change was blowing through the colony and that it portended nothing but good; the governor, and the few loyalists with the courage to speak out, naturally took the opposite view, while between them stood the majority of Virginians, who could see nothing for 1775 but trouble—and they wished it would go away.

Had Virginia housed a British military garrison, it is conceivable that Dunmore might have used it to arrest the principal troublemakers and that, apart from a few minor skirmishes with the more rabid patriots, he might have scotched the revolutionary movement, at least for the time being. Much would have depended on the reaction of the essentially neutralist "don't know or don't care" element of the population. Having no troops to back him, the governor's only other military approach would have been to hoist the royal standard and issue a proclamation calling on all true Englishmen to rally to it. Such an act would have automatically plunged the colony into the civil war he was trying to avoid, and he would undoubtedly have been blamed for it both in America and at home. Dunmore had, therefore, really no alternative but to sit tight, to do as little as possible to rock the boat, and to rely on the steadying influence of the neutralists and middle-ground conservatives to keep it afloat.

Lord Dunmore's own popularity, regardless of his recent testimonials, was not very great. He was, after all, the symbol of parliamentary oppression, and as the King's governor he had to be officially opposed to every "patriotic" outburst which threatened or offended the dignity of royal authority in the colony;

furthermore, he was a Scot, and all Scots were born avaricious and uncivilized. As one Scots merchant in Norfolk put it, Dunmore was as "popular as a Scotsman can be amongst weak prejudiced people." [7] We may safely conclude, as Dunmore must have done when he sat down to review the situation on Christmas Eve, that the affection and respect of the colonists as a whole did not weigh very heavily when it came to balancing his assets. There was not even much comfort to be drawn from telling himself that he had friends in the other royal governors and that they were all in the same straits together. Dunmore did not have an entente with his neighbors; indeed, the governor of Pennsylvania, John Penn, had little love for him, believing him responsible for much of the trouble on that colony's western frontier. If Dunmore paused to consider, as he doubtless did, he must also have realized that all the governors were not in the same predicament.

In the first week of January 1775 Lord Dunmore had an opportunity to compare notes with his closest neighbor, Josiah Martin, governor of North Carolina, who with his family was on his way back to New Bern from New York. Martin, then aged thirty-eight, a retired lieutenant colonel of infantry, was a man with considerable personal charm as well as long experience of colonial affairs. He had succeeded the unpopular Governor Tryon in 1771, shortly after the first colonial civil war confrontation at the battle of the Alamance, and he had found himself saddled with an assembly weighted with malcontents who became ever more vociferous as tensions between Britain and the colonies increased. Martin's difficulties had therefore been of longer standing than Dunmore's; he had inherited the aftermath of a revolt, whereas Dunmore had followed a governor who had been revered throughout Virginia. Martin had used his personality to win respect in his colony and he had enjoyed some measure of success; but Dunmore, apart from his military exploit had done little to impress people with his moderation and

[7] James Parker to Charles Steuart, Jan. 27; CSP.

understanding of their problems. Besides, when the two men met in Williamsburg in January, Governor Martin was in distinctly the more enviable position in that he could reasonably count on the loyalty of the large numbers of highland Scots who had settled in his colony, and regardless of their dubious social graces he could not want for better fighters.

Although no records survive to tell us of the two governors' conversations, the remarkable parallels between their approaches to the trials of 1775 would suggest that they carefully considered their strategy. Dunmore had long feared the possibility of a slave uprising, and it is highly probable that the discussions turned more than once to the role the Negroes might play if actual fighting should begin. In an attempt to envisage Dunmore's views we may usefully recall his comments to the Secretary of State more than two and a half years earlier.

At present the Negroes are double the number of white people in this Colony, which by the natural increase, and the great addition of new imported ones every year is sufficient to alarm not only this Colony, but all the Colonies of America. . . . in case of a war which may probably often happen with Spain, or indeed any other Power, that might make an attack upon this Colony, the people with great reason tremble at the facility that an enemy would find in procuring such a body of men, attached by no ties to their masters or to the Country; on the contrary it is natural to suppose their condition must inspire them with an aversion to both, & therefore are ready to join the first that would encourage them to revenge themselves, by which means a conquest of this Country would inevitably be effected in a very short time. . . .[8]

Here was something worth thinking about, something that could only be discussed in lowered voices behind locked doors and that, if overheard, might provoke an explosion in Virginia and North Carolina that would shatter the windows of Whitehall.

[8] Dunmore to Hillsborough, May 1, 1772; PRO,CO 5/1372.

If the citizens of Williamsburg knew that the two governors
were discussing matters of grave import, the fact was never
mentioned in the press: the *Virginia Gazette* noted only that
Josiah Martin and his family had stayed with Lord Dunmore
from Saturday to Wednesday and then had gone upon their
way. It is, of course, very easy and smugly satisfying for the
historian to point knowingly to the seeds of great events and to
belittle those contemporaries who had failed to recognize them.
It may perfectly well be that nobody gave the Dunmore-Martin
visit any thought, and it is even possible that no plans were laid
and no ploys discussed—though I doubt it. Be this as it may,
there was one paragraph in the January 7 *Gazette* whose
significance no one could have foreseen. It said only that "The
Magdalen armed Schooner, Capt. Collins, is arrived at Norfolk,
from the Northward."

Norfolk was the largest town of colonial Virginia, with a
population of about 6,000 and a size about four times that of the
administrative capital at Williamsburg. It possessed, as it still
does, one of the finest harbors on the eastern seaboard, well-built
wharves and warehouses, many stores and merchants' offices, a
town hall, poor house, and churches. It was a town of considerable wealth, though not a great deal of culture; in short it was
little different from any sizable British port of the period, such
as Portsmouth or Gravesend. Williamsburg, on the other hand,
was the product of a society specifically Virginian. It was
established in 1699 to replace the unsatisfactory Jamestown,
which by that time had declined into a community of tavern
keepers whose business boomed only four times a year, when the
courts and assembly were in session. Because the colony existed
on the profits of its land, the majority of the colonists needed
ground of their own. So, when their fear of Indian attack had
been dissipated, they moved away from the protection of
community life to live on farms, either as landowners or tenants.
But because they had little concept of how to make the best use
of their soil, they proceeded to cultivate it until it was played out
and then cleared some more. There was, to be sure, a great deal

of land; nevertheless, the best of it was soon built up into a comparatively small number of great estates, driving the little man into their employment or into the interior.

When the seat of government was moved from Jamestown to Williamsburg the same structure prevailed. Although supporters of the new location claimed that the town was strategically placed between the York and the James rivers and would receive shipping from both, docking in College and Queen's creeks, Williamsburg was not a port and therefore it did not receive the maritime business enjoyed by Norfolk, Yorktown, or Fredericksburg. Furthermore, Williamsburg had no industries and only a few tradesmen; indeed, its total population in 1775 was about 1,600, of which half were Negroes. It did possess numerous taverns, as well as a fair array of stores, all of which slept away the months when the courts and general assembly were not sitting. Like seasonal floods, the advent of the courts in spring and autumn suddenly swelled the town until it burst at the seams. Up to 6,000 people were wont to pour in from all over the colony; legislators, lawyers, plaintiffs, witnesses, merchants, peddlers, players—anyone with a shilling in his pocket and a desire to do business, seek a job, meet friends, or just raise hell. There was not a bed to be had, unless you were prepared to squeeze one more into a cot with six feet protruding from it already. The streets were jammed with carriages whose wheels raised clouds of dust while their drivers cursed their horses and each other; peddlers' stalls covered the market square, and amongst them youths tried their luck chasing greased pigs, cudgelling, or yelling themselves hoarse at the sight of steel spurs slashing through feathers and flesh at a cockfight. If they still had any breath left they could compete in a foot race down the mile length of Duke of Gloucester Street from the College of William and Mary at one end to the handsome brick Capitol at the other. But in doing so, they may have had difficulty avoiding the carriages, chairs, cart ruts, and cattle that obstructed its entire length. The victor could win himself anything from a pair of silver buckles to a pint of ale, the latter only being attained after fighting his way through a crowd of planters gathered at the steps of the Raleigh to bid on a new consignment of slaves or to listen to the result of a lottery. Inside, the smell of liquor, food, and sweat contrasted sharply with the elegance of lace cuffs, brocade waistcoats, and silver buttons. It was here, and in other taverns like it, that planters traded their tobacco and made deals with factors and ships' captains, drawing up agreements on which their fortunes and their futures hung and gambling on the honesty of agents and the chances of a fair wind to England.

Unfortunately many English and foreign visitors saw Williamsburg only in the heat of "Public Times," and what they saw they heartily disliked. A French traveler who stayed there in 1765 declared: "Never was a more disagreeable Place than this at Present. In the Day Time People hurrying back and forwards from the Capitoll to the Taverns, and at Night, carousing and drinking in one Chamber and Box and Dice in another, which continues till Morning commonly. . . ." [9] But when the courts or assembly adjourned the town emptied just as quickly as it had filled; only streets churned up like an Ocean City beach after Labor Day, a market square littered with broken bottles, torn advertising and discarded packaging, and a community of tired tavern keepers bore witness to the chaos that had reigned. Like modern resorts after the last beach umbrella has been blown inside out, Williamsburg settled down to a somnambulant pace with nothing much to do except clear up the mess, patch up the paint, restock the stores and cellars, count the money, and wait for next time.

Visitors who passed through the town in the sleeping seasons received an entirely different impression of it. Nicholas Cresswell thought it the finest town he had seen in Virginia, and he described both the college and Capitol as "large and elegant brick buildings"—though he was less impressed by the governor's palace, which he considered "a good brick building, but it

[9] Goodwin, *Williamsburg*, 224; quoting "A French Traveller in the Colonies, 1765," *AHR*, XXVI (July, 1921), 742–3.

does not make a grand appearance. Here is only one Church," he added, "none of the grandest, and I suppose there may be about 250 houses in town." [1]

The Reverend Andrew Burnaby had visited Williamsburg in 1759, and his description, which was first published in 1775, was rather more detailed than Cresswell's, though his opinion was much the same.

It consists of about two hundred houses, does not contain more than one thousand souls, whites and negroes; and is far from being a place of any consequence. It is regularly laid out in parallel streets, intersected by others at right angles; has a handsome square in the center through which runs the principal street, one of the most spacious in North-America, three quarters of a mile in length, and above a hundred feet wide. At the ends of this street are two public buildings, the college and the capitol: and although the houses are of wood, covered with shingles, and but indifferently built, the whole makes a handsome appearance. There are few public edifices that deserve to be taken notice of; those, which I have mentioned, are the principal; and they are far from being magnificent. The governor's palace, indeed, is tolerably good, one of the best upon the continent; but the church, the prison, and the other buildings, are all of them extremely indifferent. The streets are not paved, and are consequently very dusty. . . . Upon the whole, it is an agreeable residence; there are ten or twelve gentlemen's families constantly residing in it, besides merchants and tradesmen: and at the times of the assemblies, and general courts, it is crowded with the gentry of the country: on those occasions there are balls and other amusements; but as soon as the business is finished, they return to their plantations; and the town is in a manner deserted.[2]

It seems that most visitors were inclined to condemn the town with faint praise. Nevertheless, it was the social and cultural center of the colony, and even when Williamsburg was sleeping it possessed a nucleus of educated people drawn from

[1] *Cresswell*, 207–8; April 29, 1777.
[2] Burnaby, *Travels*, 4–5.

the governor's staff, the faculty at the college and the families of
the merchants, city officials, and near-by planters. It was for
these that organ concerts were given at Bruton Parish Church,
occasional plays were performed by the college students, dancing masters held classes, and visiting lecturers offered anything
from a discourse on phrenology to an exhibition of mechanical
marvels. Readers of the *Virginia Gazette* [3] learned that on
Saturday, January 7, they would be treated to Mr. Wall's
demonstration of electricity with "Real Lightening." Thomas
Wall was a temporarily retired actor who made a living as an
itinerent music teacher and lecturer on such subjects as "heads"
and "noses." His knowledge of electricity was newly acquired
and presumably small, though not, he hoped quite as small as
that of his prospective audiences. The lecture was to be given at
the home of Mr. Gabriel Maupin, opposite the church, and for
the substantial price of three shillings and ninepence the amazed
public was invited to enjoy three "courses," the first offering
"Electrical sparks visible to the eye, and sensible to the touch,"
an electrical football, and a free shock for anyone wanting to
stick his hand into a basin of water. The second course was a
little more advanced and included "A small shower of artificial
snow. Ditto of rain." The third featured "The electrical kiss"
along with further shocks for the more adventurous members of
the audience. This section of the program also contained a
discourse on the horrors of thunderstorms and offered advice on
how to protect one's home against them. Although the whole
thing was advertised as being "For promoting religion, morality, useful knowledge, the instruction of the curious, and for the
benefit of persons afflicted with paralytic disorders," one cannot
help wondering whether Mr. Wall may not also have doubled as
a lightning rod salesman.

No eyewitness accounts survive to give us a description of
the electrical demonstration, and no space was given to it in the
next issue of the *Gazette*, perhaps because it was too concerned

[3] Pinkney, Jan. 5.

with printing accounts of calculatedly insolent resolutions passed at committee meetings in Caroline, Richmond, and Charles City counties. The seeds of discontent, which were sown in the taverns and fertilized with a weekly dose of printers' ink, produced only a small thorn to torture the governor's already smarting flesh. More important than tavern gossip were the opinions of the members of his council and of the House of Burgesses, and more important still, the reaction of his Majesty's government to his letter of December 24th. It was probably this last consideration that prompted Lord Dunmore to postpone the meeting of the general assembly scheduled for February 2, until May 4, thus giving him time to receive further instructions from the Secretary of State. It also, as it happened, gave the political situation plenty of time to go from bad to worse. The governor's proclamation received only minimum space in the Dixon and Hunter *Gazette* of January 21, possibly because Pinkney had given it a double-column splash on the very day of issuance, adorned incidentally with the same ornamental cut showing shipping before a castle beneath the arms of the colony, which had embellished his masthead until it had been scrapped in December of the previous year.

If Pinkney's Thursday placing of his proclamation had been accepted by Dunmore as right and proper, Dixon and Hunter's issue of January 21 must surely have stifled any affection for the press which his Lordship might have been generating. The entire front page was devoted to a day-by-day account of the previous September's proceedings of the Continental Congress. It was not exactly hot news, but it could be relied on to stoke any fires which might have been cooling during the winter. Lord Dunmore's gesture of christening his daughter, Virginia, along with the celebration of the Queen's birthday at the governor's palace, were dismissed in a single two-sentence paragraph. If this was not intended as an affront, such slender recognition following the long Continental Congress coverage could hardly have made his Lordship very happy. He may also have noted that he was given less attention than the next item recording the

marriage of Beverley Randolph Esq. to Miss Martha Cocke, an
occasion which prompted the editors to a small poetic excess,
informing their readers that

> In this amiable couple every manly and tender virtue conspire
> to render the marriage state completely happy.

> "Perpetual harmony their bed attend,
> "And Hymen still the well-matched fair befriend,
> "May she, when time has sunk him into years,
> "Love her old man, and cherish his white hairs;
> "Nor he perceive her charms through age decay,
> "But think each happy turn his bridal day."

If Dunmore was scratching about for some faint consolation, he
might have found it in the thought that at least he had been
spared this melancholy little verse with its self-destroying
spelling error in the second line. However, the bottom of the
same column did contain a word of cheer; though not being
clairvoyant, the governor could not have fully appreciated it.
The item was datelined Portsmouth, Virginia, January 12:

> Last week a deputation from this town waited upon Capt.
> Montagu, and the other Gentlemen officers on board his
> Majesty's ship the Fowey, and delivered them a card of
> thanks for the important aid they afforded at a late alarming
> fire in that town, and for the constant readiness they have
> always shown to assist every trading vessel in distress.———
> The address was politely received; and Captain Montagu
> having thanked them, was pleased to say, "He ever would be
> disposed to grant every assistance in his power, when
> consistent with his duty."

It was a nice change to find citizens of a Virginia community
with a good word to say for an officer of the Crown. At the same
time, Montagu gave a suitably proper and loyal response. He
would be worth watching.

The last January issue of the *Gazette* concluded its front-
page coverage of the autumn deliberations of the Continental
Congress, ending with an advertisement for "The Whole
Proceedings of the Grand American Continental Congress (in a

pamphlet, just published, Price 2/6.) to be Sold by Dixon and Hunter only at the Post Office, Williamsburg." We do not know how many customers rushed there to obtain their unabridged pamphlets, or whether, perhaps, the crowd at the door was actually seeking the address of the two gentlemen of King and Queen County who, according to the paper, had made a rather remarkable discovery—a technique for extracting molasses from pumpkins. "The pumkins yielded liquor of a good quality, and in such quantities that two rendered three quarts fit for distilling.——This being the case, the colony may, with a proper use of this information, be thoroughly supplied with rum without extra-imports of molasses." [4] Here at least was a piece of news to be appreciated and applauded by patriots and Tories alike, unless, of course, they happened to be in the imported liquor business. Another small news item, this time from New York, was less gratifying; it reported that "The Company of Comedians, with Mr. Douglass, the manager, are preparing to embark for the island of Jamaica, and they will not return to the continent, until its tranquility is restored."

The Douglass Company was well remembered by Virginia theatergoers; originally known as "Lewis Hallam's select Company of Comedians," it had arrived in Williamsburg in the summer of 1752 fresh from Goodmansfields, London, offering new scenery and new plays, which would be performed "in as polite a manner as at the Theatres in London." By way of a small contradiction it had opened with the *Merchant of Venice;* but new or not, the players' efforts were well received. Subsequently the Hallam Company toured the colonies with a largely contemporary repertoire which included Farquhar's *The Beaux' Stratagem,* Congreve's *Love for Love,* Colly Cibber's *The Careless Husband,* and Steele's *The Conscious Lover.* When the troupe returned to Williamsburg in 1760, Hallam had died and David Douglass had taken over both the management and the late manager's widow and leading lady, marrying her after a

[4] Dixon & Hunter, Jan. 28.

suitable period of mourning. The Douglass Company included the new Mrs. Douglass's two sons, Adam and Lewis Hallam, Jr., the latter's small-talented wife, Sarah, and Mrs. Douglass's much-admired niece, Nancy. Lewis eventually earned himself his place in theatrical history as the first great actor of the American stage, while Nancy became the toast of wherever it was she happened to be. The company was in Williamsburg in the spring and fall of 1770, and between June 16 and 28 George Washington bought tickets for ten performances. Thomas Jefferson was equally devoted and went to see the plays (and Nancy Hallam) thirteen times between October 23 and November 8.

The company presented what was to be its last Williamsburg season during the general assembly meetings of February to April, 1772, and again Washington was a frequent member of the "very crowded and splendid Audience." [5] The players had been so long a part of the Williamsburg scene that, even after an absence of two years, the news that they were leaving the country must have left many a playgoer with the feeling that this was the end of an era. Others less sensitive and with fewer cherished memories of Nancy Hallam and magic moments behind the footlights, probably dismissed them with a grunted comment on rats and sinking ships. Among those voicing such views may well have been Sarah Hallam, who had herself been abandoned by her husband in Williamsburg more than eleven years before. As for Nancy and the rest of the troupe, none of them would be seen again in Williamsburg; indeed, by 1780 the theater, too, had gone, although for another seven years its foundations protruded from the ground like a graveyard of the arts.

In London, in January 1775, the theatrical season was in full swing, the highlight being the opening, on the seventeenth, of a new play by the young Mr. Sheridan, entitled *The Rivals*. Unfortunately it proved to be something of a bomb. *Lloyd's*

[5] *Virginia Gazette* (Purdie & Dixon), April 2, 1772; quoted by Jane Carson, *Colonial Virginians at Play*, 236.

Evening Post thought it required "much castigation, and the
pruning hand of judgment, before it ever can pass on the town
as even a tolerable piece." The reviewer for the *Morning
Chronicle* declared unequivocally that he had never seen "a
performance more disgraceful to a Theatre-Royal," and complained that one of the principals could not remember two lines
in a row and that when he fluffed them "he tried to fill the
interval with oaths and buffoonery." Another actor caused the
same critic to assert that "of all disgusting attempts that ever
was damned in a strolling company, nothing ever came up to
this. . . ." [6]

Three days later the voice of another critic was raised in
loud condemnation when "the Great Commoner," William Pitt,
Earl of Chatham, rose in the House of Lords to reply to Lord
Dartmouth after the latter's delivery of the most recent dispatches from America. Sad faced, and bent with age and long
years of sickness, Chatham began by proposing that the King
should order the withdrawal of his troops from the town of
Boston.

I wish, my Lords, [he said] not to lose a day in this
urgent and pressing crisis; an hour now lost in allaying the
ferment in America, may produce years of calamity; for my
own part, I will not desert for a moment the conduct of this
mighty business, from the first to the last; unless nailed to my
bed by the extremity of sickness . . . I will knock at the
door of this sleeping and confounded Ministry, and will rouse
them to a sense of their important danger.

When I state the importance of the Colonies to this
country, and the magnitude of danger hanging over this
country, from the present plan of misadministration practised
against them, I desire not to be understood to argue a
reciprocity of indulgence between England and America. I
contend not for indulgence, but justice for America. . . .
But his Majesty is advised that the union in America cannot
last. Ministers have more eyes than I, and should have more

[6] Hampden, *Journal*, 134; quoting *Lloyd's Evening Post* and the
Morning Chronicle for Jan. 18.

ears; but from all the information I have been able to procure,
I can pronounce it, an union, solid, permanent and effectual. . . .

The spirit which now resists your taxation in America, is
the same which formerly opposed loans, benevolences, and
ship-money in England:—the same spirit which called all
England *on its legs*, and by the Bill of Rights vindicated the
English constitution:—the same principle which established
the great, fundamental, essential maxim of our liberties, *that
no subject of England shall be taxed but by his own
consent.* . . .

Lord Chatham's speech was long and eloquent, full of
phrases to quicken the heart and thoughts to stir the conscience
of the King. He called again on the government to withdraw the
troops and repeal the acts that denied the colonists the rights of
Englishmen.

*They must be repealed,—you will repeal them; I pledge
myself for it, that you will in the end repeal them; I stake my
reputation on it:—I will consent to be taken for an idiot, if
they are not finally repealed.* . . .

To conclude, my Lords: if the Ministers thus persevere in
misadvising and misleading the King, I will not say they *can*
alienate the affections of his subjects from his crown; but I
will affirm *that they will make the crown not worth his
wearing*. I will not say that the King is betrayed; but I will
pronounce, *that the kingdom is undone.* . . .[7]

In his closing words Chatham spoke of himself as "aged and
infirm,"[8] but his speech was vibrant with life and would give
strength to many men far younger than he. However, it failed to
win the approval of the House, which, when it divided, voted 68
to 18 in support of the government.

Lord Chatham's speech would not be read in Virginia until
April; in the meantime there would be other speeches and

[7] Ibid., 136–9; quoting Hugh Boyd, *The Miscellaneous Works of
Hugh Boyd*, with an account of his life and writings by Lawrence
Dundas Campbell (London, 1800), I, 255 ff.

[8] *Virginia Gazette* (Dixon & Hunter), April 15.

proclamations to engage the attention of colonial patriots. If the governor so much as announced that yesterday's weather was horrible, he could expect a score of voices to be raised in protest at so gross a slight on the climate of the colony. The *Virginia Gazette* [9] for January 28 carried a quite innocuous proclamation wherein Lord Dunmore recalled the reciprocal terms of the recent treaty with the Indians and ordered that all Virginians should refrain from further encroachments on Indian territory and that magistrates should see to it that the Indians were protected by every means in their power. The support of Indian rights to property and human dignity has never been America's strong suit, and so it may have been this which prompted a *Gazette* reader to edit, in ink, the proclamation's closing "GOD SAVE THE KING," to read: "GOD DAM THE KING." We may safely assume that the scribe enjoyed the same sense of misspelled satisfaction that is to be obtained from scratching obscenities on washroom walls. It was, to be sure, a small and infantile gesture, but it probably represented the only mark that that patriot would leave on the page of history, surviving long after his own name had been forgotten. It may not be much of an epitaph, but it certainly provided a concise prologue to the drama of the months to come.

[9] Dixon & Hunter.

[*II*]

FEBRUARY

In *Virginia February began quietly; but*
across the water in England it was heralded by a storm of
terrifying proportions. A lunatic prophet near Greenwich had
foretold that the town would be swallowed by an earthquake,
thus causing many of its inhabitants to take to their heels. At
Portsmouth, and at other towns along the English Channel, the
tide rose higher than at any time in living memory, flooding
streets of houses and drowning hundreds of cattle. It was, all in
all, a fittingly ominous prelude to the storms being spawned in
parliament, which would continue to rock its houses for many
days to come.

On Wednesday, the first of the month, Lord Chatham
outlined a bill in the House of Lords which he called "A
Provisional act for settling the troubles in America, and for
asserting the supreme legislative authority and superintending
power of Great-Britain over the Colonies." It was no surprise to
anyone that this was a conciliatory proposition; it proposed that
no taxes should be levied in America "except by common
consent in their provincial assemblies." It accepted the Crown's
right to send its armies where it wished, but added the rather
ineffectual reservation that no military force should be used to
violate or destroy the rights of the people. The bill also called
for legalizing a meeting of the Continental Congress in May—to
give it an opportunity to recognize the authority of parliament
over the colonies, and to enable the delegates to make a "free
grant to the King . . . of a certain and perpetual revenue,

subject to the disposition of parliament, and applicable to the alleviation of the national debt."

It is doubtful whether the bill would have earned much sustained applause in America, and it is likely that Lord Dartmouth quickly realized it, for instead of condemning it out of hand he paid tribute to its noble author and declared that it required to be maturely and fully considered. But the lords supporting the administration were not in the least impressed by the bill nor were they awed by its author; instead they leapt upon it as viciously as hounds upon a fox. In presenting the bill, Lord Chatham had explained that it was put forward only in an embryo state and he had begged for the assistance of the House in digesting the raw material. He did not get it. As the *Annual Register* noted, bills of any stature at all, regardless of their form, would merit more than one reading and considerable debate. This bill was condemned out of hand, and its manner of presentation was declared "irregular, unparliamentary, and unprecedented. . . ."[1] The administration lords contended that the whole thing was, in effect, an acceptance of American demands and of American actions. After a series of heated exchanges the bill was rejected by a vote of 61 to 32, the opposition figure probably somewhat swollen by the votes of those who felt that so peremptory a dismissal of an elder stateman's brain child was an insult to him and unworthy of the House.

On the next day the Prime Minister, Lord North, rose in the House of Commons to outline some of his proposals for bringing the colonies to heel. In a long speech retelling the history of America's disenchantment, he laid most of the blame on New England malcontents and claimed that the seditious spirit nurtured there was being fed from both sides of the Atlantic. Rather than withdrawing the troops from Boston, as Lord Chatham had urged in January, he proposed to reinforce General Gage with four more regiments. As for the fears of the

[1] *Annual Register, 1775*, "History of Europe," 58 ff.

adverse effects on trade resulting from the congressional ban on imports and exports, the Prime Minister assured the House that it would come to nought. Furthermore, he would see to it that the weapon was turned upon its own creators; if America would not trade with Britain, then British ships would prevent the New England colonies from commerce with any other country. In addition, the navy would also deny them access to the Newfoundland fishing banks.

Lord North then moved that an address be presented to the Throne declaring that the recently transmitted American dispatches had been thoroughly studied and that it was the considered opinion of parliament that the Massachusetts Bay colony was in a state of rebellion and that all necessary measures should be taken to put it down. This was, in reality, a call for a declaration of war, and many members looked upon it with considerable misgivings; they were not at all certain that Massachusetts was in a state of rebellion and they made no bones about saying so. But when it came to a division, the address was approved by 296 to 106. Afterwards Horace Walpole noted in his *Journal* that it was "*a vote for a civil war. . . .*"[2]

The Commons' decision was by no means the end of the matter, and a few days later an opportunity arose to reopen the debate. By that time the members had had an opportunity to consider in the privacy of their own hearts the implications of their previous vote, and it was moved that Lord North's address should be re-examined. The resulting debate was even more vitriolic than before; the Ministry was condemned by the Opposition and warned that a conquest of America would only ensure its eventual loss, while its supporters countered that "the Americans had long been aiming at independency; and that as soon as they thought themselves able, and a pretence occurred, they insolently and openly avowed their eagerness to put the design in execution. . . ." It was the duty of all Englishmen,

---

[2] Hampden, *Journal*, 146, quoting Horace Walpole, *A Journal of the Reign of King George III, 1771–1783* (London, 1857), I, 455.

the administration supporters contended, to "crush the monster in its birth" [3] and to bring the wayward and misled colonies back, repentant, into the fold. The debate kept the Commons' candles burning late into the night, and it was past two in the morning when it agreed to vote on the almost forgotten issue of whether or not the address to the King should be recommitted. The vote was 288 against, and 105 in favor of the motion—the address would stand.

Upon receipt of the address the King quickly sent his answer back to parliament, urging it to press forward with its plans with all possible speed. On February 10 the Prime Minister moved that he be allowed to introduce a bill to restrain the trade, not only of the Massachusetts colony, but also of New Hampshire, Connecticut, Rhode Island, and Providence Plantation. As only Massachusetts Bay had been named in the address as being in a state of rebellion, the inclusion of the others provoked a storm of objections in the House. Nevertheless, when it came to a division the members lined up as usual to give the administration an overwhelming majority. The debate continued throughout the month as the bill passed from reading to reading, and it is unnecessary to pursue it any further. The Southern colonies figured hardly at all in the arguments, the government firmly believing that once the New England colonies were chastened the others would be only too happy to forget the whole thing.

I realize that it is cheating a little to discuss these parliamentary developments in February when news of them would not reach Virginia until mid-April. I have chosen to do so simply because these highly dramatic debates set the seal on what was to follow. In addition, they help us to see how strong was the power of the administration. There was not the slightest hope that the supporters of American liberties would win more than respect for their rhetoric. It is very tempting to see Lord Chatham and the rest of the Opposition as the knights of

---

[3] *Annual Register, 1775,* "History of Europe," 68.

integrity tilting against the black Lord North and the hell-hounds of his government. But the lines are not so easily drawn; the administration had certainly maneuvered itself into an extremely embarrassing situation, but it could and did argue that any lack of firmness now would be exploited a hundredfold in the future. A deteriorating political situation demands a bold remedy. If the choice is force, then that force must be massive and sustained until the desired ends are achieved. There can be no time for moral reappraisals, no pauses for fear of what others may say or think, no softening of the blows in the hope that history will be lenient. Success, however achieved, will acquire an aura of respectability, of "rightness"; only failure will be condemned. These were the kinds of arguments that were voiced in England in support of a hard line in dealing with the escalating unrest. The British government of 1775 was doubtless morally wrong, but there was good reason to suppose that it might be politically and militarily right.

Having taken this position the government benches were stunned when, on February 20, Lord North proposed the resolution that if the colonies would themselves raise money to contribute their proportion to the common defense, the Ministry would forbear to "levy any duties, tax or assessment, except only such duties as may be expedient to impose for the regulation of commerce." Neither side of the House could believe its ears; almost before the ink was dry on a series of highly punitive measures, the Prime Minister was reversing himself and proposing the kind of conciliatory motion which, if offered by the Opposition, would have been hounded out of Westminster. Nevertheless, Lord North urbanely proceeded to defend his position at considerable length, explaining that his proposal in no way detracted from the authority of the previous coercive resolutions, but simply demonstrated parliament's willingness to be fair. At the same time, it would, he contended, provide "an infallible touchstone to try the sincerity of the Americans. . . ."

The Tories found it hard to see the logic of their leader's argument, and vehement objections were voiced from the government benches. The members saw only that the resolution called for them to "give up every ground they had gone upon in the whole course of American measures," and "that it was a contradiction to all the acts and declarations of parliament." [4] Lord North admitted that he did not expect that the American patriots in general would favor the proposition, but he contended that it might serve to divide them. He argued that if but one colony would accept the offer, the entire confederacy would be broken. Eventually, after much more heated debate, the government members decided to support the motion rather than side with the Opposition, and it was carried with the wide margin of 186 votes. The good word would now be passed on to the various colonial governors and it would be up to them to try to sell it to their respective legislatures.

Although Virginia would not react to the events in London for some weeks, it did get something of a preview of those events when the ship *Caroline*, six weeks out of London, lay to in the Potomac and unloaded, among other things, a copy of the King's address on the opening of parliament at the end of the previous November. Most of it had been devoted to the problems of Massachusetts, where, it was declared, "a most daring spirit of resistance and disobedience to the law still unhappily prevails . . . and has, in divers parts of it, broke forth in fresh violences of a very criminal nature." The King went on to state that this lawlessness was being approved of and encouraged in other colonies. "I have," he declared, "taken such measures, and given such orders, as I judged most proper and effectual for carrying into execution the laws which were passed in the last session of the late parliament . . . and you may depend upon my firm and steadfast resolution to withstand every attempt to weaken or impair the supreme authority of this legislature over

[4] Ibid., 95–100.

all the dominions of my crown; the maintainance of which I consider as essential to the dignity, the safety, and the welfare, of the British empire. . . ." [5]

The King's address was printed in the *Virginia Gazette* on February 4 and left little doubt that the Crown intended to remain, as it said, "firm and stedfast" in its resolve to use any means, however harsh, to chasten Massachusetts and any other colony whose radicals could not be controlled by their governors. The Secretary of State had mailed a copy of the address to Lord Dunmore on December 10, but it seems that he first read it in the *Gazette*—which must have been a little irritating. The paper, as I have noted, published the address on February 4, and on February 7 Dunmore wrote to Lord Dartmouth acknowledging receipt of correspondence dated November 2. He did not acknowledge the arrival of the December 10 letters until March 14, at which time he had to admit that "His Majesty's Declaration & the Resolution of both Houses do not seem to produce the happy effect in the Colony which Your Lordship reasonably expected from them; but the People still pursue their Schemes of Opposition & Resistance with the utmost Obstinacy." [6]

Dunmore might well have added that the people of Virginia were being encouraged in their opposition by a constantly needling press, whose weekly sowing of the seed would today be condemned as downright seditious. The front page of the February 4 *Gazette* [7] devoted its entire first column to what purported to be a letter from a senior British officer at Boston written to "a noble Lord," calling on him to use his influence on behalf of the colonies. The letter abounds with well-worn phrases and equally well-worn arguments regarding the rights of Englishmen and the iniquity of taxation without representation; the Prime Minister is seen as "violent and tyranni-

---

[5] *Virginia Gazette* (Dixon & Hunter), Feb. 4; also *Annual Register*, *1774*, "State Papers," 263.

[6] Dunmore to Dartmouth, March 14; PRO,CO 5/1353.

[7] Dixon & Hunter.

cal . . . mowing down whole communities, merely to indulge his hereditary hatred of liberty, and those who are attached to her. . . ." The letter reads remarkably like a piece of concocted propaganda intended to illustrate the very real doubts which many British officers felt toward their Boston assignments. Its use in the *Virginia Gazette* was simply that of a disguised editorial.

Apart from a single paragraph on a treaty concluded with the Indians by the governor of South Carolina in the previous October, the rest of the *Gazette*'s front page was devoted to news from Boston, datelined January 5. The principal item concerned the deliberations of the freeholders of Boston on December 30, when they prepared an answer to a recent statement by General Gage discussing his punitive activities in Massachusetts. This provided some splendidly inflammatory copy, as did the last item, which was claimed to be an extract from a letter received in Boston describing the christening of the great bell for the Roman Catholic cathedral in Quebec. The *Gazette* justified its inclusion on the grounds that it would ". . . *serve to convey some idea of the ceremonial nature of that religion which is now established there by an act of the British Parliament.*"

. . . Pere Montgolsia came down from Montreal to stand godfather, and Madamoiselle Delary stood godmother; the coadjutor, or Deputy Bishop, performed the ceremony of christening, and very awkwardly indeed. However, after saying mass, and playing several tricks with the candles, the young lads holding up the tail of the gown, putting on and pulling off the cap, holding it, &c, he was introduced to the bell, which was at a small distance from him, preceded by two Priests, who brought the *eau benite* (holy water) and two small brooms made of twigs, who fell to washing the bell like mad, outside and in, then to wiping it with two very fine white napkins, which were made black enough before they had done cleaning of it from the impurity of heretical hands; after this it was well smoked with incense, then followed the ceremony of the oil, salt, &c. as to infants, only they marked or crossed it in three different places, and went three times round it at each ceremony of the oil, salts, &c. They then wrapped round it a piece of fine new linen, which they called a shirt, then over it a piece of crimson damask, by way of waistcoat, and after this a piece of light blue damask, to serve as a coat. After its being thus dressed, and a few more capers, it was then undressed, and by a great number of people conveyed under the belfry and hung up, in doing which one man was killed by a fall from the top, who was pronounced to have gone immediately to Heaven, without stopping at Purgatory, as he was serving the Lord.

The above-mentioned bell, which was a present from the Bishop of Quebec, weighed 2500 lb. and was baptised by the name of LOUISA.[8]

Since the passing of the Quebec Act of 1774, the slogan "No Popery" was almost as popular in America as the cry of "Liberty." Consequently the account of the Quebec ceremony was designed to remind readers not only that Catholics were idiots but that the British government approved of them. The paper did not add that if American rights were not protected, papist mumbo jumbo would come creeping back into Protestant churches; it was much better to let the customers draw their own conclusions. But just to be sure that the seed took root, it was given a dab of fertilizer on page two by inserting a passing reference to rumors of American emissaries visiting the Pretender with unspecified but doubtless hideous and unspeakable proposals.

The rest of the week's news was nicely balanced between the sweet and the sour; it was being said in London that General Gage had asked to be relieved of his American command and would be replaced by General Howe; the congressional ban on imports from Britain was proving so effective that the poor were starving to death in Staffordshire and Yorkshire; and the activities of Americans in general were so disturbing to Lord North's sleep that "as soon as his Lordship is seated at the head

---

[8] *Virginia Gazette* (Dixon & Hunter), Feb. 4.

of the Treasury Bench he falls as fast as a church, which sometimes produces none of the most agreeable fumes." Morocco was reported to have declared war on Spain, the Russians were marching into Poland, and Lord Clive, the founder of Britain's Indian empire, was dead. The *Gazette* rather surprisingly failed to reveal that Clive had died by his own hand, probably, as it was rumored, by cutting his jugular vein with a penknife.

The Russian rebel Pugachev, whose capture had been reported in January, was now said to be on his way to Moscow, "fastened down to the bottom of his cage." Although of little concern to America, Pugachev's rebellion against the Empress Catherine had been watched with considerable interest both in Europe and in England. Coming as it did, when Russia was already involved in a war with the Turks, the appearance of Pugachev claiming to be Catherine's murdered husband, Peter III, threatened to upset many a European applecart. Although the rebellion had been successful at the start, Pugachev was not much of a tactician and was repeatedly defeated in a series of increasingly bloody battles east of the Volga, the last of which forced him to swim the river and to hide in the deserts of Astrakhan. There, starving and having been reduced to eating his horse, he was captured and carted ignominiously to Moscow, where he was interrogated with some thoroughness but with little apparent effect. The *Annual Register's* comment on Pugachev's questioning has a surprisingly contemporary ring to it: "It is, however, to be remembered, that facts transpire with great difficulty through the walls in which such examinations are taken, and the reports given out for the gratification of the people, only wear the momentary colour, which at the time, it is thought necessary to give them." [9]

By the time that the *Virginia Gazette* learned of Pugachev's caged journey to Moscow, he was already dead. Brought to madness (or feigned madness) through his ordeals in the desert

[9] *Annual Register, 1774*, "History of Europe," 15.

and at the hands of his captors, a merciful error spared him a final agony. ". . . By a mistake, his head was first severed from his body, and then his hands and feet; these were then shown to the spectators, and afterwards his head. . . . It is generally believed the executioner will lose his tongue for mistaking his orders, and cutting off the rebel's head, before he cut off his limbs. . . ." The Russians were not a gentle people —nor, for that matter, were all Virginians, as the *London Chronicle* was at pains to point out.

Much has been said of late concerning the treatment which those unfortunate beings, the negro slaves, meet with at the hands of their masters in the British Colonies. It seems, indeed, wondrous strange, that those very people who so loudly complain of infringements of their liberties, and so speciously declaim about the natural rights of mankind, should themselves have so little consideration for the sufferings of [those] of their fellow creatures who have the misfortune to fall into their power. The Rev. Mr. Wesley . . . has given two remarkable instances of this notable inconsistency in the Colonists, exemplified in copies of two advertisements, published in the newspapers of Virginia and North Carolina. They are as under—"Ran away on the 10th inst. a lusty negro, named Bob. The said fellow is outlawed, and I will give ten pounds for his head, severed from his body; and forty shillings if brought alive." The second advertisement breathes the same diabolical spirit of revenge. "Ran away from the subscriber, a negro fellow named Zeb. aged 36. As he is outlawed, I will pay twenty pounds currency to any person who shall produce his head severed from his body; and five pounds if brought home alive. John Mosely."

However cheap these advertising tyrants may hold the liberties of others, and even the lives of those who happen to wear a complexion darker than their own, surely the souls of their poor slaves can never be half so black as those of their unhuman task-masters; whose cruelties can only be equalled by the unfeeling barbarity of drovers and carmen, the very scum and outcasts of a civilised nation! [1]

[1] Hampden, *Journal*, 133, quoting the *London Chronicle*, Jan. 10–12.

Drovers and carmen were apparently renowned for their ill-treatment of their horses, and as the English have always considered themselves the horse's best friend, the analogy was aimed straight at the heart. No doubt many a reader who had never been closer to Virginia than a London tobacco shop had horrible visions of thousands of cloven-hoofed planters being presented with recalcitrant Negro heads on silver platters.

There is no denying that slavery was a barbarous institution, and we can certainly take time out to denounce the prosperous merchants of England and New England who benefited so handsomely from it. But to the Southern plantation owner who had inherited an economy and way of life based on slave labor, there was little difference between this and the feudalism of medieval Britain. Admittedly, slaves were chattels to be bought and sold, and no human being should be so treated —nevertheless, because they were *property* it was to the advantage of the owners to look after them and to see to it that their investment did not deteriorate. Besides, the idea was that the slaves should work, and they were more likely to do so if they were reasonably happy than if they were moved by fear alone. Wesley's picture of the planters rushing around screaming "Off with their heads!" could only have been drawn by Tenniel from an idea by Carroll.

It is quite true that the pages of every Southern newspaper were filled with advertisements offering rewards for runaway slaves. The *Virginia Gazette* of February 4 contained six of them; but none of the owners were offering money for heads— they wanted their property back, sound and in one piece. It is highly likely that they beat the slaves when they were retrieved to discourage them from trying it again. It is equally probable that white apprentice William Johnston received similar punishment on being returned to the brig *Innermay*, from which he had absconded in December. His master, James Belches, was advertising in the same *Gazette* and offering fifteen shillings for the lad's return. My point is simply that we must not judge eighteenth-century America by our own sponge-soft standards, nor must we suppose that harsh punishments were reserved for the slave population alone. There were some two hundred capital offenses on the English Statute Book, and they had little regard for color or sex. In 1771 a young woman with her child at her breast was taken to Tyburn and hanged for stealing a few pieces of muslin, and in 1773 another woman, who had murdered her husband, was chained to a stake and publicly burned. The London crowd which turned out for this free spectacle was so large that the executioners had difficulty in setting up the faggots. Three years later a girl of fourteen received a similar sentence for hiding a few tin-plated farthings which her master planned to pass for silver, and on February 14, 1775, a convict was hanged at Tyburn for stealing sixpence from a farm boy. Punishments at sea were equally barbarous, and many a sailor who declined to obey an order found himself roped and pitched over the starboard stern and raked along the barnacled keel to the port bow. That he was hauled aboard at the end of it was rarely of any interest to the victim, but rope was not cheap and it needed to be untied. These are the standards against which our judgments must be based.

The venerable dictum that the rod was sanctified by God had considerable mileage left in it, and Virginia counties still maintained their public whipping posts along with their stocks, pillories, gallows, and occasional ducking stools. But the whip was not a powerful deterrent to the prospective escaping slave, and some owners allowed their overseers to adopt other methods. Said one Virginia seneschal: "Whipping of any kind does them no good, for they will laugh at your greatest Severity." He offered a variety of alternatives, prescribing: "For Sullenness, Obstinacy, or Idleness. . . . Take a Negro, strip him, tie him fast to a post; take then a sharp Curry-Comb & curry him severely til he is well scrap'd; & call a Boy with some dry Hay, and make the Boy rub him down for several Minutes, then salt him, & unlose him. He will attend to his Business afterwards!" For extracting information from a Negro the same overseer offered another method, which he was proud to claim as his own invention. "Lay upon your Floor a large thick plank, having a peg about eighteen Inches long, of hard wood, & very Sharp, on the upper end, fixed fast in the plank—then strip the Negro, tie the Cord to a Staple in the Ceiling, so that his foot may just rest on the sharpened Peg, then turn him briskly round, and you would laugh at the Dexterity of the Negro, while he was releiving his Feet on the sharpen'd Peg!" [2] The diarist, Philip Fithian, from whose journal these helpful hints are derived, took a very poor view of Virginians' treatment of their slaves and commented frequently on it. This is hardly surprising; he came from New Jersey, had enjoyed an austere Presbyterian up-bringing, and had studied for the ministry, a combination un-likely to generate much affection for the Southern way of life. Fithian spent a year as tutor to the children of Robert Carter of Nomini Hall in Westmoreland County, during which time he kept an extremely full diary. This journal provides us with one of the finest extant pictures of life on a colonial plantation in the period immediately preceding the Revolution. He recalls with dismay how Carter "entertained" [3] his family at breakfast one day with an account of his visit to a neighboring plantation, where he found the coach of a fellow guest parked outside, without its horses, but with the Negro coachman still seated on the box. Some time later he looked out of the window and noticed that the coachman was still perched there. When he asked the reason for this odd behavior, he discovered that the slave was chained to his seat as he was apt to run away.

The slave population of Virginia at the end of the colonial era was approximately 200,000 as against about 300,000 Europeans, although, as we have seen, Lord Dunmore did not agree, claiming a ratio of two to one in favor of the Negro. The majority of slaves could neither read nor write, and many of the first generation died without acquiring anything but the vaguest idea of the English language. Consequently they lived out their captive lives and departed this earth without leaving any mark

[2] Fithian, *Journal*, 38–39; Sept. 23, 1773.
[3] Ibid., 84; March 24, 1774.

behind them. Ironically, it is generally only those who got into trouble who are remembered.

CAESAR, a Fellow about 6 Feet high, very thick, strong made, and about 30 Years of Age, ran away, last *August,* from Mr. Robert Donald's in *Warwick;* he has not been long in the Country, and speaks *English* very badly—The Subscribers will give 3£. Reward to the Person who takes him up. . . .

RAN away from the Subscriber, the 8th Instant, a clear Mulatto Fellow named NICK, by Trade a Mill-wright, is about 25 Years of Age, about 5 Feet 5 Inches high, well set, speaks and walks very quick, has a Scar over one of his Eyes, and his Fingers much marked, by being often cut. He generally wears Leather Breeches, and a gray Great Coat, but has a variety of Clothes. Some little time since he was whipped, and has many fresh Marks upon his Back. Whoever brings him to me shall have 3£. Reward, or 40s. for securing him in any Gaol, so that I may get him again. He is so very artful that he will escape from any One who is not extremely careful. He ran away some Time ago, and hired himself as a Freeman at a Saw Mill, either in *Isle* of *Wight* or Nansemond, and it is supposed may take the same Route.

BENJAMIN HARRISON

The foregoing notices from the *Virginia Gazette* [4] are typical of those to be found on the back pages of every newspaper in the Southern colonies, and more often than not the runaways had not absconded for the first time. Most of our information about trades, clothing, appearance, and idiosyncrasies of the slave population relates to the minority of supposed miscreants who were unwilling or unable to accept their lot.

It would be wrong to suppose that the life of the average slave was that of a shackled and imprisoned animal. Those who were household servants were able to move freely about the towns doing their various duties. On Easter Monday, 1774, Fithian noted in his diary "a general holiday; Negroes now are

[4] Dixon & Hunter, Feb. 4.

all disbanded till Wednesday morning & are at Cock Fights through the County. . . ." [5] The following Sunday he noted that on the plantation the slaves were passing the day cockfighting around the stables and tending the plots of land given to them for the growing of their own vegetables.

As early as the 1740's there had been talk of founding a Negro school in Williamsburg, and in 1760, at a London meeting of a philanthropic group known as Dr. Bray's Associates, the project was revived, thanks in part to the advice of Benjamin Franklin, who had recently been made a member. The school was duly established and continued to operate until the death of the teacher, Mrs. Anne Wager, in 1774. The records of its work are scant, but it appears to have been reasonably well attended by children between the ages of four and ten, though their owners rarely allowed them to stay the full three years prescribed by trustee Robert Carter Nicholas. The instruction was basically religious, yet it is clear that the Associates were anxious not only to preserve the pupils' souls but also their livers, for among the books sent over from England were a dozen copies of *Friendly Admonitions to the Drinkers of Spiritous Liquors.*

The English traveler, John Ferdinand Dalziel Smyth, frequently commented on the harsh treatment meted out to slaves by overseers and on the hardness of their labor. But he also noted that after the day's work was done, the slave "generally sets out from home, and walks six or seven miles in the night, be the weather ever so sultry, to a negroe dance, in which he performs with astonishing agility, and the most vigorous exertions, keeping time and cadence, most exactly, with the music of a banjor (a large hollow instrument with three strings) and a quaqua (somewhat resembling a drum), until he exhausts himself, and scarcely has time, or strength, to return home before the hour he is called forth to toil next morning." [6] Most contemporary writers who had anything at all to say about the

[5] Fithian, *Journal,* 91; April 4, 1774.
[6] Smyth, "Tour," *VHR,* VI, No. 2 (April, 1853), 85.

plight of Virginia's slaves commented on their delight in
dancing and their resulting ability to forget their troubles.
Nicholas Cresswell observed that "Their Dancing is most
violent exercise, but so irregular and grotesque. I am not able to
describe it. They all appear to be exceedingly happy at these
merry-makings and seem as if they had forgot or were not
sensible of their miserable condition." [7] Smyth voiced much the
same opinion, saying: "It is fortunate for humanity, that these
poor creatures possess such a fund of contentment and resignation in their minds; for they indeed seem to be the happiest
inhabitants of America, not withstanding the hardness of their
fare, the severity of their labour, and the unkindness, ignominy,
and often barbarity of their treatment." [8]

Seventy years earlier Robert Beverley contended that slaves
in Virginia were "not worked near so hard, nor so many hours
in a day, as the husbandmen, and day-labourers in England." [9]
However, the overwhelming weight of evidence does not suggest that this happy state of affairs existed in 1775. But even if
it can be argued that there were thousands of supposedly free
Englishmen in the slums of London who were physically worse
off, there can be no denying that most colonists of sensibility
abhorred the principle of slavery. On the Easter Monday
already mentioned Philip Fithian discussed the morality of the
system with his employer's wife. It is doubtless significant,
however, that he chose to wait to do so until the master of
Nomini Hall had retired to bed.

Wrote Fithian in his journal:

We both concluded, (& I am pretty certain that the conclu-
sion is just) that if in Mr. Carters, or in any Gentlemans
Estate, all the Negroes should be sold, & the Money put to
Interest in safe hands, & let the Lands which these Negroes
now work lie wholly uncultivated, the bare Interest of the
Price of the Negroes would be a much greater yearly income

[7] *Cresswell*, 19; May 6, 1774.
[8] Smyth, "Tour," 82.
[9] Beverley, *History of Virginia*, 172.

than what is now received from their working the Lands, making no allowance at all for the trouble & Risk of the Masters as to the Crops, & Negroes.—How much greater then must be the value of an Estate here if these poor enslaved Africans were all in their native desired Country, & in their Room industrious Tenants, who being born in freedom, by a laudable care, would not only inrich their Landlords, but would raise a hardy Offspring to be the Strength & the honour of the Colony.[1]

Tobacco farming, on the scale needed to keep the planters in the manner to which they had become so lovingly accustomed, could not be sustained by single tenants tending rented plots. It might have been achieved by freemen working in a kind of commune, but this would have rather defeated the idea of productivity through private enterprise. Another alternative would have been to increase the number of indentured servants, who, after serving their term, would go off to farm for themselves. But this would have called for ever-increasing supplies of land— which could only be obtained by grabbing it from the Indians. Furthermore, the supply of workers of worthwhile quality was equally limited. The only large supply of labor would have been from the ranks of the English poor, and more often than not the indigent were also indolent.

One of the principal sources of labor, at a variety of levels, was created by the severe economic blight then being experienced by the Scots. But, as already noted, "Scotchmen" were not too highly regarded in Virginia. Quite apart from the fact that they were stingy, avaricious, and without any sense of humor, they were also only very slightly civilized and were liable to revert to native barbarism at the drop of a sporran. This rather biased but widely held opinion was not confined to the colonists; either they or their parents had been weaned on such prejudice before they left England.

After traveling with three Scotsmen for some days, Nicholas Cresswell noted in his journal that he found them very good

[1] Fithian, *Journal*, 92; April 4, 1774.

company, a fact that surprised him, as he had always had a particular dislike for their country "owing to the prejudice of [his] education. I was taught to look upon them as a set of men divested of common humanity, ungenerous and unprincipled. . . . I most heartily condemn this pernicious system of education by which we are taught to look upon the inhabitants of a different nation, language or complexion, as a set of beings far inferior to our own." [2] Cresswell's condemnation had, of course, little impact on English upbringing, and the educated upper-class Englishman went on believing precisely that for another hundred and fifty odd years.

The popular view of the Scots had been vividly displayed in a letter to Pinkney's *Virginia Gazette* of January 19, when an anonymous contributor declared:

> It is generally believed, by this time, that the Scotch have all signed the association [against British imports]. If they have, I would ask if it is not through compulsion? Will they not so represent it to the Ministry? And if we should be so unhappy as to come to a rupture with Great Britain will they not be ready to come at our backs, and cut our throats? Let us then, my friends, whilst the disorder is still cureable, purge this our sickly colony of such filth.

Throughout February irate and indignant Scotsmen penned their replies both to Pinkney's and to Dixon and Hunter's *Gazette*s. Writing to the latter (a fiendish "Scotchman's" device to create disharmony between the two papers), "A SCOTCH ASSOCIATOR" referred to the author as a "malevolent scribbler" and asked: "can such ill-timed scurrility, such low and unmanly abuse, have a tendency to make one friend, or some thousands of foes? Or can this man be a Virginian, and possess any of those manly sentiments and refined feelings, inseparable from the mind of every real friend to liberty?" In conclusion, he wrote, "Mr. Pinkney must pardon me, for I am really a friend to the liberty of every press, but in my opinion such *filth*, as in the

---

[2] *Cresswell*, 205; April 26, 1777.

before-mentioned paper is held out to the publick, can dignify none."

The Scotch Associator's letter had been dated January 29, and before Dixon and Hunter could print it, Pinkney had already been prompted to excuse himself. "Nothing gives the printer of this paper greater pain," he declared, with eyes turned piously to heaven, "than to be concerned in the publication of *controversial* pieces; that which was inferred against the *Scotch*, of the 19th ult. has had this tendency. He can with the utmost truth declare that it was his ardent wish to have dropped it, which certainly would have been the case, had he thought it consistent with his duty; but every impartial person must be convinced that even the motto of his paper will not permit him, at all times, to act agreeable to his inclination." [3] The motto, you may recall, was "Open to ALL PARTIES, but influenced by NONE."

Had Pinkney really wanted to avoid controversy he would have allowed the mudslinging to proceed no further. Instead, he inserted the following gem into his February 23 issue preceded, of course, by a suitably partisan editorial note:

The printer received the following *witty* and *ingenious* letter by one of the posts last Saturday; and, in order that it may not lose any of its *merit*, he will not attempt to make the least alteration or correction, for fear that he may diminish the *poignancy* of the satire, and thereby gain the *censure*, instead of the present *good-will*, of his *delicate* correspondent.

Pinkney

You print for the benefite of Clementina Rinds children do you, You are a low lif,ed Rascal that I can tell you. The origenal of you & many of your countrymen may be easily Traced filth,e You scoundrel you are the Author of that pice in the paper yourself For which the first time I come to Wmsburg I.ll break your head make your shorter by the head or kick your Arse and this depend upon from

GREGOR McGREGOR.

[3] *Virginia Gazette* (Pinkney), Feb. 2.

One rather doubts whether Pinkney wrote the original letter, but I cannot help wondering whether he may not have written this one. Indeed, I am apparently not alone in doubting the identity of Gregor McGregor, for early in March Pinkney published a letter from one Charles M'Carty of Richmond County in which this correspondent referred to "the meritorious performance of the fictitious Gregor McGregor" and went on to claim that it was he, M'Carty, who wrote the original attack on the Scots. He added that if "the Caledonian"⁴ wanted to attack him he was to be found near Farnham Church, but that McGregor would be advised to bring along five friends to help him.

I have pursued this journalistic exercise for some distance because it well illustrates the kind of devices which colonial newspaper publishers used to exacerbate the prejudices and rivalries of their readers, while masking their purpose behind a guise of good-humored impartiality.

Not all the problems that were bothering the people of Virginia in February 1775 were political or even new; among their more pressing minor irritations was a lack of money. There was a most parlous shortage of small change. This had been brought about in a large degree through the fact that Virginia's principal currency was tobacco; it was accepted by storekeepers in exchange for goods, one could pay one's taxes in it, and it was even used to pay clergymen's salaries. Small merchants transferred their accumulated stocks and promissory notes to larger firms, which in turn collected and shipped the tobacco to England. Some planters shipped their own and bought their furniture, clothes, table wares, tools, and the products of fashion in England through English agents. In this way large transactions took care of themselves, and people with prospects could live on credit until their crops were in. There was little occasion for them to need hard cash; not so the poorer people, who had no tobacco to harvest, nor the travelers, who

⁴ Ibid., March 9.

would not appreciate receiving promissory notes instead of coinage as change for their own gold and silver.

Surprisingly little English coinage was circulating in the Southern colonies in the years prior to the Revolution; what money was available was largely Spanish and French silver, which was frequently cut up into small segments to parallel the bullion value of the lower English denominations. At no time did the term "small change" more accurately describe the contents of a poor man's purse; so minute were many of the cut pieces that they were no larger nor much thicker than a little fingernail. They could be guaranteed to escape through the smallest hole in one's pocket, and if dropped on the store floor the chances of finding them again would be as small as the money.

In 1769 the general assembly had authorized the purchase of £2,500 worth of the current English copper halfpennies, and the Colony's treasurer, Robert Carter Nicholas, started the interminable negotiations that would eventually result in the shipping of five tons of copper halfpence specially minted for use in Virginia. Although gold and silver coins were generally worth their weight in bullion, copper coins were not, and consequently their circulating value was regulated by decree. In England copper halfpennies and farthings (there were no pennies) were considered to have a circulating value of their weight coupled with the cost of production, which meant that their copper value was approximately half. This, of course, was why counterfeiting was such a popular crime in England and why it was so harshly punished. If you took twelve official halfpennies and used them to buy six pennyworth of copper, you could take the metal home and forge yourself approximately twenty-four halfpennies, and thus double your money.

It was because of an interminable series of misunderstandings and disagreements between Virginia and the Secretary of State regarding the value of the coins that their minting was so long delayed. Matters were further complicated by the retirement of Lord Hillsborough as Secretary of State and the appointment of his successor, Lord Dartmouth, making it necessary to repeat certain steps of the original negotiations. Then came disagreements over the design of the coins, followed by more delays at the mint caused by the dilatoriness of the engraver, who had not provided all the necessary tools. It was not until September 1773 that the finished pieces were actually shipped to Virginia, and their arrival was not reported in the *Virginia Gazette* until February 23, 1774. The colonists might reasonably have supposed that this was the end of the matter and that within a day or two the coins would be clinking in their pockets. But no; the Treasurer and presumably the governor believed that they could not issue the money without a royal warrant, and none had come with the shipment. On February 7, 1775, almost a year later, we find Lord Dunmore writing to Lord Dartmouth with as much irritation as a subordinate could permit himself, saying: "I am obliged to remind your Lordship that a Coinage of Halfpence which had been procured by this Colony has lain some time here waiting for His Majesty's or necessary Proclamation to give them Currency and many of the People of the Colony are desirous of having them circulated." [5]

It is highly likely that the ship carrying Dunmore's letter to England passed one only a few miles off the Virginia coast bringing instructions from the Secretary of State. Among Lord Dartmouth's missives was one dated December 1, 1774, saying that there was "no longer any impediment" to the distribution of the coins and enclosing a copy of the necessary royal proclamation. The proclamation itself was dated November 16, 1774, and, after summarizing the history of the related legislation and describing the appearance of the pieces, it announced that five tons of them were "now ready to be exported to Our said Colony of Virginia. . . ." [6] Somebody presumably forgot to mention that the coins were already in Virginia and had been sitting there in their kegs quietly turning green for the past seven months. The governor had no authority to edit the King's

[5] Dunmore to Dartmouth, Feb. 7; PRO,CO 5/1353.
[6] PRO,CO 5/1375.

missive and he had no alternative but to release it as it stood, and it was duly published in the *Virginia Gazette* [7] of February 23, thus giving the Crown's critics a fine opportunity to argue that the King was palpably out of touch with the problems and affairs of his American colonies.

A somewhat ironic footnote to the issuance of the Virginia halfpennies was to be found further down the same column of the *Gazette* in an announcement by the Committee of Safety for Surry County stating that it had sold certain prohibited imported goods, which had been ordered by three Southampton firms before the ban had been imposed and which had arrived on board the ship *Thomas* after the first of December, when the embargo came into effect. The unspecified "European goods" were disposed of in exchange for £138 11s. 9d. worth of "halfpenny *Virginia* currency. . . ." Right from the first days of issuance the new coins were being acquired for hoarding rather than circulating. With the winds preceding the storm already blowing through the tobacco fields of Virginia, many colonists believed that hard cash—even copper coinage—would weather that storm a good deal better than would promissory notes for crops that might never be harvested. Besides, in the event of a shooting war the metallic value of the coins would almost certainly rise above their official monetary worth.

As February went out, colonial farmers began to think of spring, and on Colonel Daingerfield's plantation, where diarist John Harrower was in service, the hands were plowing the land for "his croop of Indian corn." [8] But in the field of politics the future seemed far less predictable; the papers continued to print their rumors and to squash the fingers of authority in their presses whenever an opportunity presented itself.

Mr. Pinkney's concern for the public good prompted him to publish lengthy extracts from a pamphlet entitled *American Independence the Interest and Glory of Great Britain*, originally printed in London and supporting American rights—including

[7] Pinkney.
[8] *Harrower*, 86; March 1.

the right to do wrong in the right cause. "I must therefore repeat," declared the author, "that the destroyers of the tea at Boston, were, in my opinion, a band of virtuous patriots, whose names, when once made public, will doubtless be held in eternal veneration by their countrymen, and that the glorious *illegality* (if every statute, whether just or unjust, be properly comprehended in the word law) they atcheived, was an act of absolute moral and political necessity, and therefore exempt from even good laws. . . ." [9]

In a supplement to his issue of February 16, Pinkney offered further teatime intelligences from Boston, where on January 18 sixty pounds of tea had been publicly burned on the quay at Portsmouth. The importer was "so convinced of his error in exposing that condemned commodity to sale, that he set fire to it himself, in presence of a great number of people." If the unfortunate importer felt a hint of intimidation in the attitude of the crowd, General Gage must certainly have found it in the events of February 2—which were also reported by Mr. Pinkney. On that date

the minute company of the Massachusetts town of Lunenburg, consisting of fifty-seven able bodied men, appeared in arms on the parade, at ten o'clock, A.M. and after going through the several military manoevres, they marched to a public house, where the officers had prepared an elegant dinner for the company, a number of the respectable inhabitants of the town and patriotic ministers of the town adjacent. At two o'clock P.M. they marched in military procession to the meeting house, where the reverend Mr. Adams delivered an excellent sermon, suitable to the occasion, from Psalm xxvii. 3 [Though an host of men were laid against me, yet shall not my heart be afraid: and though there rose up war against me, yet will I put my trust in him.]. . . . On the day following the freeholders and other inhabitants of the town being assembled in a legal town meeting, voted one hundred pounds for the purpose of purchasing firearms, with

[9] *Virginia Gazette* (Pinkney), Feb. 16.

bayonets and other implements of war, agreeable to the advice of the late provincial congress.

These news items from Boston were not of major importance; the inhabitants of that city, and of Massachusetts in general, were by now quite used to the bizarre union of tar and feathers, the sounds of breaking tea chests, and the sight of minute men drilling on village greens. Not even the fact that in Bristol, Rhode Island, some of those amateur warriors were under fourteen could cause much of a sensation. A large, fever-ridden British army was encamped at Boston, and the masts of the British navy choked its harbor; as long as they remained, any acts of opposition on the part of the citizenry would not be thought remarkable—they were simply to be expected. But in the Southern colonies the roar of mobs and the tramp of marching soldiery were sounds heard only in the heads of the more explosive patriots. Consequently the newspapers were busily making it their business to enliven their pastoral scenes with martial noises from the wings. Mr. Pinkney, for example, chose to lift from the *Newport Mercury* the single paragraph story about the Rhode Island boys and elevated it into his lead item for February 23.

The town of Bristol, in this colony, affords an instance which would astonish the most accomplished soldier. About fifty young gentlemen, the eldest not exceeding the age of four-teen, stimulated by the most laudible emulation, have formed themselves into a regular company, under the direction of a young master of their own body, for rendering themselves expert in the military exercises. The proficiency they have made, in the manual exercise in particular, is amazing. From a strict observation, no irregularity can be discovered in their motions.

AN OLD SOLDIER

It was really quite astonishing that the Virginia publishers could unearth so many completely disassociated scraps of information and use them for the same inflammatory purpose, apparently without changing them in any way. The fact that the celebrated portrait painter Charles Willson Peale designed a banner for the Baltimore Independent Company might not seem of much interest to anyone outside Baltimore. But to the busy Mr. Pinkney it was manna of the most succulent variety. Because the design was much admired (presumably by the members of the B.I.C.) Pinkney hoped "that the insertion of it will not be disagreeable to our readers----- 'LIBERTY trampling upon TYRANNY, and putting off SLAVERY, who is represented by a SKELETON on the right hand side. Behind the figure of SLAVERY is a SEA. By the figure of LIBERTY is a column to denote STABILITY, and an extent of country. The motto, REPRESENTATION, OR NO TAXATION.' " [1] Here wrapped in one choice capsule we have an independent military unit receiving the patronage of the foremost American painter of his day (suggesting acceptance of independent military action by men of culture) and a fine opportunity to set out the "Up Liberty and down the British" idea in bold upper-case type. If the governor chose to complain, Mr. Pinkney could quickly counter that he was simply printing the news as he received it and that any attempt to restrain him would be an assault on the freedom of the press.

Because the newspapers had an irritating habit of getting the news before he did, Lord Dunmore had no alternative but to read every edition, now three pills to be taken each week, perhaps at *teatime*—one of the few little private defiances the governor and his family could permit themselves. As Nicholas Cresswell noted in his journal on February 28, "This is the last day Tea is allowed to be drank on the Continent, by an act of Congress. The ladies seem very sad about it." [2] But ladies will always have their way, as Helen Maxwell of Norfolk reminds us. Speaking of her father, she said:

I remember him coming in one evening in fine spirits, laughing and saying to my mother and all of us, "Well, now,

[1] Ibid., Feb. 23.
[2] *Cresswell*, 58.

take notice, one and all of you, that I have joined the *Association* (against tea), and you must drink no more of it— at least, not in my sight, for if you do, I shall be obliged to break your China for you." So we banished the teapot from the table, but as we could not give up our tea, and saw no good to come in spiting ourselves in that way, we used to sip a little, now and then, by ourselves, And sometimes, too, my mother, waxing bold, would venture to pour it out to us before his eyes—but, *nota bene* from a *coffee pot*, to which, of course, he could make no objection.[3]

[3] Maxwell, "My Mother," *LNCVA*, I, 98–99.

[*III*]

MARCH

The tired adage that if March comes in like a lamb it will go out like a lion was never more valid than in 1775. The first weeks were much like February, a time to stay at home, grumble by the fireside, and perhaps write rude letters to the newspapers. But the end of it carried the scent of spring, and, as every good revolutionary knows, it is a time to be up and doing. The colonists, of course, were not revolutionaries, simply patriots; nevertheless it was also a time for them to be about their business—the business of electing delegates from their county committees to send to the spring meetings of each colony's provincial congress. The Virginia congress or convention would meet on March 21; already the majority of the delegates had been chosen, and there was not much the governor could do to prevent it. In North Carolina the convention would meet at the beginning of April, and Governor Martin believed that a proclamation was in order, one which would serve to remind the colonists of their duties and true loyalties. He duly conceived it on the first of March.

The proclamation was somewhat intemperate in its condemnation of the leading Carolinian patriots, referring to them as "evil-minded and designing men" who through their "tyrannical and arbitrary Committees" were doing the most cruel and unpardonable violence to the rights and liberties of their fellow colonists. It reminded the people that they already possessed a perfectly good and legally constituted assembly through which their grievances could be heard. They therefore had no reason to join "such meetings, cabals, and illegal proceedings, which artful and designing men [the phrase weakening with repetition] shall attempt to engage them in, and which can only tend to introduce disorder and anarchy, to the destruction of the real interest and happiness of the people, and to involve this Province in confusion, disgrace, and ruin." [1]

Unfortunately the effect of the governor's proclamation was the reverse of what he had intended; instead of discouraging the local committees from sending their delegates to the convention at New Bern, its vehement yet empty exhortations suggested that Martin was rattled and his authority slipping, an interpretation which only strengthened the resolve of the patriots.

Although he was unaware of it, Governor Martin was not alone in his belief that the committees and conventions were the destroyers of liberties rather than their defenders. Lord Dartmouth had the same idea, and he began his month by saying as much in a letter to Lord Dunmore.

The Steps which have been pursued in the different Counties of Virginia, to carry into execution the Resolutions of the General Congress, are of so extraordinary a nature, that I am at a loss for words to express the Criminality of them, and my Surprise that the People should be so infatuated as tamely to submit to Acts of such Tyranny & Oppression: It is however an evil, which, from the Situation and Circumstances of Virginia, where the People must ultimately depend for Subsistance upon an Export of the Produce of their Lands, will, I should conceive, work out its own Cure, and that the Promoters of those violent Measures will soon be convinced of the Folly of their Conduct, tho' not perhaps until some of them fall victim to that Resentment of the People which will be the inevitable Consequences of the Distress they must, in the end, be exposed to. . . .[2]

This sounded like good sense if one happened to be reading

---

[1] Jones, *Revolutionary History of N.C.*, 157–8.
[2] Dartmouth to Dunmore, March 3; PRO,CO 5/1375.

it in London—and if one had no personal knowledge of the temper of the colonies. The letter would be of little comfort to Lord Dunmore; on the contrary, it would serve only to make matters worse. If the Virginia patriots had been operating in our own age they would almost certainly have had the governor's palace at Williamsburg thoroughly "bugged" with hidden microphones. Instead, they had their own, still undetermined methods of obtaining classified information, and they were able to read official dispatches almost as soon as the governor broke their seals. Consequently they were to make considerable hay out of one of the Secretary of State's closing comments concerning Dunmore's long epistle of December 24, 1774. Wrote Dartmouth, "I shall only add that the Communication to Parliament of that part of your Letter, which relates to the Proceedings of the People in the different Counties of Virginia, will probably occasion the Restrictions proposed to be laid upon the Trade of the New England Governments being extended to Virginia." [3] Thus the blame for any restrictions which might be imposed could be squarely laid at Dunmore's door. If he had not misinterpreted the colonists' just intentions and desires when writing to London, none of this would have happened—at least that is how Virginians would have looked at it. But as it turned out this trade restriction did not then come to pass—though through no fault of Lord Dartmouth, who had clearly worked hard to see that it would.

On March 21, when the New England Restraining Bill came up in the House of Lords for its third reading, the Secretary's prophecied amendment was moved, proposing that the restrictions on commerce and fishing should be extended to the colonies of New Jersey, Pennsylvania, Maryland, Virginia, and South Carolina. The evidence of letters from the various colonial governors was duly produced to show their provinces were just as culpable as those of New England. The noble lords agreed in a vote of 52 to 21, and the amendment was appended;

[3] Ibid.

they then proceeded to a vote on the bill as a whole and carried it with 72 to 21, twenty more administration lords apparently having been whipped out of the peers' washroom in time for the second vote.

Up to this point Lord Dartmouth's machinery had performed with satisfying smoothness, but it lost a wheel as soon as the bill was returned to the Commons. It was there rightly pointed out that the title of the bill specifically identified it as being directed toward New England, and therefore the body could not be amended to include other provinces. The Commons thereupon rejected the amendment, and when their objections were explained to the lords the latter agreed to withdraw it. Thus the government's maneuver was scuttled on a technicality which it certainly should have foreseen.

We may suppose that the acrid smoke of recrimination hung over the offices of the Secretary of State for days to come, and his Lordship could, with some reason, maintain that his advisers had let him down. In Williamsburg, Lord Dunmore had similar problems. It was getting harder and harder to know whom to trust. Two years earlier he had written to the then Secretary of State, Lord Hillsborough, recommending that John Page, master of the great Virginia plantation of "Rosewell," should be appointed to the council. Page was, he thought, "a young gentleman of singular good parts, of a most amiable character. . . ." [4] The governor had since had time to change his mind, and he now wrote to Lord Dartmouth saying: "It has been a Matter of no small Concern to me, to find how much I have been mistaken in the Character of Mr. John Page, whose Name your Lordship will observe upon the List of the Council, and whom I recommended from the public opinion of his good Qualities. . . ." [5] He now found him "undutiful" and "inconsistent" and accused him of supporting the council with one breath and siding with the opposition as soon as he was out of the chamber.

[4] Dunmore to Hillsborough, Nov. 16, 1772; PRO,CO 5/1372.
[5] Dunmore to Dartmouth, March 14; PRO,CO 5/1373.

The truth of the matter was not that John Page had
suddenly turned into a scoundrel but that he, like the majority of
thinking Americans, had been forced to take stock and determine where his allegiance lay. It was to his King and to his
homeland; but his home was Virginia, and if he had to choose
between them he was a Virginian first and a subject second.
When Page was appointed in 1772 it was inconceivable to him,
and to most colonial Americans, that any such choice would ever
have to be made. There were wide differences, to be sure; but
these were parliamentary matters, misunderstandings and disagreements between children and parents—and family quarrels
are not, as a rule, resolved through patricide. It was only natural
therefore that John Page should be loyal to his King, and by
extension to his governor, and that he should be proud to serve
on the council, to help guide the affairs of the colony toward a
closer kinship with England. Although Lord Dunmore may not
have been aware of it, Page had been critical of British
government policy long before he took his seat on the council.

In 1768, when the radical and outlawed John Wilkes was
campaigning for a seat in parliament amid loud vituperation and
even rioting, John Page wrote to his English agent crying:

In what an unhappy situation was Great Britain! Unsteadi-
ness in her Councils, Confusion, Riots & Tumults, little short
of Rebellion in her very Metropolis; Discontent in all her
colonies, each, & every one justly complaining of the Arbitrary Proceedings of Parliament; and many of them provoked
at the Severe Restrictions on their Trade, are ready to give a
Stab almost vital to the Trade of G-t B-n. Great God! Was
ever any Nation under Heaven capable of being happier than
the British—Our most invaluable Constitution; and the im-
mense extent of the British Dominions filled with the most
loyal Subjects in the World, one would think would make the
British Empire the most flourishing & glorious that ever
existed. And so it must be, whenever that excellent Constitution shall be strictly observed & when the loyal People shall
be treated like British Subjects. But unhappy for us, unhappy
for G-B, the rising Prospect of that Glorious Empire is

obscured if not the View entirely & forever intercepted, by the Gross Vapours of Ministerial Ignorance or Villainy.[6]

Nearly two hundred years later, archaeologists digging on the site of the Page plantation would find a buckle which had been thrown away shortly before Page was seated on the council, and on that buckle were the words NO EXCISE, one of the slogans so loudly shouted by the supporters of John Wilkes. It would seem that Dunmore's "young gentleman of singular good parts" was even then a liberal.

As the governor sat writing to Lord Dartmouth in March 1775 he was probably wondering how many other vipers he had been clutching to his bosom. In theory the council was composed of carefully chosen men of culture and position in the colony who could be relied on to support the status quo. They were the Lords, and the burgesses the Commons; the latter were elected by the freemen, and you could never be sure what loud-mouthed malcontent would turn up there. But the council was hand picked, they were the King's men; some of them might disagree from time to time on minor issues, that was only natural. But in the final analysis they knew what had to be; they knew where their duty lay—didn't they?

Appended to Lord Dunmore's letter of March 14 was a list of the members of his council. It read as follows: "Thomas Nelson, President, Richard Corbin, William Byrd, John Tayloe, Robert Carter, Robert Burwell, George William Fairfax, Ralph Wormeley junr., Reverend John Camm, and John Page." Nearly all of them were men of great property who had inherited both their lands and their sense of responsibility from families with a long history of service to the colony. But it was not on background alone that these men had risen to the council; there were men of lineage and property among the burgesses too, but whose political views were not atrophied by traditional loyalties—men such as Peyton Randolph, Thomas Jefferson, George Mason, Richard Henry Lee, Benjamin Harrison, Robert

---

[6] John Page to John Norton, Aug. 26, 1768; *Norton Papers*, 64–65.

Carter Nicholas, Carter Braxton, and, of course, Colonel George
Washington. All those burgesses, and many more besides, were
due to represent their counties at the March convention of
delegates in Richmond. For the King's governor in Virginia,
friends were becoming hard to find and enemies less prone to
hide—even in the council.

The March newspapers continued to keep the pot boiling
with a liberal supply of hot rumors, not the least of them being
an impending attack by France upon England. Second hand
from London came word that "the most formidable preparations
are making in France, and that they wait only till our troops and
fleets are engaged in America, to strike some fatal blow to this
country." [7] On the same page readers were told that apart from
garrison troops Britain could only muster 7,000 enlisted men to
protect the homeland, while "France is known to have at this
instant 25,000 foot, besides a formidable and well provided
train of artillery." Four items further down the page we find a
report that "a neighbouring power has offered the Americans
assistance by sea and land, in case of a rupture with Great
Britain, on certain advantageous conditions." Two weeks later
came further rumors from London: "It was yesterday morning
strongly reported in the city, that the French had sent a powerful fleet into America, which is cruizing at the back of the
Western Islands; and, that their project might pass undiscov-
ered by the English, the ships of which this fleet is composed are
said to have sailed one at a time from different ports in
France." [8] A week later, though quoting an earlier London
source, the *Gazette* revealed that "Two large ships laden with
arms, &c. are said to have lately sailed from France to America;
in consequence of which, orders are said to have been given for
two sloops of war to go in quest of them." [9]

The same issue of the *Virginia Gazette* also reported from
London that the French were opening up a profitable trade with

[7] *Virginia Gazette* (Dixon & Hunter), March 4.
[8] Ibid., March 18.
[9] Ibid., March 25.

the American colonies, selling "tea and piece goods," which they shipped into the back settlements and carried overland to the principal towns. In exchange they carried home American corn and other colonial provisions. "The French seem highly pleased at England's quarrelling with her colonies," noted the correspondent, "which has thrown a considerable branch of trade into their hands." [1] This kind of news was major propaganda material for the patriots, one of whose greatest problems was to convince their friends that the rejection of English trade ordered by the Continental Congress would not drive them all into bankruptcy. Thus a report from Jamaica that the Dutch islands of Curaçao and St. Eustatius were being fitted out as "magazines" [2] for trading with the colonies was received with pleasure and relief. That the Dutch would take advantage of any opportunity to trade with the colonies was only to be expected; indeed it had been going on for years, regardless of the British Navigation Acts, which prohibited the export of most commodities to America unless loaded from English ports aboard English ships. The Dutch possessed a major trading port at Paramaribo in Surinam, where colonial American ships in the slave trade did much other business on the side, a fact immortalized by the Philadelphia painter John Greenwood in his famous picture, "American Sea Captains Carousing in Surinam."

It is hard for us today to appreciate how large a role ships and shipping played in the life of the average eighteenth-century American. We are so accustomed to finding what we want at the stores that we rarely stop to wonder how the merchandise got there. For a freighter to be wrecked is now a sufficient rarity for it to be reported in the American press even if no United States property or personnel are involved. But in 1775 shipwrecks were so common that they were reported largely to enable owners of cargoes to be aware of their losses. The winter of 1774/75 had been particularly bad, and the March *Virginia*

[1] Ibid., March 18.
[2] Ibid.

Gazettes were the mirror of it: "The Martin, [Captain] Clarke, from Virginia to London, is totally lost near the mouth of the harbour of Milford; the Captain, and part of the crew, drowned." [3] A handful of relatives would mourn, merchants would scratch a few lines through their ledgers, but nobody would be surprised.

Somewhat more sensational was a report from London of the December storms in the North Sea, where "The damage done by the late tempestuous weather on the coast of Suffolk and Norfolk, is almost incredible; the sea, for several days, has been covered with wrecks of ships and dead bodies, so that the people who live at Dunwich, and the adjacent places near the sea, have had great employ in burying the dead bodies (which they found cast on shore whilst they were looking out for plunder) in the sand. By the wrecks, we find that most of the vessels lost are Dutch and French." [4] The same storm took the ship *Industry*, which was driven on shore six miles from Aberdeen, where it quickly went to pieces with the loss of all hands. The paper reported that "The body of a man, with a mourning ring on his finger, had come ashore when these accounts came away." [5] Another English ship was dashed to pieces in the harbor at Oporto, while at Madeira two successive storms took heavy toll of ships of a variety of nationalities:

On the 8th of December last the gale came on, which obliged all the shipping then in the bay to put to sea, among which a large Dutch ship bound for Surinam was drove ashore, and totally lost; also a Portuguese brig, of which no account has been received since, and is supposed to have foundered at sea.

On the 17th, being fine weather, and the wind easterly, the shipping all returned to anchor in the bay of Fynchall. It continued fair till Sunday the 18th, about 3 o'clock P.M.

[3] Ibid.
[4] Ibid., March 4.
[5] Ibid.

when a sudden and heavy squall came on from the south, and
continued to blow with such unrelenting fury, as to prevent
the shipping from getting out, attended with thunder, lightning, and rain.

About midnight six sail out of seven were dashed in
pieces. . . . Capt. Stewport, of the ship Dawkins, from
London, for Jamaica, was the only vessel that rode out the
storm, having parted one cable, and the other near going,
when the dreadful tempest abated. So terrible and tremendous a gale has never been known in the memory of the oldest
man living in Madeira.[6]

Just as today most air crashes occur on landing or shortly
after take-off, so, in the days of sail, most wrecks happened in
sight of land. In England the mariner's nemesis was waiting
outside the great convoy-assembling basin of the Downs off the
coast of Kent. Through the centuries the Goodwin Sands had
taken hundreds, thousands of ships, and even in medieval times
they were known as the "shippe swalower." America had its
own ship swallower, the Diamond Shoals off Cape Hatteras, and
the toll they took was enormous. On October 4, 1774, Nicholas
Cresswell, en route from Barbados to Virginia, found cause to
remember the shoals. "By reckoning we are pretty near Cape
Hatteras. Still lying to under F. Sail. Blowing very hard at N.E.
Shipped several heavy Seas, one of which has carried away our
Starboard Quarter Rails with three bags of Cotton. Two of them
belong to me. This is all my venture, I am now a beggar."[7]

Three years later Cresswell returned to England and in
doing so provided us with a splendidly graphic yet succinct
account of a storm at sea. "The sea a roaring," he wrote, "the
ship a rolling, the rigging breaking, the masts a bending, the
sails a rattling, the Captain swearing, the Sailors grumbling,
the boys crying, the hogs grunting, the dogs barking, the pots
and glasses breaking, the Colonel ill of the C--p in bed. All from
the top Gallant truck to the keel, from the jibb boom to the

[6] Ibid., March 18.
[7] *Cresswell*, 41.

taffrail in the utmost confusion. Few of the Fleet in sight. I am confoundedly sick." [8]

Shipbuilding was an important industry of colonial America, where timber was so much more plentiful and available than in England. While Virginia was more concerned with the exporting of timbers and spars than with actual construction, private yards on the Potomac and on the Rappahannock produced small vessels of good quality. One such, a brig, was advertised in the *Gazette* on March 23: ". . . burthen about 125 tons, now on the stocks, and ready for launching. Her upper timbers are altogether of black walnut, cedar, locust and mulberry. The terms of sale will be made known to any person inclining to purchase by applying to the steward at *Stratford*, the seat of the honourable Philip Ludwell Lee, esquire, in *Westmoreland* county." [9]

Philip Ludwell Lee had died on February 28, leaving an empty seat on the council. The *Gazette* reported that "the day following his Lady was safely delivered of a son, and on Friday his remains were attended to the place of interment by a very numerous company of relations and friends." [1] The Lee family was only second to the Carters as the greatest landowners of colonial Virginia, and if Philip had died a year earlier it would have been reasonable to assume that he was buried with all the pomp befitting a man of his station. But now times had changed, and the Continental Congress had directed in Article 8 that frugality and economy should be encouraged, and it specifically stated that the colonists were "to lessen the expenses of funerals; to discontinue the giving of gloves and scarfs, and the wearings of any other mourning than a piece of crape or ribbon." [2] Thus was fired the first shot in the war on the cost of the American funeral.

Even before the Continental Congress concerned itself with

[8] Ibid., 273; July 22, 1777.
[9] *Virginia Gazette* (Pinkney).
[1] *Virginia Gazette* (Dixon & Hunter), March 11.
[2] *Annual Register, 1775*, "History of Europe," 27.

the expense of funerals, thinking men were rebelling against what seemed to them to be unnecessary ostentation. Robert Carter of "Nomini Hall" announced one Saturday night to a slightly surprised gathering that he "would have no splendid, nor magnificent Monument, nor even Stone to say 'Hic jacet.'— He told us he proposes to make his own Coffin & use it for a Chest til its proper use shall be required." Carter's wife added that she wanted a plain stone bearing the simple legend, "Here Lies Ann Tasker Carter." Their children's tutor, Philip Fithian, noted the conversation in his diary, observing that "with these things for my consideration I left them about ten and went to my cold Room, & was hurried soon to bed; Not however without reflecting on the importance of our preparation for this great Change!" [3]

Our other tutor diarist, John Harrower, has provided us with one of the most detailed extant descriptions of an eighteenth-century Virginia burial. Following the death of a visitor to his master's plantation, he wrote: "Freiday 10th March 1775. This Night the young Ladys Mama died her[e] and none knew it until the morning notwithstanding her Daughter and a Niger waiting maid was in the room all night." The lady in question was Mrs. Priscilla Dawson of Williamsburg, the widow of a past president of the college, and whose death was later announced in the *Virginia Gazette*. On the following night Harrower sat up with the corpse, along with two women servants and the plantation overseer. At sunset on the twelfth the body was dressed "in a Calico Goun and white apron," was wrapped in a sheet, and laid in a black walnut coffin with pinchbeck handles and lined with flannel. Again Harrower spent the night with the corpse, and at ten the following morning he screwed down the lid and accompanied the coffin, which was carried on a "Chair Carriage" to the graveyard. Harrower notes that the grave was between five and six feet deep and that he, his master, and a few associates saw the grave half filled with earth

[3] Fithian, *Journal*, 61; Jan. 29, 1774.

and then overlaid with planks. It was now left until the next day, when the mourners were joined by "Mr. Mann Page's Coach with 4 or 5 Gentlemen in it and after dinner they in Compy. with the Coll. his Lady and the daughter of the deceased went to the grave & heard the service of the dead read by one Mr. Wilson after which the grave was fully closed up." [4] Harrower was presumably not present at the final stages of the proceedings; otherwise he would surely have known whether the coach contained four or five men and he would also have noted whether or not Mann Page was among them. Page was another of Virginia's foremost landowners and the half brother of John Page of "Rosewell," but what, if anything, he had to do with the deceased Mrs. Dawson remains obscure.

There can be no doubt that the funeral was a reasonably simple, even disorganized affair; but whether this was in respect for the wishes of the Continental Congress, or simply because the colonel was unexpectedly saddled with a dead widow he did not want, is anyone's guess. The coffin was undoubtedly simple, as was indicated by the use of pinchbeck handles instead of silver or brass; but then he might have stooped to iron or even to no handles at all. On the other hand, Harrower *screwed* the lid down. It would have been a lot cheaper to have nailed it. The most curious aspect of the entire affair was that the coffin was half buried one day and not read over until the next. A possible explanation is that the parson had not arrived and that the coffin had already been around the house too long. Whatever the explanation, it must have been a relief for Harrower to have been freed from his vigil.

Eighteenth-century Anglican clerics did not enjoy the respect that they would in the Victorian era, probably because they were prone to worldly excesses, which blended rather poorly with their spiritual advice for others. In Virginia their image had been tarnished by their agitation for larger salaries, which began with the celebrated "Parson's Cause" of 1763 and

---

[4] *Harrower*, 87–88.

continued until the "Twopenny Act" was passed in 1769, leaving them where they were when they started. Young Fithian, who came from New Jersey, found the Virginia clergy less than exemplary, but one has the feeling that he also thought that the Virginians had the clerics they deserved. "A Sunday in Virginia dont seem to wear the same Dress as our Sundays to the Northward—Generally here by five o-Clock on Saturday every Face (especially the Negroes) looks festive & cheerful— All the lower class of People, & the Servants, & the Slaves, consider it as a Day of Pleasure and amusement, & spend it in such Diversions as they severally choose—The Gentlemen go to Church to be sure, but they make that itself a matter of convenience, & account the Church a useful weekly resort to do Business." [5] Nor was Fithian impressed by the quality of the singing in most Virginia churches. On being pleasantly surprised by the voices at one small church, he was prompted to note in his journal that when the psalm began he heard a large number of voices raised, "entirely contrary to what I have seen before in the Colony, for it is seldom in the fullest Congregation's, that more sing than the Clerk, & about two others!" He found that the remarkable improvement had been occasioned by the recent presence in the community of a singing master, who had inspired the congregation to "the respectable Method which they, at present pursue." [6]

At his own Nomini church Fithian found a notice attached to the door (bearing Sunday's date) advertising pork, which was to be sold the next day "at 20/. per Hundred." [7] The gentry did not enter the church until after the service had begun and sometimes the clerk had to go out and call them in, whereupon they entered in a body. After the service was over they would linger in the churchyard to talk and bargain. Sunday churchgoing was then, as now, an occasion to amaze one's neighbors with a bank-breaking display of fine clothes. Watching the twentieth-

[5] Fithian, *Journal*, 137; July 10, 1774.
[6] Ibid., 195; Sept. 25, 1774.
[7] Ibid., 29; Dec. 12, 1773.

century godly on their way to church, one is constantly
reminded that it is more desirable to be "in fashion" than it is to
express one's own taste, thus causing daughters, mothers, and
grandmothers to sally forth looking equally ridiculous, if for
different reasons. It seems it was always thus. "Almost every
Lady wears a red Cloak," wrote Fithian, "and when they ride
out they tye a white handkerchief over their Head and face, so
that when I first came into Virginia, I was distress'd whenever I
saw a Lady, for I thought she had the Tooth-Ach!" [8] The
women may not have suffered with a universal toothache, but
they were quite prepared to suffer considerable discomfort and
even pain to be in vogue. Ever since fashion designers discovered that all women were not the same shape and so could not all
wear their creations with success, they have been working on
the female form to make it fit the designs. In 1775 women were
going through a particularly trying period, and elaborately
boned stays were at the bottom of most of their troubles.

Young Mr. Fithian, whose seminary training might have
aimed his thoughts at higher goals, was able to diagnose a
lady's discomfiture with clinical accuracy.

She was pinched up rather too near in a long pair of new
fashioned Stays, which, I think, are a Nusance both to us &
themselves—For the late importation of Stays which are said
to be now most fashionable in London, are produced upwards
so high that we can have scarce any view at all of the Ladies
Snowy Bosoms; & on the contrary, they are extended down-
wards so low that whenever Ladies who wear them, either
young or old, have occasion to walk, the motion necessary for
Walking, must, I think, cause a disagreeable Friction of
some part of the body against the lower Edge of the Stays
which is hard & unyielding—I imputed the Flush which was
visible in her Face to her being swathed up *Body* & *Soul* &
limbs together. . . .[9]

Fithian was writing in July, and so apparently was exploring

[8] Ibid., 29; Dec. 13, 1774.
[9] Ibid., 130; July 4, 1774.

different ladies than those encountered by Nicholas Cresswell, who found them remarkably well shaped. "I have not seen three crooked women in the country," he wrote. "Few, or none of them wear stays in the summer and there are but few that wear them constantly in the winter, which may be a principal reason why they have such good shapes." [1] Nevertheless stays were the fashion, and sufficiently desirable to merit a specific advertisement in the *Virginia Gazette:* "JUST COME TO HAND, and to be sold at JOHN CARTER'S store, for READY MONEY only, A VARIETY of women's, girls, and childrens STAYS." [2] We may pity the unfortunate children who were confined in such armor. But it serves to remind us that the children of the eighteenth century were dressed as miniatures of their parents, helping them to pass quickly through childhood into the precocity of the "young adult," a state which is today considered more American than English. But even accepting this rapid transformation as part of our modern way of life, we are still likely to raise a jaded eyebrow if an aspiring cleric speaks of our fourteen-year-old daughter as "a slim, puny silent Virgin . . . & I dare say from her Carriage that her Modesty is invincible." [3] Indeed, our much denigrated twentieth-century morality is still well laced with Victorian prudery, and it would be equally shocked by the antics of Robert Carter's eight- and twelve-year-old daughters, whom Fithian discovered "stuffing rags & other Lumber under their Gowns just below their Apron-Strings [and who] were prodigiously charmed at their resemblance to Pregnant Women!" Fithian commented that the amusement was "no less merry than natural," [4] which, in a way, it was.

Writing of the Southern colonies in general (i.e., those south of New York) Nicholas Cresswell observed that most women married before they were twenty-two and often before they were sixteen, and an old maid was hard to find. They were

[1] *Cresswell*, 270.
[2] *Virginia Gazette* (Pinkney), Feb. 9.
[3] Fithian, *Journal*, 124–5; June 24, 1774.
[4] Ibid., 193; Sept. 20, 1774.

generally "good natured, familiar, and agreeable upon the whole, but confoundedly indolent." He also noted that they had very poor teeth: "Very few of them have a good mouth at twenty-five." And he added, "It is said that eating so much hot bread and fruit is the reason why their teeth decay so early." In summation, he found the colonial South "a paradise on Earth for women, the epicure's Elysium, and the very centre of freedom and hospitality." [5]

Accounts of clothing styles in the Southern colonies in 1775 are far from helpful, and it is uncertain how great an effect the Continental Congress's demands for economy had on the ladies. English goods seized by the zealous county committees were put up for public sale and were advertised in the *Gazettes*. On February 16, the citizens of Cobham, Virginia, could purchase "womens silk BONNETS, RIBBANDS, and mens SHOES . . . by the owners delivered to the committee to be sold, agreeable to the tenth article of the continental congress." [6] Another advertisement declined to say where the goods came from, but offered "A LARGE assortment of *Irish* LINENS, ladies black and other coloured silk quilted petticoats, ladies neat black calimanco pumps, white, figured, and striped lustrings, ladies and gentlemens silk, thread, and cotton stockings, mens grey thread, spun silk and worsted ditto; some pieces of beautiful coloured *Irish* muslins, fine buff coloured dimity, suitable for ladies riding dresses. . . ." [7] By and large it would appear that both men and women continued, as best as they could, to keep themselves sartorially abreast of the times.

George Washington, whom one often thinks of as a man concerned with more practical matters than the length of a coat, was not above chastening his London tailor for having cut a coat three inches too long in the skirt or for having made his stepson's breeches too tight in the seat. In ordering a waistcoat for the

[5] *Cresswell*, 270–2.
[6] *Virginia Gazette* (Pinkney).
[7] Ibid., Feb. 23.

young man, he asked for it to be of "Superfine Scarlet Cloth with
a Neat light gold Embroidery (if Embroidery is in Fashion,
if not then to have a gold Lace on it). In short he wants a fash'e
Winter Waistcoat which you please to let this be." For his own
wardrobe Washington also desired to be in the mode and so
specifically ordered "A Fash'e Suit of Cloaths made of a
handsome Super'e Broad Cloth for dress" and "A Fash'e Ditto
made of Cassimer for Summer Wear, well fancied and only
faced and Lined in the foreskirts." [8]

Washington was equally anxious that his family should be
in fashion. Amid a long list of items ordered for his step-
daughter, Martha Parke Custis, we find "A Suit of Fash'e Lace,
Includ'g a Cap with Lappits, Ruffles, Tippet (or handkerchief
&ca), not to exceed £40; 2 Very handsome Caps of Min't Lace;
A handsome Suit of Tambour Worked Muslin; A hand'e and
fash'e Sattin Bonnett; A handsome Velvet Collar with an Indian
Pearle Bow to it; A string of Amber beeds; A Sett of Firestone
Necklace and Earrings set round with Paste with Pins &ca. to
them, not to exceed £7; A Guinea's worth of Hair Pins set with
Paste and Garnett; . . . A pair of Fash'e and handsome
Garnett Shoe Buckles." [9]

Later, in 1775, we catch a glimpse of the attire of some of
the lower echelon of Washington's plantation family, namely
Thomas Spears, a twenty-year-old joiner from Bristol, and
William Webster, a Scots bricklayer ten years older—both
runaway servants. Spears had taken with him "a coat, waistcoat
and breeches, of light brown duffil, with black horn buttons, a
light colored cloth waistcoat, old leather breeches, check and
oznabrig shirts, a pair of new milled yarn stockings, a pair of
old ribbed ditto, new oznabrig trowsers, and a felt hat, not much
the worse for wear." Webster was less well attired and had
thoughtlessly omitted to pack as many spares. He had taken

[8] Washington to Thomas Gibson, July 15, 1772; *Writings*, III,
95–96.

[9] Invoice of goods to be shipped by Robert Cary, July 15, 1772; ibid.

only an "olive coloured coat, pretty much worn, with black horn buttons, duffil waistcoat and breeches (same as Spears's) oznabrig trowsers, and check and oznabrig shirts." [1]

Some of the clothing of servants and slaves was passed down from the big house and so gave the wearer an air of tattered elegance; but much of it was of stout serviceable quality, made on the plantations from materials bought for that purpose. In 1770 Mann Page of "Mannsfield" wrote to London for great quantities of supplies, among them "24 yds. Duffle with Buttons & Mohair for Servants Coats; 1100 yds. Cotton; 1600 yds. Oznabrig from 7d to 8d"; also "6 Dozn. Monmouth Caps; 10 pr. coloured Stockings for Servants; 10 plain Hats for —d[itt]o." [2] In the same year a less affluent planter wrote to his agent, John Norton, in London, explaining that he was in sad straits and assuring Norton that as soon as he grew some good tobacco he would ship it over, but what little he had produced in recent years had "been sold in the County to cloath my Negroes and the rest my Credrs. has got." [3] Two years later Governor Dunmore's steward wrote to the same firm in London ordering supplies and saying that he enclosed "the Colours of the Cloath &c for his Lordship, also Patterns of the Cloath &c for his Servants." [4]

John Harrower, in a letter to his wife in the summer of 1774, told her: "I suppose you wou'd scarce know me now, there being nothing either brown, blew, or black about me but the head and feet, I being Dressed in short cloath Coat, vest Coat, and britches all made of white cotton without any lyning, and thread stockins & wearing my own hair curled round like a wigg. At present a suite of Cloaths costs five and twenty shillings here of making which I really think verry high." [5] This

[1] *Virginia Gazette* (Pinkney), May 4.

[2] Mann Page to John Norton, invoice of Feb. 15, 1772; *Norton Papers*, 124–5.

[3] Colonel Bernard Moore to John Norton, July 25, 1770; ibid., 140.

[4] James Minzies to John Norton, June 12, 1773; ibid., 328.

[5] *Harrower*, 57; June 14, 1774.

would have seemed to be a pleasantly cool attire in which to pass a hot southern summer, though it was, perhaps, a little impractical for a schoolteacher handling inky children.

The mark of the lower classes was generally the lack of embellishment in their dress, particularly an absence of quality metal buttons and buckles, tinned brass or copper generally substituting for silver among the luckier and bone and pewter sufficing for the rest. Nicholas Cresswell, who spent much of his sojourn in America in a modicum of financial distress, decided in the summer of 1775 to leave his assets with a friend before making a trip into the disputed territories beyond Fort Pitt. Those assets comprised his "watch, Buckles, Breast Buckles, Stock Buckle and silver buttons," and he left them "with a paper directing how I would have them disposed of if death should happen to be my lot, as everyone tells me that I am running a great risk of being killed by the Indians." [6]

Servants, by and large, appear to have worn much the same clothing in summer as in winter, though in the hot weather they wore only a waistcoat over their shirts. Advertisements for runaway slaves show that they, too, merely went without their coats in summer, though many of them were not stated to have been wearing waistcoats at any season. As for the slave women, the majority were described only as wearing petticoats and coats. The following notices from the March 25 *Virginia Gazette* [7] speak for themselves on matters of clothing—and on other subjects besides:

> Run away last *October*, a middle sized Negro Wench named HANNAH, she pokes her Neck out very much, is long thin visaged, and wants an upper fore Tooth, had on a Check Petticoat, one brown Linen Ditto, and a blue Stuff jump Jacket. She may probably be lurking about *Occoquan* Works, or at Mr. *William Bailey's* Quarter in *Loudoun*, as she has a Husband at each. . . .
> Run away, or stolen, the 1st of *December* last, a *Virginia*

[6] *Cresswell*, 101; Aug. 13.
[7] Dixon & Hunter.

born slave named SAM, about 5 Feet high, pretty well set, has
a remarkable Scar on his Breast, which seems as if occasioned by the Lash of a Whip, his Sides and Back are much
scarified by Whipping, had a Wart of an uncommen Size on
the Top of his left Shoulder, is very dim sighted, and in the
Night Season almost entirely deprived of Sight. He had on,
when he went away, a Jacket and Breeches made of Blanket-
ing, a very coarse Rolls Shirt, an old patched Hat, but neither
Shoes nor Stockings. . . .

The latter advertisement is, in itself, a grim indictment of
slavery; but we are here concerned only with his clothing, which
was as poor as could be imagined—though no worse than that of
the free poor of eighteenth and nineteenth century England.

Like so many of his fellow slaves, Sam's harsh and hopeless
life had left him unable or unwilling to make the most of what
few opportunities offered themselves to him in captivity. Too
unprepossessing to become a house servant, not smart enough to
learn a trade, his fate was to be a field laborer for the rest of his
days. Those who aspired to a trade fared better, dressed better,
and when they escaped stood a better chance of passing for free
—as did the mulatto Stephen and his wife Phebe.

Stephen was bright, light skinned and twenty-two years old,
and his owner thought enough of the pair to run an eighteen-
line advertisement and a £10 reward for their capture. Sam had
only been worth 40 shillings. When he escaped, Stephen was
wearing a "Negro Cotton Waistcoat and Breeches, Osnabrig
Shirt, and a Pair of blue Gambadoes." Said the ad, "his Hair is
cut close off the Top of his Head, and the Front Part combed
back. His wife PHEBE went away with him, a remarkable white
Indian woman, about the same Age, and was with Child; she
has long black Hair, which is generally clubbed, and carried off
with her a blue Negro Cotton Waistcoat and Petticoat, a
Virginia Cloth Bonnet. She can spin well, and I imagine they
will both endeavour to pass as free. . . ." [8]

Worth as much in reward as Stephen and Phebe put

[8] Ibid.

together was an unnamed convict servant from London who
stood an even better chance of getting away—though he must
have been somewhat encumbered by the quantity of his baggage:

> He had on, and took with him, a *Virginia* Cotton Kersey
> wove Coat, *Russia* Drill Breeches, a Pair of old *English*
> Buckskin Ditto, a Wilton Jacket mixed with Red, a blue
> Jump Jacket without Sleeves, and very coarse, a Pair of
> white Cotton Stockings, a Pair of pale blue *Virginia* Yarn
> Ditto, one Pair of Sale Do. mixed with Red, a Pair of old
> Shoes, a Pair of turned Pumps, and I think he had a Pair of
> Silver Buckles, a Stone set Brooch, a fine Holland Shirt, an
> Osnabrug Shirt, a Muslin Neckcloth, and a small fine Hat,
> almost new. . . . As I had my House robbed the Night
> before he went away, I suspect him to be the Thief, and to
> have taken away two new Cotton Shirts.[9]

He was clearly a bright lad, destined to go far, and his master
thought so too; the reward was for £5 if caught in the colony
and £10 if apprehended and returned from beyond it.

Any absconding slave or servant would have been advised to
have traveled cross country and to have kept away from the
roads, at least until he was well beyond the area in which he was
known. Such routes were not kind to clothing, and the mud and
briars drew no distinction between enslaved, indentured, or free,
so colonist travelers into the back country dressed accordingly.
Nicholas Cresswell recalled that his companions on a journey
along the Kentucky river had not two pairs of breeches among
them. "The rest wear breechclouts, leggings and hunting shirts,
which have never been washed only by the rain since they were
made."[1] Nevertheless these choice garments were carefully
looked after. "It is a custom with our company," wrote
Cresswell, "as soon as it begins to rain to strip naked and secure
their clothes from the wet. I have attempted it twice to-day, but

[9] Ibid.
[1] *Cresswell*, 84; June 10.

the drops of rain are so disagreeable to my skin, that it obliged me to put on my shirt." [2]

Cresswell had left some of his clothing in the custody of acquaintances while on his travels into Indian country, but when he got back he found that "These rascals have wore out all the clothes I left here, so that I am now reduced to three ragged shirts, two pair linen breeches in the same condition, a hunting shirt and jacket, with one pair of stockings." [3] In short, Cresswell's wardrobe was no better, and perhaps a good deal worse, than that of many a runaway slave. I hasten to add that I am not inferring that this has any great sartorial significance. On the contrary, when you have put all the advertisements, letters, bills, and journals together, you find only that you could not necessarily identify a gentleman by the cut of his coat any more than you can today by the size of his bank account.

There are a great many misconceptions in the mind of the layman regarding life in eighteenth-century America. When and if he considers colonial Virginia, he envisages two brands of inhabitants: a plantation-owning gentry perpetually dressed as though it were just on its way to a ball at Versailles and a cowed and broken army of slaves wearing little but a coating of dried blood. Admittedly it would have been possible to find examples of both in the Virginia of 1775, though neither would have been representative of the whole. There was, as I have said earlier, a lack of a large, industrious middle class, and so in the Tidewater one did find a contrast between the large plantation-owning elite and the lower classes, whose lives, one way or another, were devoted to serving it. But the Tidewater was by no means all of Virginia, and as you journeyed inland to the mountains and the Indian frontiers, you found settlers farming much smaller land grants, communities not so very different from those of the westward movement in the nineteenth century. Cresswell was not impressed by the caliber of many of the frontier adventurers

[2] Ibid., 91; June 27.
[3] Ibid., 97; July 18.

and considered it "an asylum for rascals of all denominations." [4]
Of Western Augusta County, he wrote tersely, "Nothing but
whores and rogues in this country"; [5] and he found a certain
Major Crawford of that county a particularly choice example: "I
set out this morning to Major Crawford's, but met him at his
Mistress's. This woman is common to him, his brother, half
brother, and his own Son, and is his wife's sister's daughter at
the same time." [6] It took all sorts to make a colony.

It would be fair, I think, to say that the veneer of Southern
gentility was only coast deep, and the further west one went the
rougher became the company. But this is hardly surprising. The
low coastal plain was all parceled out, and latecomers had to
hack their farms out of the wilderness beyond—further and
further beyond as the population increased. It had been this
need for land that had led to the recent clash with the Indians
and had caused the Secretary of State to instruct the governors
to refrain from issuing further grants without specific royal
sanction.

America is still considered a land of opportunity, where,
with a little effort, the have-nots can have. It was always thus.
The original Virginia colonists in the seventeenth century came
either because they had failed to succeed at home or because they
thought that they could make a fast ducat and return to a life of
affluence. Some of the settlers were third- and fourth-class English gentry whose rank gave them a leadership it would never
have produced at home, and these became the legislative fathers
of the colony. By 1775 a handful of families that had risen to
prominence in the late seventeenth century were now the colony's
aristocracy with roots three and more generations deep.

The English have a tendency to look on American aristocracy with ill-concealed merriment, while Americans themselves
tend to be apologetic when mentioning their history and back-

[4] Ibid., 84; June 11.
[5] Ibid., 98; July 27.
[6] Ibid., 100; August 9.

ground to an Englishman. What both fail to remember is that the bulk of English titles are no older than are the first families of the American colonies, nor have most of their holders contributed as much to their country as have the Americans. It is true that the *great* plantation houses of colonial America look like rather ornate outhouses when compared with the grandeur of Blenheim, Chatsworth, or Longleat. But those are not the yardsticks by which the plantations must be judged. If comparisons must be made (and they are always dangerous) then we must look to the English country squire who through his own labors—not through royal favors—founded an estate, and whose son or grandson in the eighteenth century built himself a suitably "genteel" home. A great many of those houses no longer survive, but there are enough to show that the degrees of affluence were not as far apart as we might suppose.

In essence the Virginian plantation owner was no different from his English provincial counterpart. Most of his time was devoted to running his estate, selling his crops, feeding his servants and field hands, and playing some part in the political and judicial life of his county. For recreation the Virginia gentleman read the same books as his English cousins, drank the same wines, watched the same plays, attempted to perform on the same musical instruments, and above all enjoyed the same love of horses.

The Virginian was happy to wager away his fortune at a horse race, but happier still to spend it equipping himself for the hunting field. Appropriately fashionable attire there was every bit as important as one's appearance on Sundays. In 1772 George Washington ordered himself "A Riding Frock of a handsome Drab colour'd broad Cloth with plain dble gilt Button's; A Riding Waistcoat of Superfine Scarlet Cloth, and gold Lace with Button's like those of the Coat." [7] The supposedly traditionally hunting pink was a much later innovation. In addition to his coat and waistcoat, Washington sent to London

[7] Washington to Thomas Gibson, July 15, 1772; *Writings*, III, 96.

for "A Gentleman's Hunt'g Cap, Coverd with black Velvet, to
fit a pretty large head, cushioned round or stuffd to make it sit
easy thereon. A Silk Band, and handsome Silv'r Buckle to it."
He also wanted "1 pr. of Silver Spur's of the new'r Fashn," and
"1 Best whole hunting Whip, pretty stout and strong, cap'd
with Silver and my name and the y'r engravd thereon." [8]
Hunters have always been fond of accessories.

In March of 1775 a sportsman's fancy was none too lightly
turning to thoughts of stud, and he was to be found scanning the
columns of the *Virginia Gazette* [9] for a likely match. There was
Fearnought, and Cripple (a somewhat discouraging name),
Jupiter, Regulus, Sloe—or Pilgrim: "A Fine black horse, 5 Feet
2 Inches high, high blooded, and only 7 Years old, now stands
in the upper end of *Spotsylvania*, in the highest Order, and will
cover Mares this Spring at 6s. the single Leap, 20s. the Season,
or 30s. to ensure." If this seemed suspiciously cheap, there was
John Willis's Rockingham, which would "cover Mares at 20s.
the Leap, and 41. the Season, *Virginia* Money." For that price
one was offered "Good Pasturage for the Mares, and Entertainment for Gentlemen's Servants, gratis." For the man who was
prepared to starve his family to pursue what would later be
dubbed the "sport of kings," the same newspaper offered him
an opportunity to buy the late Philip Ludwell Lee's thorough-
bred Dotterel. "He is full 15 Hands 3 Inches high, and
remarkable for the Strength and Beauty of his Form, being in
every Respect worthy of his high Descent, which is from the
best Stock in *England*, as may be seen by his Pedigree, in the
Hand Writing, and signed by *Sir John Pennington*, who bred
him. The Gentlemen of the Turf are well acquainted with
Dotterel's Performances in *Great Britain*, and that he was
esteemed the swiftest Horse in *England* (*Eclipse* excepted.)" [1]
The price was not given; for that you had to apply in person to

---

[8] Invoice to be shipped by Robert Cary & Co., July 15, 1772; ibid.,
92.

[9] Dixon & Hunter, March 25.

[1] Ibid.

the steward at Stratford. It is significant that Dotterel's colts were described as being "uncommonly beautiful and fit for the Turf or Road." Most of the horses whose services were offered in the *Gazette* were of racing lineage, though only the most valuable would have been kept for the turf alone.

The names of the stallions that appeared in the March *Gazette*s were among the royalty of the English studbook. Fearnought as a six year old had won three King's Plates and was a grandson of the incomparable Godolphin, one of the three oriental progenitors from which most modern thoroughbreds are descended. Fearnought had been brought to Virginia in 1764 by the planter John Baylor, who is reputed to have paid £1,000 for him. Now twenty years old and no longer owned by Baylor, Fearnought was still earning 30 shillings "the cover." The oddly named Cripple was a son of Fearnought, a distinction enabling him to draw 15 shillings "the leap." Jupiter, a colt of Janus, a horse that has been described as the most perfect in colonial America, was another whose strain would live on into our own time. John Smyth was expansive in his praise of Virginia horses, saying that "nothing can be more elegant and beautiful than the horses bred here, either for the turf, the field, the road, or the coach; and they have always fine long, full, flowing tails. . . . even the most indigent person has his saddle-horse, which he rides to every place, for in this country nobody walks on foot the smallest distance. . . . In short, their horses are their pleasure, and their pride." [2] On a visit to Colonel John Tayloe's handsome Palladian mansion, "Mount Airy," in Richmond County, Philip Fithian was particularly impressed by the presence in the dining room of portraits of "twenty four of the most celebrated among the English Race-Horses, Drawn masterly, & set in elegant gilt Frames." [3]

Horse racing was one of Virginia's favorite sports, and the oval one-mile track was to be found on the outskirts of most of the principal towns in Tidewater. Fithian recalled a visit to a

[2] Smyth, "Tour," *VHR*, VI, No. 2 (April, 1853), 16–17.
[3] Fithian, *Journal*, 95; April 7, 1774.

race at Richmond Courthouse, where a field of only two horses
ran the mile course for a purse of £500 "besides small Betts
almost enumerable." He added that "The Assembly was remarkably numerous; beyond my expectation and exceeding
polite in general." [4] Less polite by far were the back country
quarter races (a sport that had originated in Tidewater but that
was not considered vulgar) where two fast but comparatively
short-winded horses would sprint over a quarter-mile course
down a village street, country road, or any open space that
presented itself. Meets of this sort were well attended by those
frontier gentry whom Cresswell found so distasteful, and they
involved a good deal of whiskey tippling and playful badinage,
which often ended in fist fights and broken heads. It was at one
such gathering that an incident occurred that helped to stimulate the Indian troubles of 1774.

A small group of white settlers and two Negroes had been
murdered by Indians; some months later the only man to escape
was attending a frontier horse race when he saw in the crowd
two men and one Indian woman whom he believed to have been
among his attackers. Governor Dunmore later reported to Lord
Dartmouth that "The Man immediately fell upon the Indians &
murdered one of them notwithstanding the Interposition of all
the other People [;] all they could do was to save the other
Indian and the Woman." [5] No one apparently thought of
apprehending the murderer, for both Dunmore and the local
magistrate offered £50 for his capture. History does not record
whether the incident dampened the spirits of the racegoers; in
all probability it merely added a welcome diversion to the day's
entertainment.

The "sporting" instincts of the lower classes of white
colonists were rather more basic than the term might now lead
us to believe. Nevertheless they were the same instincts, and the
same sports, that they had learned at their father's knees in
England, Scotland, or Ireland. Boxing was a favorite spectator

[4] Ibid., 24; Nov. 25, 1773.
[5] Dunmore to Dartmouth, Dec. 24, 1774; PRO,CO 5/1373.

sport—with rules much in need of a Marquis of Queensbury. "They conduct themselves," noted one foreign spectator, "with a barbarity worthy of their savage neighbors. The ferocious practice of stage-boxing in England, is urbanity, compared with the Virginian mode of fighting. In their combats, unless specially precluded, they are admitted (to use their own terms), 'to bite, b-ll--ck, and goudge,' which operations, when the first onset with fists is over, consists in fastening on the nose or ears of their adversaries, seizing him by the genitals, and dexterously scooping out an eye; on which account it is no uncommon circumstance to meet men in the prime of youth, deprived of one of those organs." [6] It naturally followed that if the bouts could be arranged between Irishmen and Englishmen, or better still Englishmen and Scotsmen, the frolic would be that much more diverting.

The *Virginia Gazette*'s running diversion, which had been so entertaining in its attack on the Scots in February, came to a somewhat sobering halt in March. Two Scotsmen, neither identified by name, wrote long and shaming letters to the Pinkney and to the Dixon and Hunter *Gazette*s regretting what had been written about their countrymen and asking that their fellow Virginians should judge each Scot on his merits. The arguments of one of them are worth pondering.

At a time when the press in general, and your paper in particular, teems with abuse against the Scotch, permit an old fellow, who first drew breath on the north of the Tweed, to have a few minutes hearing on the other side of the question. You must know that I came into this country young, and that, from a residence in it of upwards of forty years, I had long ago begun to look upon myself as a *Virginian*, when some pieces in your late papers made me feel very sensibly from what country I sprung. . . .

In vulgar and uncultivated minds nothing is more prevalent than national prejudice; they imbibe it, as it were, with their mother's milk, and it generally sticks by them to the end of their lives. There are few, Mr. Printer, very few, who can

[6] Chastellux, *Travels in North America*, II, pp. 601–2, n. 7.

truly say, *I am a citizen of the world.* I judge a man's
principles from his conduct, not from the spot on which he
first drew breath; and I equally esteem the honest man, of
every country and every profession. It is a general observation, that of all nations under the sun the English, amongst
the lower ranks, are most commonly addicted to this low,
illiberal, manner of thinking. Ask them their sentiments of
the French: They are a race of faithless coxcombs. Of the
Spaniards: They are a set of stiff, formal fools. Of the Dutch:
They are dull, plodding nation, whose only pursuit is gain.
Of the Scotch: They are a selfish, beggarly people. And of the
Americans, or rather the Bostonians: They will tell you that
they are a set of enthusiastic, unprincipled knaves. I have
instanced the English, in support of my position, because
they are the nation from which most of the Virginians boast
their descent, and a nation which, take it all in all, is, inferior,
in few respects, to any which the sun visits. From this we
ought to learn to be cautious how we form general characters
of any nation, or set of men, from vulgar prejudice; and, from
the opinion of most among the English of the Bostonians, we
ought to observe how a people, struggling in the noblest
cause, may be abused, and how their actions may be misrepresented and misinterpreted.[7]

Unfortunately, as the anonymous writer himself intimated,
reason cannot dispel prejudice; it is a canker that lurks in the
innermost recesses of one's being, impervious and unassailable.
Nevertheless, the arguments of the two Scotsmen were so
couched that they must surely have reminded men of good will
that they should stand firm against extremists and not be
swayed by the emotions of assemblies.

There were other words of counsel for these men of good
conscience, again published in the columns of the *Gazette;* this
time from a transcript of the charge to the Charleston, South
Carolina, grand jury by Judge William Henry Drayton on
December 12 of the previous year. The speech received considerable attention (as is attested by its appearance in the *Virginia
Gazette*) because it dwelt so eloquently on the value of civil

[7] *Virginia Gazette* (Pinkney), March 23.

liberties and in particular on a man's priceless right to trial by jury. Judge Drayton apparently feared that any diminishing of civil liberties through government action would lead to a denial of jury trial and thence to despotism. The words may have been uttered two centuries ago, but they are still as valid and as disturbing today:

> You are now met to discharge one of the most important duties in society; for you are assembled arbiters of the innocence or guilt of such of your fellow citizens who are so unfortunate as to have afforded occasion, however slight, for the laws to take cognizance of their conduct. You are authorized to pass judgment, in the first instance, upon the apparently guilty wretch; and by your acquitting voice, you have power to shield apparent innocence from a malicious prosecution; such powers have the constitution of your country vested in you; powers no less important than truly honourable when exercised with a fearless integrity.

The judge went on to speak of the various freedoms that were in his opinion threatened by the actions of the English parliament, and he urged the assembled jurors to hold their civil liberties "dearer than your lives, a lesson at all times proper from a judge, but particularly so at this crisis, when America is in one general and generous commotion touching this truly important point." Speaking of the jury law, Judge Drayton declared:

> This law carries in itself an indelible mark of what high importance the legislature thought it when they enacted it, and it carries in itself also a kind of prophecy that its existence, in its native vigour, would in after times be endangered. . . . A learned judge says "Every new tribunal erected for the decision of facts, without the intervention of a jury, is a step towards aristocracy, the most oppressive of absolute governments; and it is therefore a duty which every man owes to his country, his friends, his posterity, and himself, *to maintain, to the utmost of his power*, this valuable constitution in all its rights, to restore it to its ancient dignity, if at all impaired, to amend it wherever it is defective, and,

above all, to guard, with the most jealous circumspection, against the introduction of new and arbitrary methods of trial, which, under a variety of plausible pretences, may, in time, imperceptibly undermine this best preservative of English liberty." Mr. Justice BLACKSTONE terms the English trial by jury the glory of the English Law: Let me tell you *our* trial by jury is that kind of glory, in full meridian lustre, in comparison of which, the English mode appears only with diminished splendour." [8]

This was good stirring stuff to fill the jurors (who would probably have preferred to be somewhere else) with a fitting sense of responsibility, as well as pride in their tasks. While the judge had no evidence that South Carolinians were about to be deprived of jury trials, it is conceivable that he saw in the Quebec Act, the Administration of Justice Act, and the Massachusetts Government Act of 1774 the beginning of a much broader assault on the rights of all the colonies to administer their own justice. Nevertheless, to the layman reading the speech in the newspaper, it seemed as though the judge knew something that the reader did not, and so it served to increase his apprehension. So also did news, reported in the *Gazette*, of a narrowly avoided Negro revolt in New York.

It seems that Johannes Schoonmaker of Ulster County overheard a conversation between two of his Negroes in which they were discussing the quantity of powder they would need and the sources of support for the plot. The idea was that the slaves should set fire to their owners' houses and then kill the families as they came out. The conspirators were apparently concerned that they should "have drums enough to prevent hearing the cries." [9] To those outside the plot this might have appeared a rather unnecessary refinement, for when you awoke in the night and saw your neighbors' homes burning briskly all around, the beating of drums would not have been very much more reassuring than the sound of their cries for help.

The two plotters were duly arrested, as also were seventeen

[8] Ibid., March 2.

[9] *Virginia Gazette* (Dixon & Hunter), March 18.

or eighteen of their associates, along with considerable quantities of powder and ball shot. The conspiracy involved Negroes in the towns of Kingston, Hurly, Keysereck, and Marbletown, and it was rumored in New York that the Negroes were to be joined by five or six hundred Indians, though this was thought to be unfounded. But regardless of whether or not Indians were involved, the very idea of a Negro plot in New York served to arouse the worst fears of newspaper-reading Virginians. There had been that case only last September in Westmoreland County in which Thomas Sorrel's Negroes would have murdered him in his bed if his wife had not waked in time. It was true that at their trial the slaves claimed Sorrel's brother had put them up to it. But nobody was sure whether they were lying. Fithian, in relating this affair, observed that he thought the life of slaves was such that it would "almost justify them in any desperate attempt" to improve their lot, and he concluded "I sleep in fear too, though my Doors & Windows are all secured!" [1] Who could tell? The Negroes might only be waiting for the colonists to become embroiled in some open breach with the governor, to rise up as one against them. It could even happen around the countryside while the plantation owners were away at their conventions. The sight of the slave gangs working the fields was no longer one to promote complacent satisfaction. Now there was the fear that they had arms hidden in the barn, and that behind their docile eyes and servile speech they were secretly saying: "And on Friday night, my master, when the moon is dark, we shall cut your throat." What of the house servants? Did they know of the plot? Were they part of it? And old Sam, who had been like one of the family since heaven knows when— would it be he who would unlock the door and let them in? Such thoughts were almost too chilling to contemplate. But if it could happen in New York, how much more easily could it occur in Virginia—perhaps even now, while the delegates were assembling in Richmond for the March convention.

The purpose of this, the second Virginia Convention, was

[1] Fithian, *Journal*, 187; Sept. 8, 1774.

initially to ratify the resolutions of last autumn's Continental Congress and to establish the necessary machinery to implement them in the colony. The names of the delegates who assembled at St. John's Church on March 20 read like a Virginia edition of Burke's *Landed Gentry:* Thomas Jefferson, Edmund Pendleton, Benjamin Harrison, George Washington, Thomas Marshall, Lewis Burwell, Patrick Henry, Robert Carter Nicholas, Carter Braxton, William Aylett, Richard Bland, Francis Lightfoot Lee, Richard Henry Lee, Mann Page, Jr., Dudley Digges, Thomas Nelson, Jr., Champion Travis, and a host of others. Chosen president was the revered Peyton Randolph, representative from Williamsburg; and as clerk, John Tazewell. As expected, the resolutions of the Continental Congress were unanimously approved, and the delegates from Virginia were officially applauded for their part in formulating them. Thus, Monday, Tuesday, and Wednesday passed smoothly and without surprises, and at the outset it looked as though Thursday would follow suit.

The morning began with the reading of a petition to the King by the Jamaican assembly, in support of American rights. Having heard it, the Virginia delegates adopted a resolution of thanks to their Jamaican cousins, ending with the assurance that it was "the most ardent wish of this colony . . . to see a speedy return to those halcyon days, when we lived a free and happy people." To Patrick Henry, the effervescent young representative from Hanover County, all this gentlemanly somnambulance was too much to take. Three days had gone by and no one had said "Down with King George!"; no one had offered to shoot Lord Dunmore—instead, they just wanted to get back to the way things used to be. The last thing in the world Henry then wanted was the restoration of the status quo, no matter how halcyon it might have been. He therefore decided to set the ball rolling himself, and much to the surprise of his more timid colleagues he proposed that an independent militia be immediately established for the defense of the rights and liberties of the colony.

The delegates gulped, and one by one their most influential spokesmen rose to urge moderation. Pendleton, Nicholas, Bland, and Harrison all pointed out that the colonies had many good friends in the English parliament, and that it would be most unwise to embarrass those supporters. The nonimportation resolves had already hurt Britain's manufacturing interests, and the merchants were clutching their bleeding pockets and calling for a settlement. Even the King himself was showing signs of relenting and looking upon America's "sufferings with an eye of pity." Surely, argued the moderates, this was hardly the time to rock the boat. Besides, the colony was in no position to defend itself against the might of the British crown, "A nation ready and armed at all points! Her navies riding triumphant in every sea; her armies never marching but to certain victory!" What possible outcome could there be "but to yield up *this country* an easy prey to Great Britain, and to convert the illegitimate right which the British parliament now claimed, into a firm and indubitable right, *by conquest?* The measure might be brave; but it was the bravery of madmen. It had no pretension to the character of prudence; and as little to the grace of genuine courage." [2]

In the face of such a vehement counterblast anybody but Patrick Henry would have quietly withdrawn his resolutions. But he was not that kind of man; instead he rose again to deliver what has long been considered one of the greatest speeches in the annals of American oratory. He told his colleagues that this was no time to prevaricate, and he considered it his duty to speak his piece no matter whom it should offend. He scoffed at the previous speakers' hopes that all would yet be well. Did they really believe that the King was moving toward a reconciliation?

Are fleets and armies necessary to a work of love and reconciliation? Have we shown ourselves so unwilling to be reconciled, that force must be called in to win back our love? Let us not deceive ourselves, sir. These are the implements of

[2] Wirt, *Henry,* 116–8.

war and subjugation—the last arguments to which kings resort. I ask gentlemen, Sir, what means this martial array, if its purpose be not to force us to submission? . . . . Has Great Britain any enemy in this quarter of the world, to call for all this accumulation of navies and armies? No, sir: she has none. They are meant for us: they can be meant for no other. . . . And what have we to oppose to them? Shall we try argument? Sir, we have been trying that for the last ten years. Have we anything new to offer upon the subject? Nothing. . . . We have petitioned—We have remonstrated —We have supplicated—We have prostrated ourselves before the throne. . . . *There is no longer any room for hope.* If we wish to be free—if we mean to preserve inviolate those inestimable privileges for which we have been so long contending . . . we must fight!—I repeat it, sir, we must fight!! An appeal to arms and to the God of Hosts, is all that is left us!

Judge Tucker of Williamsburg, who read Henry's speech later, said of this passage that it was as though the delegates were hearing Cato in the Roman senate and seeing the writing as it appeared on the wall of Belshazzar's palace. Henry continued:

They tell us, sir, that we are weak—unable to cope with so formidable an adversary. But when shall we be stronger? Will it be next week, or next year? Will it be when we are totally disarmed; and when a British guard shall be stationed in every house?—Sir, we are not weak, if we make a proper use of those means which the God of nature hath placed in our power. Three millions of people, armed in the holy cause of liberty, and in such a country as that which we possess, are invincible by any force which our enemy can send against us. . . . The battle, Sir, is not to the strong alone; it is to the vigilant, the active, the brave . . . it is now too late to retire from the contest. There is no retreat, but in submission and slavery! Our chains are forged. Their clanking may be heard on the plains of Boston! The war is inevitable—and let it come!! I repeat, sir, let it come!!!

. . . Gentlemen may cry, peace, peace—but there is no peace. The war is actually begun! The next gale that sweeps

from the north, will bring to our ears the clash of resounding
arms! Our brethren are already in the field! Why stand we
here idle? What is it that gentlemen wish? What would they
have? Is life so dear, or peace so sweet, as to be purchased at
the price of chains, and slavery? Forbid it, Almighty God!—I
know not what course others may take; but as for me, give me
liberty, or give me death! [3]

William Wirt, Henry's ebullient biographer (from whose
narrative the preceding account is derived), declared that when
this Cato sat down "No murmer of applause was heard. The
effect was too deep. After the trance of a moment, several
members started from their seats. The cry, 'to arms,' seemed to
quiver on every lip, and gleam from every eye! . . . . That
supernatural voice still sounded in their ears, and shivered along
their arteries. . . . They became impatient of speech—their
souls were on fire for action." Nevertheless, regardless of Mr.
Wirt's colorful picture, the delegates did not draw their swords
and dash out to do battle with any Tory in sight. Instead, the
convention continued with its business through the week, even
to including a unanimously approved resolution expressing the
colony's thanks to Lord Dunmore "for his truly noble, wise, and
spirited conduct on the late expedition against our Indian
enemy:—a conduct which at once evinces his Excellency's
attention to the true interests of this colony, and a zeal in the
executive department, which no dangers can divert, or difficulties hinder, from atchieving the most important services to the
people who have the happiness to live under his administration." [4] As Thomas Jefferson later explained, the older
delegates, who opposed Henry's eagerness to toss them into the
maelstrom, were all men of good conscience whose principles
were essentially the same as those of their more spirited young
associates. "Sensible," said he, "of the importance of unanimity
among our constituents, although we often wished to have gone

[3] Ibid., 121–3.
[4] *Virginia Gazette* (Dixon & Hunter), April 1.

on faster, we slackened our pace, that our less ardent colleagues might keep up with us." [5] Even so, the concluding days of the convention were not devoted to backpedaling.

The delegates agreed to see to it that more contributions were forthcoming to enable Virginia to continue to send aid to the people of Boston; lawyers, suitors, and witnesses were called on to refrain from attending the next session of the general court; in short, a temporary suspension of the administration of justice. Other unanimously approved resolves encouraged the Virginia brewing of malt liquors to remove the need for imported beverages; also to be promoted were the making of gunpowder, paper (for cartridges), iron wire, nails, and steel. However, the bulk of the time was spent in consideration of the proposals of Patrick Henry's committee, which had been charged with evolving a plan for embodying, arming, and disciplining three regiments of militia.

Henry's proposals were founded on good colonial precedent, on an old act of 1738 for the better regulating of the militia, whose provisions had long been allowed to lapse. It was recommended to each county in the colony that they raise at least one company of infantry and one troop of cavalry and that these should be trained and ready for any emergency. Each company of infantry should comprise sixty-eight men, one captain, two lieutenants, one ensign, four sergeants, and four corporals, plus a drum and colors. Each man should "be provided with a good rifle, if to be had, or otherwise with a common firelock, bayonet, and cartouch-box [cartridge box], and also with a tomahawk, one pound of gunpowder, and four pounds of ball at least, fitted to the bore of his gun." They thought of everything. "Every man should also be clothed in a hunting shirt, by way of uniform," and furthermore he should "use all endeavor, as soon as possible, to become acquainted with the military exercise for infantry, appointed to be used by

[5] Wirt, *Henry*, 126-7.

his majesty in the year 1764." Here, we may note, was one
occasion when what was good enough for King George was
good enough for Patrick Henry.

The cavalry troops were each to consist of thirty men,
excluding officers, and each man should "be provided with a
good horse, bridle, saddle, with pistols and holsters, a carbine,
or other short firelock, with a bucket (a saddle socket for the
gun), a cutting sword, or tomahawk, one pound of gunpowder,
and four pounds of ball, at the least; and he should use the
utmost diligence in training and accustoming his horse to stand
the discharge of fire-arms, and in making himself acquainted
with the military exercise for cavalry." [6]

When the convention adjourned for the week end, Patrick
Henry had every reason to feel pleased with himself. He had
whipped up a gathering of quietly unhappy Englishmen into a
band of militant Americans. It has even been claimed that
Robert Carter Nicholas, who initially opposed Henry's militia
resolve as too aggressive, once it was adopted became so enthusiastic that he wanted to enlarge the whole enterprise, and instead
of arming a militia he proposed that the colony should raise ten
thousand regulars for the war. His proposal was not accepted,
but it must have caused Henry considerable satisfaction to see
how readily one might turn a conservative into a fanatic if fed on
a suitable diet of oratory. However, Thursday's triumph was not
enough, and on Monday Henry rose again to take another
whack at the roots of royal authority.

On March 2, Governor Dunmore had issued a proclamation
stating that it was the King's wish that all vacant lands within
the colony should be put up for public sale, "and that the
highest bidder for such lots shall be the purchaser thereof, and
shall hold the same, subject to a reservation of one halfpenny
sterling *per* acre, by way of annual quitrent, and also of all
mines, of gold, silver, and precious stones." [7] In the words of
biographer Wirt, Henry saw this proposal as "an innovation on

[6] Ibid.

[7] *Virginia Gazette* (Pinkney), March 23.

the established usage of granting lands in this colony . . ."
and therefore "not only an usurpation of power, but a great
subduction of the natural wealth of the colony, and the creation,
moreover, of a separate band of tenants and retainers, devoted to
the vilest measures of the crown." [8] To thwart such foul
designs, Henry proposed that a committee should be set up to
study the proclamation and to report back to the next assembly
or convention; in the meantime no one should purchase land on
the conditions contained in it. The resolve was approved, and it
will come as no surprise to learn that P. Henry was chosen to
head the committee.

On the preceding Saturday the convention had elected its
representatives to attend the Second Continental Congress,
scheduled to meet at Philadelphia on May 10, and those chosen
were Peyton Randolph, George Washington, Patrick Henry,
Richard Henry Lee, Edmund Pendleton, Benjamin Harrison,
and Richard Bland. On Monday, as something of an after-
thought, it was resolved that Thomas Jefferson should be
appointed to stand in for Peyton Randolph if he should be
unable to attend.

The election of the delegates to go to Philadelphia proved to
be a clear violation of a proclamation issued by the governor that
called on "all magistrates and other officers, to use their utmost
endeavours to prevent any such appointment of deputies, and to
exhort all persons whatever within this government, to desist
from such an unjustifiable proceeding, so highly displeasing to
his Majesty." [9] This proclamation was hurriedly issued after
Lord Dunmore had received the Secretary of State's January 4
circular letter to his colonial governors calling on them to do all
they could to prevent the election of delegates to the congress.
Unhappily, the order arrived a little late, and it was March 28
before Dunmore could issue his proclamation—three days after
the election and one day after the convention had adjourned.
Nicely gauged to increase his Lordship's embarrassment was the

[8] Wirt, *Henry*, 128.
[9] *Virginia Gazette* (Pinkney), March 30.

Virginia Gazette's [1] placing of the proclamation immediately after its report of the concluding session of the Richmond convention.

In writing to Lord Dartmouth, Dunmore did not reveal that the proclamation was issued too late to do anything but fan the coat tails of the departing delegates; the inference was that the colonists merely ignored it. "As I expected," he wrote, "it had no other effect than exciting the further insults of the Enemies of Government here, in their free Animadversions upon Administration, and giving them occasion to urge, to the People, a Stronger Necessity of Continuing their unwarrantable Practices." [2]

Dunmore then went on to summarize the results of the convention, laying obvious stress on the resolution to raise a military force and also referring to the rejection of the government's land sale proposal. It is curious that his Lordship should mention both of Patrick Henry's contributions to the proceedings without any mention of the man himself. Similarly the *Gazette*s published details of the resolutions but omitted any word about the "Liberty or Death" speech. Nor did Washington mention it, either in his diary or in the letter to his brother that he wrote from Richmond two days later. He said only that he had been offered the command of the Richmond Independent Company and intimated that he would accept it, adding: "it is my full intention to devote my Life and Fortune in the cause we are engaged in, if need be." [3] Washington had also been chosen to command the companies of Fairfax, Albemarle, Spotsylvania, and Westmoreland Counties, the latter his brother's home. In all fairness, one must admit that Washington was neither easily impressed nor an expansive letter writer. On the very day that he wrote to his brother he was chosen to be a Virginia representative to the congress, yet he failed to mention it.

[1] *Virginia Gazette* (Dixon & Hunter), April 1.

[2] Dunmore to Dartmouth, March 14; PRO,CO 5/1353.

[3] Washington to John Augustine Washington, March 25; *Writings*, III, 276–7.

Therefore, his failure to discuss Patrick Henry's oration need not suggest that it was less inspiring than bright historians and fading memories later claimed it to be.

That volatile Scotsman from Norfolk, James Parker, wrote to his friend Charles Steuart, giving his account of what Patrick Henry had said: "You never heard anything more infamously insolent than P Henrys speech," he declared. "He called the K— a Tyrant, a fool, a puppet & tool to the Ministry, Said there was now no Englishmen, no Scots no Britons, but a Set of Wretches Sunk in luxury. . . ."[4] Regardless of the content of Henry's pyrotechnical display, one fact is indisputable. The majority of the delegates came away still believing that in the end reason would prevail and a just and happy settlement would be reached with the mother country. Life would go on as usual.

With spring in the air, there were more immediate crises to worry about—such as the servant problem. One could not expect to run a neat plantation without adequate staff, and good tradesmen were hard to find. It was fortunate that Captain Kidd's *Justitia* had just arrived in the Rappahannock with a cargo of indentured servants and time-serving convicts; they might be worth looking over. There were 130 of them, including carpenters and joiners, bricklayers and plasterers, shoemakers, barbers, weavers, cutlers, bakers, a tanner, tailor, stay maker, blacksmith, painter, printer, bookbinder, a miller, stocking weaver, a schoolmaster, a hatter, and a silk dyer, as well as farmers, country laborers, and gentlemen's servants. They would be put up for sale at Leedstown, and the sale would continue until all had been bought.[5]

Felons found guilty of capital crimes whose sentences had been commuted to transportation were indentured for fourteen years, while those paying the price of lesser lapses served seven. On the other hand, people who sold themselves into servitude as the price of a new start in a new land were bonded for periods of three to seven years depending on their worth. John Harrower

[4] Parker to Steuart, April 6; CSP.
[5] *Virginia Gazette* (Pinkney), March 16.

was, as we have seen, a man of intelligence, and as a schoolmaster he would be free after four. At the end of it his master,
Colonel Daingerfield, was required by Virginia law to provide
him with "freedom dues" amounting to £3 10s., though in
Harrower's case his indenture specified £5. In South Carolina
he would have been entitled to fifty acres free of quitrent for ten
years, but in Pennsylvania two suits of clothes and a new ax
were the statutory fruits of service.

The yardstick against which a servant's capability and
length of bondage were computed was a combination of the
price of his passage from England and a reasonable (or
sometimes unreasonable) profit for the ship's captain or the
agency which undertook to pay his passage out. The actual
indenture stating the length of service was agreed upon and
signed in advance, and it was up to the captain on arrival to get
the best possible price for his cargo by any means short of
tampering with it. The purchaser, for his part, was not hiring
an employee as we might today, he was investing in a piece of
livestock, a short-term slave who would be his, in body if not
soul, until he worked out his term or, alternatively, expired.
Most indentured servants were already trained to a trade, and
more important most of them came of their own free will, just as
John Harrower had done. It is true that the "free will" was
often closely allied to an escape from creditors or a simple flight
from jobless starvation, and if the man was a victim of his own
flaws rather than of circumstances, he would probably continue
to be a failure here. However when one bought an indenture one
was able to talk to the man and size him up. The same was true
of the cheaper convict labor, though, as we shall see later, the
trick was to hang onto it. But neither was nearly as chancy as
buying a newly landed slave, when all you could do was to check
his teeth and his muscles and make sure that he was not unduly
damaged.

Besides the need for servants there was that little matter of
the parlor wall paper; it could never last another year. The

obvious answer was to send for John Lockley's newly arrived decorator:

THE Subscriber begs Leave to acquaint the Public in general, and his Friends in particular, that he has engaged a Person, from *London*, who is a Proficient in PAINTING, PLASTERING and PAPER-HANGING, and hopes to give general Satisfaction to all those who please to employ him; which will much oblige

Their humble Servant,
JOHN LOCKLEY

N.B. *Stolen out of my Yard, last Night, a white* MUSCOVY DUCK, *and a* SUMMER DRAKE. *Whoever brings them to me shall have 5s. Reward.*[6]

The spring was a good time to consider enhancing the social graces of one's family. It might not be a bad idea to send the boys to Dr. Joseph De Sabbe to improve their fencing, a proficiency which might serve them in good stead one of these days. The doctor advertised that he was about to offer "his services to those gentlemen who have an inclination to learn the manly art of FENCING, with the small-sword, and begs leave to inform them that he intends taking a room in *Williamsburg* and *York;* in the first of which places he will attend four days in every week, in the latter two. His price will be a guinea entrance money, and fifteen shillings per month. The doctor does not by the above intend to decline his practice as a physician, but would be still glad of the favours of the public." [7] One wonders whether the doctor had fallen on hard times and had hit on this novel method of obtaining patients.

If the boys were to learn fencing in Williamsburg, perhaps the girls should go along too, in answer to another advertisement from the same page of the *Gazette:* "LADIES who are inclined to learn the GUITTAR may be instructed on that

[6] *Virginia Gazette* (Dixon & Hunter), March 18.
[7] *Virginia Gazette* (Pinkney), March 30.

instrument by a lady lately arrived. Enquire of the printer." [8]

Even the *Gazette*'s poetry editor (Mr. Dixon or Mr. Hunter?) felt it was time that his readers turned their thoughts from the vendettas, fears, and crises of the winter to a somewhat higher plane; so he gave them a poem on hang-overs entitled "Next Morning":

What means this fury in my veins?
This fire that hisses through my brains?
　　Ah me! my head! my head!
My pulses beat; parch'd by my tongue;
Dry are my palms; my nerves unstrung;
　　And every sense is fled.

Now nauseous qualms my bosom heave,
And, Oh! such sad sensations give,
　　Too exquisite to name!
In dizzy mists my eye-balls swim;
A languor creeps o'er every limb,
　　And all unmans my frame.

Through ten verses the poet told of his downfall; how a friend had brought this horror upon him through taking him to a party and introducing him to bottles hitherto unknown.

Oh! fatal and accursed hour,
And claret's more pernicious power:
　　How could a friend do this?
To cheat me with a seeming joy,
And in a moment to destroy
　　Whole years of treasur'd bliss.

　　.　.　.　.　.　.　.　.　.

But farewell peace, and farewell riot:
For sober ease and decent quiet,
　　The bottle I resign;
Firm to pursue this better plan,

To drink small-beer, and make the man,
Fair temperance, ever thine.[9]

If we still retain doubts that eighteenth-century Americans thought very much as we do today, "Next Morning" must surely remove any lingering suspicions that their senses were different too. The poet knew of what he wrote, and so do I—and so, I suspect, do you.

As the poet so graphically pointed out, the merry hours of night are quickly followed by the jagged light of day; last night's joyously accepted rumor that Lord North and Lord Dartmouth were about to be replaced and America was to receive full redress seemed to lose their substance and to drift away into improbability once the sun came up. Much more tangible than that "buz" from the court at London was the *Gazette*'s report of another act of "infamy" by the King's officers right here in the colony.

The item came from Northampton on Virginia's eastern shore, was dated March 26, and was headed: "VIRGINIANS, The following is meant for you as a caution which is worthy of your strict attention." [1] It seems that the navy schooner *Magdalen* under Lieutenant Collins (whose arrival at Norfolk was noted in Chapter I) was now cruising in the Chesapeake Bay in search of contraband. On March 22 Collins's men boarded a sloop in Hungar's Harbor belonging to a certain Mr. B——— and found it to carry only oats, corn, and two hogsheads of molasses, all legally imported, and with papers to prove it. After searching the ship and examining the papers the boarding party left, apparently satisfied. But that night they returned and hid aboard the vessel until noon of the following day, when they proceeded to hoist a distress signal. Mr. B——— saw it, and sent one of his apprentices to see what was happening. As soon as he went aboard, the boy was grabbed and taken to the *Magdalen*, where he joined another boy seized from the sloop the previous night.

[9] *Virginia Gazette* (Dixon & Hunter), March 25.
[1] *Virginia Gazette* (Pinkney), March 30.

The boys were threatened, cajoled, and even tempted with substantial bribes to reveal where the rest of the sloop's crew was to be found.

It would appear that the *Gazette*'s correspondent was none too clear on a number of details. We do not know what Collins expected to find aboard the sloop nor why he wanted to locate the crew. Neither do we know what he hoped to gain by hiding on the ship (and for so long) and then hoisting the distress signal. It was all very odd. However, the reporter was obviously satisfied with his account and he ended it as follows:

This is a plain representation of the conduct of the officers and men aboard the *Magdalen.*—Pusillanimous and dastardly! Why did not captain [Lieutenant] Collins, to whom Mr. B------ had sent his compliments to come ashore and dine with him, why did he not go, and tell Mr. B------ that he had information against his vessel, and should seize her? No. He skulked in his vessel, and would not be seen. The nature of the action may always be known from the conduct of the agent. What a man is ashamed of he will decline appearing in; an infamous cause even captain Collins was ashamed of, and therefore would not appear in, but left the management of the business to his inferiors in infamy.[2]

These editorial comments did nothing to clarify the cause or even the result of the incident. The *Gazette*'s readers knew only that Lieutenant Collins had been up to some rather curious capers in the night. But if they were surprised by these, they were destined to be flabbergasted by his nocturnal efforts in April.

[2] Ibid.

[*IV*]

APRIL

For Mr. *Jefferson the month of April was* unusually short; it ended on All Fools' Day. That morning he and Mrs. Jefferson were found dead in their bed with their throats cut. This is an item of history not particularly well known, possibly because the Jeffersons lived at Deptford, near London, and not at Monticello.

All Fools' Day or April Fools' Day was enjoyed to the utmost in eighteenth-century England, and the delights of making asses of one's friends and neighbors were savored as richly as they are by children today. Numerous contemporary writers speculated about the origin of the practice, and most of them traced it back to remote antiquity. One scholar suggested that it began with the April first on which Noah let the dove out of the ark before the waters had subsided, another thought it began with Herod's fruitless search for the infant Christ, and yet another was sure that it all started with the rape of the Sabine women. Just how much fun colonial Americans had on April 1, 1775, remains in doubt, though the *Virginia Almanack* for 1775 noted that it was, indeed, All Fools' Day.

The Dixon and Hunter *Virginia Gazette* that came out on April 1 did not find life very amusing. Its columns were largely filled with a report of the recent Richmond convention; what was left was devoted to advertising and a report from the Nansemond County Committee exposing the sins of the rector of Suffolk parish. It grieved the members of the committee to have "to hold up for public censure the conduct of any man," but in

the case of the Reverend John Agnew they knew they were
dealing with an enemy to America and, at the same time, one
who was no friend to the excellent constitution of Great Britain.
He had accomplished this somewhat gymnastic feat by declaring that the resolves of the Provincial Congress were rebellious
and the proceedings of the Continental Congress were resisting
the King and parliament, and that to do so was rebellion. For
good measure he added that he could see nothing wrong with
the Ministry's Administration of Justice Act. The committee
ordered the Reverend Mr. Agnew to attend one of their
meetings for the purpose of atonement, but he decided that he
would rather not. Complainants therefore gave evidence against
the rector in his absence, one indignantly relating how he had
told Agnew that he resented hearing sermons attacking the
patriot cause; to which the rector had had the audacity to reply:
"If you do not like such sermons, you can only leave your seat."
The committee declared itself horrified by such an attitude, and
it found that Agnew had been "industrious in propagating false
and erroneous principles, not only in private discourse, but in
blending detestable tenets in his angry orations from the pulpit,
in order to gain a party in opposition to the common
cause. . . ." In short, it was a crime to say anything in public,
or indeed in private, that could be construed as supporting the
established government of the colony.

The Reverend John Wingate of Orange County was another
April victim of the paper pillory. The committee of that county
discovered that Wingate was in possession of a number of
loyalist pamphlets, and it demanded that he give them up.
Wingate refused on the grounds that they were not his to
surrender but belonged to a Mr. Mitchell of Fredericksburg.
The committee thought this an outrageous excuse and warned
him that if "he regarded his association engagements, the
favour of the committee, or the good of the public, he would not
deny so reasonable a request." Wingate weighed these heavy
responsibilities on the balance of his principles and again
refused to hand over the pamphlets. However, he did offer to let

the committee look at them providing that it would return them undamaged; naturally it refused. Exactly what happened then is far from clear, but according to the committee's published report it decided that "there was no prospect of working on Mr. Wingate by arguments or entreaties" and it simply demanded the surrender of the pamphlets, promising that it would no longer be defeated in its intentions. It seems improbable that the Reverend Mr. Wingate would be so easily frightened into submission, but according to the report he was.

It was then late on Saturday, and the committee decided to adjourn until Monday, thus giving its members time to read the pamphlets before passing judgment on them. What they read quite spoiled their week end, though it enabled them to assemble on Monday filled with patriotic indignation and possessing a splendid opportunity to rattle their sabers in public. Among the offending publications were such disgraceful titles as *The Congress Canvassed* by A. W. Farmer, *Free Thoughts on the Proceedings of the Continental Congress* by "a Farmer," and *Short Advice to the Counties of New York* by "a Country Gentleman." Damned Tory poison in every line of them! If the committee of Orange County could have laid its hands on "a Farmer" and on "a Country Gentleman" it would have surely hung them up by their heels. Instead, it had to make do with publicly burning the pamphlets, which it did before an audience of the recently formed Independent Company "and other respectable inhabitants of the said county, all of whom joined in expressing a noble indignation against such execrable publications, and their ardent wishes for an opportunity of inflicting on the authors, publishers, and their abettors, the punishment due to their insufferable arrogance, and atrocious crimes." [1] Clearly the worthy inhabitants of Orange County were deeply affronted by the contents of the pamphlets, though one wonders how they had managed to read them when only five publications were involved and these had been in the hands of the Committee for

[1] *Virginia Gazette* (Dixon & Hunter), April 15.

only a day before they were burned on the Monday. Equally intriguing were the questions that were apparently neither asked nor answered: Why did Mr. Mitchell of Fredericksburg (who was said to be a "hearty friend to the [patriot] cause") have the offending literature in the first place? Why did he pass it on to the Reverend Mr. Wingate, and who told the committee that Wingate had it? There would seem to have been more to this affair than met the committee's eye.

The outcome of the affair was that the Reverend Mr. Wingate ended up with his name in the paper, knocking another nail into the coffin of disaffection that had been developing for many years between the people and the clergy. These unfortunate gentlemen seemed to lose out on every score. Nicholas Cresswell, who would probably have applauded the attitudes of both Agnew and Wingate, continued to have bad luck in his own churchgoing. On Sunday, April 2, he noted that at Leesburg there was no parson available. "It is a shame," he added, "to suffer these people to neglect their duty in the manner they do." [2]

Other people were more fervent in what they believed to be their duty, and a sharp eye was kept for any seeming violations of the nonimportation resolution of the congress. In February the merchant vessel *Elizabeth* had docked at Norfolk for repairs, and her master, Captain Sampson, had asked permission to unload a cargo of salt while the repairs were being made. The Norfolk committee gave its consent, the salt was unloaded, and the work on the ship completed. Instead of taking the salt on board again, Captain Sampson proceeded to load a cargo of lumber. The committee sent for the captain and told him what it thought of him, whereupon he sought the protection of the British ship of war then lying in the harbor. The committeemen felt that this was cheating, and they unanimously declared Sampson a "violater of the association, and an enemy to *American Liberty*," [3] and they called on all merchants to have

[2] *Cresswell*, 60.
[3] *Virginia Gazette* (Pinkney), April 6.

no further dealings with him. The measure seems to have been successful, for by the end of March the *Elizabeth* had left Norfolk for Bristol, England, taking back the same cargo of salt that she had brought out.

Like most statements issued by the local committees, only one side of the story is preserved in print, and many rather obvious questions are never answered. In the case of the *Elizabeth* one wonders what became of the cargo of lumber, which was apparently already aboard before the committee issued its condemnation. The report places Captain Sampson in the worst possible light, and doubtless the average newspaper reader thought him a pretty fair scoundrel, a man whose word was not to be trusted and who returned courtesy with knavery. It is possible that he did break his word, but at the same time one cannot overlook the fact that he, too, had a valid point of view.

Captain Sampson was simply the master of a merchant ship whose job was to carry Mr. X's cargo and deliver it, as addressed, to Mr. Y. He would then attempt to obtain another cargo and carry that back to someone else. To provide this essential service the captain spent the best part of his life in cramped quarters aboard a small and vulnerable cockleshell. He had enough trouble with his ship, his crew, the weather, disease, his King's enemies, pirates and privateers without having to worry about whether the recipient of his cargo would accept it when he got it there. Seafaring men had a reputation for being short-tempered, and not without some reason. Consequently we might spare Captain Sampson a moment of sympathy. He had brought his cargo safely across the Atlantic only to find that a committee of hot-headed radicals was able to prevent him from completing his mission, and that the King's officers would or could do nothing to support him. On top of it all, the captain found himself publicly robbed of his good name and accused of being a violator of an association to which he had not been a party in the first place. It is likely that Captain Sampson was rather a hard man to serve under during the long trip back to

England, as were probably the masters of a Liverpool brig and a ship out of Glasgow, both of which were likewise sent back without unloading.

The same issue of the *Virginia Gazette* that contained the sad story of Captain Sampson and his salt also included part of a quasi-biblical satire called the "American Chronicles of the Times," a thinly disguised commentary on current events:

> And behold about that time there came another TEASHIP from the land of Britain, and cast her anchor in the river of York, in the land of the Virginites, and the sons of liberty and the Virginia rangers assembled themselves together, and the TEA and their TEA-CHESTS ascended up in a pillar of fire and smoke, and vanished out of sight.
>
> But the ship being innocent, and the owner thereof a righteous man, and knowing nought of the matter, for his sake therefore they suffered her to depart to the isles afar off.

Thus another disgruntled ship's captain sailed homeward, a voyage made the more galling by the fact that he had been allowed to make it at all thanks only to the unctuous magnanimity of the "Sons of Liberty."

For those who cared to notice it, the April papers provided further details of the wreck of the Virginia ship *Martin* off Milford Haven, a loss that had been briefly reported in March. The vessel was quite large, 300 tons, and carried a cargo of 463 hogsheads of tobacco and some 10,000 barrel staves; all were lost except for a few water-ruined casks of tobacco, some of the staves, and part of the rigging, which washed ashore. Seven seamen were able to escape in the longboat, but the captain, mate, and eight others drowned. The report noted that the ship had had a long voyage of eleven weeks and was short of provisions. "Neither of the seamen were acquainted with this channel, which was the cause of this sad misfortune. The rocks whereon the ship struck are horrible, and the destruction which appeared the following morning on the shore for near a mile long, is beyond all description." [4]

[4] *Virginia Gazette* (Dixon & Hunter), April 8.

The loss of the *Martin* was followed in the *Gazette* by an account of another maritime disaster, which again served to underline the dangers that beset those who daily hazarded their lives on the water. The report came from New London, Connecticut, and described one of those accidents that still happen today and are always greeted with amazement.

Capt. Arwell from the West Indies, advises, that a sloop, Jacob Goodwin, master, who sailed from this port the 16th of December, fine wind at N.W. on the evening following, between 10 and 11 o'clock, being bright moon light, under her mainsail and head of the squaresail, run down a large sloop, Timothy Pierce, master, from Fort Dauphine, belonging and bound to Rhode Island. She was lying too, about 3 leagues from Block Island; she sunk immediately, when the Capt. and crew; all but one man (who was sick in the cabin) saved themselves by catching hold of Captain Goodwin's shrouds. The cargo lost consisted of sugars, coffee, and molasses. The Captain had 200 half johannes in his chest, which went down with the sick man, &c.[5]

Throughout April the tide of rumor flowed a good deal more than it ebbed, and the newspapers were filled with reports of feverish activity, most of it boding little good for the colonies. From London, datelined January 19, came word that the government had no intention of repealing any of the acts aimed against America; instead it was to pursue even more vigorously aggressive policies. Six men of war with two regiments aboard were bound for America, and all officers belonging to regiments already in America were to join their corps immediately. In addition, it was reported that bills of attainder were to be passed against the Bostonians, in effect declaring them guilty of high treason and so open to arrest and conviction without trial.

On the credit side, the supporters of nonimportation could derive some satisfaction from the news that in London the price of tobacco had risen by twopence a pound "in consequence of the expected non-importation from America."[6] But this cheer-

[5] Ibid.
[6] *Virginia Gazette* (Pinkney), April 28.

ing thought was more than offset by reports that the merchants of England were not all clamoring for capitulation, as previous stories might have led one to believe. A petition from the merchants and manufacturers of Birmingham had been presented to parliament in January—a petition not calling for placating the colonies but demanding that the authority of the mother country should be firmly enforced. Earlier reports that the trade of the town of Leeds had been so hard hit that its people were reduced almost to starvation were now firmly denied in a public letter issued by the mayor, recorder, vicar, and various local business houses.

Rumors of cabinet changes, which had been circulating for some months, now persisted with even greater frequency— though with little more authority. The *Gazette* for April 22 [7] was a particularly fine example of the way any story, however wild, could find a printed place in posterity, even if it had to share it with another, contradictory rumor in the adjacent column. A report that Lord North would resign within fourteen days was followed by another claiming that the resignation had already taken place. Although placed in the *Gazette* within a dozen items of each other, they did stem from sources almost two weeks apart. Further support was to be found on page three, coming from a Liverpool ship that had just arrived in the James river, whose captain told how a "Gentleman of undoubted varacity" had come aboard just before he sailed "and informed him that a change in the Ministry, had actually taken place, which, it was generally thought, would occasion a turn of measures in favour of the Americans." With three such reports in one paper there certainly should be some truth in them—there should have been, but there wasn't.

Equally false was the assertion that General Gage had been relieved of his command and was already on his way home. This was followed by an oblique reference to Lord North's dissatisfaction with Gage's diligence since he had been commander in

[7] Dixon & Hunter.

chief. In the next column we find an editorial comment on the virtues of the General: "It is well known that no man ever accepted a commission with more reluctance than General Gage did the command of the troops against the Americans. His lady is the daughter of an inhabitant of Boston. . . ." What more could one say? One could (and someone did) point out that the same gentle general purchased four hundred copies of each issue of James Rivington's *New-York Gazetteer* and distributed it "among the army, navy, and such others as are thought most proper to promote the infamous plan of enslaving this country." It was the dastardly Mr. Rivington who had printed the pamphlets that had brought down the wrath of the Orange County Committee upon the head of the Reverend Mr. Wingate and who, much earlier, had commented favorably on the character of Lord Dunmore. Not only were Rivington's lies being served to the troops in weekly doses, the papers were being paid for out of American revenues. "Thus, Americans," declared the Rhode Island writer, "you already begin to see your own money employed for enslaving yourselves and your children." [8]

Fortunately the generally darkening pages of the newspapers were touched with occasional flashes of satisfying irony, as shown in the same April 22 *Gazette*, which carried, without comment, a letter written by Samuel Adams thanking the people of Virginia for sending donations to the beleaguered citizens of Boston, donations carried to Salem aboard the schooner *Dunmore*.

On occasion the papers even offered their customers a straightforward funny story, and as an example of what made Virginia laugh in 1775 I submit the following rib-tickling anecdote:

A young Gentleman, who is clerk in a public office, enjoying one evening, an agreeable *tete a tete* with his mistress, they were unexpectedly disturbed by the Lady's father knocking at the door; and not thinking it prudent for him and Quildrive

[8] *Virginia Gazette* (Dixon & Hunter), April 22.

to have an interview, it was judged proper that the latter
should be secreted, and the place of his retreat was fixed to be
in a tub, in which was held salt; and as he was neither in bulk
nor stature a Goliath, it very conveniently held him: But the
old Gentleman bringing home some sprats for supper, and
being very particular in his mode of dressing them, undertook to go through the operation himself; when, unluckily
going for some salt to the identical tub in which was our hero,
and being in the dark, the inhabitant of the wooden tenement
bit his finger pretty severely; on which the old man lustily
roared out "A rat, a rat!" and going for a candle, in order to
wreak his vengeance on the author of his pain, in the mean
time the supposed little animal made his escape, boasting,
that however cunning the old Don might think himself, yet he
was not sagacious enough at all times "to smell a rat."

For those who preferred the quick-fire topical gag there was
the one about Lord North needing a stick to support himself
when speaking in the Commons, thus producing the comment:
"There are some very *sad sticks* on the Treasury Bench who
yield him *no support at all*." Or how about this one? "We hear
that the troops have finished the fortifications on Boston Neck. It
is now *neck or nothing*."

These and other similar gems adorned the Dixon and
Hunter *Gazette*'s lead column on April 22, a time in which
levity seemed least appropriate. But then, of course, news of the
shot heard round the world would take another week to reach
Virginia. Nevertheless, although events containing the seeds of
disaster were happening within shouting distance of the printing office; the paper's principal front-page story concerned a
murder in Amiens last November. Admittedly it was a good,
juicy story, one that any modern tabloid would be delighted to
carry—and if Messrs. Dixon & Hunter were prepared to let the
Virginia news wait for it, why should we not do likewise?

Early in the morning a baker's man found a child, new born,
at or near the door of his master's house, in a basket. The
child was neatly dressed, and in the basket was deposited,
with the poor infant, a bag containing a thousand livres. The

fellow put the money in his pocket, but the child he put into the oven, which had been just heated for baking bread. When the master came to the oven, he found a strange offensive smell, and receiving no satisfactory answer from the man to his enquiry after the cause of it, he searched the oven, which presented a sight too horrid for description. He seized the wretch, who confessed the deed, but had the address to tempt his master to conceal it, by offering him the money which had induced him to commit so abominable a crime. In fine, the villain was delivered into the hands of justice, was tried, convicted, and sentenced to be baked alive in an oven, in the public market place of the town where the murder was committed. An oven was accordingly built for that purpose, which was heated from six in the morning till noon; in which the miscreant was sacrificed to the manes of the poor infant, and perished a just victim to the law of retaliation, in the sight of many thousands, without a tear of pity from an individual eye to moisten his ashes.

On the yardstick of sensationalism a baked baker is hard to beat; but in spite of surprisingly poor newspaper coverage, Lord Dunmore's effort of April 21 was a worthy competitor. On that date he carried off the colony's stock of gunpowder from the public magazine in Williamsburg and had it put out of reach aboard Lieutenant Collins's *Magdalen.* Transferring the King's supplies to a place of greater safety—that was how the governor explained this exploit. The colonists called it something quite different.

The background to Dunmore's highly provocative act has been debated from that day to this, but as no new evidence has come to light we are really no better informed now than were those who were in Williamsburg at the time. There was, of course, one person who did know all the answers, and he was the governor himself; but he chose to give one explanation to the Virginians and another to the Secretary of State. However, he could have had little reason to distort the facts when writing to Lord Dartmouth, and so we may reasonably assume that here is at least part of the story:

My Lord,

The series of dangerous measures pursued by the People of this Colony against Government, which they have now entirely overturned, & particularly their having come to a Resolution of raising a Body of armed Men in all the Counties, made me think it prudent to remove some Gunpowder which was in a Magazine in this place, where it lay exposed to any attempt that might be made to seize it, & I had reason to believe the People intended to take that step.

The letter goes on to say that when the citizenry complained, he thought it wiser to conceal the true reason.

I thought proper, in the defenseless state in which I find myself to endeavour to sooth them and answered verbally to the effect that I had removed the Powder [,] lest the Negroes might have seized upon it [,] to a place of security from whence, when I saw occasion I would at any time deliver it to the People. . . .[9]

Because Lord Dunmore was not the only colonial governor that April to be concerning himself with keeping arms and supplies out of the hands of potential rebels, some historians have supposed that they were all responding to a single directive from London. But if Dunmore had received specific instructions to seize the Williamsburg powder he would hardly have written as he did to Lord Dartmouth, nor is he likely to have neglected to acknowledge receipt of such important instructions. Aggravating though they might have been had they fallen into the wrong hands, they would hardly have been so secret that they were to be read and destroyed without acknowledgment. It would seem therefore that no such orders existed and that his Lordship was prompted, as he said, by the aggressive resolutions of the recent Richmond convention.

The desire to prevent ammunition from reaching those who might fire it back at the government was not an April whim. In London, on October 19, 1774, an Order in Council (updating another of 1756) had been issued preventing, for a period of six

[9] Dunmore to Dartmouth, May 1; PRO,CO 5/1353.

months, the exportation of "Gunpowder or any sort of Arms or Ammunition out of this Kingdom." On the same day Lord Dartmouth sent out a circular letter to the colonial governors advising them of the decision and instructing them to "take the most effectual Measures for arresting, retaining and securing any Gunpowder, or any sort of Arms or Ammunition which may be attempted to be imported into the Province under your Government." [1] In addition there was a section in Lord Dunmore's original commission from the King that gave him authority to build fortifications "and furnish with Ordnance, Ammunition, and all sorts of Arms fit and necessary for the security and defence of our said Colony," [2] and also to demolish or dismantle them as he thought fit. Using such authority very loosely, the removal of the powder might be seen as a dismantling job to promote the security and defense of the colony. Furthermore, his commission had specifically called upon him to "vanquish" any "Enemies Pirates or Rebels" by whatever means necessary. The only trouble was that the colony considered that the contents of the magazine belonged specifically to it and not to the Crown.

At some time during Easter week (April 10–16) his Lordship told the Keeper of the Magazine, John Frederick Miller, that he wanted the keys to it, and they were duly handed over. Miller later testified that there were then in the building: "twenty one barrels and half of Powder . . . three hundred and forty two new Muskets, lately cleaned, and in complete order, others that wanted but small repairs, and a large number of old Muskets, and other small Guns, almost useless. . . ." [3] According to historian John Burk, whose account of the affair was published in 1805,[4] Miller informed the town authorities that the governor had taken the locks (firing mechanisms) from

[1] Dartmouth circular letter to the "Governours of the Colonies," Oct. 19, 1774; *American Archives*, 4th ser., I, 881.
[2] Hillsborough to Dunmore, Dec. 21, 1770; PRO,CO 5/1372.
[3] *JHB*, 223; June 13.
[4] Burk, *History of Virginia*, III, 409, footnote.

the muskets and was planning to carry off the stock of powder. As a result, the local volunteer company mounted guard on the magazine over the Easter week end, and were still doing it on the night of the twentieth. The building, which survives today, was an octagonal brick structure surrounded by a high protective wall pierced by a single, heavy, and very locked gate—to which the governor now had the key. Had the volunteer guard been able to perform its duty from inside, history might have taken a slightly different turn. Instead, the guard had to pass the night outside on the square, listening to friends enjoying themselves in the nearby taverns and watching the lights in upper windows going out, one by one, as the town went to sleep. For the first night or two the novelty and excitement of the thing kept the guard on its toes, but when nearly a week had passed without anything happening, the project became a bore. By the time you have received the plaudits of your neighbors and have challenged everything that moves across the town square in the night (seven drunks, five slaves, one horse, four dogs, a goose, and three members of the guard) there is not much left to do but to go home to bed—which is what the volunteers did in the small hours of April 21.

I mentioned earlier that the governor's security was not of the best and that the patriots knew what was going on at the palace almost before it happened. On this occasion, however, the spy system must have broken down, for nobody knew that on the night of April 15 Lieutenant Collins had arrived there with a detachment of fifteen marines. The palace stood on the northern edge of Williamsburg with extensive park lands behind it, thus making it possible to enter or leave it without passing through the town. Thus the unobserved arrival of the soldiers was fairly easily accomplished; much less simple was the task of hiding them there for five days. Nevertheless, they managed it, and by midweek the pre-Easter scare had subsided.

We may suppose that while the volunteer guard watched the magazine, a marine scout watched the guard. As soon as they departed, he hurried back to the palace and gave the word

to go. No details of the sequence of events have survived beyond
the fact that the wagon used in the project was a small one and
that it belonged to the governor. Whether its wheels and axles
were greased, or the horses' hooves muffled—or even whether
there was one horse or two—is all conjecture. Equally debatable
is the route taken by Collins and his wagonload of marines;
though it seems likely that they came out of the stable yard and
turned into North England Street rather than taking the more
open route down Palace Green. The side street would have
given them fair cover until they reached the market square; once
there, they could have crossed the grass and stopped in the
shadow of the new courthouse until they were certain that Duke
of Gloucester Street, the main thoroughfare, was deserted.
From there it was only about 230 feet to the magazine gate and
to the deep shadows cast by the building and its wall. The entire
trip from palace to magazine should not have taken more than
five or six minutes at walking pace.

We do not know what the weather was like, but by the
calendar there was more moon than was desirable: it was five
days past full. The time was between three and four A.M., and it
would not be too long before the first servants were stirring. The
sun would rise around five-thirty. All in all, the timing was excellent, though it left little room for dalliance. The powder would
have to be loaded and the wagon out of town before the first eye
was opened. This could not be accomplished at the gallop, for the
whole point of this nocturnal adventure was that the powder
should be spirited away without anyone realizing that it had gone.
Consequently Lieutenant Collins had to allow himself sufficient
darkness to creep away as silently as he had come. Once clear of
the town he could travel as fast as he liked along the rough country road leading to Burwell's Ferry and the waiting schooner
Magdalen, a distance of some four miles from Williamsburg.
The final stage of the plan was that the *Magdalen* should immediately up anchor and proceed down the James river to Norfolk,
where the powder would be transferred to the man of war *Fowey*,
commanded by Dunmore's friend Captain Montagu.

Just what went wrong, history does not reveal. Perhaps someone saw a light in the magazine or heard the rattle of harness as the wagon headed out of town. One fact alone is certain—someone saw or heard enough to know that Collins was absconding with the colony's powder and at once raised the alarm.

In his letter to the Secretary of State Lord Dunmore wrote rather shamfacedly ". . . but tho' it was intended to have been done privately, Mr. Collins & his party were observed, & notice was given immediately to the Inhabitants of this place, Drums were sent through the City—the Independent Company got under Arms." The townspeople gathered on the steps of the courthouse, where they made a great deal of noise. "Continued threats," wrote Dunmore, "were brought to my House, that it was their Resolution to seize upon, or massacre me, & every person found giving me assistance, if I refused to deliver the Powder immediately into their Custody." [5]

Eventually, regardless of the threats of the more pugnacious members of the gathering, the mayor, John Dixon, and his aldermen and Common Council decided to present the governor with a petition regretting the incident and asking for their powder back on the grounds that they feared a slave rebellion. It was, as Lord Dunmore later admitted, "in reality milder in Terms than I expected." [6] But when he saw the mayor and his colleagues approaching down Palace Green, backed up by the armed members of the Independent Company, Dunmore had no idea what might happen. Lieutenant Collins and his marines had gone, and his only defenders were the members of his family and household. Had the mayor chosen to force his way into the palace, he could undoubtedly have taken it, and the governor as well, without much effort. Instead, the Independent Company halted halfway down the green and the mayor and council came on alone to present their petition. Relieved though his Lordship must undoubtedly have been, he made it clear that he resented the manner in which he was approached and

[5] Dunmore to Dartmouth, May 1; PRO,CO 5/1353.
[6] Ibid.

considered it "if not a treasonable proceeding, at least nothing less than one of the highest insults that could be offered to the Authority of His Majesty's Government." [7]

Fortunately the Mayor's petition gave Dunmore room to maneuver. The face-saving section ran as follows: "We further beg leave to inform your Excellency, that from various reports at present prevailing in different parts of the Country, we have too much reason to believe that some wicked and designing persons have instilled the most diabolical notions into the minds of our Slaves, and that, therefore, the utmost attention to our internal security is becoming the more necessary." [8] It seems improbable that both the mayor and governor would have independently used the fear of a slave rising as the reason for (a) removing the powder and (b) wanting it back. It is more likely that when the mayor mentioned the possibility of a slave insurrection, Dunmore seized on it as the reason for taking the powder in the first place. Without this excuse, his only possible explanation would have been the real one—that the citizens of Williamsburg were not to be trusted with it.

No one has ever proved whether there was or was not a genuine danger of a slave uprising, though there was, as we have seen earlier, a real *fear* of what might happen if the slaves did coordinate in some sort of plot. The recent newspaper report of the attempt in New York had done nothing to assuage those fears. Nevertheless it is probable that because both the mayor and the governor were anxious to avoid a direct confrontation between the colony and the Crown, each made use of the Negro scare to justify his actions. Having been able to clutch at this straw, Dunmore clambered onto it with a will, and in an explanatory proclamation he later stated ". . . I think proper to declare that the apprehensions which seemed to prevail throughout this whole Country, of an intended insurrection of the Slaves, who had been seen in large numbers in the night time about the Magazine, and my knowledge of its being a very

[7] Ibid.
[8] *American Archives*, 4th ser., II, 371.

insecure depository, were my inducements to that measure, and I chose the night as the properest season, because I knew the temper of the times, and the misinterpretations of my design which would be apt to prevail if the thing should be known." [9] Here for the first time the fears are turned into figures, and according to the governor we have slaves actually creeping about round the magazine—though what they were supposed to be doing is left to the imagination.

When discussing the affair at his council meeting in the palace Dunmore was less inclined to prevaricate, declaring that he had every right to take what steps he thought necessary for the safety of the colony, and it really did not matter "whether I acted in this manner (as my indispensible duty required) to anticipate the malevolent designs of the enemies of order and government, or to prevent the attempts of any enterprising negroes. . . ." [1]

A modicum of substance was given to the rumors of a rising when the *Virginia Gazette* reported on April 29 that sentence of death had been passed on two Norfolk Negroes "for being concerned in a conspiracy to raise an insurrection in that town." [2] The nature of the evidence was not revealed, and two suspended Negroes do not make a scotched rebellion. However, they do show that the fear of one was immediate enough to provide both governor and colonists with a valid argument.

The outcome of Mayor Dixon's confrontation with the governor was that Dunmore assured him that if the insurrection materialized he would have the powder back in half an hour. Of course he could not have handed it over at once even if he had wanted to. By this time Lieutenant Collins was well on his way down river and totally out of reach. In any case, Dunmore added, he certainly would not give the powder into the hands of the motley lot outside, the very people who an hour or two before had been threatening to murder him. It was much better

[9] Ibid., 371; proclamation May 3.
[1] Ibid., 464; May 2.
[2] *Virginia Gazette* (Dixon & Hunter), *Supplement*, April 29.

to leave things as they were for the time being. Realizing that this unsatisfactory answer was all Dunmore was prepared to offer, Dixon and the assembled officials declared themselves reconciled to the situation. With the customary obeisances they withdrew, returning to the green and to the almost impossible task of explaining to the populace why they had returned without either the powder or any assurance that it was about to be put back.

As everyone expected, from Dunmore downward, the return of the mayor and corporation caused a good deal of brouhaha on the green and around the courthouse, punctuated no doubt with waving pitchforks, scythes, and whatnot, for no demonstration against authority is complete without a display of agricultural implements. It is still slightly surprising to relate that reason did prevail and the crowd quietly dispersed. How this minor miracle was achieved no one knows; but the fact remains that the citizens accepted the news that they were not about to get their powder back with surprising stoicism.

The passage of time in these events is hard to determine. Some authorities see the townspeople gathering at the courthouse immediately after the pell mell departure of Lieutenant Collins and his wagon—and perhaps they did, running down the still dark streets with a burning torch in one hand, tugging at their breeches with the other, and all the while trying to keep their nightcaps from flopping over their eyes. But even if this was the way of it, it is unlikely that they marched to the palace before dawn or that they left it before nine or ten in the morning. The governor was obviously up and ready to receive them, and furthermore he was able to see that it was the Independent Company that backed up the mayor and city officials. Even if we accept the argument that Dunmore had been up to see Collins on his way (which he really had no necessity to do), it seems likely that it was quite a reasonable hour before the deputation came knocking at his door.

Apart from telling the mayor that he could not have his powder back, the governor made it clear that he did not propose to surrender to threats and that he would arm his family and servants and defend the palace to the death. Logic and the bulk of available evidence suggest that Collins loaded the confiscated powder (all fifteen and a half barrels of it) onto the *Magdalen* and sailed down river to meet Captain Montagu, who would have been waiting to receive it aboard the *Fowey*. However, in his letter to Lord Dartmouth on May 1, Dunmore stated that "There happened to be then in Town Captain Montagu Commanding the Fowey with his Captain of Marines a Mr. Stretch and Lieutenant Henry Collins the Officer already mentioned . . ." [3] One can only presume that the governor meant later in the day, though even so it is odd that he should have said that the officers just "happened to be then in town." They could hardly have been party to the seizure of the powder and then have turned up in Williamsburg independently and by sheer coincidence. The only passably logical explanation for their presence must have been that on completion of their task they hurried to town to see what the citizens' reaction had been. If this is the correct explanation, their appearance would seem militarily foolhardy, as they represented the entire command of the King's force then in Tidewater Virginia. Besides, what reason could Dunmore have had for failing to say to Lord Dartmouth that the officers returned to see what service they could render? Instead he said only that they happened to be in town and so "immediately joined themselves to my little party and offered me all the Assistance which could be spared from on board the Ship and Schooner which only amounts to between thirty and forty Men." Dunmore went on to relate that he "was not long after unexpectedly informed [that] the People by the persuasion of Mr. Peyton Randolph and Mr. Nicholas the Treasurer, had dispersed and appeared satisfied with the Answers which [he] had returned." [4] Although we do not know how long it took for the crowd to disperse, Dunmore's statement that the officers offered their aid beforehand certainly makes it

[3] Dunmore to Dartmouth, May 1, PRO,CO 5/1353.
[4] Ibid.

extremely unlikely that they would have had time to personally attend to the shipment of the powder aboard the *Fowey* and then get back to Williamsburg—all before the morning's angry crowd broke up. There is clearly something wrong somewhere.

The fact that Montagu and his colleagues did offer to reinforce the governor's meager household may well have generated the rumor that marines from the *Fowey* had landed and were marching on the capital. The alarm was raised late in the day, and again everybody turned out. As though to make up for previous laxity, armed citizens rallied round the magazine and vigorously guarded it. But when night came and nothing had happened, most of them went home, leaving only a small patrol to keep watch. The marines had not landed.

April 22 was a miserable anticlimax: the night had passed without incident, and during the day groups of armed patriots bustled into town from the surrounding counties all ready for something to happen—but nothing did. That morning the Williamsburg physician Dr. Pasteur called at the palace to attend an unnamed patient. While he was there the doctor happened to bump into the governor, "who introduced a Conversation relative to what had passed the preceding day, and seemed greatly exasperated at the Peoples having been under arms." [5] Pasteur later testified that he tried to placate his Lordship by explaining that what had occurred had been the unthinking result of confusion and overhasty action; he added that "most of the People were convinced they were wrong." But Dunmore's ruffled feathers were not so easily smoothed, and, and, as the doctor told it, "His Lordship then proceeded to make Use of several rash expressions and said that tho' he did not think himself in Danger yet he understood some injury or insult was intended to be offered to the Captains *Foy* and *Collins*, which he should consider as done to himself as those Gentlemen acted intirely by his particular Directions." [6]

Pasteur's testimony was given to the "Commotion Commit-

[5] *JHB*, 231.
[6] Ibid.

tee" set up by the House of Burgesses, and, being experienced
in saying what the patient wanted to hear, it is possible that he
pictured the governor in a more frenzied state than was entirely
truthful. According to the report which Pasteur carried back to
the townspeople, Dunmore "swore by the living God that if a
Grain of Powder was burnt at Captain *Foy* or Captain *Collins*,
or if any Injury or insult was offered to himself, or either of
them, that he would declare Freedom to the Slaves, and reduce
the City of *Williamsburg* to Ashes." He went on to declare that
he was prepared to raise the royal standard and call on all loyal
Virginians to rally to it, and he added that he believed that if he
did so, the majority of white colonists and all the slaves would
take up arms in the King's cause. Recalling his exploits against
the Indians in 1774, Dunmore roared that having once fought
for the Virginians, now "by GOD, he would let them see that he
could fight against them!" [7] In case the doctor was not sufficiently impressed, he concluded by declaring that it would not
take him long to depopulate the entire colony.

Pasteur reported the governor's threats to the city fathers,
who were not particularly intimidated. Around the town the
patriots brandished their tomahawks and made warlike noises
into their beer; but nobody did anything. Even now the prospect
of assaulting the palace and hanging their governor was too big
a step to be taken by any save the most rabid revolutionaries. To
demand one's rights was one thing, but to murder the King's
representative was quite another. Indeed, so undecided were the
patriots that Captains Foy, Stretch and Collins walked around
town the day after the powder seizure entirely unmolested.

But although no violence occurred, the governor's threat to
free the slaves sliced into the patriots' Achilles' heel. No
conceivable threat could be better guaranteed to strike fear into
the hearts of the entire white population. But if he expected that
out of fear would come obedience, he was wrong. The only
obvious result was an intense anger and a stiffening of the

[7] Ibid.

patriots' will to resist. In a letter to Lord Dartmouth, General
Gage later wrote that Dunmore's threat had "startled the
Insurgents." [8]

His Lordship was also due to be startled, for on or about
April 23 he learned that a large body of armed men was
gathering in the vicinity of Fredericksburg and that it was their
proclaimed intention to dispose of him. On the morning of the
twenty-third Dr. Pasteur was again attending his patient at
the palace when he ran into the governor, who had just heard the
news. Dunmore gave Pasteur another message for the city
fathers, saying that if any large body of men came below
Ruffin's Ferry (a point on the Rappahannock about thirty miles
from Williamsburg) he would immediately carry out his previous threat. Two of the principal citizens had already removed
their families to the safety of the country, and Dunmore's
second message doubtless caused others to seriously consider
following suit. As for the governor himself, he hastily set about
putting the palace in a state of defense. He had already told
Pasteur that he had two hundred muskets loaded and ready,
muskets which, incidentally, were part of the colony's defense
supplies just as were those in the magazine. Writing two weeks
later, James Parker, the Norfolk loyalist, proudly compared
Lord Dunmore with Charles XII of Sweden, adding that "he
has fortified his Home, with Swivel guns at the Windows, Cut
loop holes in the Palace, and has plenty of Small Arms." [9]
Parker was doubtless thinking of Charles's stubborn defense of
Stralsund in the Great Northern War; but the analogy was not
wholly happy in that Charles was renowned as a military egoist
who cared nothing for the suffering of his people and who
ultimately received a soldier's crowning reward—a two-inch
aperture in the temple, the product of a sniper's bullet.

The extent of Dunmore's defensive measures is uncertain.
Historian John Burk later asserted that "he immediately armed
his servants together with the Shawanese hostages" and that

[8] Gage, *Correspondence*, I, 399; May 15.
[9] Parker to Steuart, May 6; CSP.

"Parties of negroes mounted guard every night at the palace." [1]
Burk's "Shawanese" were those Shawnee whom Dunmore had
brought back to Williamsburg after concluding his treaty with
the Indians in the previous December. Whether or not he had
actually armed his slaves at this point remains open to debate. In
writing to the Secretary of State on May 1 Dunmore said that he
would do so if the need arose. But it is possible that he was
meaning his "Porto Bello" plantation hands as opposed to the
palace Negroes, who may already have been armed. No one but
Parker made mention of loopholes being cut in the palace walls,
and as the building was liberally slashed with windows, it would
seem more reasonable and convenient to have barricaded them
and to have cut his gun slits through the folding, interior
wooden shutters. But then Parker also has guns in the windows,
although nobody else seems to have noticed them. Burk was
probably closest to the mark when he wrote that the palace "was
in some measure fortified." [2] If Dunmore was to be suddenly
attacked by the Williamsburg patriots he, his family, and his
servants would defend themselves as best they could. To this
end they undoubtedly barred the doors and closed the shutters.
But the palace was no citadel; as the governor wrote to Lord
Dartmouth, "I shall remain here until I am forced out but
. . . I cannot expect to be able to make any effectual Resistance
in this place. . . ." [3] If the odds became heavier against him
Dunmore planned to withdraw to Yorktown and the protection
of Captain Montagu's guns.

Monday, April 24, was a quiet day in Williamsburg, or as
quiet as armed patriots with nothing to shoot could be expected
to make it. If an army was gathering in Fredericksburg it was
raising very little dust, and there was no significant news from
the north. There was none from the south either, for that
matter, but it was in the making.

The month had been a bad one for Governor Martin of

[1] Burk, *History of Virginia*, III, 407, 409.
[2] Ibid., 409.
[3] Dunmore to Dartmouth, May 1; PRO,CO 5/1353.

North Carolina. He, like Lord Dunmore and the other royal
governors, had received the Secretary of State's circular letter
calling on them to discourage any attempts among the colonists
to elect delegates to attend the second Continental Congress. On
April 3 the North Carolina Provincial Congress met at New
Bern with the prominent patriot John Harvey as its moderator.
The same week the official Provincial Assembly was also in
session and as the two bodies consisted of almost entirely the
same membership (Harvey was also Speaker of the House) they
were able to deal with the King's business and their own at one
and the same time. The Provincial Congress duly elected its
delegates to go to Philadelphia; and on April 8 Martin dissolved
the Provincial Assembly.

The governor had no military force to enforce his authority;
the assembly was against him more or less to a man, and, as in
Virginia, his council was weak and divided in its sentiments. As
early as the middle of March, Martin had written to General
Gage asking for military aid, and a copy of the letter had fallen
into the hands of the patriots—much to Martin's embarrassment. As no aid came from outside, the governor hastily tried to
assemble a loyalist force from among the Highland Scots. At the
same time he set about defending his palace and drawing up a
number of pieces of artillery in front of it.

On April 24, while Martin was in session with his council, a
party of armed patriots suddenly appeared and hauled away the
guns. The first the governor heard of it was when he looked out
of the window and saw them departing. The meeting was
hurriedly adjourned, and that evening he packed up and
withdrew from the palace to the greater safety of Fort Johnson
at Cape Fear. His flight marked the end of normal British
government in North Carolina. Step by step, the fortunes of
Josiah Martin followed or preceded those of his Virginia
neighbor. He, too, threatened to free and arm the slaves, and he,
too, was forced to utter his threats with only the guns of a single
British warship to back him. Had Lord Dunmore been able to
watch Governor Martin's ignominious departure he might well

have been reminded of Belshazzar and that rude message on the wall. But fortunately he was unaware of what was happening.

News of the powder seizure in Williamsburg appeared in the April 22 issue of the *Virginia Gazette* [4] and was vociferously digested over the week end. County committees began meeting early in the following week to decide what action should be taken, and it was as the result of such gatherings that some of the independent companies set out for Fredericksburg. The Gloucester Committee was one of the first to go on record as condemning the governor's removal of the powder. It also declared "that his lordship's verbal answer to the address of the mayor, recorders, aldermen, and common council, of the city of Williamsburg, is unsatisfactory, disrespectful, and evasive." It was resolved that Lord Dunmore "by this and other parts of his conduct which have lately transpired, has justly forfeited all title to the confidence of the GOOD PEOPLE OF VIRGINIA." [5]

So unequivocal a statement from a county close to Williamsburg and inhabited by some of the colony's most influential people can have left the governor with few illusions as to the reactions of the more distant committees. It was possibly for this reason that Dunmore made some small attempt to show that the powder was actually the King's property, having been deposited at the magazine from on board the British man of war *Rippon*. But as he made no such statement in his letter to Lord Dartmouth, we must suppose that it was untrue and that he simply tossed it out to see if anyone would catch it. Nobody did; though the committee formed by the House of Burgesses later made some inquiries and reported that it had "applied personally to his Majesty's Receiver General for that purpose," but could not find "that any Powder had been lodged in the Magazine from on board the Rippon, Man-of-War, or any other of his Majesty's Ships." [6]

[4] Dixon & Hunter.
[5] *Virginia Gazette* (Pinkney), April 28.
[6] *JHB*, 224.

It is not clear exactly when Dunmore tried the *Rippon* ploy, but it would seem that he was still standing by his original statement on April 28. Around one in the afternoon of that day a mud-splattered and exhausted horseman rode into Williamsburg from Fredericksburg. He had made the journey in about twenty-four hours of hard riding, an impressive accomplishment made more so by the fact that he headed back again the same evening. The rider was Mann Page, Jr., of "Mannsfield" in Spotsylvania County, and he had been sent by the council assembled at Fredericksburg to obtain first-hand information regarding the powder affair and the reactions of the patriot leaders on the scene. With him, he brought news that messengers had been sent into several counties, and "it was expected that upwards of two thousand men" [7] would have gathered at Fredericksburg by that evening. In addition, the militia of Caroline County would be arriving around ten o'clock the next morning. It sounded like a very formidable army—at least it did to Lord Dunmore, whose own force could not top a hundred.

If the resolutions of the county committees were Page's yardstick of public opinion, he was probably mightily surprised to find Williamsburg in a state of comparative calm and to learn that the city fathers were satisfied with the governor's statement that he would return the powder if a need for it arose. Even Peyton Randolph, Speaker of the House of Burgesses, declared himself reasonably satisfied with the present state of things, and he gave Page a letter to his council strongly urging that they should desist from their punitive intentions.

Mann Page hastened back to Fredericksburg, apparently as quickly as he had come, arriving in time to lay both his information and Randolph's letter before the council on Saturday the twenty-ninth. Page could also report that that day Peyton Randolph was starting on his way to attend the Continental Congress in Philadelphia and that he intended to stop at

[7] *American Archives*, 4th ser., II, 426.

Fredericksburg to repeat in person what Page had already delivered in writing. As it happened, Randolph's verbal reinforcement was not necessary. After a long and heated debate the council (comprising 102 members, including delegates of the Provincial Convention and officers and special deputies of fourteen companies of light cavalry) prepared a resolution condemning the governor's actions but adding that they, "justly dreading the horrours of a civil war, influenced by motives of the strongest affection to our fellow-subjects of *Great Britain*, most ardently wish to heal our mutual wounds, and therefore prefering peaceable measures, whilst the least hope of reconciliation remains, do advise that the several companies now rendezvoused here do return to their respective homes." Lest this anticlimactic resolve should be read as a sign of weakness, it concluded by asserting that "we do now pledge ourselves to each other to be in readiness, at a moment's warning, to reassemble, and by force of arms, to defend the Law, the Liberty, and Rights of this or any sister Colony, from unjust and wicked invasion." [8] So it was that the couriers who had last week gone out to call on the independent companies to gather at Fredericksburg, now set out again to tell them to turn back. The council members, their ardor somewhat cooled, were able to take stock; they had trodden on the brink of revolution, and it was only now as they drew back that they realized the full consequences of such a step. An inch further and they could have brought the might of Great Britain down upon the bare heads of their families, neighbors, and friends, causing the destruction of their homes, properties, and businesses. There might eventually be no alternative, but to risk everything now over fifteen barrels of gunpowder would be more foolhardy than heroic. This sense of relief was expressed in a letter to George Washington on April 30 from Alexander Spotswood, one of those who came with their companies to Fredericksburg, who concluded: "I am extremely glad to inform you, that, after a

---

[8] Ibid., 443.

long debate, it was at last agreed we should not march to *Williamsburgh.*"

In all fairness to Spotswood, one must add that his relief was not born of cowardice or lack of enthusiasm for the cause. On the contrary, his letter's purpose was to make sure he was up at the front when the war came and the jobs were being given out. "It is imagined," he wrote, "that the first thing which will come on the carpet at the meeting of Congress, will be that of establishing regular armies throughout the Continent on pay. If such a thing should take place, there is not the least doubt that you will have the command of the whole forces in this Colony. In that case I shall ever esteem you as my best friend, if you will use your interest in procuring me a commission. . . ." [9]

Had Patrick Henry been at Fredericksburg on April 29, it is possible that the council would have found itself swept halfway to Williamsburg on a wave of oratory; for, as Jefferson's friend Dr. Philip Mazzei noted, to sway such an assembly "it is necessary to have the proper terms ready, as well as a selection of choice phrases, which are often more effective than sound reasoning." [1] But with Randolph's letter before it, the council had listened to the carefully composed voice of reason. When the resolution to disperse reached Patrick Henry, it found him in no mood to listen to anyone. He was still gathering his forces to embark on his march to Fredericksburg, and, late as he was, he had no intention of being stood up. If the halfhearted council was to be so easily satisfied, that was their business, but as for Patrick Henry, he had declared himself for liberty or death, and he would march on Williamsburg by himself. Well, not exactly by himself; some estimates of his strength ran as high as 1,500 men, though James Parker wrote that 60 was "all he could raise of the boasted thousands." [2] Nevertheless, Henry did march, but it would be May before he would be heard from again.

In the meantime the entire picture changed. Another hard-

[9] Ibid., 447.
[1] Mazzei, "Memoirs," *WMQ*, 2nd ser., IX:4, 250.
[2] Parker to Steuart, May 6; CSP.

riding messenger galloped into Williamsburg carrying dispatches from Philadelphia, and on the morning of April 29 the
whole countryside knew of the fracas at Lexington and Concord.
The messenger had arrived late in the evening of the twenty-
eighth, just as Pinkney's printers were putting the Saturday's
Gazette to bed. But curiously enough it was not this news which
made him issue a supplement, but the arrival of much older
information from London. "Our paper was entirely prepared for
the press; but just as we were going to publish it we were
informed of the arrival, in York river, of the snow Martin,
captain Wood, in six weeks from Liverpool, by whom we
received papers as late as the 11th of March, from which we
have only time to select the following intelligences." The first
described the scene in the House of Lords when Lord North,
instead of offering a "grand concilating plan," revealed that he
was extending the powers of his New England Restraining Act
to the other American colonies. Another letter from New York
revealed "on unquestionable authority" that General Gage had
received a royal proclamation declaring the inhabitants of
Massachusetts Bay rebels and giving him a blank commission to
seize, try, and execute their leaders. In case there should be any
doubt in his mind as to who they were, a list of their names was
thoughtfully attached to the proclamation: among them Samuel
Adams, John Adams, John Hancock, and Peyton Randolph of
Virginia.

These pieces of news, if true, meant that Virginia and the
other Southern colonies were now to be subject to the same
oppressive acts as were their Northern cousins. As far as
Pinkney was concerned it was this information that warranted
issuing a supplement. The Lexington and Concord battle story
was tucked away in small print at the back, next to (and in type
of the same size as) an advertisement inserted by George
Washington offering a reward for the detention of two runaway
servants, a joiner and a brickmaker. Indeed, so poor a place does
the Concord news occupy that one wonders whether Pinkney
would have bothered to issue a supplement for it at all if the

news from London had not come in on the same evening.

It would seem that the messenger from Philadelphia brought a variety of missives pertinent to the Concord encounter. Pinkney ran two letters describing the fight, the numbers involved, and the estimated casualties. Alexander Purdie issued a broadside on the next day using these two letters and adding a few editorial comments.

The Blow (so much dreaded by our noble Friend Lord *Chatham*) is now struck, a great Deal of Blood spilt, and much more, it is likely, than the present Advices communicate. That great Man, in his Speech upon the Necessity of withdrawing the Troops from Boston (delivered in the House of Lords the 20th of *January* last) says: "Perhaps, even whilst I am now speaking, the decisive Blow is struck, which may involve Millions in the Consequences; and, believe me, the very first Drop of Blood that is spilled will not be a Wound easily skinned over; it will be *irritable vulnus*, a Wound of that Rancorous and festering Kind, that, in all probability, will mortify the whole Body."

It was a well chosen passage—even if it did look a bit like speaker's notes thrown away by Patrick Henry at the Richmond convention. Then Purdie concluded with a paragraph coined in Williamsburg, whose final sentence has secured its place in history as the epitaph for 1775. It read: "This Morning the Committee of Correspondence met, and have determined to send Expresses to the southward.—It is now full Time for us all to be on our Guard, and to prepare ourselves against every Contingency. The *Sword is now drawn*, and *God* knows when it will be sheathed."

Initial reaction varied all the way from "Now we know where we stand" to plain disbelief. Lord Dunmore professed the latter, declaring that he considered the reports entirely without truth. It would be some days before the full story would be available, and even then there would be endless variations from which to select one's own version of the facts. But even while the smell of brimstone still hung amid the trees around Concord, the open-letter writers were at work to make sure that Americans everywhere would catch a whiff of it. Wrote "JOHANNES IN EREMO" of Salem, Massachusetts:

> Great Britain, adieu! No longer shall we honour you as our mother; you are become cruel; you have not so much bowels as the sea monsters towards their young ones. We have cried to you for justice, but behold violence and bloodshed! Your sword is drawn offensively, and the sword of *New-England* defensively; by this stroke you have broken us off from you, and effectually alienated us from you. O *Britain!* see you to your own house.
>
> King *George* the Third, adieu! . . .
>
> General Gage, pick up stakes and begone. . . . The call of Heaven is to arms! to arms! . . . . What unheard-of barbarity has been committed on the sickly and helpless grey hairs and innocent babes, by the *British* troops! [3]

There was a great deal more in the same vein, ending, somewhat predictably, with a call on the Almighty, "Judge of all the earth," to wake up and lend a hand.

The Dixon and Hunter *Gazette* came out on Saturday, April 29, carrying, rather inappropriately, an item from London stating "the late dispatches from Boston make no mention of any acts of hostility being committed between the King's troops and the provincials." That bland statement had been made as early as February 17, reminding us once again that news, good or bad, did not travel fast in the eighteenth century. But Dixon and Hunter were not left completely at the post, and they, too, brought out a supplement carrying the same letters printed by Pinkney and Purdie (though with considerable variation in punctuation and spelling) and claiming that the messenger had reached Williamsburg on the morning of the twenty-ninth rather than on the preceding evening as indicated by their competitors. Dixon and Hunter, however, did hold the laurels for producing the largest supplement, a full four-page issue. But they, too, chose to hide the Lexington and Concord story away

[3] *American Archives*, 4th ser., II, 369.

in the middle, while giving most prominence to reports from London.

The lead item gave the text of Lord Chatham's abortive Provincial Act, which had been so roughly handled by the House of Lords earlier in the year. In it, Chatham called for an assurance "that no military force, however raised and kept according to law, can ever be lawfully employed to violate and destroy the just rights of the people." The act also declared no British freemen in America should be taxed by the Crown without consent of a Provincial Assembly; it further stated that the forthcoming Continental Congress should be declared a lawful gathering, and that its deliberations should include a resolution to levy a self-imposed "free grant to the King" to help pay for the national debt.

As Lord Dunmore had already made it very clear that the Crown took the deepest exception to Virginians even electing delegates to attend the Philadelphia Continental Congress, Chatham's bill must have provoked a few bleak smiles from its readers. But hardly anyone would have found much to smile at in the next item—a long excerpt from Dunmore's letter of December 24 to Lord Dartmouth. It was in this that he had referred to the patriots as "infatuated people" whose nonimportation and like acts would eventually defeat their own purpose and bring their adherents to ruin. He had also described the colonists as "being very far from naturally industrious" and added that the poorer people would eventually realize that they had been duped by their richer spokesmen who bore little of the burden of their self-imposed restrictions. It was, of course, this part of the governor's letter that was now printed in the *Gazette*'s April 29 supplement and that James Parker noted galled "the very Souls" of the patriots "& more expecially as it is all strictly true." [4]

On page two we find a detailed account of Lord North's

[4] Parker to Steuart, May 6; CSP.

statement to parliament on proposed taxation, wherein he made
it abundantly clear that every person under any government
should be compelled to contribute to that government, according
to his ability and the support he derived from it. The American
colonies were no exceptions, and until they accepted this fact
and paid what was considered to be their share of the empire's
costs, they could not expect any relaxation of the measures being
taken against them.

Next came a report from New York dated April 17
containing the already noted comments on the rumored royal
proclamation declaring the inhabitants of Massachusetts Bay to
be rebels and giving the names of American leaders on General
Gage's not-so-confidential black list. The same report gave news
of four regiments of light dragoons on their way to Boston from
Ireland, as well as a formidable convoy of Navy ships with
orders to create a blockade against all European goods bound
for America. Dragging at the heels of this news came the
sketchy accounts of the disagreement at Lexington and Concord, followed by a stale rumor from London that Lord North
had offered his resignation to the King and that it had been
refused. Toward the end of the same page was the item Pinkney
had considered most important—Lord North's March 9 proposal to extend the Restraining Acts to include all the American
colonies.

The entire Dixon and Hunter supplement seems as confused
as the news it reported, the items being scattered haphazardly
about, leaving the reader to decide for himself which were
significant and which were not. Although the editors refrained
from comment, it was obvious that nine-tenths of the stories
boded nothing but ill. But regardless of the tenor of the times,
Dixon and Hunter remembered their promise to their readers
that whatever should be sent them "for the PUBLICK GOOD"
would "be published with cheerfulness," and in keeping with
that policy they included in the supplement "A Serious Admonition to the Inhabitants of Williamsburg" written by an unknown loyalist calling himself "Civis."

The writer expressed relief that reason had prevailed over the affair of the powder. "Though we had committed our unruddered bark to the mercy of a stormy sea," he wrote, "we have providentially recovered the firmer element, on which we may tread in security and peace; and here let us rest." But he declined to take his own advice, and instead went on to argue in support of the legality of the governor's action.

. . . Even admitting the powder, which was removed, to have been purchased by this country (a fact I do not pretend to be acquainted with) yet the money given for that purpose could be constitutionally given only to the King: The powder must therefore be under this direction, to be employed indeed for the benefit of the country, but how, and in what manner, as long as our government exists, is in the discretion of the King, or his representatives. . . . How frantic then would it appear in us to think of acting on the idea of reverted power, and of appealing to Heaven upon no other inducement than the Governor's exertion of a right certainly vested in him by the constitution, which, for what we know, might have been necessary to our welfare, and which, after the information his Excellency has been pleased to give to the Corporation, cannot, without the most causeless breach of good manners to him as a man, and of that respect and decorum which are due to him as our Governor, be conceived not to have been so, at least in his Lordship's opinion.

Elsewhere in the letter Civis called again for coolness. "A decent representation of grievances ought certainly to precede, and much, very much, ought to be borne, before the people can be justified in restoring to their natural power, in the reclaiming of which so much disorder and confusion must necessarily arise."

But in the minds of many Virginians the tide of reason was already well on the ebb, and some would elect to go out with it. The final page of the Dixon and Hunter supplement contained no less than three notices of impending departures. William Craig said simply (but in large type) "I INTEND to leave the Colony soon." S. Henley of the college said that he "designed" to leave shortly and so offered for sale "A COLLECTION of valuable BOOKS, either separately or together, a Port Folio of ENGRAVINGS, ETCHINGS, and MEZZOTINTOS (all fine impressions, and many of them *Proofs*) by the most celebrated Masters." The third ad was inserted by "Edward & J. Charlton"— Edward, a well-patronized Williamsburg barber, and "J." his recent bride, Jane Hunter, who ran a millinery shop on the opposite side of the street. In their announcement they called on their customers to pay their bills so that the businesses could be wound up. As it happened, the Charltons did not leave the colony, and we can only wonder whether perhaps the advertisement was simply a device to prod their debtors into paying. Thanks to the discovery of one of Edward Charlton's account books in a Williamsburg attic, we know the names of some of his delinquent customers, among them Patrick Henry and Thomas Jefferson.

If Edward and Jane Charlton's impending departure was a hoax, there was no doubting the substance of a heavily laden coach which left the governor's palace on the last day of April and headed down the road to Yorktown. In it were Lady Dunmore and all her children, plus the necessary baggage to sustain them in their new quarters—aboard the *Fowey* man-of-war.

Lady Dunmore was, as we have seen earlier, both popular and respected in the colony, and consequently many Virginians saw her departure as a scar upon their honor. Loyalist John Randolph later testified that "he thought Lady Dunmore had no reason but the Timidity of her Sex, to suspect any Injury would be done her or her Family, nor did he know that Lord Dunmore had just Cause to apprehend Danger, unless he gave Credit to the Reports coveyed to him, which were of such a Nature as to justify an Opinion that his Person was not safe." [5] But at this time the governor had very real grounds for concern—at least for his own safety. Patrick Henry and his Hanover County

[5] *JHB*, 232.

warriors were heading for Williamsburg, and there was little likelihood that they would be satisfied with anything short of the powder or its equivalent. If Henry was really prepared to oppose the King's will with force, he was guilty of treason and liable to be sentenced to death. He would have nothing more to lose. Once that bridge had been crossed, an assault on the palace would pose no problems, and the King's governor could well expect to find himself suspended—from a tree on Palace Green.

[V]

MAY

"Come lasses and lads, take leave of your
dads, and away to the May-pole hie; for every he has got him a
she, and the minstrel's standing by. For Willy has gotten his Jill,
and Johnny has got his Joan"—but not, it appears, in Virginia.
The ancient rites and delights of Maying, dancing round the
Maypole, romping through the woods in search of floral gar-
lands, and all the other traditions of May Day still survived in
England and through most of Europe, but they seem never to
have taken root in the colonies, at least not in the South. It is
possible that that omission is an illustration of the fact that,
contrary to popular belief, Virginia and her neighbors were not
really the true-born daughters of Britannia that they are
supposed to have been.

The rituals of May Day are believed to have originated with
the annual festivals in honor of the forest goddess Flora and as
such were really fertility rites. Whatever the truth of this
derivation, the fertility aspects of it are in no doubt. "I have
heard it credibly reported by men of great gravities, credite, and
reputation," declared the Puritan John Stubbes with eyes
turned hopefully heavenward, "that of fourtie, threescore, or a
hundred maides goyng to the woode over night, there have
been scarcely the thirde parte of them returned home againe
undefiled." [1] It was in all respects a very rural festival, though
simply for the fun of it the gentry frequently horned in. But in

---

[1] Brand, *Popular Antiquities*, I, 213; quoting John Stubbes, *Anato-
mie of Abuses* (1585).

England, by 1775, much of the earlier appeal had been lost; in the cities the day had been taken over by the chimney sweeps, who made it an occasion for hooliganism rather than a celebration of the birth of summer, and in the country only the farm hands and milkmaids besported themselves as of yore. A wedge of sophistication hammered home by education had divided the upper from the lower classes and had robbed the former of many a simple pleasure. Thus in Virginia the plantation-owning gentry neither brought with them nor sustained the May Day tradition; while at the other end of the scale there were no deblacked chimney sweeps nor petal-cheeked milkmaids to keep it alive. Both of the latter roles were played by enslaved Negroes for whom the white man's spring held little promise; and it was this above all that ensured that Virginia could never be looked upon as another English shire across the water.

Although that misconception was widely held by his Majesty's ministers in London, his governor in Williamsburg was painfully aware of the differences. These people might make much of their claims to be free-born Englishmen, but a damn sight too many of them had the hearts and souls of foreigners. "Every person who has manifested the least partiality to the King's Government are now become suspected by their furious Countrymen and are in the greatest danger of falling Victims to the Rage and Violence which accompany all the Transactions of these People pretending to contend for Liberty." So wrote Lord Dunmore, who spent his May Day writing his long and self-revealing report to the Secretary of State, a document at first perhaps salted with fear, then leavened with irritation, and rising toward the end into a belligerent anger. He proposed to call on all loyal citizens to come to his aid; if they failed to appear in sufficient numbers he intended to declare the entire colony in a state of rebellion "and myself at Liberty to annoy it by every possible means and . . . I shall not hesitate at reducing their houses to Ashes and spreading devastation wherever I can reach." [2]

[2] Dunmore to Dartmouth, May 1; PRO,CO 5/1353.

As well as writing to London, the governor also wrote to General Gage asking for military assistance and to Admiral Graves in the hope of obtaining a large man-of-war. "The Appearance of such a ship in the interior parts of this Country where the great depth of Water in the Rivers here will permit it to go, would," he thought, "strike the greatest Awe. . . ." Warming to these punitive prospects, Dunmore assured Lord Dartmouth "that if His Majesty should think proper to add to a small Body of Troops to be sent here a Quantity of Arms[,] Ammunition and other requisites for the Service, I would raise such a Force from among the Indians[,] Negroes and other persons as would soon reduce the refractory People of this Colony to obedience." [3]

All this was more or less what Dunmore had told Dr. Pasteur on their two chance meetings in the palace. But while the doctor then described the governor's statements as being made in the anger of the moment, it is significant that now, after time for sober review, they were being laid before the Secretary of State as a considered course of action. It can, I admit, be argued that Dunmore was unable throughout this period to indulge in sober reviews or create considered courses of action; the prospect of Patrick Henry's Hanoverians descending on the indefensible palace, Dunmore's Dunsinane, could banish reason. John Page would later say that in his opinion the governor and Patrick Henry were mutually afraid of each other, and modern historians have described Dunmore as becoming "frantic," [4] and in "a state bordering on what would appear to have been frenzied desperation." [5] If these are fair descriptions of the governor's state of mind, they were certainly out of step with the evidence of his fortitude and bravery both past and future. Dr. Pasteur probably came closest to the mark when, on the occasion of their meeting in the palace on April 23, he described Dunmore as seeming "greatly exasperated at the Peoples having

---

[3] Ibid.

[4] Berwick, *Loyalties in Crisis*, 29.

[5] Caley, *Dunmore*, 463.

been under Arms" [6]—exasperation at the people's apparent disloyalty to the Crown and frustration at being too weak to bring them to heel. Both of these emotions were very probably sustained through to May 1, but, regardless of whether they were or not, Dunmore's intention to raise an army from wherever it could be drawn and to put the homes of the rebels to the torch were neither the whims of a man distraught nor were they new to the annals of war. Fire and retribution had gone hand in hand through history, and they would do so again in Virginia in the War of 1812 and throughout the Civil War. However, at the beginning of May 1775 the threat was just that, the only weapon that Dunmore could use in his defense until the troops and man-of-war were sent from Boston—*if* they were sent. There was no guarantee that they would be, and certainly no prospect of their being in time to defeat Henry's forces. Thirty years later historian John Burk would say of Dunmore: "He might rave in the council room and issue the brute thunder of proclamations, but unsupported by fleets and armies, his rage was regarded in no other light than the phrenzy of a chained and imprisoned man." [7]

As we have seen, the governor was under no illusion that the palace could withstand a direct assault. In his dispatch to Lord Dartmouth he explained that he intended to "retire towards the Town of York where the Man-of-War[,] a Twenty Gun Ship[,] and an armed Schooner lie[,] under the protection of the Guns of which and under Cover of a little Entrenchment which I shall throw up[,] or at worst aboard the Man-of-War[,] I shall wait for His Majesty's orders." [8] It would be a long wait, as his Lordship well knew. In the meantime a show of support from his council would be reassuring, and possibly break the stride of the rebels; the members were requested to meet on May 2.

The meeting got off to a poor start, the members gathering

[6] *JHB*, 231.
[7] Burk, *History of Virginia*, III, 418.
[8] Dunmore to Dartmouth, May 1; PRO,CO 5/1353.

in their chamber at the Capitol only to find that Lord Dunmore did not propose to venture from the palace and that he required them to meet there. Having duly presented themselves they first heard a review, or rather the governor's view of the recent developments, beginning with the now-familiar affair of the powder. At one point they were told that there was some reason to fear that the volunteer companies might have been tempted to seize the magazine and to carry off its contents, an action which would have brought down on their heads "the vengeance of insulted majesty." [9] Such a suggestion was later loudly denied and ridiculed. But was it, we may wonder, entirely coincidental that on April 21, the night after Dunmore removed the powder from the Williamsburg magazine, a band of rebels broke into the arsenal at Charleston, South Carolina, and carried off both arms and ammunition? News of that exploit would not reach Williamsburg for another twenty-two days.

Lord Dunmore concluded his summary by expressing surprise that the colony was not grateful for his action in protecting the Williamsburg powder, and proposed that the council should draft a proclamation calling on the people of the colony to abjure violence and to uphold the laws. It was a speech of moderation, and although it warned of dire consequences for those who would not listen it was delivered without histrionics. The council would doubtless have proceeded to their task of drafting the requested proclamation had not John Page pitched a rock into the pond by asking whether, if the council advised it, Dunmore would return the powder. According to Burk, the governor's wrath "displayed itself in rude and indecent terms." It is tempting to read into this outburst the cracking of Dunmore's veneer to reveal the molten fear and "phrenzy" bubbling beneath. On the other hand it could equally well have exposed nothing more than his well-documented dislike of John Page and his irritation with himself at having put Page on the council. We do not know exactly what Dunmore said (perhaps it

---

[9] Burk, *History of Virginia*, III, 413.

is just as well), but it evoked nothing more than an embarrassed silence. No one seconded Page's motion and for some minutes the council members sat looking at each other and uneasily examining their quills. Eventually the governor, "having resumed his politeness," rose and told them that he proposed to leave them to themselves so that they could pursue "a free and unbiassed deliberation." [1] The meeting was then adjourned until the next day.

The firstborn of that free deliberation was a scabrous and searing proclamation drafted by the strongly loyalist Ralph Wormeley; but although other members of the council inclined to his views, they proceeded to tone down the proclamation into a form that might be swallowed by the people without permanent damage to their throats. Indeed, it seemed as much concerned with assuring the colonists that the members of the council were fellow countrymen as it was with censuring "that licentious and ungovernable spirit that is gone forth, and misleads the once happy people of this country." [2] Nevertheless, regardless of its toothless admonitions, the governor professed to be pleased with what he read, and the meeting broke up on a note of optimism.

But there was still Patrick Henry. By this time, he had advanced into New Kent County, and on May 3 he was encamped at Doncastle's Ordinary, about sixteen miles from Williamsburg. In England an ordinary was a place where meals were bought, but in Virginia there was no difference between an ordinary and an inn where travelers could lodge and imbibe as well as eat. After sampling the joys of such establishments in 1773, the English traveler John Smyth declared "They are all very indifferent indeed, compared with the inns in England: and three fourths of them are in reality little better than mere shelters from the weather; yet the worst of them is by no means deficient in charging high." [3] It was ever thus: in 1676 the

[1] Ibid., 414.
[2] *Virginia Gazette* (Dixon & Hunter), May 20.
[3] Smyth, "Tour," *VHR*, VI, 2, 87.

inhabitants of Jamestown were said to have made their living "by keeping ordnaries, at extreordinary rates." [4] However, the wayside ordinaries provided an essential service, particularly to horses who were less fastidious and demanding than English travelers. Unfortunately no one has left us a description of the services provided at Doncastle's Ordinary, but, good or bad, that hostelry was destined for a permanent, if shallow niche in history as the scene of the first direct confrontation between the Crown and the patriot leadership in Virginia.

On May 2, or early on May 3, Patrick Henry had detached a small contingent of sixteen men, under Ensign Goodall, to raid "Laneville," the home of Receiver General Richard Corbin, in King and Queen County, the object being to seize Corbin as a hostage or to obtain monetary compensation for the Williamsburg powder. Goodall's men duly surrounded the house—if a little thinly, the mansion being 194 feet in length and 27 in depth, probably the largest residence in the colony. In any case Goodall was wasting his time; only Mrs. Corbin was at home, and she explained to the somewhat sheepish insurgents that not only was her husband in Williamsburg but so was the King's money. She added that the latter was always kept at the Receiver General's office and never at his home—which seems obvious and makes it surprising that Henry should have expected otherwise.

Goodall and his party immediately withdrew from "Laneville," and following the rest of their orders they proceeded at once to rejoin the main body at Doncastle's Ordinary, arriving at sunset on May 3. That same evening the influential planter Carter Braxton was among those who met with Patrick Henry to determine what he proposed to do next. According to the recollection of Mrs. Corbin, Braxton warned Henry that if he insisted on marching into Williamsburg, Lord Dunmore would use cannon mounted at the palace to fire on the town, while the guns of the British warships would do the same to Yorktown.

---

[4] *James Towne in the Words of Contemporaries*, compiled by Charles E. Hatch, Jr., and Edward M. Riley (Washington, 1955), 28.

Thus any precipitous move by Henry would bring death and destruction about the ears of many innocent people.

There seems to be no extant evidence that Lord Dunmore did intend to fire into Williamsburg or that he had given orders for the ships to bombard Yorktown. It is possible that Mrs. Corbin was combining the governor's threat to burn Williamsburg if attacked with Captain Montagu's warning, which would not be issued until the next day and which we shall discuss later. The important fact at this point is that, regardless of what he may have told Henry, Braxton was able to get him to agree to remain at Doncastle's Ordinary while he, Braxton, rode into Williamsburg to try to prevail on Corbin to pay for the powder.

Braxton was not the only rider carrying tidings to Williamsburg that night; a merchant's clerk from New Kent courthouse was traveling the same road, probably only a few minutes ahead of him. The clerk's name is not recorded, but the author of a partially allegorical account of the affair described him as "a lying spirit" who warned the governor, saying: "provide thyself, for thy life is in danger." [5] In much plainer English he must also have told Dunmore that Henry's force was not nearly as large as had been rumored. Just how big it really was is still not clear. Historian John Burk at one point claimed it to have numbered about five hundred, but in a later chapter reduced it to "more that 150 men, all said to be men of property, well accoutred, & exhibiting a very martial appearance." [6] James Parker of Norfolk, as we have seen, contended that there were fewer still. But even sixty men in the hands of a firebrand were not to be ignored, and at about midnight Dunmore sent a messenger to Captain Montagu of the *Fowey* at Yorktown calling for military assistance.

We do not know whether Carter Braxton called on the governor, though it seems probable that he did, for the Receiver General was unlikely to give anything to anybody without Lord

[5] *Virginia Gazette* (Pinkney), May 25.
[6] Burk, *History of Virginia*, IV, 14.

Dunmore's sanction. Richard Corbin was in an unenviable position; being responsible for the gathering of taxes and duties for the Crown he was therefore the symbol of the principal cause of the colonists' disaffection with the British government. The writer of the allegory previously cited said of Corbin: "Now Richard is slightly afflicted with the palsy, *and grievously afflicted with the love of money*, and he was frightened, and his trembling encreased greatly, and he hesitated: But the deputies admonished him and Richard took of the gold of Rehoboam one hundred and four-score and three shekels, and with a sigh, and a deep groan, he put it into the hands of the deputies. For the parting of Richard and gold is always as the parting of true friends, he letteth it go with reluctance, and hopes soon to repossess it." [7] While this was doubtlessly all very amusing to the readers of the *Virginia Gazette*, it was not entirely true. Corbin did not have any gold, Rehoboam's or anyone else's; he had lent what he had to Robert Carter Nicholas, the treasurer, and to demand that he should pay up would have hurt the colony more than the Crown.

Corbin did offer to give Braxton an order payable on Nicholas, but Braxton did not think that Henry would find it acceptable. These negotiations were attended by Thomas Nelson, president of the council, who offered to provide a bill payable in Philadelphia for which he would accept Corbin's order on the treasurer. To make sure Henry realized that this was no trick, Nelson proposed to go back to Doncastle's Ordinary with Braxton, and in the small hours of Thursday morning the two tired men mounted their horses and rode out of Williamsburg. At the same moment forty other men were approaching the town from the east.

On receipt of Lord Dunmore's midnight message, Captain Montagu routed his marines from their hammocks and sent them ashore, presumably clear of Yorktown with orders to proceed at once to "Porto Bello," the governor's farm on

[7] *Virginia Gazette* (Pinkney), May 25.

Queen's Creek, and from there to march to Williamsburg. Montagu also sent the sloop *Liberty* to the mouth of Queen's Creek with orders to take the governor and his household on board should their retreat down the York Road be cut off. We do not know exactly how Dunmore phrased his call for help (if we did, we might be better able to judge his emotional stability at that time), but somehow or other Montagu was led to believe that the palace was threatened with an attack at daybreak. He therefore expected that his troops would be fired on before they reached Williamsburg, and in an effort to avoid this, he wrote a letter to Thomas Nelson warning him that such an assault would be quickly followed by his bombardment of Yorktown. Now Nelson was not only a respected moderate, he was also the most prominent citizen of that town and the owner of an impressive brick house there, which would be one of the gunners' principal targets. Consequently Montagu could reasonably expect that his letter would prove effective. What he did not know was that Nelson was neither in Yorktown nor Williamsburg, but was on his way to Doncastle's Ordinary and could not possibly receive the letter in time.

While Montagu waited, his forty-three marines and sailors commanded by Captain Stretch and Lieutenant Sandys completed the long first leg of their march and arrived at "Porto Bello" unmolested. Indeed, it was not until they reached there that anyone spotted them. The news was immediately brought to Captain Innes, commander of the Williamsburg volunteer company, and he hurried from house to house to muster enough men to halt the marines before they could enter the town. At the same time the governor's secretary, Captain Foy, was also going around Williamsburg urging restraint and promising that the detachment would not enter it, but would be brought through the park to the palace—the same route that Collins's men had taken before the removal of the powder. Foy assured the nervous citizens that the troops had no evil intent and were coming simply to protect the governor, and once his need of protection had passed they would be promptly withdrawn. While Foy talked, the volunteers wavered, and before they could make up their minds Captain Stretch and his men arrived at the palace, their mission accomplished. The governor was now strong enough to make a reasonable showing if Patrick Henry decided to reject Nelson's bill of exchange.

Henry did not reject the bill, though Mrs. Corbin contended that it was "with much difficulty" that he was prevailed upon to accept it. This evidence may reasonably be doubted, for Henry had himself named his valuation of the powder—a humiliatingly exorbitant £330 (the convention subsequently agreed that it was worth only £110 12s 0d), and he had not the slightest reason to doubt that Nelson's bill would be honored. Anyway, accept it he did, and that same day Henry wrote to Robert Carter Nicholas saying that "The affair of the powder is now settled, so as to produce satisfaction to me, and I earnestly wish, to the colony in general." He went on to add that he feared that the colony's treasury might no longer be safe in Williamsburg and if Nicholas would like to help to remove it elsewhere he and his men would be delighted to offer their services.[8] That such a move might provoke a violent reaction from the governor did not seem to concern him. On the contrary one might read into this bold suggestion an eagerness to provoke the conflict which Corbin's payment for the powder had just averted.

Nicholas, though deeply committed to the patriot cause, was a conservative who preferred to make haste slowly. James Parker called him "our thick headed treasurer, who finds it more difficult to extinguish a flame than kindle it." [9] But this one he could and did snuff out, replying to Henry that he considered the treasury quite safe where it was and politely declining his offer. So with no other exploits in view, the Hanover patriots and their adherents went home.

Although Henry had declared that the affair of the powder was closed, the pot was kept boiling a while longer by the publication of Captain Montagu's letter to Thomas Nelson. It is

[8] Burk, *History of Virginia*, IV, 14–15.
[9] Parker to Steuart, May 6; CSP.

not clear exactly when the letter was made public, though Burk suggests that it was opened and read in Williamsburg, in Nelson's absence, on the morning of May 4 and that it was only then that anyone learned of the approaching marines. Pinkney's *Virginia Gazette* of that same day included a number of hot news items, including the following wry comment: "It is imagined that captain Montagu . . . will meet with some extraordinaly mark of his majesty's approbation, as he has displayed the most exalted courage on a late occasion, by threatening to bombard the defenceless town of York, when the news of the INSURGENTS from Hanover was imported to him." If the *Gazette* was actually issued on the given date it would imply two things; first that Montagu's letter was not the first time that he had threatened to fire on Yorktown, and second that neither the existence nor the contents of the letter were public knowledge when the *Gazette* went to press, though the arrival of the marines was reported. We should therefore deduce that it was not the letter, but the report of an observer that warned Williamsburg of Captain Stretch's approach. However, it is more plausible to suppose that the paper's publication had been delayed.

The *Gazette* provided two details of the troops' progress that are absent from other sources, the first claiming that "In order to prevent any interruption in their progress to the capital, they were armed with cutlasses, swords, and bayonets. It is imagined they were to be supplied with fire arms from the spoils of the vanquished." The editor obviously thought that the absence of muskets was peculiar, and it looks equally odd today. There were, as we have seen earlier, sufficient arms stored in the palace to furnish the detachment, and St. George Tucker, who was in Williamsburg at the time, later wrote that "It was *these* Arms I suspect, that Lord Dunmore put into the hands of the Marines." [1] But as Montagu was fearful that his men might be fired upon en route, it is remarkable that he gave them nothing

[1] *WMQ*, 1st ser., XXII, 257.

with which to defend themselves. Such a decision becomes even more illogical when we remember that Virginia was abuzz with rumors of the success of patriot marksmen along the road from Concord.

It is perfectly true that Captain Stretch and his force could make much better time if they were not encumbered with the heavy, eleven-pound "Brown Bess" muskets. Yet even without them, according to the *Gazette*, their progress was not exactly that of a gazelle: "the marines from on board the Fowey not being accustomed to marching, were so fatigued when they reached the confines of the Palace, that several of them tumbled into a ditch. . . ."

Even if Pinkney did not know about the Montagu letter in time to get it into his May 4 issue, its existence was revealed very soon thereafter. The Dixon and Hunter *Virginia Gazette* of May 6 reported that the Yorktown Committee of Safety had obtained a copy and in a mood of high indignation had passed certain resolves. The first condemned Montagu for having "testified a spirit of cruelty unprecedented in the annals of civilized times" and further stated that in sending the letter to Nelson when he was unable to influence the course of events Montagu had "added insult to cruelty," revealing "the most hellish principles that can activate a human mind." The second resolution called on all citizens of Yorktown and York County to henceforth refrain from entertaining Montagu or showing any other mark of civility beyond "what common decency and absolute necessity require."

One wonders what sort of a hellhound George Montagu really was. In January the people of Portsmouth had thought him a pretty fair fellow; yet he was to become a close friend of the governor, though that may have been bred of the fact that they would find themselves in the same boat—the *Fowey*. Setting aside the indignant shouts of the patriots, there is little to be gleaned from Montagu's actions beyond an impression of a competent career naval officer attempting to serve his country with what means he had at his disposal. Forty odd marines

would not go very far if an armed rebellion broke out; General
Gage had lost many more men than that on his first encounter.
The only big stick Montagu possessed took the form of the
Fowey's guns, and their only targets were the homes of
the rebels. However, behind this rationalization there lurks the
niggling possibility that there was more (or perhaps less) to
Captain Montagu than meets the eye. The clue is provided by
Pinkney's rather ponderous Biblical allegory, verses 58 and
59:

> And he made great preparation, and he felt a strange
> emotion, a spark of spirit was kindled within him, *and he
> thought valiantly.* But the Yorkites regarded not his menace,
> they dispised his threats, and laughed at his preparations.
> The damsels of the Yorkites said, in derision, is not this
> the *Jemmy Jessamy captain, who weareth a mask on his face,
> and gloves of the skins of chickens on his hands?* Of a truth,
> the noise of cannon distracteth him, and the smell thereof
> offendeth him much. He can only bear the sound of the gentle
> tabor, an odour of roses doth his nose delight in. Fear him
> not.[2]

What, we may well ask, had George Montagu been up to? The
term "Jessamy" was a corruption of the white-flowered jasmine,
and a "Jemmy Jessamy" generally meant an effeminate dandy
—a mantle that fits poorly on the figure of Montagu the resolute
commander, Montagu the sun- and salt-hardened seadog. Yet so
out of character are the allusions that one can hardly doubt that
they spring from some now-lost truth.

The Pinkney *Gazette* of May 4 had suggested that Montagu's marines would seize muskets from the colonists, and
although everyone must have known that they could be well
supplied from the palace it is possible that some of the less
intelligent readers feared a further nocturnal trip to the public
magazine. Consequently that very night they made one of their
own and absconded with "a great number of guns, cartouch
boxes, swords, canteens, &c. for which his Excellency the

[2] *Virginia Gazette* (Pinkney), May 25.

Governor has ordered a diligent search to be made." [3] Although, according to Burk, the governor would not venture out of the palace to meet with his council, the *Journal of the House of Burgesses* [4] indicates that soon afterwards he did emerge long enough to join the mayor of Williamsburg, John Dixon, and the magazine's Keeper, John Miller, in an inspection of the rifled building. Dixon later testified that they found many weapons lying haphazardly about where they had been dropped by the looters. He reported too that the governor announced that he had ordered the burying of the remaining barrels of powder in the magazine yard to ensure that it was not touched off by open lights carried by subsequent intruders. There were then eight barrels in the building, though the contents were not all fit for use.

Throughout the tour of inspection Keeper Miller attempted to demonstrate that even if he was not too adroit in protecting the arsenal he was fully aware of the condition of its contents. He was at pains to point out to the mayor that of the muskets that were otherwise in good order a large number had had their locks removed; whereupon "his Excellency rebuked him for taking notice of that Circumstance." Whether this was achieved through a stage whisper or a kick on the shin, history fails to relate.

At a meeting of Williamsburg's Court of Common Council on May 8, the matter of the second painless extraction from the magazine was reviewed and the following statement issued:

> Whereas it has been represented to this Hall, that on the 4th instant, in the night time, some person or persons unknown had broke into the public magazine, and taken from thence sundry fire-arms belonging to his Majesty:
>
> We, the Mayor, Aldermen, and Common Council, of the said city, being desirous to maintain peace, order, and good government, do hereby declare our abhorrence of such unlawful proceedings; and do require the inhabitants to use

[3] *Virginia Gazette* (Dixon & Hunter), May 6.
[4] Pp. 223–4.

their utmost endeavours to prevent the like outrage in future, and exhort all persons who may be in possession of any of the said arms to return the same immediately, to be replaced in the magazine.[5]

It is likely that Lord Dunmore obtained a rare moment of satisfaction from reading this published statement in the *Virginia Gazette*, for taken at face value it appeared to confirm his previously voiced fear that the powder removed in April had been unsafe in the magazine. In addition, the Common Council seemed to agree that the arms stored there were the property of the King. This, you will recall, had been one of Dunmore's various contentions when defending his right to extract the powder. Legally, however, it was a simple matter for the mayor and council to extricate themselves from either commitment, for the preamble to their statement began with the words: "Whereas it has been represented to this Hall. . . ." They had been told that such and such was the case, and on the basis of that information they reacted as stated. Similarly they had been *told* that the arms were the property of the King. It is quite possible that if they really did not know who took the arms, some may have suspected that Lord Dunmore himself was again responsible. However, for reasons that will be apparent later, there is good cause to suppose that some of the city dignitaries knew exactly where the weapons were hidden.

The Common Council's statement concluded by recommending that Mr. Gabriel Maupin, who lived on the edge of the market square immediately west of the magazine, should be appointed its keeper. It is significant that once again the councillors made it clear that they were following instructions from the governor, though they spoke for themselves when they announced that they had "no authority to lay any tax for that purpose;" but if Lord Dunmore chose to appoint someone to the office, they would concede that it might be a useful step toward maintaining law and order. The statement made no mention of

[5] *Virginia Gazette* (Dixon & Hunter), May 13.

John Miller, and we can only suppose that his overzealous attention to unnecessary detail had cost him his job.

In the days following Patrick Henry's triumphant withdrawal many county committees issued statements commending him for his actions and offering support should he need it in any subsequent foray. In a vain effort to discourage such saber-rattling resolves, Lord Dunmore issued a proclamation on May 6 charging "all Persons, upon their Allegiance, not to aid, abet, or give Countenance to, the said *Patrick Henry*, or any other Persons concerned in such unwarrantable Combinations; but, on the Contrary, to oppose them and their Designs by every Means; which Designs must, otherwise, inevitably involve the whole Country in the most direful Calamity, as they will call for the Vengeance of offended Majesty and the insulted Laws, to be exerted here, to vindicate the constitutional Authority of Government." [6]

This did not mean, as has sometimes been thought, that Patrick Henry was outlawed, for no mention was made of denying Henry his rights under the law. The proclamation was simply a toothless roar intended to frighten his supporters. Privately, of course, there can be little doubt that the governor would have been delighted to have received Henry's head on a platter, for as Dunmore indicated to the Secretary of State, the man had been making a nuisance of himself in the wilderness for much too long, being "of desperate Circumstances and one who has been very active in encouraging disobedience and exciting a Spirit of revolt among the People for many years past. . . ." [7]

The Spirit of '75 was a-bubble on all sides, and it was now apparent that only a massive British military triumph or a change of heart by the Continental Congress at its meeting in Philadelphia could stem the tide. Neither seemed to be forthcoming. Wrote Lord Dunmore: "even in the Place where I live Drums are beating, and Men in uniform dresses with Arms are continually in the Streets, which my Authority is no longer

[6] Enclosed in Dunmore to Dartmouth, May 15; PRO,CO 5/1353.
[7] Ibid.

able to prevent." [8] But although the drums beat and the bagpipes skirled, James Parker was unimpressed. "These Shirt men, or Virginia uniform, are dressed with an Oznabr Shirt over their Cloaths, a belt round them with a Tommy hawk & Scalping knife. They look like a band of Assassins & it is my opinion if they fight at all it will be in that way." [9]

It would be wrong to suppose that the entire colony was standing about striking martial poses; on the contrary, most of the inhabitants were busy about their own business—or that of their owners and masters. John Harrower noted that on Colonel Daingerfield's plantation, "the Colls Nigers finished planting Indian Corn" [1] on May 3, while on the following Saturday he himself set up forty-one hills of cotton seed, followed on the Monday by twenty-two of water- and mush-mellon seeds. Life had to go on—though not for Messrs. Pitman, Gray, Wood, and Watkins, who died on the Williamsburg gallows on May 12th, their respective crimes having been the murder of a Negro boy, two robberies, and a rape. In London the Old Bailey sessions just concluded had resulted in fourteen such convictions, for two crimes of highway robbery, nine house breakings, one cattle theft, one horse stealing, and the theft of two warrants. For lesser crimes, miscreants were constantly being shipped to the colonies to serve out their sentences, and there had been a number of convicts among the holdful of miscellaneous talents that Captain Kidd had sold at Leedstown in March.

The trouble with convicts, of course, was that unlike people who indentured themselves of their own free will, they were there on sufferance and were apt to abscond when the opportunity arose. Mr. Andrew Leitch, who had invested in two of them, failed even to get them home, and a month later, at the beginning of May, he inserted the following reward offer in the *Virginia Gazette:* [2]

[8] Ibid.
[9] Parker to Steuart, June 12; CSP.
[1] *Harrower*, 95.
[2] *Virginia Gazette* (Pinkney), May 4.

Run away from the subscriber, living in *Dumfries*, two convict servant men, just imported from *London* in the *Justitia*, Captain Kidd, lying at Leedstown: WILLIAM PEARCE, a stout, likely fellow, 5 feet 8 or 9 inches high, with red hair; he has a fair complexion, tolerably well dressed, and is about 25 years of age. RALPH EMANUEL, about 6 feet high, strong made, and likely; he has darkish coloured hair, is well dressed, has a chocolate coloured surtout coat, with a red cape, a small hat, bound round with ferret, and a black band round the crown; he is about 22 years of age. They left the company in which they were travelling, a few miles above *Leedstown*, and will certainly endeavour to pass for sailors. To those used to the smell of servants just from a ship they will be easily discovered. . . .

One might have expected that Mr. Leitch would have had his fill of convict labor—he had lost a convict tailor and a convict sailor only last November. Nevertheless he was offering £10 for the recovery of his runaway property. But smell or not, there was a fair chance that the men had gone for good, the convicts probably having spent most of their days aboard ship savoring the prospects of escape.

Life on shipboard for convicts, or even for servants, could be unbelievably unpleasant. The day after John Harrower had arrived at Fredericksburg a servant from the ship had "returned on board from Liberty so drunk that he abused the Capt. Cheif Mate & Boatswan to a verry high degree, which made to be horse whipt. put in Irons and thumb screwed. An houre after he was unthumbscrewed, taken out of the Irons, but then he was hand cuffed, and gagged all night." [3]

Much worse was in store for a young Irish blacksmith named John Cunningham, whose description was published in the May 4 *Virginia Gazette* [4] and who had made and passed a dud doubloon. All sheriffs and constables were instructed to "make hue and cry after him, from town to town, and from county to county, as well by horsemen as footmen" and to seize

[3] *Harrower*, 38; May 11, 1774.
[4] Pinkney.

him in the name of the King. Coining was a treasonable offense
and so punishable with the harshest penalty on the books, that of
being drawn to the place of execution on a sledge, being hanged
(though not necessarily killed), and having one's bowels cut out
and burned. Women were less horribly treated—though not
much. On April 23, 1775, Lord North submitted a petition to
the King requesting the commutation of a sentence of death by
burning which had been passed on one Martha Latimer.
Reduction of the penalty was asked on the grounds that she was
only the servant of a Mr. Harris, who was the principal
criminal. The King later advised Lord North that in consideration of his personal interest in the fate of Martha Latimer the
sentence should be reduced to transportation to the colonies.
Perhaps she would subsequently be able to offer a few useful
tips to John Cunningham.

Mr. Cunningham was not the only person whose troubles
were broadcast in the May 4 issue of the *Virginia Gazette;*
declared William Northen: "I hereby give notice that I will pay
no debts that my wife *Abigail Northen* shall or may contract from
the date hereof." Mrs. Northen's credit rating thereupon plum-
meted, doubtless ensuring that she could not take advantage of
the bargains offered on page four. There Mrs. Catherine Rathell
advertised the contents of her store in Williamsburg, saying
that as she proposed to go to England until liberty of importation should be allowed, she was put "under the necessity of not
parting with a single shilling's worth, without cash. . . ."

The shop's stock included an infinite range of haberdashery
to delight the female eye and precisely the kind of things that
the 1774 Continental Congress had thought should be forsworn
in these belt-tightening times:

> . . . a great variety of black, white, and other coloured silk
> petticoats, patent net aprons and hoods, superfine fancy and
> dress caps, stomachers and knots . . . cane and silk hats,
> *French* flowers for trimming ditto, silk gloves and mits,
> leather and brown thread ditto, fine stamped *Irish* muslins for
> ladies gowns, which are remarkable for their beautiful

colours, salmon coloured, plain and striped dimities, silk and lawn pocket handkerchiefs, ladies riding hats and feathers . . . fans, garnet set in gold, plain gold and paste broaches and lockets, set combs, paste bows, crosses, springs, and pins . . . marcasite and paste necklaces and earrings . . . swan skin and silk powder puffs, tooth brushes and picktooth cases, a large quantity of *Irish* linen. . . .

She also offered a "second hand guittar"—just the thing for anyone wanting to take those lessons advertised last March.

Mrs. Rathell was leaving for England because her business was being damaged; others were going for the same reason or because they could not in good conscience sign the Association, which the county committees demanded of them. Each week the *Gazettes* carried notices inserted by more and more of these, some trying to sell their lands and belongings, and others trying to get customers to pay their bills. Much has been made of those wayward debtors who supported the coming breach as a means of avoiding payment to English creditors. The case of Thomas Macknight of Currituck County, North Carolina, may therefore come as something of a surprise, as, indeed, it must have been to many of those who read about it in the *Virginia Gazette* [5] on May 6.

Macknight had been a delegate from his county to the convention that had met at New Bern in April, and when required to join his colleagues in signing the Association approved by the previous Continental Congress he had astonished everyone by refusing. Even more astonishing was his reason. He explained that "he owed a debt in Britain, which the operation of the nonexportation agreement would disable him to pay, and that he could not approve of a conduct in a collective capacity, which, as an individual, he should blush to acknowledge." He added that in principle he was in favor of the Association and that he would cheerfully comply with the nonconsumption and nonimportation clauses. Furthermore he would give passive agreement to the nonexportation section

[5] Dixon & Hunter.

providing it did not prevent him from sending the money or produce he owed to England. The delegates did not think that this was good enough, so Macknight declined to put his name to the paper. In doing so he asked permission to put his reasons in writing and to present them the next day so that they could be entered into the minutes. The convention agreed; but when he presented his statement it was not permitted to be read. He was then asked whether he would agree to sign if he declared that he would "accede" to the requirements of the Association. This he agreed to do, and the motion was carried sixteen to fourteen. But the minority was not to be defeated and they declared that "if any subscription, different from theirs, was accepted from him, they would withdraw from the convention." At this point Macknight rose and announced that rather than cause any more dissension he himself would withdraw.

After Macknight's departure a vote of censure was passed against him, branding his conduct "as inimical to the cause of American liberty," declaring him to be "a proper object of contempt to this continent," and recommending that "every person break off all connexion, and have no further commercial intercourse or dealing with him." Such was the reward of an honest man at the hands of the Sons of Liberty. In all fairness, one must add that the rest of the Currituck delegates walked out in support of Macknight, as also did those from Pasquotank County—but they were five, and twenty-three remained.

In these early, uneasy, and suspicious days even the most honest patriot was in danger of being bitten by his own dogs, and longtime friends of the family were transformed overnight into enemies of the people. John Norton and Sons, of London, the factors who had aided and supported most of the first families of Virginia through their lean years, now found themselves publicly assailed by the citizens of Gloucester and York counties, and all over two half-chests of tea. So closely was this firm tied to the interests of the colony that the founder's son had managed the Virginia end of the business at Yorktown and was married to a girl from Elizabeth City County. Their son,

John Hadley Norton, was born in Yorktown in 1745, and when his father went back to England to direct the London end in 1764, John Hadley took over the Yorktown management. He was to all intents and purposes a Virginian, and he stoutly espoused the colonial cause; but that did not prevent the Gloucester County Committee from declaring his father "guilty of a daring insult upon the people of this colony, to whom he owes his all . . ." and asserting that he had "forfeited all title to the confidence of this county, and that we will not in future consign tobacco, or any other commodity to his house, until satisfactory concessions are made; and we recommend that same resolution to the rest of the colony." [6]

The cause of all this fuss was, as I have said, two half-chests of tea, one of hyson and the other green, both ordered by the merchants John Prentis & Son, of Williamsburg, early in 1774. The order was received by John Norton in London in June, but in view of the growing dissent he waited to ship the cases until August, expecting all the while that Prentis would cancel the order; but he did not. Toward the end of the month the cases were consigned to the ship *Virginia*, under Captain Howard Esten, who left London early on the morning of September 16. The previous evening (too late to stop the *Virginia*, whose cargo was in bond) came news of the Virginia Convention's resolution banning the importation of tea after November the first. A message was rushed to Captain Esten, whose ship had reached the Downs off the coast of Kent, instructing him that if he failed to deliver the tea before the closing date, he should lay his case before "the committee and other Gentlemen of Virginia, immediately on his arrival . . . and that, if he found it was disagreeable to the inhabitants that the tea should be landed, stored, or returned in the ship, he was then to propose destroying it; but by no means attempt the landing it without leave." [7]

Captain Esten did not arrive before the deadline; he had

[6] *Virginia Gazette* (Pinkney), Nov. 24, 1774.
[7] *Virginia Gazette* (Dixon & Hunter), May 6.

missed it by almost a week. He therefore followed his orders and explained the whole unfortunate story to the House of Burgesses in Williamsburg. But while they were deliberating, the York-town Committee of Safety made up its own mind, boarded the *Virginia*, hoisted the tea chests out of the hold, and tossed them into the river. The ship was subsequently forced to leave without a cargo.

Now, in May, we find John Norton writing from London to explain his position and apologizing for having offended his erstwhile friends, the friends who must have known full well that they were accusing him unjustly. Like any local "enemy of the Association" Norton published his apology and assured the colony that his "avowed principles are, that the Parliament of Great Britain have not the least shadow of right to tax America . . ." and that "far from having any connexion with the Ministry, that my person is even unknown to any of them, and that I never was in their presence, except when I attended about the copper coinage for Virginia, in which I was employed instead of a better agent." [8] No one could have wished for a more complete explanation and apology—except perhaps the committee of Gloucester County.

The same issue of the *Gazette* that published Norton's statement also printed two new Gloucester resolutions:

> *Resolved*, That we will not ship a single hogshead of tobacco to Great Britain until the determination of the Continental Congress, respecting exportation, be known.
> *Resolved*, that we deem the resolution of our committee last November, not to ship any tobacco in future to Mr. Norton's house, as still oblagatory; the ship Virginia having arrived without the concessions then required.

There could be no denying that the embargo on importation and exportation was having its effect on both sides of the ocean. Three months later John Norton would write to his son at Yorktown telling him that he proposed to sell the *Virginia*. "I

[8] Ibid.

have offered her at £2800 rather than keep her to look on, she
has always been unfortunate & for many reasons shou'd be glad
to part with her at that price. . . ." [9] The late Philip Ludwell
Lee's new brig was still without a buyer, and another was in
search of an owner in Suffolk: "FOR SALE, A NEW BRIGANTINE,
now rigging, and may be soon got ready for Sea, Burthen 122
Tons. She is a handsome well calculated Vessel, built of
excellent Materials, ornamented with a Figure Head and other
carved Work. Credit will be allowed for one Half of the Money
on giving proper Security. If not sold shortly, would accept of a
Freight." [1] But this was not a good moment to enter the
mercantile business, and shipbuilders could expect to be
saddled one way or the other. Virginia's shipbuilding industry,
though never a match for the yards of Massachusetts, New
York, or Pennsylvania, had produced a creditable number of
vessels in the past decade. The year 1765 had been the best,
with a total of forty-seven ships of various sizes reaching the
water. Better than average was 1773, with thirty vessels
launched, so dramatizing the virtual sinking of the industry in
the first gusts of the political northeaster that blew down in the
following year. The total output that year was only seven keels,
all of them quite small, one schooner, two sloops, three brigs, and
a ship, having a total cargo capacity of only 475 tons. Once the
lines had been drawn the shipbuilding picture would undoubtedly improve, prompted either by a resumption of normal trade
with Britain or by an increase of coastal commerce, coupled
perhaps with the opening of a new and lucrative trade with
France, Spain, and Holland. All would be well—providing one
could afford to wait.

The prospect of France and Spain becoming militarily
involved was always in the air, ozone for those who contended
that the colonies could take up arms against Britain and win. A
London rumor, published in the *Virginia Gazette* [2] of May 6,

[9] *John Norton & Sons, Merchants*, 389; Sept. 5.
[1] *Virginia Gazette* (Dixon & Hunter), May 27.
[2] Dixon & Hunter.

had it that France was readying herself for an attack on Ireland, once the British troops camped there were shipped to America, and that a large Spanish fleet was assembling for an assault on Jamaica. As for the British themselves, they were certainly coming, but the papers took every opportunity to suggest that they would not have their heart in their work. An extract from a letter written at Cork on March 1 stated that "most of the troops destined for America are arrived here. Both officers and men never went upon an expedition with greater reluctance than on the present intended one." [3]

Pinkney's *Gazette* of May 18 devoted half of its front page to a remarkable letter ostensibly written by an Irish immigrant in Botetourt County, to his brother in Ireland, who had enlisted to serve in the American expedition. The writer explained his desire for this rather public avenue for his private missive by saying that it would be more likely to reach his brother this way than through the mail. He also begged Mr. Pinkney to correct his spelling and phraseology as he was "but a mean scholar." The kindly editor duly went to work and tidied the thing up— but "only as far as was indispensibly necessary"—and out came as fine and provocative an editorial as any patriot could hope to read. One small excerpt will suffice:

I dare believe there is not a single soldier in any of the *Irish*, nor even in any of the *British* regiments, but has relations and friends among those he is about to slaughter. Those brave soldiers I pity, because they are deceived [having signed on to fight the French or Spaniards]. They never suspected their generous spirit was to be employed in such unnatural wickedness. But *you*, my brother, *you* enlisted of your *own* accord in this very service. What have you to plead in your justification? You come premeditatedly to ruin all your friends, all your relations, in *America*, to ruin *America* herself, and, with her, the only recourse of every *poor*, every *oppressed*, every *outed* family *in the three kingdoms*. My dear brother, rather end your days with a pistol than be instrumental in those abominations.

[3] *Virginia Gazette* (Dixon & Hunter), May 6.

It was, you must agree, a splendid effort; and so thoughtful of the writer to use this novel method of encouraging his brother to shoot himself—his brother and all his brother's brothers-in-arms. If one read Mr. Pinkney carefully, one might have taken added heart from the fact that even if the Irishman's brother did not do as he was asked, he would, in any case, very quickly live to regret that he had signed on. According to a report from Hartford, Connecticut, a British soldier who had been at Lexington declared that "the militia had fought like bears, and that he would as soon attempt to storm Hell as to fight against them a second time." [4] From London it was learned that two generals appointed to American commands had refused to take them.

There could be no denying that a goodly proportion of the British senior officers looked upon the American adventure without enthusiasm. When General Sir William Howe had stood for election as Member of Parliament for Nottingham in 1774, he had assured his procolonial merchant constituents that he would never accept a commission that would require him to fight against the Americans. But he did; and before he sailed he tried to explain his change of heart by lamely contending that "My going thither was not of my seeking, I was ordered, and could not refuse without incurring the odious name of backwardness to serve my country in distress." [5] General Sir Henry Clinton said much the same thing; so, too, did General "gentleman Johnny" Burgoyne, though of the three his was the most ready acceptance. In a speech in the House of Commons following his appointment he asked: "Is there a man in England (I am confident there is not an officer or soldier in the King's service) who thinks not the Parliamentary rights of Great Britain a cause to fight for, to bleed and die for? . . . The reason of the nation has been long convinced; the trial now only is, whether we have spirit to support our conviction." If the

[4] *Virginia Gazette* (Pinkney), May 11.

[5] Thomas A. Fleming, "The Enigma of General Howe," *American Heritage*, XV, No. 2 (February 1964), 8.

nation was not prepared to stand up for its rights in the face of American defiance, he declared, "I agree that the sooner a formal surrender is made the better; let Great Britain revert to her primitive insignificancy in the map of the world, and the Congress of Philadelphia be the legislature to dispense the blessings of empire. Let us spare the blood of our subjects, let us spare the treasures of the state; but let us at the same time confess we are no more a people." It was only after all this (and more) that Burgoyne added that "it might be thought I sought the situation in which I am going to be employed. I publicly declare I did not seek it. I will take leave to say on the part of my colleagues, it was sought by none of us, but it was accepted with that submission which is due from servants of the Crown, and with that sense of gratitude to his Majesty which the importance of the trust required." [6]

On April 22 Burgoyne and his drafted but dutiful colleagues, Generals Howe and Clinton, boarded the frigate *Cerberus* for a trip that would earn them little glory on either side of the water. The name of the vessel could hardly have escaped the attention of pro-American wits, and it did not. Both Pinkney and Dixon and Hunter reported that "A correspondent thinks it an odd circumstance, that the Cerberus (whom the poets feign to be the three headed dog that guards the mouth of hell) should be the ship appointed to carry over to America the three Generals appointed to tame the Americans." [7] Even more coincidental (but apropos of nothing in particular) was the fact that the commander of the *Cerberus*, Captain Shads, had been with Howe when, as a young colonel, he had led the assault on the Heights of Abraham at Quebec, and it was aboard Shads's vessel that General Wolfe had been carried after the victory. If General Howe was in search of omens, shipping with Shads might reasonably have been deemed favorable—unless it meant that the price of victory would be more dead generals.

[6] *Virginia Gazette* (Dixon & Hunter), June 3.

[7] *Virginia Gazette* (Pinkney), April 28; *Virginia Gazette* (Dixon & Hunter), May 6.

Soldiering in the eighteenth century was a very much more gentlemanly activity than it is today, at least it was for the officers. Their personal baggage accounted for a high percentage of the load carried by each regiment, and an officer of substance could be expected to carry with him his wines, porcelain tea services, clothes for every occasion, even a billiard table. According to a report from New London, the *Cerberus* man-of-war carried no troops other than its three first-class passengers—and the twenty-five horses they brought with them "to take their pleasure in this delightful country." [8] The *Gazette* noted without comment that it learned from London that "The transports getting ready for Boston are ordered not to be crowded full of men, as they usually have been, that there may be sufficient room for the officers to take as much baggage as they think proper." [9]

Another traveler bound for America was Benjamin Franklin, and the speed of news being what it was, the report of his departure was published in Virginia three weeks after he arrived in Philadelphia. Nevertheless the item is of interest in that it voiced some of the speculation regarding Franklin's stay in London. His departure was thought to have been somewhat precipitous, prompting some experts to consider it merely the result of having received news of his wife's death, while others were convinced that he was carrying highly secret proposals to be laid before the Continental Congress.

But although the February 20 attempt at conciliation had still to be played out, any hopes for an accommodation had faded. As Governor Dunmore observed, something might be achieved "if the People of this Country were still under the influence of reason, or had not already thrown off every inclination to an accomodation of differences: it is no longer to be doubted that Independence is the object in view; and I am of opinion that no warning will deter, nor offer divert them from

[8] *Virginia Gazette* (Pinkney), June 22.

[9] *Virginia Gazette* (Dixon & Hunter), May 27.

making every attempt their leaders advise to establish it." [1] In the long run, of course, Dunmore was right; but at the Continental Congress the voices of moderation were still loud and strong. The war, which had already begun in the North, was euphemistically described as being with the Ministry and not with the Crown, and the British troops, the despised "boiled crabs," were known as "ministerialists" rather than soldiers of the King. The Declaration of Independence was still more than a year away—except, perhaps, for North Carolina.

The present seal of North Carolina bears in its field the date "May 20, 1775," and the same legend figures prominently on the state flag. Both proudly recall the day when the committee of Mecklenburg County, meeting at Charlotte, drew up its own Declaration of Independence, resolving unanimously:

That we, the citizens of Mecklenburg County, do hereby dissolve the political bands, which have connected us with the Mother Country, and hereby absolve ourselves from all allegiance to the British Crown, and abjure all political connection, contract, or association with that nation, who have wantonly trampled on our rights and liberties, and inhumanly shed the blood of American patriots at Lexington.

That we do hereby declare ourselves a free and independent people;—are, and of right ought to be, a sovereign and self-governing association, under the control of no power, other than that of our God, and the general government of the Congress;—to the maintenance of which independence, we solumnly pledge to each other, our mutual coöperation, our lives, our fortunes, and our most sacred honor. [2]

Two further resolves were concerned with the striking down of existing colonial laws and establishment of officers among the committeemen to "preserve peace, union, and harmony" in Mecklenburg County.

This remarkable document was allegedly written by Ephraim Brevard, chairman of the committee, and read to it by

[1] Dunmore to Dartmouth, May 15; PRO,CO 5/1353.
[2] Jones, *Revolutionary History of N.C.*, 298.

him at noon on May 20. Having been unanimously adopted, the
declaration was then read publicly before the courthouse door.
According to an eyewitness, it was received with great acclama-
tion. Someone called for three cheers, which were loudly
forthcoming, the men tossing their hats into the air so vigorously that some of them landed on the courthouse roof—from
which their owners later had trouble retrieving them. Thus
supported, the committee then gave a copy of the declaration to
Captain James Jack of Charlotte, with instructions to carry it to
Philadelphia and lay it before the Congress. But when he got
back, Jack reported that although the members, "individually,
manifested their entire approbation of the Mecklenburg citizens," [3] they considered the document premature and advised
against officially presenting it; and that was that.

Nothing more was heard of the Mecklenburg Declaration of
Independence until it was brought to light in an editorial in the
Raleigh Register of April 30, 1819. The original document had
seemingly been destroyed along with other Mecklenburg committee records in a fire in about 1800. John Adams read a
reprint in the *Essex Register* of Salem, Massachusetts, and he
promptly wrote to Thomas Jefferson asking how the declaration
could have "been concealed from me to this day." Adams went
on:

Had it been communicated to me in the time of it, I know, if
you do not know, that it would have been printed in every
Whig newspaper upon the continent. You know, that if I had
possessed it, I would have made the Hall of Congress echo
and re-echo with it fifteen months before your Declaration of
Independence. What a poor, ignorant, malicious, short-
sighted, crapulous mass is Tom Paine's Common Sense in
comparison with this paper. Had I known it I would have
commented upon it from the day you entered Congress till the
fourth of July, 1776. The genuine sense of America at that
moment was never so well expressed before nor since. . . . [4]

[3] Ibid., 308, footnote.
[4] Ibid., 296.

Inside the portrait, lower left:
John IV Earl of Dunmore
Captain in Regiment of Lord Gordons
1755. Governor of Virginia 1770.

1. *John Murray, fourth Earl of Dunmore, by Sir Joshua Reynolds, 1765.*

THE ALTERNATIVE OF WILLIAMSBU

*Showing either the Burgesses forced by their Constituents
to the signing of an Agreement of Non-Importation,
or else the Loyalists forced to such an Association
by the Sentiment of the aroused and angry Publick*

III. *"A Society of Patriotic Ladies at Edenton in North Carolina," mezzotint published in London, March 25, 1775.*

IV. *A Virginia copper halfpenny of 1773, issued in the colony in 1775. Excavated in Williamsburg.*

eft: *"The Alternative of Williamsburg," aved from a mezzotint published in London, February 16, 1775.*

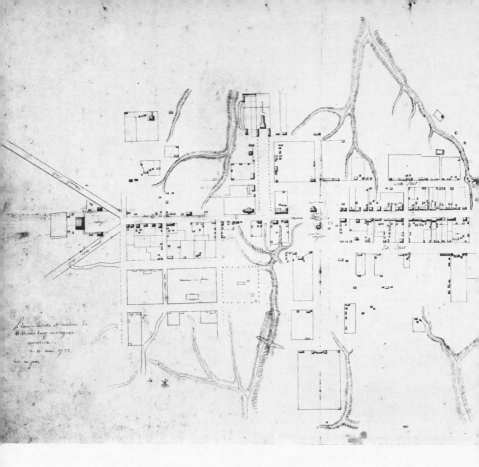

v. Above: *A French cartographer's map of the city of Williamsburg,* circa 1782.

vi. Right, Top: *A Chinese export porcelain soup plate enameled with the crest and arms of Lord Dunmore. Found on the site of the Governor's Palace.*

vii. Right: *Deck plans of H.M.S.* Fowey *drawn at Sheerness, March 24, 1772.*

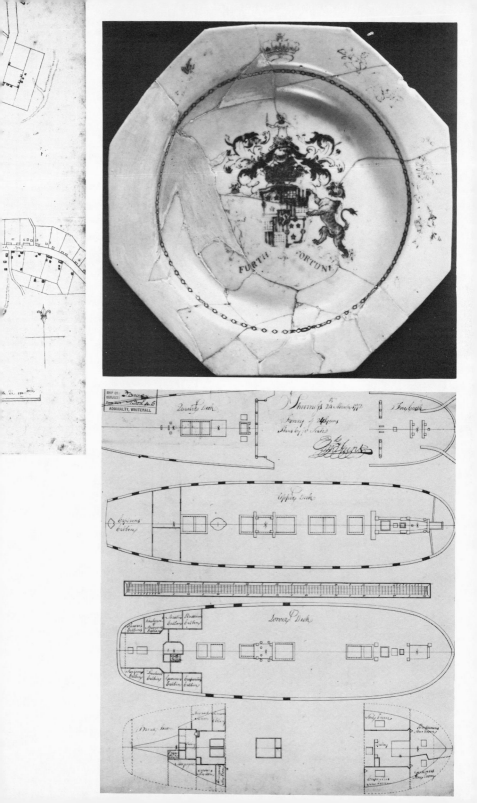

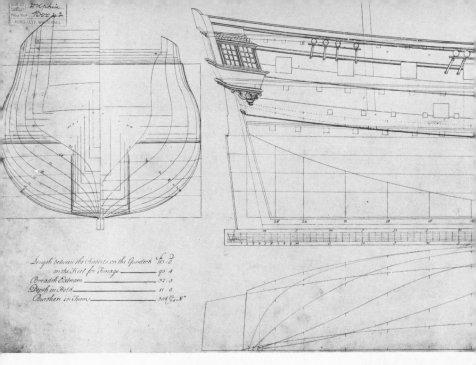

VIII. Above: *Master sheer draught for a 24-gun ship of the same class as H.M.S. Fowey. The name Dolphin was added later, obscuring the fact that this was a preliminary draught for the entire class (1745-50) and did not represent one individual ship.*

IX. Right: *Detail from "A View of the Town of York, Virginia, from the River"; water color probably by John Gauntlett, 1755. Thomas Nelson's house stands to the right of the flagstaff, and the three principal ships are identifiable as (from left to right) a brig, sloop, and shallop.*

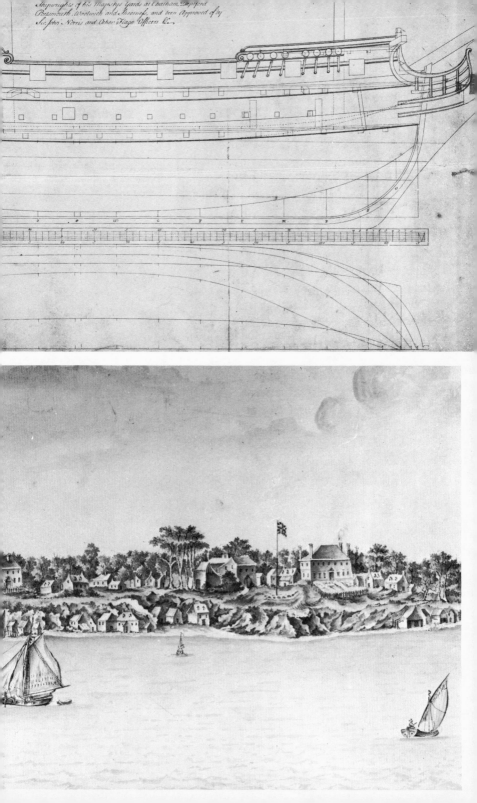

New P'news

To York

N.P. Creek

Seyla

Salt c

Armstead's mill

St George

Hook Back River Road

HAMPTON

B

C

A

D

Hampton Creek

Mills Creek

Point Comfort

x. Detail from "A Sketch of the East End of the Peninsula Where on is Hampton," circa 1775. Soundings are in feet, and the numbers on the land indicate the distance in miles from Hampton. The letters are identified as follows: A, shipyard; B, Little England; C, not identified; D, Little Scotland; E and H, guard houses; M, not identified. The map is orientated with the north to the right; the James River is seen at the left and the road running westward past Newport News as part of the "Great Warwick Road to Williamsburg."

XI. Right: *The Honorable Peyton Randolph, by John Wollaston, circa 1755.*

XII. Below: *George Washington in the uniform of a colonel of the Twenty-second Regiment of Virginia Militia, by Charles Willson Peale, 1772.*

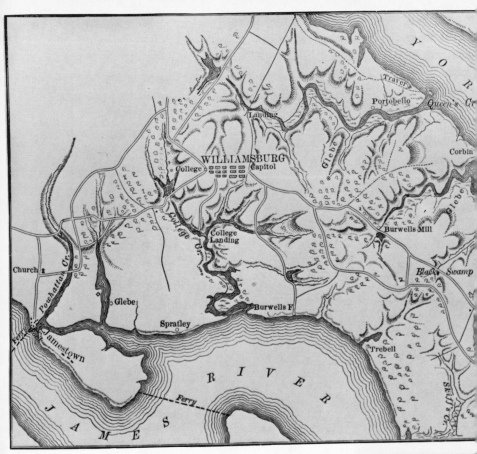

XIII. Above: *A section of the first U.S. survey of the Virginia Peninsula (1818) showing the relationship between Williamsburg and the adjacent creeks, and the landings and roads as they were in 1775.*

XIV. Right, Top: *A tall-case clock made in Glasgow, circa 1765, and reputed to have been among the furnishings left behind in the palace by Lord Dunmore.*

XV. Right: *"Sea Captains Carousing in Surinam," by John Greenwood, circa 1758.*

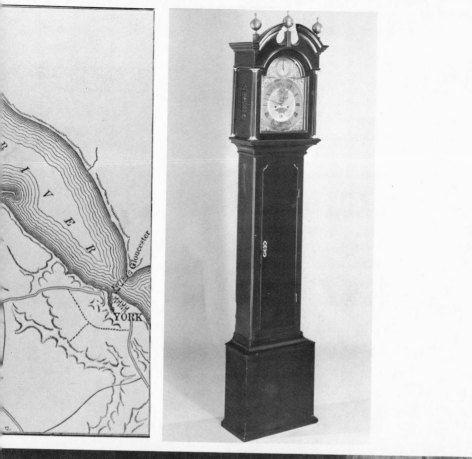

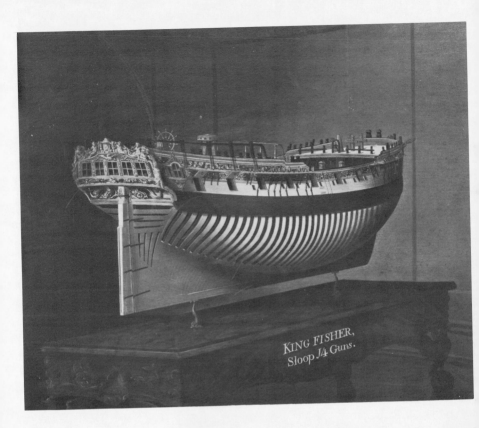

KING FISHER,
Sloop 14 Guns.

xvi. Above: *Model of his Majesty's sloop-of-war Kingfisher, painted in oils by Joseph Marshall, 1775.*

A MAP of
the moſt INHABITED part of
VIRGINIA
containing the whole PROVINCE of
MARYLAND
with Part of
PENSILVANIA, NEW JERSEY AND NORTH CAROLINA
Drawn by
Joshua Fry & Peter Jefferson
in 1775.

XVIII. Above: *A colonial tobacco wharf; title ornament from the Fry-Jefferson map of Virginia and Maryland, 1775 edition.*

XVII. Below: *Examples of paper money issued by order of the Virginia Convention in July 1775. Left: Regular half crown and five-shilling notes. Far left: Twelve- and one-pound bills issued in 1775 on James River Bank forms after the treasury ran out of paper.*

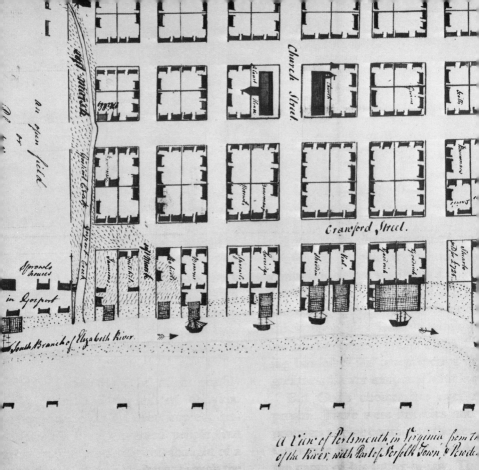

Within the map image, the following text is visible:

Church Street

An open field

Cransford Street

Sprowls houses in Gosport

South Branch of Elizabeth River

A View of Portsmouth in Virginia from the
of the River, with Part of Norfolk Town, & Powde

XIX. Above: *"A View of Portsmouth in Virginia from the
East Side of the River with Part of Norfolk Town and
Powder Point,"* attached to the claim of loyalist John
Agnew, January 22, 1788, in the Public Record Office,
London.

XX. Right, Top: *A Grenadier of the Fourteenth Regiment
in the uniform prescribed by the King's Regulations of December 19, 1768; a contemporary water-colored drawing.*

XXI. Right: *An undated manuscript map of Norfolk and
Princess Anne Counties probably drawn late in 1775 or
shortly thereafter. The British fort at Great Bridge is clearly marked "Fort Murray," though it is shown to the west
of the road rather than to the east as depicted in the battle
plan, Pl. 21. The American defenseworks to the south are
lightly sketched in. The lower right corner of this map
points approximately north.*

Light House

Cape Henry

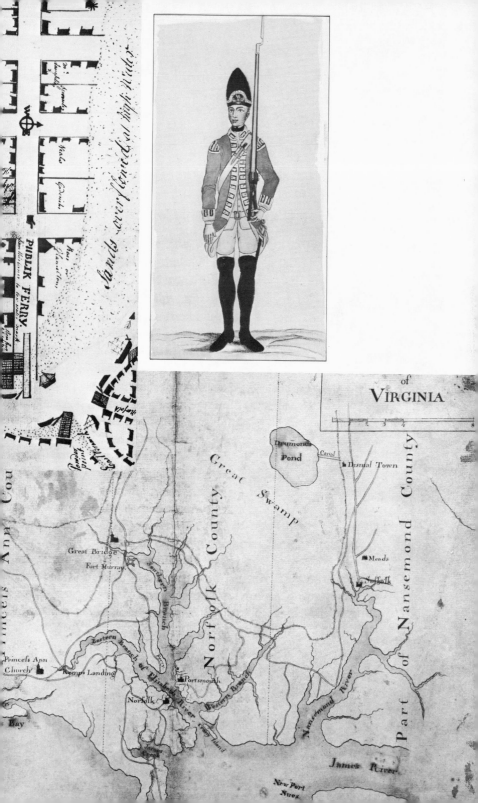

A View of the Great bridge near Norfolk in Vir=
=ginia where the action happened between a Detachment
of the 14th Reg.t & a body of the Rebels.
A. A Stockade Fort thrown up before the action by the Regulars.
B. Entrenchments of the Rebels. C. a narrow Causeway by which the Regulars were
forced to advance to the attack. D. The Church occupied by the Rebels.

XXII. "A View of the Great Bridge near Norfolk, Virginia," undated, but
presumably drawn shortly after the battle.

However, far from agreeing that the document represented a genuine sense of anything, Jefferson wrote back that in his view the thing was a fake, and that he would continue in that opinion until someone produced evidence to the contrary. No one ever did; though in 1834 John Seawell Jones published a lengthy treatise entitled *A Defence of the Revolutionary History of the State of North Carolina from the Aspersions of Mr. Jefferson.* The purpose of this work was to establish the authenticity of the Mecklenburg Declaration. But although Seawell Jones managed to dig up a few venerable eyewitnesses, he could produce no documentary proof that the Mecklenburg meeting of May 19–20, 1775, conceived anything more memorable than the general fuming that was emanating from every colonial committee of safety at that time. The Seawell Jones evidence is certainly intensely interesting, but it was too little—and too late—to have convinced Thomas Jefferson.

In the nineteenth century many loyal and prominent North Carolinians were convinced of the validity of the Mecklenburg Declaration—which was how "May 20, 1775," found its way onto the state's flag and seal and how the text came to be written into the published colonial records. Today the document has fewer supporters (most of them from Mecklenburg County), and when state officials are asked to comment on the date on their emblems, they generally begin to steam beneath their collars and hastily suggest that the new state house is a fine place to visit. I have chosen to include the Mecklenburg Declaration, not because I am convinced by the evidence put forward in its favor, but because no one has finally proved that it did not exist. If it did, one can only echo Adams and salute the Mecklenburg Declaration of Independence as one of the most impressive documents in American history. But if we do that, we are left wondering why it was not read at Philadelphia, even if it was to be subsequently rejected. There were undoubtedly plenty of delegates there who would have been only too happy to introduce it. Besides, the Mecklenburg resolves contain phraseology that is disconcertingly akin to that of the final paragraph of the 1776 Declaration; too alike, one might think, to be dismissed as mere coincidence. Either way, somebody was cribbing from someone. All in all, it is more logical to reject Mr. Ephraim Brevard as the sower of the seed of '76, and instead to hail the editor of the *Raleigh Register* as the father of the most audacious hoax in American political history.

Even if the words of farewell were not yet on paper, the slamming of doors in the face of the Ministry's offer of compromise were loud in the wind. "The News-Papers have already begun to prejudice the People against it," wrote Lord Dunmore, "and to call it only a Ministerial device to divide the Colonies. . . ." [5] On May 12 Governor Penn of Pennsylvania laid the British government's conciliatory proposal before that colony's general assembly at Philadelphia. "You have," he assured the members, "in the resolution of the house of commons, which I have authority to tell you is entirely approved by his majesty, a solemn declaration that an exemption from any duty tax, or assessment, present or future, except such duties as may be expedient for the regulation of commerce, shall be the immediate consequence of proposals on the part of any of the colony legislatures, accepted by his majesty, and the two houses of parliament, to make provision, according to their respective circumstances, for contributing their proportion to the common defense, and the support of the civil government of each colony." [6] This was the previously discussed proposal of February 20, which said, in effect, we still want the revenue, but you can have the privilege of levying the taxes. The assembly reacted as expected, declaring that offering individual colonies the opportunity to come to terms was an attempt to divide them—which it was. Without a single dissenting vote it decided that "Having weighed and considered this plan with the temper, calmness, and deliberation that the importance of the subject, and the present critical situation of affairs, demand, we are sincerely sorry that *we* cannot think the terms pointed out

[5] Dunmore to Dartmouth, May 15; PRO,CO 5/1353.
[6] *Virginia Gazette* (Pinkney), May 25.

afford a just and reasonable ground for a final accommodation between Great Britain and the colonies." [7]

In Williamsburg the middle of the month saw a return to something approaching the town's normal rural tranquillity. Patrick Henry had gone to Philadelphia, and the confusion over the powder seemed to have run its course. On May 12, the governor felt sufficiently reassured to bring his wife and family back to the palace, an event which Purdie's *Virginia Gazette* noted was "to the great joy of the inhabitants [of Williamsburg], and we make no doubt, of the whole country, who have the most unfeigned regard for her Ladyship, and wish her long to live amongst them." [8] Soon afterwards Captain Stretch and his marines returned to their ship—though not before secretly making some improvements in the security of the public magazine.

Acting on advice from his council, Lord Dunmore issued a proclamation convening the Virginia General Assembly to meet on the first Thursday in June. He had previously prorogued it until September 7; but by that date the Philadelphia Congress would have reached conclusions that would almost certainly make the Virginia Burgesses even more difficult to handle. It was reasonable to expect that a June meeting could attempt to deal with the colony's business without rocking the boat too violently.

That pause before the storm, when the wind drops and the sky seems to lighten, can be relied on to encourage the unwary from their shelters. After the return of his family, Lord Dunmore frequently ventured out from the palace to visit the home of his friend John Randolph a quarter of a mile away. However there is not the slightest reason to suppose that the governor failed to recognize the lull for what it was—though he could hardly have anticipated the storm that broke over the palace on the afternoon of May 22. In the course of a few minutes three hundred odd window-panes were broken, not by

[7] *Virginia Gazette* (Dixon & Hunter), May 20.
[8] *Supplement*, May 12.

irate colonists but by hailstones of prodigious size, some weighing up to an ounce apiece. The storm suddenly appeared out of the northwest, having previously spawned a tornado that had raced through King and Queen County. "It seemed to rise from two thunder clouds meeting in the west;" said an eyewitness, "about one o'clock its course was easterly, and tore up every thing in its way near a quarter of a mile wide. Many poor people have felt its direct effects; no less than eight plantations are swept in as many miles, some not having a house left, 4 persons, viz. a young man, a woman, a boy, and a child in its mother's arms, were crushed to death, and several so much bruised and wounded that their recovery is doubtful. In short, such a scene of horrour and devastation was never seen before by winds in this country." [9]

A week later a black cloud again blew down from the northwest, but this time the storm would not content itself with breaking windows; it would eventually shake Lord Dunmore right out of the palace. It was not so much the cloud itself, but rather the winds that surrounded it that would do the damage. On Tuesday, May 30, Peyton Randolph was on his way back from Philadelphia, having surrendered the chair of the Second Continental Congress to fulfill his duties as Speaker of the Virginia House of Burgesses. Doubtless to his surprise, he was met at Ruffin's Ferry (some thirty miles from Williamsburg) by a detachment of cavalry from the town's volunteers "in their uniforms, well mounted and equipped." Recalling that Peyton Randolph's name figured on General Gage's wanted list, the volunteers expressed their concern for his safety and offered him their services "to be exerted at the expense of every thing a freeman ought to hold dear." At the end of their short formal address they called on heaven to grant Randolph long life, and dubbed him "FATHER OF YOUR COUNTRY AND THE FRIEND TO FREEDOM AND HUMANITY." [1] Randolph's paternity would be short-lived, but it was doubtless gratifying while it lasted.

[9] *Virginia Gazette* (Dixon & Hunter), June 3.
[1] *Virginia Gazette* (Pinkney), June 1.

Classical students might have looked for laurels and a touch of purple as the procession made its way toward Williamsburg. Two miles from the town the procession was joined by a company of infantry, and the whole martial display made its way to Randolph's house on the market square, only a block from the palace. This exhibition, according to the *Virginia Gazette*, "gave great satisfaction to the spectators. The bells began to ring as our worthy delegate entered the city, and the unfeigned joy of the inhabitants, on this occasion, was visible in every countenance; there were illuminations in the evening, and the volunteers with many other respectable Gentlemen, assembled at the Raleigh, spent an hour or two in harmony and cheerfulness, and drank several patriotic toasts." [2]

Meanwhile, Lord Dunmore sat glumly in the palace wondering whether calling the June assembly had been such a good idea after all.

[2] *Virginia Gazette* (Dixon & Hunter), June 3.

[*VI*]

JUNE

The first of June found Nicholas Cresswell struggling upstream against the rapids and currents of the Kentucky river, while in Williamsburg Governor Dunmore was about to be engulfed by the mainstream of public opinion. It was the first day of the general assembly, and his Lordship was due to make the traditional opening speech, a piece of ceremony which in the past had been received with equally traditional acclaim. It would be again, if the governor chose to avoid controversy and agreed to restore the status quo—a synonym for fifteen barrels of gunpowder. But the assembly could not expect that he would do either; and he did not.

The speech was devoted to a review of Lord North's remarkable attempt at conciliation of February 20, the one that had already been rejected by the Pennsylvania Assembly and that Dunmore had told Lord Dartmouth would fare no better in Virginia. Nevertheless he spoke earnestly, if not convincingly, of his hope that nothing would remain "after a just consideration of the nature and tendency of that resolution, to prevent you seriously exerting yourselves to bring the disputes, which have unhappily raged between the mother country and the colonists, to a good end." He assured the burgesses that their "well founded grievances, properly represented, will meet with that attention and regard which are so justly due to them." He told them that there was no thought of treating one colony any differently from another, but that just as they would all share common rights, privileges, and advantages, so they would be asked to give financial support for their governments and common defense. The colonies' civil governments were already maintained; all that was being asked was that they should share with the mother country the cost of securing and maintaining their mutual safety. "No specific sum is demanded of you for these purposes," the governor went on, "that your justice and liberality may be left to their full scope, and that your gift, if you should be induced to offer any, may be, in the completest manner, free." If the assembly would just show the "justice, equity, and moderation" which had prompted the government to make these proposals, all would be well; the halcyon days would dawn again, and they would find that the King had "no object nearer his heart than the peace and prosperity of his subjects in every part of his dominions." [1]

The assembly heard the governor out without any obvious derision; but they must have known that he knew just how hollow the phrases sounded, and what is more he must have known that they knew he knew.

The answer of the assembly would be some days in the making, but it was really unimportant to Lord Dunmore; the longer it took, the longer he could sustain the charade that an agreement would be reached, and the better chance he would have of receiving aid from Boston before it was too late. On the first of June, with the Assembly in session, there was little to be done other than to go home and read the paper, specifically Pinkney's *Virginia Gazette*,[2] fresh from the press. In it he must have found some new information regarding his own activities. Proper names were disguised by the use of only the first and last letters, but it called for little intelligence to read them as Stretch, Sandys, *Fowey*, Montagu[e], York, Majesty's, *Magdalen*, Corbin, (for the next gap choose any appropriate piece of the King's anatomy), Chaplain Gwatkin, council, Wormeley, and palace. This is what it said:

[1] *Virginia Gazette* (Dixon & Hunter), June 3.
[2] June 1.

A correspondent observes that the operations of the campaign are settled; that a certain nominal itinerent governor, who for some time past has been suspected of acting the part of an incendiary in this colony, is to take the field as generalissimo at the head of the Africans; he is to be supported by the bold and daring captain S----h, and *little* lieutenant S---s, with a detachment of *boiled crabs* from his majesty's ship the F---y, the magnanimous captain M----e is to carry on the bombardment of Y--k town, and his m-----'s schooner of war, the M----n, is to cover the landing of the detachment under the gallows, which by some is thought ominous.

Another correspondent observes that R. C----n, junior, is actually appointed powdermonkey to the general, and is soon to embark for London, to kiss his majesty's ---- on his preferment, though some are of opinion that that station will be too hot for his *maccaroni* constitution. The reverend Mr. G----n is to act in the capacity of a spy, he being thought well qualified for that office, as he carries about him much falsehood and treachery, under the deceitful appearance of a *simpleton*. The honourable the c----l are to issue out weekly proclamations against the real and undaunted friends of America, accusing them with a design of overturning the constitution, and branding them with the odious epithets of *rebels;* and R. W-----y, junior, has solicited to be appointed executioner to hang up the *rebellious crew* in half dozens, and expose their estates to public sale.

N.B. The Black Ladies, it is supposed, will be jollily entertained in the p----e.

The nature of the supposed palace entertainment for the "black ladies" has never been revealed; but whatever it was, or was claimed to be, it was still remembered at the end of the year. In a public review of Lord Dunmore's iniquities, Theodorick Bland accused him of providing the Negroes with "convivial banquets, and . . . lewd and nightly orgies within the walls of your palace." [3]

It was true that Dunmore was arming his personal servants

---

[3] *Bland Papers*, 43–44; no date.

and that he had threatened to free all slaves, but he had not freed them yet, and he would undoubtedly avoid doing so as long as other recourses remained open to him. Indeed, in an earlier *Gazette* Pinkney had reported that "We are credibly informed that several negroes made a tender of their services to a certain noble lord when the attack from the west was expected to have been made on his sacred person. It must, however, be observed, to the honour of his lordship, that he threatened them with his severest resentment, should they presume to renew their application." [4]

In the eighteenth century the blade of satire was honed to an edge that has not been matched since, and even if Pinkney's offerings were closer to the cutlass than the rapier, the victims still bled. Shortly after the June 1 *Gazette* came out, a party of marines from the *Fowey* went ashore at Yorktown and destroyed the waterfront gallows, a pointless reaction which delighted the patriots. The next *Gazette* naturally picked it up and dropped a pinch of salt in the wound, informing its readers that "the crew of the F---y have destroyed that ill-boding memento of their merits; but lest they might hope to offend with impunity, they would do well to remember that there are many lofty trees on the banks of the river." [5]

The departure of Richard Corbin, Jr., mentioned in the Pinkney column was hardly news; he had been advertising a phaeton for sale in May, explaining that he was about to leave for Great Britain. The powdermonkey reference almost certainly stemmed from the fact that the Receiver General's son had been staying at the palace. Early in May a rumor had been circulating to the effect that one of the Reverend Thomas Gwatkin's servants had been seized by the watch and found to be carrying a letter to the governor warning him that a plot was being hatched to seize Corbin's son; possibly, we may suppose, in the hope of forcing the Receiver General to surrender Crown

[4] May 4.
[5] Pinkney, June 8.

monies as ransom. The story was loudly denied, and nothing
came of it. Nevertheless, Richard Corbin, Jr., did plan to leave
the country.

The same kidnap rumor probably prompted the Pinkney
comments regarding Gwatkin's descent into the world of espio-
nage. Gwatkin came in for a handsome share of the spring mudslinging, but it is hard to decide whether he was Dunmore's
private Rasputin or simply a clergyman owing allegiance to his
God and to his King. In a letter to the Secretary of State in June
1774 the governor had described Gwatkin (then principal
master of the William & Mary grammar school) as a man "of a
most exemplary good character and great literary abilities."
This letter was now published in the June 8 *Virginia Gazette* [6]
to remind readers that any friend of Dunmore's was no friend of
theirs; nor did the newspapers neglect the attack direct. On May
25 the pseudonymous "Virginius" recalled that five years earlier
Gwatkin had arrived in Virginia "a flaming American patriot . . . a staunch republican, an utter enemy to supremacy,
both in church and state. . . . Behold him now resplendent in
the rays of despotism, a ministerial champion, and pontifex
maximus to his most catholic excellency l--d D-----e. From
such hypocritical priests, good Lord, deliver us." [7] At first
reading this is a straightforward attack on Gwatkin, but is it not
also a smear on the religious beliefs of the governor? It might be
read as such.

The term "catholic" then meant universal, just as it does
now; but as a dictionary of 1671 pointed out "the Title of
Catholick is attributed to the King of *Spain*, as a maintainer of
the Catholick Faith." [8] It is possible then that the *Gazette* writer
was promoting the idea that Lord Dunmore was soft on popery.
If this was the intended inference there is little evidence to
support it, other than Charles Inglis's equivocal comment on
Dunmore's arrival in New York and the fact that Dunmore's

---

[6] Pinkney.

[7] *Virginia Gazette* (Pinkney), May 25.

[8] E. Phillips, *The New World of Words*, London 1671.

father was a leading supporter of the Stuart cause in 1745. But many a politician has been ruined by less.

The governor was, of course, in a much better position to suffer the slings and arrows than were his Virginian friends. It would be unlikely, under the circumstances, that eventual defeat in the colony would be held against him, and when he returned home he would be able to slough off the patriots' mud like last year's skin. But for those whose lives and fortunes were invested in America, there was no such easy and cleansing exit. Hardest hit was the Attorney General. John Randolph, a man of "a most estimable good character," [9] was considered by Dunmore to be the best lawyer in the colony, but ever since he had opposed the assembly's resolves regarding the Stamp Act, he had "been employed but upon very few occasions." In June the governor wrote to Lord Dartmouth on Randolph's behalf saying that "The Fund for the Support of Government Ceases when the exportation of Tobacco Ceases, which is to be after the first of September next, when we shall all be destitute; but the Attorney General, who has little or no private fortune, will be entirely ruined." [1] Dunmore proposed that the Ministry should grant Randolph a salary or pension and added that such a gesture would give encouragement to other supporters of government. He did not say, however, whether he expected the Crown to follow this encouragement with handouts for all.

In the same letter Lord Dunmore offered comments on other members of the council; and, as the lines were being finally drawn at this time, it will be as well to see who stood where. It was a distinctly lopsided roster; the distinguished Virginia names supporting the patriots stretched halfway from Williamsburg to Philadelphia; but those siding with the Crown barely reached from the palace steps to its garden gate, and only a handful of these were scions of old Virginia families: notably Corbin, Randolph, and Ralph Wormeley. The last wrote a private letter to Dunmore in mid-June declaring his loyalty to

[9] "Journal of Augustine Prevost," July 5, 1774.
[1] Dunmore to Dartmouth, June 25; PRO,CO 5/1353.

the Crown, but saying that if his support was not always as vocal as he would wish, it was caused by the fact that he saw no point in aggravating the situation, knowing that his single voice would make no difference to the outcome. He feared for the safety of his family and declared that his stands to date had "drawn on me the popular odium, and my situation, on this account, will be critically dangerous when all the forms (for the essence has long vanished) of the constitution are abandoned." [2] Wormeley had a good deal to lose. His family had built up a large estate in Middlesex County in the seventeenth century, where he now lived in the handsome brick mansion "Rosegill," 87 feet long and 40 wide, with two brick wings extending forward from it another 33 feet on either side. By colonial standards it was a substantial property. In addition he owned quarters elsewhere and was involved in the shipping business. If the patriots should actually decide to fight for independence and, by some improbable chance, should win, he stood to lose the lot. Even if they lost, there was every likelihood that he would be destroyed in the process.

In his letter Lord Dunmore inferred that he could rely to some degree on William Byrd of "Westover" in Charles City County. Byrd was, he felt sure, "averse from the violent proceedings in the Country." Averse he may have been, but that did not necessarily make a reliable supporter. Byrd had inherited one of the richest estates in the colony, and had shown his worth, both in the French and Indian war and by raising and maintaining the Second Virginia Regiment out of his own pocket. But since then his lack of business acumen and penchant for gambling had brought the bottom of the pocket into sight. Even now Byrd continued to sustain a remarkably high standard of living, and, while he might wager what was left on the throw of a dice, he was unlikely to risk it for a principle.

The only other supporter on Dunmore's council was the

[2] Enclosure dated June 22; ibid.

Reverend John Camm, president of the College of William and
Mary, born in England, remembered as the clergy's spokesman
in the furor of the Parson's Cause, and so considered to be "well
effected" toward the government and the Crown. But although
it was generally agreed that he could preach a good sermon, the
very fact that he mounted a pulpit ensured that he could not
enjoy much trust or respect among the patriots. Thus his
support could be more of a liability than an asset. The same, of
course, was true of the Reverend Mr. Gwatkin. Dunmore's only
other supporter and advisor was his Secretary, Captain Edward
Foy. But Foy, like the officers of the ships at Yorktown, was
merely an Englishman on duty in Virginia, and so could have no
favorable influence on the colonists. Indeed, there were those
who thought Foy to be the puppeteer who pulled his Lordship's
strings. Any influence would have to come from Virginians,
from Receiver General Corbin (hated as the symbol of Ministerial taxation), from Attorney General Randolph (rejected as the
prosecutor of English injustice), from Ralph Wormeley (despised as a traitor to his birthplace), or from William Byrd
teetering on the brink of bankruptcy, having "reduced himself
to that Degree by Gameing, that few or nobody will credit him
for ever so small a Summ of Money." [3] As a first team, they left
something to be desired.

The only real help Lord Dunmore could hope for would
have to come from the patriot moderates, specifically from
Thomas Nelson, who was both president of the council and a
respected upholder of American rights. But Dunmore was either
too angry or not bright enough to appreciate what Nelson could
do for him, and in his letter to Lord Dartmouth he claimed that
Mr. Nelson "has shown nothing but a Care to avoid giving
offence either way, and is, from his Capacity and undetermined
Character, Merely incapable of giving any usefull assistance to
his Majesty's Government, in which he enjoys much the best

[3] Goodwin, *Williamsburg*, 224; quoting an anonymous French traveler's journal of 1765.

Office." He was, Dunmore concluded, "a very unfit person in any difficult time." [4]

Up to this point the governor's actions, though perhaps unnecessarily precipitous, can be accepted on the grounds that he was defending what in England today would be termed a rather sticky wicket. But his attack on Nelson, so soon after the latter's invaluable intervention in the Doncastle's Ordinary crisis, can be neither condoned nor reasonably explained.

On Friday, June 2, the House of Burgesses sent the governor a polite little note saying that it was studying his speech and that it would be sending a response in the near future. At the same time the House appointed a committee to draft the reply, choosing Thomas Jefferson, Robert Carter Nicholas, and Thomas Nelson, Jr., among its members. Lord Dunmore must have known that he could not expect his answer until after the week end at the earliest. It was at about this time that he decided to demonstrate his supposed faith in the Burgesses' answer by inviting some of them to dinner. We do not know exactly who was invited, but we do know that they all bit the hand that offered to feed them, and declined.

Saturday brought out another *Virginia Gazette* [5] well laced, as usual, with patriot propaganda and also containing the first details of a major American success at Ticonderoga nearly a month before. The report told how on the night of May 10 a party of some eighty-five men (commanded by Ethan Allen and Colonel Benedict Arnold) crossed the south end of Lake Champlain and in the morning surprised the small British garrison. No sentry saw them coming, and, although the fort gate was securely shut, the wicket was conveniently left open. Uttering their idea of Indian war whoops, the invaders skipped through the little door one by one—and still caught the garrison sleeping. The whole thing took only ten minutes and no one was hurt. At the end of it, Allen and Arnold had won themselves two officers, forty privates, 300 tons of lead shot, ten or twelve

[4] Dunmore to Dartmouth, June 25; PRO,CO 5/1353.
[5] Dixon & Hunter, June 3.

barrels of powder "in bad condition," and nearly two hundred pieces of miscellaneous ordnance. While this spectacular little coup gave the Americans a commanding position at the junction of lakes George and Champlain on the inland water route to Canada, it also gave the Continental Congress a free headache. The troops under Arnold had been raised at the direction of the Provincial Congress of Massachusetts, Allen's men were Green Mountain Boys from the Hampshire Grants with authority from Connecticut, and they had seized a British fort in New York. Now who was to be responsible for it? This problem was causing grave concern in Philadelphia, and some delegates were in favor of giving it back. However, although the *Gazette* report had come from that source, no hint of the controversy came with it. To the average reader, interpretation of the news was delightfully simple: the British had been caught bending. The majority of Virginians had probably never heard of Lake Champlain, and, wherever it was, it was much too far away to merit any loss of sleep over what the next move might be.

Nevertheless there was one man in Williamsburg to whom the news of the loss of Ticonderoga came like a stab in the vitals. He knew exactly where Lake Champlain was, and he had a miserably good idea of what would happen next. The man was Governor Dunmore. You may recall that he had been in the process of acquiring a considerable estate in New York when he had been so inconveniently transferred to Virginia. What neither you nor the majority of Virginians knew was that the largest of his investments bordered on Lake Champlain—to be exact, "51,000 Acres of Land on Otter Creek, Lake Champlain, in the Province of New York, with a number of Settlements on it," [6] and valued at 4s 6d an acre; an investment involving a total of £11,475, the largest single egg in Dunmore's financial nest. If it was not already lost, the capture of Fort Ticonderoga suggested that it would soon be irreparably broken.

[6] "Schedule of Losses Sustained by the Earl of Dunmore, His Majesty's late Governor of the Colony of Virginia," appended to Lord Dunmore's "Memorial" of Feb. 25, 1784; PRO,AO 13/28.

To his Lordship the rest of Saturday's news from New York was equally depressing and served only to heighten his sense of impending disaster. The *Gazette*'s lead story reported that a thousand of New York's prominent inhabitants had signed an Association to be guided by the Continental Congress and by their own Provincial Convention and to take whatever action might be necessary to implement their "resolve never to become slaves." The New York delegates to the congress had asked for advice on how to conduct themselves when the expected British reinforcements arrived. The answer was reported on page two: as long as the troops remained in barracks and made no attempt to erect fortifications or to separate the town of New York from the rest of the province, they should be left alone; but once they invaded private property or made any punitive move, the townspeople should defend themselves and repel force by force. After the attack on Fort Ticonderoga, there could be little hope that the British troops would sit quietly in their barracks.

Other news from the North told of British plans to raise an Indian-supported army in Canada to relieve Boston from the land, and, at the other end of the totem pole, was a report that the Seneca had decided to support the Americans. This last item came from Worcester, Massachusetts, as also did the following rather improbable story: "Some officers in the King's army, it is said, have sworn that the Americans fired first [at Lexington]. Their method of cheating the Devil, we are told, has been by some means brought out. They procured three or four traitors to their God and country, born among us, and took with them, and they fired upon their countrymen, which was immediately followed by the regulars. It is also said these wretches were dressed in soldiers clothing." [7]

It is debatable how many *Gazette* subscribers believed these stories, and it might be argued that, as only the more intelligent section of the population could read, it would also have the intelligence to see them for what they were. Nevertheless, even

[7] *Virginia Gazette* (Dixon & Hunter), June 3.

the most outrageous tales served a useful propaganda purpose in that they would be initially repeated in jest and would then be passed downward verbally until they reached a level that would accept them as fact. Besides, even among the educated, the funny story or obvious lie can be used to titillate deep-seated prejudices, which cannot be reached by reasoned argument. If one happened to be out of step with the policy of one's paper, reading it could be quite a tense experience, for you never could tell where the poisioned barbs might be hidden. On June 3 Catholics and adenoidal Jews got theirs in the gentle "Poets Corner."

> An unbelieving Jew one day
> Was scating o'er the icy way,
> Which being brittle let him in,
> Just deep enough to catch his chin;
> And in that woful plight he hung,
> With only power to move his tongue.
>
> A brother scater near at hand,
> A Papist born in foreign land,
> With hasty strokes directly flew
> To save poor Mordecai the Jew:
> But first, quoth he, I must enjoin
> That you renounce your faith for mine;
> There's no entreaties else will do,
> 'Tis herecy to help a Jew.
>
> "Forswear mine fait! No! Cod forbid!
> Dat would be ferry base indeed.
> Come, never mind such tings as deeze,
> Tink, tink how fary hard it freeze.
> More coot you do, more coot you be;
> Vat signifies your fait to me?
> Come tink agen, how cold and vet,
> And help me out van lettle bit."
>
> By holy mass, 'tis hard, I own,
> To see a man both hang and drown,

And can't relieve him from his plight,
Because he is an Israelite.
The church refuses all assistance,
Beyond a certain pale and distance;
And all the service I can lend
Is praying for your soul, my friend.

"Pray for mine soul! ha! ha!
    you make me laugh;
You petter help me out py half:
My soul I farrant will take care
To pray for her nown self my tear.
So tink a little now for me;
'Tis I am in de hole, not she."

The Church forbids it, friend, and saith,
That all shall die who have no faith.

"Vell! if I must pelieve, I must;
But help me out van little first."

No, not an inch without *Amen*,
That seals the whole—"Vell hear me den:

I hear renounce, for coot and all,
De race of Jews, both great and small;
'Tis de varst trade peneath de sun;
Or varst religion, dat's all vun:
Dey cheat, and get deir living pite,
And lie, and swear de lie is right.
I'll co to mass as soon as ever
I get toder side de river,
So help me out, dow Christian friend,
Dat I may do as I INTEND."

Perhaps you do *intend* to cheat,
If once you get upon your feet?

"No, no, I do intend to be
A *Christian*, such a one as *dee*,"

For thought the Jew, he is as much
A Christian man as I am such.

The bigot Papist joyful hearted,
To hear the heretic converted,
Replied to the *designing* Jew,
"This was a happy fall for you;
You'd better die a Christian now,
For if you live you'll break your vow."
Then said no more, but in a trice
Popp'd Mordecai beneath the ice.

If this was the poem of the week, the book of the week, and apparently a best seller for quite some time, was the *Manual of Military Exercise*. The *Virginia Gazette* [8] advertised that a second edition was now ready and that it could be had for only sevenpence halfpenny. You would have thought, under the circumstances, that anyone who could teach the military arts would be in great demand. The Dinwiddie County Volunteers were even advertising for an instructor. It is surprising, therefore, to find our old friend Dr. Sabbe, the physician and fencing master, packing up and leaving Williamsburg. As he made no mention of quitting the colony, we can only suppose that his pills and epées were not in sufficient demand and that he was taking his odd little practice elsewhere in Virginia.

The fourth of June was Whitsunday, and in England this week end was devoted to fairs and games: cudgeling, wrestling, racing, all the sports that were usually enjoyed in Virginia's "Public Times." Although I have found no descriptions of the entertainments that passed the hours in Williamsburg on this particular week end, there is every reason to suppose that the grim times did not cause them to be canceled. John Harrower noted in his diary for the June 3 that two of his pupils had gone to nearby Fredericksburg "to keep Whitesuntide holliday." [9] The young looked forward to these festivals for months ahead,

[8] Ibid.
[9] *Harrower*, 98.

and, while their parents concerned themselves with business and politics, the boys were free to enjoy their good, clean fun. The pages of history are littered with coincidences, and unrelated events which have inadvertently pulled out the chocks and have sent the tumbrils of disaster on their way. The fact that it was Whitsun in Williamsburg may have served such an end.

In the late hours of Saturday night the sleeping town was brought to its windows by a gun shot, a report allegedly louder than that of a musket. It was followed immediately by a good deal of shouting and yelling from the direction of the market square. Windows were thrown open, shutters flung back, and volunteers bellowed for their breeches. Someone shouted that the British were attacking the magazine, and others came running from the square swearing that it "was full of armed men and that 40 guns had been fired" at a gang of young patriots who had been trying to enter it.

When the senior citizens arrived at the magazine with their torches and lanterns they found one youth shot through the shoulder, another with two fingers blown off his right hand, and a third less seriously hurt; as for the British, none were in sight. The only defender proved to be a spring-gun (probably a short-barreled and wide-gauged shotgun) with a length of string hanging from it—in short, a trap. Another had not been triggered.

The town was beside itself. How could anyone be so fiendish as to set a trap for our sons—our fine, good, clean-living, upstanding lads? Nobody seemed to think that the attempted robbery was a crime, and there was not the slightest embarrassment that Mayor Dixon's son had been one of the ringleaders; nor, for that matter, did anyone admit that spring-guns and mantraps were then accepted devices for protecting one's game from poachers. Although they would be outlawed in England for that purpose in 1827, they are there still permissible as a defense against burglary—and there was really no other word for what the lads of Williamsburg had attempted. But as far as the town was concerned one fact was paramount: Dunmore had sunk to a new low. His own account of the affair varied in some respect from that of the newspapers and patriots—not that that should surprise us. He wrote that only two people were wounded, that the gun was only a musket loaded with large shot, and he placed responsibility for its presence on the shoulders of the Keeper, presumably the recently appointed Mr. Maupin. "The Crime in this Affair was entirely overlooked," he concluded, "but the punishment inflicted, by the hands of the Criminals on themselves irritated very much; and the Cry among the People was for vengeance." [1]

Dr. Philip Mazzei later saw the whole thing quite differently. He was sure that the governor had been hoping for many casualties, "so with the English troops, which were waiting, he could make a raid on the members of the Convention. But Dunmore had a head as weak as his heart. . . . he was unable to accomplish his evil designs." [2] Just how the spring-gun blast at the magazine and the suggested assault on the burgesses were related, or how they could have been coordinated, is far from clear. One supposes that the troops were the unfortunate marines from the *Fowey*, who would be called on to make another of their mad dashes from Yorktown. But regardless of Mazzei's supposed plot, Sunday came and went without any martial noises emanating from the palace. The second gun was found at the magazine and was brought out and shown to the angry citizens, who repeated what they had said the night before, only at greater length. Later, in an address to the governor, the burgesses explained that the heart of their objection to the spring-guns was that "the unfortunate culprit might probably have been hurried into eternity, without a moment's time for reflection." So precipitous a departure would, they contended, "do no great honour to humanity, which we should have supposed would have dictated the necessity of at

[1] Dunmore to Dartmouth, June 25; PRO,CO 5/1353.
[2] Mazzei, "Memoirs," *WMQ*, 2nd ser., II, 171.

least giving public notice that spring guns were prepared and fixed. . . ." [3]

When the assembly met on Monday morning the shot heard round the town was still the principal topic of discussion, and a committee was appointed to inspect the magazine and make recommendations on what should be done to protect it. But at midday, while the assembly was in session, a mob of townspeople converged on the magazine and again broke into it and carried off some four hundred guns. Lord Dunmore contended that some of the burgesses were actually responsible for this new outrage, but when accused they were deeply affronted and reminded him that "the House was sitting, closely engaged in public business, when this affair happened." But they did admit that "Some of our members, as we believe the Truth is, upon hearing what was going forward at the Magazine went up in hopes of preventing it." [4]

In his subsequent report to Lord Dartmouth, Dunmore softened his accusation and said only that the theft of the weapons was carried out "in the presence of several of the Burgesses." [5] If, as Parker of Norfolk contended, Saturday's effort had been led by the son of Mayor Dixon, there is certainly some likelihood that prominent citizens had been behind the Monday reprise when the unfinished rape was consummated. Fifty-eight years later, Robert Greenhow, the seventy-three-year-old son of a once prominent Williamsburg merchant, made a deposition to the effect that in 1775 he had been a member of a volunteer company of boys (captained by fourteen-year-old Henry Nicholson) who had "repaired to the magazine, and armed themselves with the blue painted stock guns, kept for the purpose of distribution among the Indians." [6] Because the

[3] Copy of address by the House of Burgesses enclosed with Dunmore to Dartmouth, June 25; PRO,CO 5/1353.

[4] Ibid.

[5] Ibid.

[6] "The Williamsburg Companies," *Tyler's Quarterly Historical and Genealogical Magazine*, IX, No. 1 (July 1927) (Richmond, 1928), 46–47.

Saturday attempt had been thwarted by the spring-gun, it must be assumed that Greenhow and his friends in arms were involved in Monday's theft; but whether they thought it up on their own over the Whitsun holiday or simply took advantage of an opportunity already created by others, we shall never know. There is little doubt, however, that Greenhow's story was true, for his recollection of having carried off Indian trade guns is borne out by evidence which I shall come to in a moment. However, it is probable that the boys were not the instigators of the affair, for in their statement to the governor, the burgesses said only that "sundry Persons unknown to us broke open the Magazine." [7] Had they known that it was the work of boys and youths, that fact would surely have been mentioned—if only in an attempt to laugh the whole thing off as a prank.

The question of the other responsibility, that of placing the spring-gun, must, I think, rest with Lord Dunmore. The general consensus was that the installation was the work of marines from the *Fowey* during their May sojourn at the palace; and that was probably the truth of it. Although Dunmore may not have specifically ordered that the building should be booby trapped, it is almost certain that he would have been told that it had been done. The fact that he did not order the guns' removal therefore left him with the responsibility for the outcome.

On the Monday afternoon, the assembly's Magazine Committee went to the palace, saw Lord Dunmore, explained their duties, and asked for a key to the magazine. Slightly to their surprise, he received them cordially and told them that while he did not personally have a key to give them, he would be glad to get one for them. The committee thanked the governor for his cooperation and departed, thoughtfully leaving a written copy of their request behind them. If they expected to be sent the key that evening, they were disappointed. Next morning there was still no sign of it, and the committee then sent its chairman, John Mercer, to remind Dunmore of his promise. When Mercer

----

[7] *JHB*, 193; June 6.

reached the palace he was peremptorily informed that his Lordship had nothing to say to him, and referred him to a note which was about to be sent to the House.

When the note eventually arrived there was no key attached; instead the negotiations had been set back to the beginning, Dunmore apparently professing ignorance of what had passed the previous afternoon. "I have received a Paper," he wrote, "without date or Signature, desiring I would direct the keeper of the Magazine, to give Access to some Persons, I know not whom, the Paper not saying who they [are], appointed by the House of Burgesses a Committee to examine into the State of the public Magazine. I send the said Paper, for the inspection of the House; and beg to be informed, whether the Persons, there alluded to, are authorized, as therein allowed, to desire Access to the Magazine." [8]

Everyone knew perfectly well that the committee was fully known to Dunmore (it included Mercer, Jefferson, Nelson, and Page, as well as many other prominent Virginians), and, as the note left by the committee was merely an abstract of their verbal request, they had thought it unnecessary to sign it. What, you may well ask, was Dunmore trying to achieve? There was nothing to be gained by stalling, and if there had been it could have been accomplished in a much more adult manner. The only explanation seems to be that he resented the fact that, after his responsive reception of the committee, it felt it necessary to put its request in writing, so casting doubt on the governor's reliability. If this is the answer, then Dunmore is revealed as a man who could be irritated into rash and petty actions. It is conceivable, though not likely, that he was actually a great deal more clever than one might suppose and that he was attempting to turn the burgesses into a pack of eighteenth-century Pavlovian dogs. One might thus explain the fact that later on the same day he sent another missive to the House, a statement of his motives for removing the powder that was almost cloyingly

[8] Ibid.

servile. He repeated that the barrels came from the *Rippon* man-of-war but said that he only shifted them because he considered the magazine insecure. "I was influenced in this by the best Motives," he assured the members, "and as I have once ventured, and if occasion Offered should again venture my Life in the Service of this Country, I had hopes the most favourable Construction would have been put upon my Conduct." He ended by saying: "I do promise you that as soon as I see the Magazine in a proper State for securing the Powder and other public Stores, I will replace it, and at all times be ready most willingly to do everything my poor Abilities are capable of for the benefit of this Colony, in which I have lived till of late in the greatest happiness." [9]

The burgesses did not know where they were; at one moment their governor was being so impossibly difficult that serious negotiations seemed almost a waste of effort, and the next he appeared to be offering grounds for conciliation. Then, just as the House seemed inclined to give Dunmore the benefit of the doubt, it received a message from the council, which was in session upstairs, telling them that a report was circulating that Dunmore had again sent for the marines, and that "Capt. Collins of the Magdalen had slipd his cable and was come up the River with a number of boats in which there were said to be a hundred armed men at least." [1] No one could imagine what had provoked this move, but the townspeople "were determined to attack the said Marines and Sailors, if they should come." [2] Again the colony appeared to be on the brink of a direct confrontation. The baffled assembly sent two envoys hurrying to the palace, Richard Corbin and Robert Carter, and they were received by Lord Dunmore with what appeared to be genuine surprise. He declared that he had no knowledge of any troops on their way from Yorktown and that he certainly had not sent for them. However, if they should appear, he assured his visitors

[9] Ibid., pp. 194–5.
[1] Dunmore to Dartmouth, June 25; PRO,CO 5/1353.
[2] *JHB*, 198; June 15.

that he would send them straight back. Once more that day the
assembly was left not knowing who or what to believe.

It would be misleading to let you suppose that the assembly's deliberations were wholly devoted to a game of
blindfolded political snakes and ladders. On the contrary, most
of their business was typical of the matters that had been
brought before it throughout the colonial years; land disputes,
people petitioning for compensation for slaves killed while in
court custody, applications for franchises. On this chaotic
Tuesday in the House of Burgesses the position of public printer
was up for grabs, and the publishers of the three *Virginia
Gazettes* were the contestants, Messrs. Purdie, Pinkney, and
Dixon and Hunter.

Following the usual procedure when more than two names
were involved, the Clerk and Sergeant at Arms carried two
glasses, one to each side of the House, and into them the
burgesses placed ballots marked with the name of the printer of
their choice. When the ballots were counted, Dixon and Hunter
had twelve, Pinkney thirty-four, and Purdie forty-four. The
choice lay between Pinkney and Purdie, and the procedure now
was that the House would divide, Pinkneys to the left, and
Purdies to the right. Purdie won, forty-seven to forty-three.

You may wonder why I have broken the thread of the
otherwise fast-moving major events to inject an item of perfectly
ordinary assembly procedure. There are two reasons: first, as I
have already indicated, we should not lose sight of the fact that
in spite of the members' fears and excitement, and regardless of
the commotion going on outside, the House of Burgesses
continued its scheduled business; and second, the appointment
of the public printer clearly demonstrated the political standing
of the three newspapers. Purdie was the patriots' choice, as was
emphasized by loyalist Parker in his letter of June 12 reporting
his version of "the affair of the SpringGuns which you will see
misrepresented by that Miscreant Purdie." [3] Pinkney was al-

[3] Parker to Steuart, June 12; CSP.

most as acceptable to the patriots, leaving Dixon and Hunter trailing far behind. The soundness of the assembly's estimate would eventually be demonstrated when Hunter left the paper to fight for the Crown. There is also a third factor that makes the printer vote important; it might provide a pretty fair count of the burgesses' own political positions: 13 per cent loyal to the Crown, 38 per cent patriotic moderates in the mold of Peyton Randolph and Thomas Nelson, and 49 per cent ready to go all the way with Patrick Henry. By this yardstick the chances for a peaceful accommodation in Virginia were thin indeed.

The final item of Tuesday's session brought back attention to the current crisis, the House directing Captain Innes, commander of the city volunteers, to mount a guard at the magazine and to maintain it until instructed by the assembly to withdraw. This move was justified on the grounds that in addition to the public arms, the magazine contained a quantity of the copper halfpennies so recently issued in the colony. This was the first time that any mention had been made of any money being stored in the building; but whether it was there or not, the mounting of a guard would seem to have been a reasonable, if belated, move. It was not the first time a patriot guard had been placed on the building; but before it had been mounted by the City—now it was a military undertaking authorized by the Assembly, without the authority of the supreme military commander, the governor. Here was the rub, and it rubbed Lord Dunmore quite the wrong way. It could have no other interpretation than that the "Command of Militia, as well as the Custody of Magazines and publick Stores of Arms and Ammunition is thus entirely wrested out of the hands of the Governor." [4] Furious though he was, Lord Dunmore did not immediately voice his objections; on the contrary, his dealings with the assembly on Wednesday, June 7, were markedly cordial.

At the opening of the day's session, beginning as usual at ten in the morning, the House of Burgesses studied Lord

---

[4] Dunmore to Dartmouth, June 25; PRO,CO 5/1353.

Dunmore's conciliatory message regarding the powder and drafted a reply commending his role in the 1774 war with the Indians and declaring that it did "sincerely lament that any event should suspend the happiness which his Lordship hath enjoyed among us." [5] The House also resolved to convert itself into a full committee to study his opening address along with the address of the Lords and Commons of February 7, and Lord North's conciliatory resolution of the twentieth. The burgesses' business was later interrupted by another message from the palace, Lord Dunmore's reply to their explanation regarding the unsigned request for a magazine key. No doubt many members expected that having deliberately exacerbated palace–assembly relations yesterday, he would follow through in the same vein today. But no; the message was that of a man wounded, saddened at his sorry treatment, but turning another cheek just the same. He considered that the Magazine Committee's failure to sign their request represented a lack of courtesy. Just, he said, "as I would by no means infringe any Rule of, or omit any Ceremony due to your House, I could not but expect to be treated with the same attention; and to give you proof of my desire to avoid every kind of controversy, I have ordered the Key of the Magazine to be delivered to the Committee, appointed by your Order of Monday." [6] Thus, without further ado, the committee got its key.

Shortly afterwards the task of preparing an inventory of the magazine's contents began, and this is what it held:

. . . nineteen Halberts, one hundred and fifty seven Trading Guns [presumably the residue of the blue-painted-stock guns left behind by Greenhow and his friends] in pretty good order, but very indifferent in kind, fifty one Pewter Basons, eight Camp Kettles, one hundred and eighty new Muskets without Locks, about five hundred and twenty seven old Muskets, the barrels very rusty, and the locks almost useless, twelve hundred Cartouch boxes, fifteen hundred Cutlasses

5 *JHB*, 199.
6 Ibid., 201.

with Scabbards, one hundred and seventy Pistol Holsters, one hundred and fifty old Pistols, or thereabouts, with and without Locks, fifty Mallets, two bundles of Match Rope, two hundred Cantines, thirty five small Swords in bad order, one Tent and Tent Poles, one Hogshead of Powder Horns, one hundred and twenty seven Bayonets, one hundred Knapsacks in the Smiths Shop, and that part of the Magazine called the Armory, also one half Barrel of Dust and rotten Powder, one half barrel and a quarter of unsifted Powder, tolerably good, in the Powder Room, that has no communication with the Armory, also five half Barrels of loose Powder buried in a Hole in the Magazine Yard, the top of which, (in quantity about two half Barrels) was totally destroyed by the late Rains, the rest very damp, but quite sound." [7]

It was the committee's considered opinion that there was little in the magazine that was worth guarding. As no mention of the copper money appeared in the inventory, we can only suppose that it had been withdrawn to some other safer repository or that it was never in the magazine at all. The only positive result of the inspection was that a rumor circulated through Williamsburg that the buried powder in the yard was linked to a subterranean fuse running to the palace, which in an emergency "would blow up the town in an instant." [8] The plot was considered particularly cunning in that the diabolical governor knew that if the alarm were sounded the volunteer company would muster at the magazine and so could be destroyed in one flick of the flint.

There can be no doubt that Williamsburg was now a singularly edgy and nervous town. You had only to shout at your dog to bring fifty volunteers to arms, or drop a cup to send half the neighbors running for cover. It mattered little that most of the tension was of the patriots' own making. The ogre in the palace and the Mephistophelean "boiled crabs" from Yorktown were expected to leap out at any moment. Nevertheless, the "diabolical" governor received a representative of the House of

[7] Ibid., 223–4; June 13.
[8] *Virginia Gazette* (Pinkney), June 8.

Burgesses without exhibiting his horns, and, on being asked
when it would be his pleasure to receive an address from the
assembly regarding some of the matters raised in his opening
speech, he advised that he would be pleased for the House to
attend him "tomorrow, at one of the Clock in the afternoon, in
the Council Chamber." [9] That evening he made his way openly
through the town to the house of John Randolph, a route he had
taken a number of times in recent weeks.

We do not know what the governor and the Attorney
General discussed, but it was seemingly merely a social visit,
and Dunmore apparently gave no hint that it was to be the last.
Yet at two o'clock the next morning he, his wife and family,
Captain Foy, and a handful of personal servants left the palace
for Yorktown and the *Fowey*. He would not be back. No one
saw them go, at least no one who was saying anything; and
when the House of Burgesses commenced its business on
Thursday morning it fondly believed that it would be delivering
its address to the governor at one. But when the council
assembled (presumably later than the burgesses) it found a
message of explanation waiting, along with the request that the
message should be sent downstairs. It began as follows:

Mr. Speaker, and Gentlemen of the House of Burgesses,
    Being now fully pursuaded that my Person, and those of
my Family likewise, are in constant danger of falling sac-
rifices to the blind and unmeasurable fury which has so
unaccountably seized upon the minds and understanding of
great numbers of People, and apprehending that at length
some of them may work themselves up to that pitch of
daringness and atrociousness as to fall upon me, in the
defenceless state in which they know I am in the City of
Williamsburg, and perpetrate Acts that would plunge this
Country into the most horrid calamities, and render the
breach with the mother Country irreparable, I have thought
it prudent for myself, and serviceable for the Country, that I
remove to a place of safety; comformable to which, I have

[9] *JHB*, 202.

fixed my residence for the present on board his Majesty's
Ship the *Fowey*, lying at York.[1]

He went on to say that the assembly should continue about its
business and that it should send down some of its members to
Yorktown from time to time to keep him informed.

The House was stunned; it spoke of "This extraordinary
Step, which none could account for . . . and we believe would
surprise the whole World, were they acquainted with it." [2] As
the news spread, the town stood gaping in astonishment, and
that astonishment lingers on to this day. It is not that Dunmore
retreated to a ship that surprises (such a recourse had probably
been in his mind since the meeting with Governor Martin at
Christmas), it is simply the timing that astounds us. Why now?
The town was tense, but not enough to prevent him from
venturing out to visit John Randolph. In its response the
assembly declared that "The City was again at rest and
continued composed, till they heard of your Lordship's removal
with your family in the *dead of night*," [3] and Randolph would
later testify that in his visits, Dunmore "received no insult as he
knows of, in passing to and from thence." [4] The most likely
place to find the truth should be in the governor's report to the
Secretary of State, but it merely repeats the fears voiced in his
message to the assembly.

It has been suggested that Dunmore may have been advised
by Randolph that the House was about to reject the Crown's
conciliatory proposals. But would that have sent him running
out into the night? He had written to Lord Dartmouth preparing
him for a "No" vote last month. Besides, the burgesses'
committee had adjourned until Thursday with its work unfinished, work which would, as it turned out, stretch through
into Friday and Saturday. If it was the assembly's rejection that
Dunmore feared, he must have known from Randolph that its

[1] Ibid., 206.
[2] Enclosed in Dunmore to Dartmouth, June 25; PRO,CO 5/1353.
[3] Ibid.
[4] *JHB*, 232; June 14.

publication was not likely to appear in a matter of hours.

Another possibility is that something happened on his Lordship's way home after leaving Randolph's house. But if he had been stoned or had received warning of an impending attack on the palace, he would certainly have mentioned it in his report to London. Then again there is a possible private reason that could not be reported, a pressure of which even the patriots were unaware. The clue to it is to be found in James Parker's letter of June 29, in which he speaks of Lord Dunmore's newly christened daughter saying "Lady Virginia is driven out of her Country before she is done Sucking; tis said the Countess is again Pregnant." [5] Is it not possible that when Dunmore returned home that evening he found his wife on the verge of a breakdown, and that she told him that she could not, and would not, stay another day in Williamsburg? Previously, of course, the family had taken shelter on the *Fowey* while the governor remained at the palace. But if Lady Dunmore's mental and physical health were now involved, it would be necessary for her husband to go with her. To have admitted this to have been the reason for leaving the palace would have been out of the question; it would have been interpreted—and rightly—as deserting his post in favor of his wife's well being. If the colony should be lost, the blame would almost certainly be laid at the door of the diplomat who fled when diplomacy was the only weapon in the Crown's Virginia arsenal. At this point the explanation is pure conjecture, but its validity would be considerably strengthened if, later in the year, Lady Dunmore should give birth to another child. In the meantime the theory's only substance lies in its ability to fit tidily into a framework of otherwise inexplicable events.

It is very tempting to dig deep into our box of clichés and to describe Lord Dunmore's flight as the beginning of the end or the end of the beginning, depending on one's loyalist or patriot sympathies. But in reality I doubt whether it made any real

[5] Parker to Steuart, June 12; CSP.

difference. On the contrary, Dunmore was right when he claimed that the palace was indefensible; if open warfare erupted, the geography of Tidewater Virginia and the small force at his disposal would give him no alternative but to rely on the Navy. His intention to withdraw had already been transmitted to London, and it was only a matter of time before it would be forced upon him. Admittedly his sneaking away like a vampire before the dawn provided ammunition for patriot propagandists; but to have made his departure an occasion for a show of force, with drums beating and colors flying, would probably have ended in bloodshed. The military pomp would, in any case, be more effective if reserved for his return, and there were those who were sure it would not be long delayed. "By the Papers You would judge us to be a Warlike people," wrote Parker from Norfolk, "believe me tis all Bully, & Calculated to figure on paper, private injuries they may do, but that will be all & I still am of opinion when General Gage begins to Act on the offensive, the Rebellion will be immediately Crushed." [6]

The days following the governor's departure were filled with jubilation, salted here and there with just a pinch of uneasiness. Hotheaded shirtmen saw only an abandoned seat of British authority, but the more responsible elements looked for an explanation and were disturbed when they could find none. The *Virginia Gazette* [7] of June 10 conveniently produced a correspondent in London who claimed that Lord Dunmore's Christmas letter to the Secretary of State had contained secret passages which were not included in the papers laid before parliament. The correspondent claimed that in this secret missive Dunmore had advised that the colony's unrest should be allowed to blossom and that the King should order the withdrawal of all the Crown officers. Left to themselves, the colonists would soon divide into opposing factions, and before long the wealthy landowners would be pleading with Britain to return in sufficient strength to restore order and the status quo.

[6] Ibid.
[7] Dixon & Hunter.

This ingenious ruse was not mentioned in relation to Lord Dunmore's flight; but that was hardly necessary.

The same newspaper provided two items of maritime news, announcing the arrival of the *Cerberus* at Boston, with its valuable supply of generals, and of the sloop of war *Otter* in Hampton Roads. The latter carried what was, to Lord Dunmore, a most acceptable cargo—a letter from General Gage advising that military reinforcements would shortly be on their way. However, it was rumored in Williamsburg that dispatches brought from Boston aboard the *Otter* had been delivered to the governor on Monday, June 5, and that it was their contents that made him decide to leave town. But odd though Dunmore's actions undoubtedly were during that week, they gave no hint of his impending departure, nor, for that matter, did his subsequent reports refer to the influence of Boston dispatches on his decision. Besides, the good news of his impending reinforcement should logically have caused him to play for more time. The military aid would not be much, but certainly better than nothing, comprising sixty men from the Fourteenth Regiment of Foot to come from St. Augustine in Florida, plus an additional company of the same regiment then stationed on the island of Providence. Of more immediate encouragement was the armed presence of the *Otter* herself, a valuable addition to Lord Dunmore's infant fleet. She dropped anchor in the York river on Saturday, June 10, and at 11 A.M., his Lordship was received aboard with a fifteen-gun salute.

Because through the rest of the year we shall be concerned with ships of various types and sizes, it may be well to pause here long enough to consider the differences between them in so far as they relate to the story of Virginia in 1775. They fall initially into three groups: warships, merchantmen, and a combination of both, which, in order of increasing size, were the cutter, sloop, schooner, brig, brigantine, snow, and ship. Unfortunately this is a wild oversimplification, as is readily apparent when one reads an advertisement in a 1768 *Virginia Gazette* offering a newly built, 176-ton hull for sale and declaring it to be suitable for rigging as a "ship, snow or brig as best suites the purchaser." [8] Thus the names more often referred to the style of rigging than to the shape or size of the hulls. It seems fair, however, to state that cutters and sloops invariably had one mast, that schooners, brigs, brigantines, and snows had two, and that ships had three.

The most frequently used term in describing the naval affairs of the months to come was the word "tender," referring not to any specific class of vessel, but to any smaller craft which served a larger. Thus a cutter could act as a tender for a sloop, while a brig could be similarly termed while serving a rated man-of-war. British naval ships were classified by rate, i.e., first through sixth rates, the rating being dependent on the number of guns carried by the vessels. First raters mounted 100 or more, while the smallest sixth rater carried from 20 to 28. Of seventeen ships in Admiral Graves's British fleet in the spring of 1775, eleven were sixth raters, and his largest were two third raters mounting from 64 to 80 guns apiece, one of which vessels, the *Somerset*, was said by Graves to be unfit to put to sea.

A study of Virginia shipbuilding in the years immediately preceding the Revolution [9] has shown that the average cargo capacity of the vessels launched were as follows: sloop, 31 tons; schooner, 34; brig, 76; snow, 105; and ship, 165. But the craft on which these averages are based varied widely within their classes, sloops ranging from 12 tons to 66 at the lower end of the scale, to ships (at the other) running from 80 to 305 tons. Although this last was the largest vessel built in Virginia in this period, it was really quite small. Merchantmen built in England for the East India trade had a capacity of about 800 tons, while men-of-war of the first rate ran to 2,000 or more tons.

Records of the complements of vessels of the various sizes

[8] *Virginia Gazette* (Purdie & Dixon), Sept. 29, 1768.

[9] William Kelso, "Shipbuilding in Virginia, 1763–1774," unpublished M.A. thesis, History Department, College of William and Mary, 1964.

and classes are few and confusing. In the first place, one can never be quite sure what was meant by a crew. To read, for example, that a certain snow had a crew of eleven sailors would not necessarily tell us how many men were aboard. The term "sailor" was more specific than it often is today; it referred to an elder seaman "employ'd in ordering the Sails, setting the Tacks on board, and steering the Ship." [1] In addition to a crew of sailors, there would be a boatswain's crew, a carpenter's crew, and a gunner's crew—all together, these often comprised a very large number of men. According to Chambers's *Cyclopaedia*,[2] the sizes of sailing crews were related to the capacity of the vessel gauged in lasts, or two-ton units. Thus a brig in the 40 to 50 last range (80 to 100 tons) would carry seven sailors and a swabber, plus another sailor for every additional ten lasts.

Lord Dunmore's newly arrived sloop-of-war *Otter* mounted 14 guns and may have had a deck length of about 90 feet. Its value lay in its shallow draft and navy complement that made it ideal for sorties up the rivers of Tidewater or for fast interception in the Chesapeake Bay. Along with the *Otter* had come the schooner *Arundle*, but nothing is known of its size or armament; the same is true of the *Magdalen*, though we do know that she carried a crew of sixty. Fortunately we fare considerably better with the *Fowey;* she was built in 1749 as a frigate of 513 tons and carried a complement of about 160 men. She was a sixth rater mounting either 20 or 24 guns, the first figure was given when a set of plans were drawn of her at Sheerness in 1772. Later, however, the zero was changed to a four. Although the Sheerness measured drawings do not include a sheer plan for the *Fowey*, they do include a plan for the entire class, which identifies most of the cabins and thus helps us to determine the amount of accommodation available for the governor and his family. Captain Montagu's cabin was located, as were all captains' quarters, at the stern, beneath the quarter deck. The plan shows two cabins forward of it, and these were presumably also used by Montagu.

[1] Bailey, *Dictionary.*
[2] Vol. I, 2nd ed., 1738.

We may suppose that he vacated all of them when Lord Dunmore took up residence. Beneath these quarters, on the lower deck, were, to starboard, the cabins of the purser, Lieutenant of Marines (Capt. Stretch), the master, and the boatswain. On the port side were those of the surgeon, the Lieutenant (Lieut. Sandys), the gunner, and the carpenter. Below these, and above the bilge and ballast, were, on the starboard side, the bread room, steward's room, and marines' clothing store; to port, the magazine, captain's storeroom, and lieutenant's storeroom. The magazine was approached by a small antechamber marked as "Passage to the Magazine," forward of which was a much larger area marked "Filling Room," where the ammunition was assembled. At the same level, below the forecastle, were the sail room, the boatswain's, gunner's, and carpenter's storerooms, and the galley. The crewmen and marines would have been housed in hammocks slung on the lower deck, as would a few of their superiors. A sixth rater of 24 guns normally carried one lieutenant, two master's mates, four midshipmen, one surgeon's mate, four quartermasters and their mates, one boatswain's mate and one yeoman, one gunner's mate and one yeoman, six or seven quarter gunners, and one purser's steward.

When the Earl and Countess arrived aboard the *Fowey* with three large boys, three blooming girls, one infant, Captain Foy, the Reverend Mr. Gwatkin, and assorted servants, Captain Montagu must have been forced into a quite agonizing reappraisal of his quartering. At the same time, Dunmore must have realized that he needed the good will of every last British officer and seaman and that the wholesale commandeering of cabins would endear him to no one.

We can only surmise how the game of musical cabins was played, but it was inevitable that at least one senior crew member ended up without a cabin at all. The governor probably took the captain's cabin, put his daughters in one of the antechambers, and his three sons plus the Reverend Gwatkin in the other. Captain Foy may have shared with Captain Stretch, and Captain Montagu may have ousted Lieutenant Sandys, who in turn would have ejected the purser or surgeon—and so on down the ranks.

The captain's cabin was almost certainly as well furnished as many a living room ashore. For a man, even a landsman, such quarters plus the deference due to a commander in chief could have provided a reasonably pleasant milieu. But for a woman accustomed to the space and comforts of a mansion, the smell of pitch and hemp, the damp, the constant lapping of the water and the creaking of yards, and rigging, not to mention the proximity of none-too-refined seamen, must have combined to ensure that the *Fowey* was a place not in the least like home. Lady Dunmore was no stranger to life on shipboard, and lying at anchor in the York presented none of the hazards of an ocean voyage. But the situation now was different, the cabins seemed smaller and the headroom lower; the Countess and her family were virtually prisoners, and there was no foreseeable or conceivably honorable end to their confinement.

In the joint address of the council and burgesses, which was made public in the June 10 *Gazette*,[3] both houses urged Lord Dunmore to return and spoke specifically of the hardship to which his wife must be subject. "It is with much anxiety," they said, "we consider the very disagreeable situation of your Lordship's most amiable Lady and family, and should think ourselves happy in being able to restore their perfect tranquility, by removing all their fears." Later, after Dunmore had rejected the assembly's assurances of safety, it again declared itself to be most sensible of "the disagreeable situation your excellent Lady must be in," adding: "But, if, after all, your Lordship is determined to persist in your Resolution of Absence, we must endeavour to rest satisfied; conscious that, whilst we have been solicitous to do justice to our Constituents and ourselves, we have not been wanting in the Respect which is due to the Representative of our most gracious Sovereign." [4]

[3] Dixon & Hunter.
[4] *JHB*, 262; June 19.

In the message to the assembly which the governor had left
behind him, he had requested that members should wait upon
him aboard the *Fowey* to report on the progress of their
business. The assembly considered this most inconvenient and
announced that it could not carry on its affairs with "any
tolerable degree of propriety" under such conditions. Nevertheless, it did appoint a deputation of two council members and
four burgesses to go to Yorktown to present the address. The
reticence of the assembly to approach the spider's web was
increased by a fast-circulating rumor that any burgesses who
ventured aboard the *Fowey* would find themselves whisked
away to England to stand trial as traitors.

The rest of June was punctuated with verbal cannonading
between the Capitol and the *Fowey*, with penned missiles
speeding in clouds of dust along the dry and unpaved road
between Williamsburg and Yorktown. The only really important shot was prepared by Thomas Jefferson; after that had
landed nothing else made any difference.

On Saturday, June 10, Jefferson's work on the assembly's
reply to Lord Dunmore's opening speech was completed, read,
and approved. It claimed to have examined the Ministry's
conciliation proposals "in every point of light in which we were
able to place it," but found that "with pain and disappointment
we must ultimately declare it only changes the form of oppression, without lightening its burden."

The address, which was dispatched to the governor, told
him that the House of Burgesses considered that it had done
everything in its power to seek a happy ending to the dispute.
"We have wearied our King with supplications; he has not
deigned to answer us; we have appealed to the native honour
and justice of the British nation; their efforts in our favour have
been hitherto ineffectual. What then remains to be done? That
we commit our injuries to the evenhanded justice of that Being,
who doeth no wrong; earnestly beseaching him to illuminate the
councils and prosper the endeavours of those to whom America

hath confided her hopes." [5] The assembly concluded by expressing wishes that even yet all would be well, but historian Burk
later dismissed those sentiments saying, "This latter was a
matter of mere form, as we have just seen them solumnly
appeal, and deliberately consign their cause to the God of
battles." [6]

The next day Jefferson left Williamsburg, bound for Philadelphia and carrying with him a copy of the assembly's
resolution to be laid before the Continental Congress. It would
be the second such rejection of Lord North's olive branch. Lord
Dunmore did not comment until June 16—after all, there was
not much that he could say or needed to say. Burk described the
answer as laconic; it read: "Gentlemen of the House of Burgesses—It is with real concern I can discover nothing in your
address that I think manifests the smallest inclination to, or will
be productive of, a reconciliation with the mother country. —
Dunmore." [7]

Until his troops arrived, Lord Dunmore was unable to do
anything more than be difficult in his dealings with the assembly, but the burgesses, on the other hand, went militantly about
their business of whipping up enthusiasm for the cause. On the
afternoon of Monday June 12, a committee of burgesses met in
a room at Mr. Southall's tavern in Williamsburg, where they
interrogated some twenty-four leading inhabitants of Norfolk
and Suffolk counties. Among those ordered to attend were such
names as Neil Jamieson and Andrew Sprowle, men whose
positions would become more clearly defined in the months
ahead. Details of the meeting survive only in a copy of the
proceedings enclosed in Lord Dunmore's dispatch to Lord
Dartmouth of June 25; [8] but it is clear that the heart of the
business was a series of ten heavily loaded questions, questions
which, in Dunmore's opinion, revealed "the malignity of the

[5] *Virginia Gazette* (Dixon & Hunter), *Supplement*, June 17.

[6] Burk, *History of Virginia*, IV, 33.

[7] *Virginia Gazette* (Dixon & Hunter), *Supplement*, June 17.

[8] Dunmore to Dartmouth, June 25; PRO,CO 5/1353.

house." Number one asked the men to consider the state of the country prior to the seizure of the powder, to which the respondents agreed that there was a "general acquiescence in the Resolves of the General and Provincial Congresses." The sixth question asked "Whether the declaration of the Governor to give freedom to the Slaves, has not been also a cause of the late disturbances, and a means of encreasing and continuing the commotion in this colony?" Only one answer could have been expected of such a question, but it was not the one it produced. The gentlemen of Norfolk and Suffolk scratched under their wigs, thought a while, and finally decided that they had "no knowledge of any declaration made by the Governor to liberate the slaves but from hearsay"; nor did they "know of any commotion having been occasioned in our parts of the Country by the Governor's declaration." The right answer to the tenth question was equally obvious. "Do you think a redress of the present grievances would establish a perfect tranquility throughout the colony, and produce a reconciliation with the parent state?" With ponderous logic they answered that as no commotion had occurred in their counties, they were in no position to reply to the question. We do not know who thought up this political quiz, but all it revealed was that some Virginians were either too stupid or too honest to be managed into responding to leading questions.

Lord Dunmore meanwhile was concerned with a question that could lead him into more problems, no matter which way he answered it. What was he to do with the Countess and the rest of his family? The assembly was perfectly right, conditions aboard the *Fowey* were totally inadequate. The obvious answer was to send them home, yet to do so would mean publicly accepting the proposition that the status quo could not be restored. Furthermore, Lady Dunmore had always been popular in the colony—as patriots had been at pains to point out in tones that inferred a strongly odious comparison. Her departure now would remove the last ties of affection that linked the Dunmore name with Virginia. The key to the question was whether or not this mattered any more. By June 16 Lord Dunmore had made up his mind, and he asked Captain Montagu to send the *Magdalen* to England with his dispatches—at least, that was the reason given in the admiralty report. She would also carry Lady Dunmore, her family, the Reverend Mr. Gwatkin, and another loyalist member of the college faculty.

On June 10 Dunmore had sent the assembly a lengthy recapitulation of all that had led up to the present crisis, as seen from his point of view. After ruminating on this for a while the House of Burgesses, on June 19, rehashed the story from theirs, using every possible device to spit with dignity into the gubernatorial eye. They spoke of Lord Dunmore's illustrious and dead predecessor, Lord Botetourt, recalling his diplomacy, his tact and benevolence, calling him the provider of the Colony's "Tranquility and Happiness." They described this paragon as having come to them straight from the King's "immediate Presence," an obvious reference to Lord Dunmore's circuitous and reluctant approach via the governorship of New York. He was, they seemed to suggest, not only a second-hand product, but one who did not have the ear of the King. The House of Burgesses' attacks were not confined to the safety of insinuation; the address also offered insolently direct advice: "Respect, my Lord, is not to be obtained by Force, from a free People. If genuine, it must be a perfect Volunteer; and nothing is so likely to ensure it, to one in your Station, as Dignity of Character, a candid and exemplary Conduct." [9]

This lengthy address had taken some five days to prepare, and in the process its creators had talked themselves into a fine lather of self-justification. But like Lord Dunmore's of June 10, it served no useful purpose other than adding another nail to a coffin already studded to the point of splitting. However, on the same day that the address was completed, the burgesses took a step of a much more practical nature. They gave their approval to three acts of the Continental Congress, banning exports to

[9] *JHB*, 253–4.

British possessions north and south of the colonial mainland, banning the sending of supplies to Nantucket, and, most important on the local scene, decreeing that no bills or drafts were to be cashed for British officers and that no British transport or store ships were to be provisioned.

Two days earlier, the council had been pushed by the burgesses into suggesting to Lord Dunmore that he should return the gunlocks missing from the magazine in Williamsburg. It was also resolved that the governor should be called upon to supply compensatory arms and powder, as there was again fear of a slave or Indian rising. The arms, it was suggested, could very well be supplied from those still in the palace. To this Dunmore replied that he had not the slightest intention of returning anything to the magazine, and as far as the arms were concerned, the palace was the proper place for the King's weapons. Not only did he not propose to return the powder, he was resolved to "apply" it if the occasion demanded.

The assembly's reply of June 21 was published on the twenty-fourth, and in it they admitted, somewhat halfheartedly that the arms in the palace might be construed as belonging to the King, but they loudly disagreed with Lord Dunmore's contention that they were safer there than in the magazine. On the contrary, they said, "had your Lordship thought fit to remain there, we should have had no apprehension of danger, but, considering these arms at present exposed to your servants, and every rude invader, the security formerly derived from your Lordship's presence cannot now be relied on." [1] Just how right they were was demonstrated that very day, when a bunch of those rude invaders broke into the palace and carried off what guns were readily available. The invaders, however, were a gang of patriot shirtmen.

This Saturday, June 24, was to be a landmark in Virginia history, for it marked the last time that the general assembly would sit as the instrument of British colonial government.

[1] *Virginia Gazette* (Dixon & Hunter), June 24.

Earlier in the week the burgesses had urged the governor to
sign various bills that were awaiting his approval, pointing out
that they were anxious to wind up their business as the
"advanced Season of the Year requires our Presence in our
several Counties." [2] They asked him to set the date for closing
the session, commenting that "Since it has been customary for
our Governors to signify their Pleasure as to adjournments, we
wish not to take Things out of their old Channel." [3] To this
Dunmore icily replied that although the convenience of the
members would "always be a strong motive to determine me, as
to the time of your meeting or Separating," [4] he would remind
them that, while they might have the power, only the governor
had the right to dissolve the assembly.

On Friday Dunmore informed the burgesses that he did not
intend to come to the Capitol to sign their bills; instead, he
would receive them on board the *Fowey* at noon on Monday. At
that time he would put his signature to those bills that met with
his approval. But by this time the vast majority of the assembly
had ceased to care whether he did or did not sign the bills. The
members had been in Williamsburg for three stormy weeks; the
weather was getting hot; they had done all their personal
business and had said all they had to say to their friends; and
now it was time to go home. The proper care of their maturing
crops was imperative at this time, and besides they were sick of
the discomfort of crowded lodgings in stinking and noisy
Williamsburg taverns. The assemblies and court sessions had
been fun in the old days, a welcome change from the daily round
of plantation life. But this time no one had had much heart for
enjoying himself. The sight of one's neighbors standing about
on street corners, dressed in backwoodsmen's hunting shirts
with "Liberty or Death" painted on them and wearing tomahawks at their belts, could be a mite disconcerting. It made one

[2] *JHB*, 274; June 21.

[3] Ibid., 280; June 23.

[4] Dunmore to Dartmouth, précis of events, June 27, appended to
letter of June 25; PRO,CO 5/1353.

wonder what was happening to the genteel life that had taken so long to establish. It was to be expected of the yeoman burgesses from the frontier counties, but to see the sons of one's Tidewater friends dressed up like savages was distinctly sobering. Of course it was all in the cause of freedom and the rights of men, and one should be proud to see such eagerness. It was stupid to expect that crusaders should always wear white surcoats; this was the eighteenth century, not the twelfth. Yet it would be reassuring if the forces of right did not look quite so much like the instruments of darkness. It would be good to get home and have time to search one's conscience, away from the influence of propagandists, rumor carriers, and the sounds of drums and martial preparation. Another week in Williamsburg would be unthinkable.

One wonders why Lord Dunmore did not realize that the assembly was sincere in its request for adjournment. It was true that it was perfectly capable of any action it thought fit, but it was equally true that it did not wish to take the step of open defiance of the Crown. At the same time it would not sit another week just to humor the whims of an absentee governor. Dunmore must have known that if the assembly took its adjournment into its own hands, the last thread of Crown authority would be severed. On the other hand, he could hardly adjourn it without signing those bills that were clearly acceptable, and at the same time precipitating a crisis over those that were not. But even that might be better than forcing the civil government to destroy itself. The governor's dilemma may have been occasioned in part by a genuine fear for his personal safety if he returned even for a few hours to the Capitol; but many of his actions smack of pique born of a frustrating impotence.

On Saturday morning the assembly adopted its final resolutions, voiced its continuing affection for and allegiance to the King—and then adjourned itself until October 12. As the burgesses filed out of the Capitol building, all but the most radical were overcome by awe at their own temerity. It was no occasion for congratulations, back-slapping, or jubilation. They had done what had been forced upon them; they had tossed their rock into the pond, but the ripples might grow into a tidal wave before they reached the shore.

Richard Henry Lee of Westmoreland County stood in sober conversation with two colleagues beneath the arches of the Capitol, and as they talked he wrote in pencil on one of the white plastered pillars the opening lines of *Macbeth:*

> When shall we three meet again?
> In thunder, lightning, or in rain?
> When the hurly-burly's done,
> When the battle's lost and won.[5]

The prophecy would not be fulfilled; but it well epitomized the feelings of most of the burgesses on that day. Lee and his friends would actually meet quite soon, at the convention scheduled to open at Richmond on July 17; but they would never meet again in general assembly at Williamsburg.

Modern historians have difficulty in coordinating and interpreting events that occurred only a few months ago, even though they are generally able to talk to the people who participated in them. But when one tries to sort out the details of happenings that are two hundred years old, inconsistencies and contradictions conspire to trip us every step of the way. The week end of June 24–25, 1775, was no exception. The assembly adjourned on Saturday, but on Sunday Lord Dunmore wrote to the Secretary of State saying that "The Assembly are still sitting, and my intention is not to give them any interruption." A little later he added: "I have received some verbal Messages to desire me to return for the purpose of passing the Bills, or to receive the House at York, or assent by Commission. I have however signified that I expect to be attended by the House on board His Majesty's ship which is equally a protection for them as for me." It seems, therefore, that on Sunday Dunmore was still unaware that the assembly had adjourned.

---

[5] Wirt, *Henry,* 157, footnote, the lines slightly misquoted.

This says little for his intelligence facilities; but under the circumstances it might not surprise us, at least not until we read on. Ten pages later in the same letter we find the following:

. . . last night the 24th of June, a considerable body of men violently forced into the Governors house, breaking open a Window by which one part entered who then forced the principal door by which the rest entered, and they carried off all the Arms they could find to the number of between two and three hundred stand, which had been always kept in the Hall of this house, and considerable number of Muskets and other Arms my own Property; what other depredation has been committed I am not yet able to learn. The streets of Williamsburg was all this time filled with People in Arms as if in expectation of some great event; and the House of Burgesses shut themselves up in their Assembly house which was guarded without by a body of men for that purpose, and Sentinals were placed to prevent any person whatever from approaching even as far as a Wall which incloses the building.[6]

Thus, on Sunday Lord Dunmore knew that the palace had been robbed "last night," yet he did not know that the assembly had gone home, an event of major political importance that had occurred some hours earlier. The governor's reference to the elaborate security precautions at the Capitol are equally puzzling. The context suggests that this guard was at its posts at the same time that the palace assault was in progress. But far from being locked up inside the Capitol, the burgesses had already dispersed. We can only suppose that Lord Dunmore was the recipient of some very garbled information, possibly from a palace servant who could report accurately on what he had seen, but who knew and understood little of what was going on in the rest of the town.

The *Magdalen* had been due to sail for England on June 25, and Lord Dunmore had presumably waited until the last minute to write his long letter so that it could contain the most recent

[6] Dunmore to Dartmouth, précis of June 27 in June 25; PRO,CO 5/1353.

information. However the wind prevented the schooner's departure, and the governor wrote again to Lord Dartmouth on the twenty-seventh, by which time he was able to report the assembly's adjournment. We can reasonably deduce that the letter of the twenty-fifth was written quite early on Sunday, before Captain Collins reported that the departure was postponed; otherwise the letter would have contained much more detailed information on the assembly's activities during the previous week, data which was subsequently given in the letter of the twenty-seventh. We still do not know exactly when Dunmore received the news that the assembly had folded its tent, and it is conceivable that it was not until the last minute, when the burgesses failed to appear at Monday's scheduled noontime meeting aboard the *Fowey*.

One can well imagine the scene on the ship as the crew busied itself preparing deck space for the burgesses, setting out chairs and tables for the council in the well forward of the poop (there would have been no room for the entire assembly to convene anywhere else), and boatswain's crews standing by to ferry the members aboard—only to find that nobody turned up. The governor's letter gives no clue as to when he learned that there would be no meeting. But had he known later on Sunday, and had there been any possibility that the *Magdalen* would sail on Monday, he would surely have added an immediate postscript to the letter written earlier that day. On the other hand it is possible that the delay in sailing was occasioned by a northeaster churning up the Chesapeake Bay, and so Collins would have known it would take at least two days to blow itself out. In that case Dunmore might again have decided to wait until the departure was imminent before bringing his report up to date; it would also give his temper time to cool. It would never do to let Lord Dartmouth think that he might be apt to let personal anger blur his objectivity. Certainly there was no hint in the letter that the assembly had made him look foolish aboard his own ship.

If Lord Dunmore was an emotional and excitable man, and

there is a deal of evidence to suggest that he was, the delayed departure of the *Magdalen* must have added to his tensions. It was, as we have seen, due to transport not only his reports, but also his wife and family. Thus Saturday night and Sunday morning must have been occupied with packing and all the preliminaries of leave-taking, which can often be more emotionally exhausting for those who stay than for those who go. Besides, it was no ordinary parting; neither Dunmore nor his wife could have felt any certainty that they would ever meet again. For four days the agony of suspended farewells continued, while the ships pitched at their moorings and the wind whined through the rigging. Thursday and its benevolent breeze off the land must have come as a merciful release for all concerned.

The citizens of Yorktown watched the bustle of activity aboard the *Magdalen* and heard the shouted commands as sails dropped from the yards. Everyone knew that Lady Dunmore was leaving. That very day Pinkney's *Gazette* [7] announced that "This week the right honourable the COUNTESS of DUNMORE sailed for England[;] this amiable lady's departure seems to give the utmost concern to every Virginian." By way of illustration, the paper carried a letter from a coy admirer named "A PLANTER," who declared:

> Your illustrious character fills the breast of Virginia with love and admiration. Wonder not, then, that your virtue, charity, and humanity, demand the public applause of an honest planter. . . . Virginia feels the warmest sympathy when she reflects that a person of your delicate sensibility, through the ungenerous treatment of a great lord, must feel a load of trouble, too ponderous not to destroy your domestic felicity. Permit me, with real concern, to lament your departure from this government. The poor will lose thy well-timed favours; the rich, your agreeable and instructive conversation, replete with native innocence.

[7] June 29. N.B.: This was doubtless one of the many occasions on which the paper was still in the hands of the compositor on the day of its scheduled publication.

We might be thinking that "A PLANTER" had slightly spoiled
the effect of his adulation by tossing in a passing crack at the
Countess's husband; but if so, we have learned little from our
six months' subscription to the *Virginia Gazette*. That was the
whole point of the letter, as becomes obvious as it goes on: "Had
your lord possessed half the engaging qualities that embellish
your mind, and render the possessor an object of universal
approbation, he would have been the idol of a brave and free
people, and not drawn upon himself their detestation."

Although Virginia's declared affection for the Countess was
frequently only a device to attack Lord Dunmore, there is no
doubt that she was widely liked. Consequently many of the
people of Yorktown who watched the *Magdalen* making ready
for sea, must have felt a real sense of loss. However, it was to be
tempered with amazement quickly fusing into delight; the
activity across the water was coming not only from the *Magdalen* but also from the *Fowey*. Her sails, too, were billowing out,
and before long both anchors came up and the two vessels were
moving away down river—soon to disappear beyond the hori-
zon.

It was all over; Dunmore had gone!

The jubilation did not last long. Soon it was rumored that
he had gone only to Boston to confer with General Gage; and
that could bode well for no one. The truth of the matter was that
the governor had gone neither home nor to Boston, but simply
on a trip as far as the Virginia Capes to see his family safely on
its way. Saturday's *Gazette* [8] accurately reported Lord Dunmore's purpose and deduced that he would soon be back. On his
return he would learn that Williamsburg had become an armed
camp and that on June 30 the Capitol had been turned into a
militia barracks and the palace park into quartering for patriot
cavalry.

These unintentionally symbolic desecrations of the seats of
royal and parliamentary government were to mark the slow
death of Williamsburg, a death from which no patriot victories

[8] Dixon & Hunter, July 1.

could save it. The dust of time and poverty would settle on its doorsteps just as the ashes of Vesuvius choked the life from Pompeii. Henceforth the town would have no sustaining purpose; to be sure, it would thrill to drums and skirling pipes and vibrate with the pounding of marching men and the rumble of artillery passing through the streets. There would be generals, flags, and regimental banners, American, French, English, and Hessian. But, besides the stimulus of the moment, these would give nothing to Williamsburg and its citizens beyond a handful of memories—memories that would not turn to gold until their great grandsons were old men. But that is another story.

Ours is June 1775, and quite a month it had been, probably the most eventful in the history of the colony. For those in places of responsibility there had been little time to think of anything but the almost frantically unfolding incidents and crises both real and imaginary. After the invariable overstatements of the newspapers throughout the month, it was somehow reassuring to find Mr. Pinkney ending on a quieter note. "We have received papers of a very late date from the northward," he told his readers, "by which we find that nothing material, since our last, has transpired in that quarter." [9] It was the understatement of the year—as anyone who had been at Bunker Hill and Breed's Hill would have told him.

[9] *Virginia Gazette* (Pinkney), June 29.

[*VII*]

JULY

I*t is always helpful when someone else has* troubles, for they take our minds off our own. The July 1 *Virginia Gazette* [1] was, by that yardstick, a most welcome palliative; many a chuckle could be extracted from the unfortunate tale of Governor Shirley of Dominica, and his bureau. It seems that the governor sold the aforesaid bureau to Lieutenant Governor Stewart, who on examining his purchase discovered a most uncomplimentary letter tucked in the back of one of the drawers. The letter had been written by the governor and contained "many things to the prejudice of [Stewart's] character." In the resulting duel Governor Shirley was killed. The moral to this story is as good today as it was in 1775: If you must libel a colleague, do not then sell him your desk without first being sure that you are a better swordsman.

The Russians were having internal troubles again, though it was not clear in the long run who was doing what to whom, or why. Letters from Italy told of the exploit of Count Alexis d'Orlow, commander of the Russian navy in the Aegean, who at Leghorn invited the Russian Princess Elizabeth to dine with him on his ship. When she arrived, the Princess and all her retinue were arrested on the grounds that she was part of a dangerous conspiracy against the government. The Russian news was always full of rumors of plots and counterplots and very weak on factual background. All that the reader could have

[1] Dixon & Hunter.

concluded from the present story was that Count d'Orlow was obviously a barbarian to treat a lady so shamefully.

Passing on to the next item one would discover that the English were in trouble in West Africa, and that large numbers of the Pholies, a tribe of Arab descent, had crossed the Gambia river and were assaulting British forts and trading posts. The Pholies' reason for this was said to result from their contention that the English "have no pretensions to the Gold Coast, it being part of the territories of their forefathers." At first glance this sounds perfectly reasonable and typical of the bases for disagreement that still exist in Africa today. On closer reflection, however, there would seem to be some geographical error on somebody's part, the Gambia river being at least 800 miles from the Gold Coast and separated from it by Sierra Leone and the Grain and Ivory Coasts. Consequently it is not clear whether the attacks were taking place in Gambia because the Gold Coast was out of reach or whether the Pholies had actually moved down through Ashanti country to assault the narrow ocean-side belt of the English Gold Coast. The report went on to state that the Pholies were "exceedingly powerful, rigid Mahometans, and well acquainted with the profits made by the gold, ivory, and slave trade; from which, and their unexcelled bravery, it is imagined they will be very troublesome to the subjects of Great Britain."

The entire West African coast from Nigeria to Senegal was one great slave market, and while it was only the section comprising Togo, Dahomey, and southern Nigeria that was actually known as the Slave Coast, French Senegal was one of the most active centers of the trade. In the same July 1 issue of the *Gazette* we find an account of a slave ship bound from Senegal to the West Indies that blew up, having been "maliciously set on fire by the black people, whereby the ship, cargo, and all the crew were lost, except four slaves, but from whom no confession could be extorted." It seems probable that the questioners tried quite hard.

In the Caribbean, the Spaniards were giving cause for

concern, attacking and plundering British ships more or less at will. A Kingston ship with a cargo valued at some £3,000 was seized and taken to Havana, as also were a schooner and two merchant vessels. These last were all attacked by a large, 74-gun Spanish man-of-war. Another Spanish warship had seized an American snow and was caught by two British frigates as she towed her prize to port. The *Gazette* reported that "an engagement ensued, and after a few broadsides, the man-of-war had her masts shot away, when the frigates retook the snow, and carried her, with the Spanish officer and men that were on board, to Jamaica." The account was as brief and as matter of fact as are those of out-of-town automobile accidents today. Such clashes were commonplace, and in 1775 the reader only hoped that if the snow carried a Virginia cargo it had not been damaged in the exchanges. The drama of battle between tall ships, the romance and color of spread sails and proud banners, the smell of brimstone and the red roar of cannon against the deep green of a Caribbean sea, all were wasted on the Americans of the eighteenth century. It takes time, generations of it, for the rosy-hued lenses of vicarious adventure to blot out the memories of savings lost, businesses ruined, and of drowned and butchered friends.

There can have been little that was stimulating or romantic for the friends and family of Captain Ward of South Carolina when they read that after a three-hour battle his ship had been captured off Glover's Reef in the Gulf of Honduras and taken to Campeche de Baranda (spelled "Campeachy" in the *Gazette*) on the Yucatan peninsula. There the crew was imprisoned and Captain Ward "inhumanly tortured to death, by beginning with drawing his teeth, finger and toe-nails, &c, a piece of cruelty frequently used by the Spaniards."

Most of the paper's readers could pass on from such an item with no more than a brief shudder and a sense of relief that it had happened to somebody else. It was far more pleasant to consider the demise of Mary Watkins, who had lived to a hundred and five. She had long led her neighbors to believe that she was poverty stricken, but when her apartments were searched after her death, a will written in her own hand was found describing where £7,000 was hidden and leaving it all to an already prosperous cooper of Henley. Mr. Richard Bottle of Lenham, England, also departed at about the same time, leaving "146 half crowns, 175 shillings, nine silver spoons, three gold rings, a pair of silver tongs, two ten pound notes, and one seventy pound note; yet so miserable was this poor wretch that it is said that he died for the want of the necessities of life!" How astonishing, we say, that people should have behaved like that, and then we remember that we read of just such an instance in Brooklyn only last week.

Although human nature does not change from age to age, almost all of man's achievements that are influenced by society do evolve. We still speak the same language as did the eighteenth-century American colonists, yet many of the words have changed their meaning. In 1775 one would have been flattered to be described as "a very curious gentleman"; today, of course, most of us would consider ourselves insulted. The word "curious" was used in its most straightforward sense, meaning interested; and a "curious gentleman" was simply a man with catholic interests, anxious to learn more about the world in which he lived. The gentry of the late eighteenth century passed much of their time in educational and creative pursuits, touring the ruins of Egypt, Greece, and Rome; dabbling in astronomy, geology, botany; experimenting with electricity; delighting in architectural form; and striving for competence in the playing of at least one musical instrument. At his "Nomini Hall" plantation, Colonel Robert Carter kept a harpsichord, forte-piano, glass-harmonica, guitar, violin, and German flutes. He apparently not only played these instruments but invented a device comprising a number of whistles, which he used to tune the harpsichord and piano. Fithian considered him to have a good ear for music and "a vastly delicate Taste." [2]

[2] Fithian, *Journal*, 30; Dec. 13, 1773.

Augustine Prevost noted that John Randolph had "two Daughters who are the two greatest beauties in America, the youngest
sings to admiration & the Oldest plays on the harpsichord &
Guitar in a masterly manner." [3] He found, too, that Lord
Dunmore's daughter the Lady Catherine was similarly talented,
though being only twelve years old her physical attributes did
not so impress themselves upon Lieutenant Prevost.

On the roof of "Rosewell" John Page undertook the first
American experiments in the measuring of annual rainfall. John
Clayton of Gloucester County, who died in 1773, was a botanist
of distinction and the author of *Flora Virginica;* he was also first
president of the Society for the Advancement of Useful Knowledge, which was founded in Williamsburg in that same year.
Most of these men could read both Latin and Greek, and some
could manage Hebrew as well. Dr. Philip Mazzei declared that
he never knew anyone in Virginia who could not read and write.
He went on to say that "Even in the houses of those who work
the land with their own hands, or who engage in any of the
mechanical arts, there are books, an inkstand and writing paper;
and it is rare that they do not know arithmetic." [4] Many of the
more wealthy planters had been educated in England and had
sent their children to English schools, though in the years
preceding the Revolution, the wisdom of doing so was increasingly questioned. Colonel Landon Carter, who had outspoken
opinions on most subjects, had this to say on the matter of
English education: "the general importers of it now adays bring
back only a stiff priggishness with as little good manners as
possible [,] especially when the particular cut of a waistcoat, the
multi oval trim of a hat or the cast of a buckle does not attract
great admiration, but if they do, then the tongue becomes
extremely multiloquous upon the learning of the foppishness of
the fancy." [5]

The College of William and Mary was the colony's princi-

[3] Prevost, "Journal," July 5, 1774.
[4] Mazzei, "Memoirs," *WMQ*, 2nd ser., IX, 247.
[5] Landon Carter, *Diary*, I, 372–3; March 23, 1770.

pal fount of learning, but this, too, had fallen into disrepute among patriots who objected in part to the dominance of loyalist clergy in the faculty. As we have already seen, the Anglican clergy was looked upon as a disaffected group—the Tory party at prayer. In 1774 Philip Fithian noted in his diary that Colonel Robert Carter refused to send his sons to the college on the grounds that "it is in such confusion at present, & so badly directed"; he added that he had known the professors "to play all Night at Cards in publick Houses in the City, and [had] often seen them drunken in the Street!" [6] Fithian went on to comment on the battle then being waged in the columns of the *Virginia Gazette* by two reverend gentlemen of the college staff, one of them John Bracken, minister of Bruton Parish Church, and the other Samuel Henley, professor of divinity and moral philosophy. The latter had taken a somewhat ungodly and certainly unphilosophical approach to being passed over when the rectorship at Bruton Parish became vacant. Nevertheless, regardless of its petty squabbling and often doubtful examples for the students, the staff of the college imparted considerable wisdom to the young men who would shape the future of Virginia. George Wythe, the college's first professor of law, was tutor and friend to Thomas Jefferson, and both were already active in the patriot cause; so, too, were many other past students.

The student body rarely exceeded 120, and as many as forty or fifty lived in lodgings around the town, providing their proprietors with a useful source of income during the draughty months when the courts and legislature were not in session. Tradesmen also relied on the college to create business during the slack seasons, and one finds advertisements describing such items as imported Staffordshire pottery as being "fit for the FACULTY." [7] This is, it is true, a slightly odd term and raises doubts as to its correct interpretation, yet none of the other meanings given in contemporary dictionaries fit the context.

[6] Fithian, *Journal*, 65; Feb. 12, 1774.

[7] *Virginia Gazette* (Rind), Sept. 27, 1770; advertisement inserted by blacksmith James Anderson.

The problems of interpretation can lead one, all unsuspecting, into the most hideous and mortifying of traps. In reading the July 1 *Gazette* [8] advertisements, I found the following trenchant little notice concerning an escaped servant: "WILLIAM LEE, by Trade a Cooper, about 5 Feet 9 Inches high, marked with the Smallpox, has a remarkable large Nose, speaks thick, and is impudent; he took with him a yellow Bull-Dog, with cropped Ears, one Side of his Face white, has a Glass Eye, and white Breast and Neck, is very fond of going into the Water, and answers to the Name of *Turk*." Here, I thought, was a fine example of Virginians' affection for animals, a trait they undoubtedly brought with them from England. What more graphic example of that affection could one wish for than a master who cared enough about the appearance of his pet to fit it with a glass eye? The very next week, however, the *Virginia Gazette* [9] carried an advertisement describing a horse that had been found in Bedford County: "a BAY HORSE about 13 Hands high, 12 or 13 Years old, has two Glass Eyes, and three white feet. . . ." This was obviously carrying kindness to animals to the point of idiocy, and a "glass eye" was clearly something other than I supposed. It was, in fact, a species of blindness in horses—and presumably in dogs. No doubt some readers will have known this from childhood, but I did not and so would have come to grief were it not for the intervention of the bay horse from Bedford. It was, it seems, a dilapidated and unhappy beast, for in addition to its two glass eyes it suffered from both a fistula and the poll-evil. Its chances of being returned to its home were marred by the fact that even its brands were substandard, being seared on "the off Buttock with Something unintelligible." It was remarkable that such a sorry nag should have any commercial value, but apparently it did, and the advertiser appraised it at seven pounds.

A beast with no value at all (except to "curious gentlemen")

---

[8] Dixon & Hunter.

[9] Dixon & Hunter, July 8.

found a place on the front page of the July 1 *Virginia Gazette*.[1]
It had been found by some workmen clearing out an old coal
mine in Stirlingshire, Scotland. They found not only the
remains of the horse but also those of his rider: "the man had
been armed, for with his bones were found a durk and sword; he
had been on horseback when dropped in, for the remains of his
foot were found in the stirrup, and part of the horse's bridle and
saddle. There was likewise found three half pence." The report
ended with the suggestion that the ill-fated horseman was a relic
of the rebellion of 1745. Here, surely, was a skein of the thread
from which ghost stories are woven.

Very few of the foreign news items that graced the columns
of colonial newspapers were any longer or more detailed than
the story of the heedless horseman, and the customers were left
to embroider them for themselves. Advertising sections of the
papers, on the other hand, were liable to describe their wares in
infinite detail—which is fortunate for the social historian. Few
notices in the *Virginia Gazette* ever capped the loquacity of Mr.
Anthony Winston in his efforts to dispose of "Huntingtour," his
plantation in Buckingham County. It is worth reading not only
for its expansive salesmanship but also because it gives us an
excellent summary of the very agreeable life that was lived by
colonial gentry on the eve of the Revolution.

The Subscriber being very desirous of getting out of
Debt, without any dependence on his ungrateful Debtors,
proposes to sell the pleasant and healthy seat of HUNTING-
TOUR, near *Appamattox* River, in the lower end of *Buckingham*, with 1500 or 2000 Acres of good Land, which
produces fine Tobacco, Hemp, Wheat, &c. The Houses are
new, and the best I have seen in the country; a large and
better Garden I believe is not in the Colony, and on this Land
are several Hundred Fruit Trees of the best Kind, many of
which were brought by water to *Richmond* Town above 80
Miles. On this Tract of Land is a large Proportion of

[1] Dixon & Hunter, July 1.

exceeding fine Meadow Land, with a Fish Pond within three Hundred Yards of the Dwelling-House, stored with various Kinds of fine Fish, sufficient for the Use of a Family the Year round. In this Neighbourhood is plenty of excellent Venison. The Air is so pure that I never knew an Instance of any Person having the Ague and Fever at *Huntingtour*. I have travelled through most Parts of *Virginia*, and I have not seen any Part that I would so willingly reside in as this Neighbourhood. If I sell this Place, I shall live on the Part of this Tract of Land which has been advertised for some Time past. I make no Doubt but *Appamattox* River will be soon cleared, and then Wheat will be carried as far as Col. *Banister's* Mill, near *Petersburg*, for 4d. or 5d. *per* Bushel. I made at this Place 100 Gallons of rich Wine in 1772, and last Year (if it had not been for the Frost) I could have made 5 or 600 Gallons, which Quantity I expect to make this Year.

HUNTINGTOUR would be a pleasant and safe Place for a Gentleman of Fortune to retreat to in the Horrours of a civil War, or in the sickly Months of many Parts of the Lowlands.

What is Honour, Grandeur, and Wealth?
All fleeting, Nothing's without Health! [2]

Those must surely have been halcyon days at "Huntingtour," idly casting one's impaled worm into the pond or wandering through the apple orchards contemplating the distances that each tree had traveled. Unfortunately life on the plantations was rarely like that, and even the most powerful planters spent much of their time simply managing their estates, worrying about the weather and the state of their crops, overseeing their overseers, and trying to trade their tobacco sufficiently advantageously to put clothes on the backs of their "family" while still leaving enough, after the most pressing creditors had been paid, to fix the roofs and repair the windows of their mansions. Lest this should be thought an exaggeration, I recall a letter written by John Page of "Rosewell" to his agent in London in 1771, discussing his need to lease part of his estate

[2] Ibid.

rather than farm it himself and adding: "As my House is very much out of Repair, I have engaged a Man to put it in a saving Condition next Spring." [3] This great brick house was one of the largest and finest in the colony and had only been lived in for twenty-eight years. Regardless of the impression conjured up by Mr. Winston's advertisement, the ever-chomping termite and the paint-blistering sun, plus a modicum of aid from dry rot and shingle-stripping winds, kept the plantation owners constantly at battle stations.

Our twentieth-century impression of colonial houses is likely to be heavily biased in favor of travel-folder architecture. We visit the restored Tidewater plantations and the well-preserved townhouses of Williamsburg and are likely to suppose that these were the mirror of all Virginia; but they were not—as John Smyth bluntly pointed out. "The houses here," he wrote, speaking of the colony in general, "are almost all of wood, covered with the same, the roof with shingles, the sides and ends with thin boards, and not always lathed and plastered within; only those of the better sort are finished in that manner, and painted on the outside. The chimneys are sometimes of brick, but more commonly of wood, coated on the inside with clay. The windows of the best sort have glass in them; the rest have none, and only wooden shutters." [4]

The truth of the matter would seem to be that then, as now, generalizations could be misleading. There is ample historical and archeological evidence to suggest that the majority of privately owned houses in the Tidewater area had both brick chimneys and glazed windows. But at the same time there were many inhabitants, white as well as slave, who lived in quarters provided for them, and it is quite possible that these would have been as primitive as Smyth described. One has also to consider regional differences (though Smyth did not), for there is reason

[3] John Page to John Norton, Oct. 11, 1771; *John Norton & Sons*, 199.

[4] Smyth's "Tour," *VHR*, VI, 87.

to suppose that the homes of the lesser freeholders of the Piedmont and frontier lands were far less desirable residences than were those of their coastal cousins.

The July 1 issue of the *Virginia Gazette* provided, in addition to Mr. Winston's gem, descriptive advertisements for two middle-ground properties, a farm in Caroline County and a townhouse in Richmond. The farm was not large; it comprised only 470 acres, a far cry from the vast 20,000- or 30,000-acre estates of the great Tidewater landowners. Nevertheless its owner, Mr. Le Roy Hipkins, considered it to be "equal to any Forest Place whatever." He stated that the house was new, measured 32 by 28 feet, and had three dormers on each side, two fireplaces downstairs and one up, and a good cellar. Like most homes of the period, it possessed a separate kitchen building, and that measured 24 by 16 feet, which was quite a reasonable size. The advertisement mentioned other new outbuildings but did not identify them. The Richmond notice referred to "A large Dwelling-House" measuring 40 by 20 feet —96 square feet smaller than Mr. Hipkins's farmhouse. It offered "two rooms below and two above, a Garden newly pailed in, a Kitchen, and all other Outhouses necessary for a Family." It is worth noting that neither house was as large as the 60-by-24-foot kitchen at "Rosewell."

It might seem reasonable to expect that Lord Dunmore's plantation house at "Porto Bello" would have been of a size befitting a royal governor; but there is no evidence that such was the case. On the contrary, the value of the estate appears to have resided in the land rather than in any improvements built upon it. In the autumn of 1773 the property was offered for sale by the widow Rachel Drummond prior to public auction in November. It is not clear whether the governor was interested in it at this point; but someone was clearly going to considerable trouble to take advantage of the poor woman.

Many people, I am told, have endeavored to undervalue this place, some of whom have made offers for it. This I take extremely unkind; for if they have not generosity enough to make a proposition worthy [of] notice, I beg they will not prevent others from purchasing agreeable to their inclinations. Can it be conceived that the above situation, attended with so many happy conveniences, which few in this country, to its size, can boast of, is worth less than the lands near Williamsburg, not so good in quality, and without even houses of any sort, or any other improvements? And why a third person will interfere in any matter which does not concern him, and which perhaps may do me a prejudice, is out of my power to determine.

This curious notice appeared in the *Virginia Gazette* [5] on November 4, 1773. Unfortunately no further details of the "Porto Bello" affair have survived, though we do know that it had originally been scheduled for auction on October 25. On the fourteenth of that month Mrs. Drummond had inserted a pre-sale advertisement in the *Gazette* describing the property as "The well known Place called PORTO BELLO, whereon is an exceeding fine Orchard with a Variety of well chosen Fruits. It is convenient to the Oyster Rocks, and great Plenty of Fish and Wildfowl may be had in their Seasons. One Third of the Purchase Money to be paid at Christmas, when Possession will be Given." [6] It is significant that no reference is made to the houses, though we know from the November 4 notice that they did exist. The land is today part of the federal government's Camp Peary, where a small, two-story brick house is still known as "Porto Bello." However on examination it is soon apparent that there is nothing colonial about it. Behind this building one can see a shallow depression, which in all probability represents the site of Lord Dunmore's farm and from which the bricks may have been taken to construct the existing dwelling.

A map of the Williamsburg area drawn by a French cartographer at the end of the Revolution showed five buildings at "Porto Bello," which might be interpreted as one residence, a kitchen, and three small outbuildings away to the west, proba-

---

[5] Rind.

[6] *Virginia Gazette* (Purdie & Dixon), Oct. 14, 1773.

bly slave quarters. However this was not the impression given
by Lord Dunmore himself when, after the dust had settled, he
applied to the British government for compensation for his
losses in Virginia. He put a value of £600 on "Two Dwelling
Houses at Porto Bello with Kitchens and other Offices" and a
further £200 on "Buildings at Porto Bello newly erected, a
Large Barn, Cow Houses, Stables, Fatning House, Work
Shopes &c." [7] Because Dunmore could not have owned "Porto
Bello" for more than eighteen months before his departure from
Williamsburg, it may be deduced that if he had built a dwelling
house it would have been mentioned among the other new
improvements. "The Furniture in His Lordships Country House
at Porto Bello" was valued at only £80 (very different from his
£3,200 loss at the palace) and this would tend to support the
impression that the plantation was more homely than handsome.
It adjoined another piece of property also owned by the governor
and known as the "Old Farm"; together they created a tract of
579 acres with a land value of 48 shillings an acre, a total of
£1,389 12s 0d. In addition, the stock and farm equipment
amounted to another £640.

Lord Dunmore has often been charged with being land-
hungry, and there is no denying that during his short stay in
Virginia he managed to treat himself remarkably well. Besides
the pleasant and convenient "Porto Bello" acres, he had acquired 2,600 more in Berkeley County and another 3,465 in
Hampshire County, as well as a house and lot in Williamsburg.
Other assets included fifty-six slaves worth about £6,000 and a
dozen indentured servants whose remaining four years of
service were valued at £24 each.

On or about July 6 the palace was again broken into, and
this time, according to the governor, "they broke open every
lock of the doors of all the rooms, Cabinets and private places,
and carried off a considerable number of Arms of different sorts,
a large collection, and valuable." He declared it to be "an

[7] "Claims of American Loyalists in the Public Records Office,
1778–1784," PRO,AO 13/28.

infamous robbery, this violation of private property, as well as [an] atrocious outrage against the King's Authority." [8] It was made the more heinous by the fact that it was led, in broad daylight, by the son of Treasurer Robert Carter Nicholas. There was little doubt in the governor's mind that the latter was privy to the robbery, and, as both he and Speaker Peyton Randolph were in town at the time, it could be construed that the project bore the stamp of official approval. It is certainly surprising that the entry into the palace should have been led by a person of such consequence, and one would be tempted to construe the move as considered policy, were it not for the fact that it was never reported in the newspapers. This being so, it may be more reasonable to see the exploit as a spur of the moment assault on the inanimate symbol of royal authority by a bunch of over-zealous young patriots. It was only to be expected that someone would take another crack at the virtually unprotected palace; the question was simply when, who, and whether patriotism or avarice would be the driving force. The park around the walled palace gardens had been taken over for the cavalry of the Independent Companies, and the shirtmen daily paraded on Palace Green. The urge to break into the mansion itself must have been well to the fore in the minds of many of the lower ranks. Who would condemn them for making sure that there were no more arms that should be commandeered for the war effort, and if the searchers happened to be wearing coats with large pockets, who would ever notice what slipped into them?

In the same letter to Lord Dartmouth in which Dunmore had reported the second break-in, he later added that "my house has been a third time rifled, and is now entirely in the possession of these lawless Ruffians." The exact date of this further outrage is not known, but in a *Virginia Gazette* [9] supplement of July 14 it was reported that "all his Lordship's domesticks have now left the palace, and are gone, bag and baggage, to his farm at Porto Bello, about six miles from town." Unfortunately there

[8] Dunmore to Dartmouth, July 12; PRO,CO 5/1353.
[9] Purdie.

is no extant inventory of the contents of the palace during Lord Dunmore's occupancy, but we do have a summary in his statement of losses. The £3,200 valuation comprised

> The Furniture of 25 Rooms completely furnished, with all the Beds, Bedding, Looking Glasses, Bureaus, Book-Cases, valuable Tapestry, Damask Curtains, Carpets &c. A number of valuable Pictures by Sir Peter Lely, and a number of costly Prints. A large quantity of very valuable China, Glass, and Household Utensils of [e]very kind. A valuable Library consisting of upwards of 1300 Volumes. 3 Organs, a Harpsichord, a Piano-Forte, and other Musical Instruments. The greatest and most valuable part of His Lordship's Cloaths, Linnen, and Servants Cloathing. The greatest part of His Lordship's private Arms which were valuable, with many Articles of Value and Curiosity. All the Beds, Bedding and furniture of the Servants Rooms; all the furniture of the Kitchen, Laundry, and other Offices. A quantity of Mahogany and other Woods; with Tools for four Cabinet Makers, and a Complete Set of Blacksmiths Tools. In short everything in and about the Palace, Gardens, Offices &c.[1]

What became of all this is anyone's guess; much of it was later put up for public auction and presumably became scattered through the homes of Williamsburg citizens. A rather ordinary tall-case clock bearing the name of a Glasgow maker is traditionally said to have been acquired by the Ambler family at that time, and descendants have now presented it to Colonial Williamsburg, which has returned it to the palace. But apart from this single exception Lord Dunmore's furniture and paintings have not retained their identity, if they survive at all. However confirmation of the quality of his "very valuable China" has come from archaeological excavations in the vicinity of the palace, where fragmentary Chinese export porcelain plates and soup dishes bearing the Murray arms have been unearthed. Other sherds from the same service have been found in widely scattered parts of Williamsburg, perhaps all that is left of souvenirs carried off during the July pilfering.

[1] *Claims of American Loyalists.*

More practical souvenirs were to be found in the palace cellars in the shape of "12 Gross of Claret, Burgundy, Champagne, Port, Hock, Sherry, Frontiniac, Creme de Noyaux &c at 32/ pr. Doz." [2] The identity of Creme de Noyaux has eluded me (was it from Noyers in central France?), but Frontiniac, according to Bailey's dictionary, was vaguely described as "a sort of luscious *French* wine." [3] These perennial perquisites of war could have been readily carried home, but much else would have had to be imbibed on the premises. There were forty-two pipes and hogsheads of wine to the value of £1,680, most of it Madeira; plus about 480 gallons of "Old Rum" and unspecified quantities of "Common Rum." A most excellent time could have been had by all.

In the stable area were housed two coaches, a chariot, a phaeton, and two one-horse chaises, besides miscellaneous carts and wagons. There was also a fine state coach, which had belonged to Lord Botetourt and which had been presented by his heir to the colony along with the portraits of the King and Queen that were hanging in the palace ballroom. The coach, which had been given to Lord Botetourt by the King's uncle, the Duke of Cumberland, was not seized, auctioned, or driven away; instead it was left in the stable, where it slowly fell to pieces. It was still there some years after the palace itself had disappeared.

We do not know how quickly Lord Dunmore heard of the second invasion of the palace, but if it reached him within the day, as it probably did, he was not deterred from returning to "Porto Bello" the next morning. Having been aboard the *Fowey* for a month and having only recently returned to his moorings at Yorktown, *now* seemed a good time for a landsman to stretch his legs, and what more obvious place could there be to do it than on one's own estate? There may, of course, have been other considerations, such as the need to show the flag among his servants. To Captain Montagu the venture meant an opportu-

[2] Ibid.
[3] Bailey (13th ed., 1749).

nity to cut a mast for one of the ship's boats. One might have
expected Montagu to have tried to talk the governor out of what
should have looked like an unnecessarily rash little project. But
instead we find both men boarding a barge in full view of the
citizenry of Yorktown and being rowed up the York river just as
serenely as if they had been aboard a Thames wherry.

It should have surprised no one that, hidden from the river
by a belt of thick woodland, a rider was galloping up the road to
Williamsburg to alert the city. Even assuming, as one surely
must, that Captain Montagu was taking advantage of the rising
tide, it is likely that the messenger arrived in Williamsburg
before the barge reached "Porto Bello." Nevertheless, the
governor and his party arrived without incident and were
warmly greeted by the servants, many of whom must have
wondered whether they had been abandoned to the enemy; there
must also have been others who had hoped that they had.
Montagu sent off his carpenters into the woods to find a tree
suitable for the mast, while he and Lord Dunmore enjoyed a
relaxed dinner at the house. Thus the largest of the Crown's
Virginia eggs were neatly assembled in one basket.

The change of diet and a good wine in the comfort of a
dining room must have been a pleasant experience for them
both, while the hot July day doubtless contributed to a satisfying after-dinner lethargy. Unhappily it was not to be savored for
long; almost as the meal ended a servant burst in to announce
that a body of armed men was in sight and quickly approaching
the house. Neither man could have been surprised, but they both
hurried out to see for themselves, and sure enough the enemy
was very much in evidence, heading, as the servant had said,
straight for the house. "We had just time," wrote Dunmore, "to
get into our boat and to escape." [4] It is evident that the
withdrawal was executed in unseemly haste and must have been
most distressing to the digestion. The descent from the house
site to the river is still long and steep, and taken at a dyspeptic

[4] Dunmore to Dartmouth, July 12; PRO,CO 5/1353.

gallop there was a more than sporting chance of tumbling wig over buckles to the bottom. A servant who either got left behind or who decided not to linger any longer at "Porto Bello" leapt into a canoe and paddled furiously down the creek after the barge, spurred on by musket fire from the bank. But the two carpenters were forgotten in the rush and were seized by the patriots and taken to Williamsburg, where, according to the *Gazette*,[5] they declared themselves to be delighted at having been freed from British service. In reporting to Lord Dartmouth, Dunmore made no reference to this aspect of the affair, but said only that they had been captured and were confined in Williamsburg under guard.

If Lord Dunmore had found life aboard the *Fowey* confining, he was about to be faced with the prospect of even greater discomfort. On July 11 a 20-gun ship-of-war, the *Mercury*, arrived in the York river with orders from Admiral Graves that it should relieve the *Fowey* and that Captain Montagu should proceed to Boston. The incoming ship had been spotted by the naval officer of the lower James river district, a man whom the governor considered to be "one of the most active and virulent Enemies of Government." [6] The officer, Wilson Miles Cary, ran true to Lord Dunmore's expectations and promptly sent word to Williamsburg that the vessel was approaching, adding, for good measure, that great numbers of troops were aboard. In response to this false intelligence Robert Carter Nicholas ordered to Yorktown a detachment of the forces then gathering in Williamsburg. So, at much the same time that the *Mercury* was dropping anchor near the *Fowey*, patriot troops were putting up tents on the heights behind Yorktown not half a cannon's shot from the ships.

All in all, July 11 was not a good day for Lord Dunmore. The presence of the patriot troops was likely to provoke an incident that could escalate into a pitched battle, and at the same time the governor's friend and strong right arm, Captain

[5] *Virginia Gazette* (Dixon & Hunter), July 8.
[6] Dunmore to Dartmouth, July 12; PRO,CO 5/1353.

Montagu, was being withdrawn. Not only that, the *Mercury* was a distinctly smaller ship than the "fine, roomy" [7] *Fowey* and would not have the space in which to accommodate him. That was not the end of it; the *Mercury* was commanded by Captain John Macartney, who had his own ideas about the duties of his Majesty's ships in Virginia. In the eyes of Admiral Graves, however, Macartney was "a very able and punctual officer, in whose Conduct and Advice respecting Naval Affairs, your Lordship may place the utmost dependence." [8]

On boarding the *Fowey*, Macartney very properly reported to Captain Montagu and gave him the admiral's instructions. This done, Macartney began to ask questions about the state of the colony, managing all the while to give the impression that he was God's gift to the navy, to Virginia, and to the world at large. He wanted to know whether Montagu went ashore and was skeptically surprised when the latter told him that he considered "the People to be in a State of Rebellion and thought it was dangerous to go." [9] The matter of going ashore seemed to be uppermost in Macartney's mind, for when he returned to the *Fowey* on July 12 to pay his respects to Lord Dunmore it arose again. He then announced that he was about to call on Thomas Nelson, the president of the council. How Dunmore reacted to this news is not recorded, but Macartney was duly rowed ashore, met with Nelson, and returned again to the *Fowey* to inform the governor that he had been invited to Nelson's house for dinner.

Lord Dunmore's reaction to Macartney's extraordinary behavior was undoubtedly explosive, but we know only that the governor told him that acceptance would be imprudent, "as the President was a man disaffected to Government, and that at his house he would most likely meet some who were then under Arms and in active Rebellion." These were the words (presum-

[7] Parker to Steuart, July 19; CSP.

[8] Graves to Dunmore, July 28; "Aspinwall Papers," MHS *Collections*, X, 751.

[9] Montagu to Graves, Aug. 7, PRO, Admiralty 1/485.

ably swabbed down) which Captain Montagu later reported to Admiral Graves on his arrival in Boston. He went on to state that "his Lordship used many arguments to shew the impropriety of Accepting the invitation without effect As he went and dined with the President and, that at that time there were three or four hundred Armed Men in the Town; From the nature of circumstances the foregoing cannot be otherwise than Awkward. . . ." [1] It was, of course, distinctly more than awkward —it was a bloody disgrace, and Dunmore would be damned if he wouldn't have the fellow's buttons.

On July 17 the governor wrote to Admiral Graves commending the conduct of Captain Montagu and asserting that "it is particularly unfortunate to his Majesty's Service that that Gentleman should be succeeded in the Command of his Majesty's Ships here by Captain Macartney who seems to be actuated altogether by Principles totally different, and to have principally at heart the making Friends among his Majesty's greatest Enemies in this Country." He went on to declare Macartney "utterly unfit for such a Command" [2] and called on Graves to relieve him of it.

That letter was but one of many items large and small that sailed for Boston aboard the *Fowey*. Graves had ordered Montagu to raise a hundred men for the fleet and bring them with him; but that was a deal easier said than done, and all he shipped out were fifty-two and these, as the admiral later complained, were mostly "very indifferent." [3] Nevertheless even fifty-two additional passengers put a strain on the galley of the *Fowey*, and it may have been this that prompted Montagu to send a foraging party ashore on a Gloucester County island near the mouth of the river. A report from Gloucester Town was short of details and was uncertain whether the raiders came from the *Fowey* or the *Otter*, but it was very sure that a farmer had been robbed of fourteen sheep and a cow. Although the

[1] Ibid.
[2] Dunmore to Graves, July 17; PRO, Admiralty 1/485.
[3] Graves to Secretary Stephens, Aug. 17; ibid.

writer admitted that the farmer had been taken completely by surprise, he assured one and all that "the People, who are now well furnished with arms, &c. will be ready to give them a warm reception, should they *favour* them with another visit." [4]

The same Gloucester source went on as follows: "*Quere*, are not the negro slaves, now on board the *Fowey*, which are under the g------r's protection, in actual rebellion, and punishable as such? Is it not high time to show administration how little they have to expect from that part of their bloody plan, by arming our trusty slaves ourselves?" This was the kind of question that had been argued ever since April, but the reference is important here in that it refers to the presence of escaped slaves aboard the *Fowey*. What was Montagu to do with them when he left? The obvious answer was to transfer them to the *Mercury*, but again Macartney added to the stigma already enshrouding him by adamantly refusing to take them aboard. He informed Montagu and anyone else who cared to listen that his principles would not induce him to "harbour the slaves of any individual in this Province." [5] It would have been hard to find a man who could make himself more objectionable to his colleagues in so short a time. There was no alternative but to move the Negroes to the already crowded *Otter*.

The Crown's position at Yorktown had been hit below the waterline by Admiral Graves's action. Lord Dunmore had to vacate the *Fowey*, but he could not move to the *Mercury*. Furthermore the presence of the rebel troops above Yorktown was making everyone nervous; wrote Dunmore: "the men are continually parading in arms along the shore close to us, and at night we hear them challenge every boat or person that approaches them." [6] The only solution would be to fall back from Yorktown and establish a land base on the coast, probably

[4] *Virginia Gazette* (Pinkney), July 13.

[5] Macartney to Paul Loyal, Aug. 12; *American Archives*, 4th ser., III, 92.

[6] Dunmore to Dartmouth, July 12; PRO,CO 5/1353.

near Norfolk, where large loyalist elements were thought to exist. Such a withdrawal would not really be a defeat, for Yorktown was no longer of any use to the governor now that he was making no efforts to negotiate with Nelson or with the patriot leaders in Williamsburg. On the contrary, the move would have the advantage of putting Captain Macartney out of reach of his new-found friends.

On July 14, therefore, the *Fowey*, with Lord Dunmore still aboard, upped anchor and headed down river, presumably accompanied by the *Otter* and *Mercury*. They put in at Portsmouth, a small new town across the Elizabeth river from Norfolk, where the governor established his headquarters. This done, the *Fowey* proceeded north for Boston, carrying with it the aforementioned letter to Admiral Graves, the fifty-two indifferent recruits, the loyalist son of Richard Corbin—and Captain Foy.

Edward Foy had had enough and had decided to return to England. This was undoubtedly one of the surprises of the year, for, as we have seen, he had been widely regarded as the power behind the governor's chair. Why, then, was he leaving now? It has been pointed out that he had been involved in some altercation with a Williamsburg shopkeeper. But although details of the dispute are not known, it could hardly have been of much consequence at this stage of the game. Did he perhaps think that the game was already lost or, at best, no longer worth the playing? Everything we know of the man points to a decisive and aggressive personality that might be expected to take unkindly to passive resistance and the confinement of life aboard ship. Then again, he was a military man himself, a hero of Minden, who doubtless thought himself more skilled in such matters than the governor he served. There is not the slightest doubt that Foy had an excellent opinion of himself, and the fact that he was still only a captain so long after his moment of glory may have gnawed at his pride—even though his own lack of a private fortune or the absence of powerful friends may have been the cause of it. One might argue, therefore, that Foy thought he could foresee disaster in Virginia and decided to seek another post before it stained his military career.

All these factors are worth bearing in mind when one reads his own explanation, as written to his friend, council member Ralph Wormeley of "Rosegill." "I am going to leave this country and, I believe, not return," wrote Foy. "Lord Dunmore's is not a character from which, in any difficult times, I should hope for any great advantage to my own, from acting under him; at the same time that I shall not fail to bear more than my share of all disgrace attending his proceedings. . . ." Here, it seems, we have two possible interpretations: one that Foy feared an eventual humiliating defeat, and the other that he disapproved of the methods Lord Dunmore was prepared to use in the name of the King. But then the letter forsakes principles and turns to more venal matters. "I have found," he said, "by five years experience that it is not an attachment to his interest, and zeal in doing his business, that can recommend a man to his Generosity, or even engage him to be just: I therefore think it necessary to quit this employment [as it] has been as little profitable as edifying [to] me." [7]

Foy's opinion of Lord Dunmore is the most damaging single piece of evidence against the governor, and it can be used to argue that not only should one condemn him for his crimes against the people of Virginia, but also despise him for having so unattractive a personality that even his *friends* could not like him. But even if that is fair comment one must remember that the pages of history are alive with brave soldiers, devout churchmen, and brilliant politicians whose personalities, so essential to their calling, made them miserable to live with and impossible to love. If Lord Dunmore was another, he is not precluded from having done his best for his government or for the colony as he saw it.

Captain Foy was, it appears, far from being the most level-

[7] Foy to Wormeley; Wormeley Papers, No. 1939. Undated, but probably written aboard the *Fowey* on or about July 12.

headed and impartial of witnesses. Less than a year later he would acquire a lucrative position as Commissary to the Brunswick general, Baron von Riedesel, who had known him at Minden. But although the Baron considered Foy a good officer, he found him to be a man who had "many positive things to say" and one who was "not to be contradicted." [8] Such traits were not generated like mushrooms overnight, and as Lord Dunmore was a man of much the same stamp it is not surprising that one might have been flint to the other's steel. Besides, Dunmore was short and Foy unusually tall, and little men and long men frequently get along poorly together. The only remarkable aspects of the relationship are that it had survived as long as it had and then that it ended when it did.

If Foy was really the good officer that Baron von Riedesel thought him, it was odd that his conscience would let him abandon his post at a time when every soldier was so desperately needed. However, another passage of Foy's letter to Ralph Wormeley indicates that he did not think that the war, as a whole, would either be long or lost, "it being impossible for the Americans in any part of the country to sustain a conflict of that nature for any length of time." Elsewhere, with an abrasive touch of hauteur, he announced: "I intend to take a peep at the *Manoeuvres* at Boston and at the end of the summer to go to England." But even if Foy could dismiss the war as a trifling irritation, he knew full well that Lord Dunmore's position was perilous and that before long the toy soldiers would be shedding real blood. He virtually admitted as much toward the end of the letter, when he asked Wormeley to keep him informed, saying that "although I am no longer interested in the fate of Lord Dunmore, I should be glad, on account of his Family which I revere, to know how he proceeds." [9]

Outspoken though Foy was in his letter, it would seem that he was able to conceal his dislike from his Lordship. Only five

[8] General Riedesel to his wife, Portsmouth, England, March 29, 1776; *Baroness von Riedesel and the American Revolution*, 163.
[9] Wormeley Papers, No. 1939.

months later Dunmore wrote to Lord Dartmouth urging that
Foy should be appointed naval officer for the Lower James
River, a lucrative post for which the latter had previously
expressed a desire. "I hope," declared Dunmore, "Captain Foy's
former Services in Germany, as well as those he has rendered
his Country here will ensure him this mark of His Majesty's
favour. . . ." [1] Under the circumstances this was an astonishing
proposal, which can be used either to demonstrate Lord Dunmore's forgiving nature or to suggest that he was such a poor
diplomat that he could not distinguish between friends and
enemies.

On July 17, the day that Dunmore wrote to Admiral Graves
calling for the removal of Macartney, another royal governor
was taking to the water. Governor Martin of North Carolina
decided that he could not properly defend himself at Fort
Johnston, and, in the face of a threatened patriot assault under
the command of Colonel John Ashe, he withdrew to the safety of
the sloop-of-war *Cruiser*, taking the fort's guns with him. When
Colonel Ashe and his troops arrived, they found "this nest of
fresh water pirates fled, [and] immediately set fire to the fort
and adjacent buildings which were consumed." [2] The carriages
for the guns were hauled away and sunk in a swamp lest Martin
should later have any idea of returning for them.

July 17 saw another setback for the Crown's position in the
Southern colonies, for this was the scheduled day when the
Virginia convention was to meet at Richmond. Later it would be
apparent that this convention marked the end of British government for the colony as a whole; henceforth the colonists would
propose and enact their own laws, levy taxes, and raise and pay
troops, without any further reference to the King's representatives. For many delegates this new license was too heady a
draught, and the more sober patriots were appalled by their
colleagues' antics. Some months later George Mason of "Gun-
ston Hall" reported to George Washington:

[1] Dunmore to Dartmouth, Dec. 6; PRO,CO 5/1353.
[2] *Virginia Gazette* (Purdie), Aug. 11.

I hinted to you, in my last, the parties and factions which prevailed at Richmond. I never was in so disagreeable a situation, and almost despaired of a cause which I saw so ill conducted. Mere vexation and disgust threw me into such an ill state of health, that before the Convention rose, I was sometimes near fainting in the House. During the first part of the Convention, parties run so high that we had frequently no other way of preventing improper measures, but by procrastination, urging the previous question, and giving men time to reflect. However, after some weeks, the babblers were pretty well silenced. . . .[3]

Disorderly though Virginia's first attempt at self-government may have been, the opening week of the convention produced some significant results. A force of 3,000 men, excluding officers, was to be raised for the defense of the Virginia lowlands, and a further 425 men were to be stationed at Fort Pitt, Point Pleasant, and Fort Gower to "watch the motions of the Indians." [4] In addition, companies of minutemen were to be assembled and trained in each county, every man being allowed full pay when on duty. These paid troops were to be in addition to the existing volunteer companies, and in case there should be any misunderstanding on that score, the newspaper announcement added that the volunteers "will still pursue their very commendable and patriotick ardour to perfect themselves in the military art." Then, in parentheses, the notice concluded as follows:

> It is now time for all GENTLEMEN VOLUNTEERS, who intend enlisting in their country's service, to be in readiness to repair to the DRUM HEAD (which will quickly sound through the different counties) where they will be kindly received, enter into present pay and good quarters, and be allowed a certain sum advance, to drink "Success to the liberties of America, and a happy issue out of all our troubles."
> GOD save the *Twelve United Provinces!* Huzza! [5]

[3] *American Archives*, 4th ser., III, 1064.
[4] *Virginia Gazette* (Purdie), July 28.
[5] Ibid.

This stirring call might be described as Virginia's first National Guard recruiting message.

There were other serious matters to be explored in the first days of the Richmond convention, not the least of them being a resolution banning the export of flour, wheat, or any other type of grain after August 4, the ban to remain in effect until repealed by the "Convention or Assembly, or the Honourable the Continental Congress." [6] The wording is interesting in that it indicates that the members of the convention had not entirely foresaken their intention to meet in assembly again at Williamsburg on October 12.

The grain resolution was an important and necessary move, and there is no evidence that it caused much dissension among the delegates. Much more provocative was old Richard Bland's angry denial of what he called "false and scandalous reports" accusing him of having applied to Lord Dartmouth for an appointment to collect taxes imposed by parliament on the Americans. The story apparently went on to tell how, in his efforts to obtain the job, he had offered to surreptitiously promote the Ministerial cause. It ended by claiming that "his conduct in General Congress had been such that he was obliged suddenly to decamp from the city of Philadelphia." [7]

The venerable Bland was not one of the most reserved of people, and, flushing with anger, he reminded his colleagues of the thirty years he had been a member of the general assembly, calling on them to remember his record and bewailing the injustice of it all. Surely, he demanded, the testimony of his life should protect a man of his age from imputations so injurious to his character. He called for a public inquiry and proceeded to name four of his accusers, two of them clergymen, the Reverends Samuel Shield and John Hurt. Eventually, after a great deal of puffing and blowing, Bland sat down, and the convention assured him that it would all be gone into at the proper time— and that would be Friday next.

[6] Ibid., Aug. 4.
[7] Ibid., postscript.

The accusations against Bland were so obviously false that they were hardly worth reviewing. Nevertheless, out of consideration for their elderly and prominent colleague the delegates wasted a great deal of time (doubtless to the irritation of George Mason) interviewing witnesses and hashing the whole affair over from every possible angle. They finally declared unanimously that "the said Richard Bland hath manifested himself the friend of his country, and uniformly stood forth an able asserter of her rights and liberties." [8] Thus Bland acquired a free testimonial and had the satisfaction of seeing it written into the record.

It is perhaps the insecurity of revolutionaries that makes them spend half their time convincing their colleagues that they are sincere and the remainder denouncing others for being traitors. The writer who called himself "Amicus" did better than most and took a righteous swing, not at an individual but at the entire population of Richmond. He denounced it for permitting "many expressions and reflections, injurious to the American cause [to be] uttered with impunity." [9] Two weeks later an answer appeared in the *Gazette* chiding Amicus for trying to set the good people of Richmond at each other's throats, and asking: "Does not the concealing your TRUE name, and the apparent design of your performance, give cause to suspect you [are] influenced more by private resentment, than a regard for public utility?" [1]

Norfolk also came in for its share of brickbats, and, predictably, the inhabitants wrote to the papers claiming that they had been most cruelly maligned. It seems that a rumor had been circulating to the effect that a party was being formed in the town to oppose the measures being adopted by the patriots. "Nothing could be more false than this," declared an indignant but anonymous correspondent. "It is true their local situation will not admit at present of offensive measures, but . . . they

[8] Ibid.
[9] *Virginia Gazette* (Pinkney), July 20.
[1] Ibid., Aug. 3.

are not neglectful of military discipline, and preparations for defence, at the same time that they are forwarding the welfare of the country, equal with its most useful inhabitants, by their industry and attention to its commercial interests." [2] But regardless of these protestations, there were a great many people who remained unconvinced, and who would continue to tell anyone who would listen that Norfolk was full of Tories, and Scotch Tories at that!

Principal targets for patriot vilification were still the unfortunate merchants and shippers who, being engaged in the import and export business, had only to comment on the state of the wind to be accused of traitorous intents. The firm of John Norton and Son, whose ship *Virginia* had been involved in the tea incident of November 1774, was in trouble again in '75. This time the vessel was the *London* and its master Captain Moses Robertson, a highly respected seaman who had been in the Virginia trade for many years. He was accused by a Gloucester County shipbuilder named John Parsons and his three apprentices of delivering banned goods to the Urbanna firm of Mills and Lorimer. According to the patriotic apprentices, they had been delivering a boat to George Lorimer and while doing so they "saw boats pass divers times in the night to and from a ship which we were told was Captain Robertson's; at the same time a Gentleman of that company stood on shore, where we saw parcels landed, which appeared to us to be goods." [3] This published accusation was written on July 10, and its somewhat qualifying tone was the result of angry offstage protestations from the merchants and captain, following the Gloucester-men's original unequivocal charges against them.

Captain Robertson was told by a friend that Parsons's accusations were to be published and so had time to insert his rebuttal into the same issue of the *Virginia Gazette*. Writing from Ruffin's Ferry on the Pamunkey river, Robertson declared that he and Messrs. Mills and Lorimer had been stigmatized in

[2] *Virginia Gazette* (Dixon & Hunter), July 22.
[3] Ibid., July 15.

the most unjustifiable manner. "I shall, without hesitation," he wrote, "take upon me to say that I did not bring any goods for them, or any other person, and am ready to make oath to this assertion whenever I may be called upon for that purpose; and my chief mate, and other officers, will attest the same." [4]

On July 17 Lorimer penned his version of the "Urbanna Affair," saying that neither he nor his firm had received any consignment from Robertson. He admitted, however, that he "dined on board his ship, with some Ladies and Gentlemen, when he [Robertson] obligingly spared me a pair of pistols and a cutteau de chasse, which he had brought for his own use, and not for sale." Lorimer added that he did not think that the ship had a shilling's worth of cargo aboard. "I never corresponded with Mr. Norton," he went on, "or received goods from that house; nor did ever James Mills and company correspond with, or receive goods from those Gentlemen, nor had they any goods by that ship, or by any other from Britain since last November." As a postscript Lorimer concluded: "It may be necessary to observe, that it must have been the apparition of one of the company which Parsons saw on the bank; I was seven miles from Urbanna, Mr. Mills spent the evening at Mr. Gregory's with company, and Mr. Cosby was in Gloucester." [5]

It would seem that Messrs. Lorimer, Mills, and Cosby were not the only people who were not at Urbanna that evening, for at least one of the three accusing apprentices was seven miles away cutting a mast, while another swore on oath that he had not seen anyone landing goods. He had simply told Parsons "that he saw a flat go out of the creek, but [did] not know to what vessel." [6] So it is possible that Parsons was not there either. Nevertheless somebody had seen something, and what it amounted to was this: Captain Robertson's ship was lying at anchor off Urbanna when, late one evening, a trader from Norfolk came up the river and decanted a group of passengers.

[4] Ibid.
[5] Ibid., July 29.
[6] Ibid.

Their baggage was later rowed ashore, as also was some sugar and two casks of wine ordered by Mills and Co. The latter were placed in that company's warehouse after dark only because the master of the trading ship wanted to make the most of a fair wind and so could not wait until morning. The Middlesex County committee held an inquiry on July 19 and heard sworn testimony from the district naval officer, Zachariah Shackleford, that the ship *London* had arrived on May 14 and carried nothing but ballast. Why this could not have been known long before is hard to imagine, but it was not; and it was only now that the committee was able to publicly declare the accusations to be "False and Groundless." Even the *Virginia Gazette* [7] offered its apologies to the merchants and captain for their having been so unjustly censured. Thus all was forgiven and forgotten—including the two months during which the good names of the accused were being dragged through the mire.

Captain Robertson took the whole thing remarkably philosophically and made very little of it when he next wrote home to Norton, saying only: "Another Attempt has been Made to Injure You by a Villian of Gloster County have.g Report'd that I had brot. in a Quant. of Goods for Mills & Co." Recalling the previous trouble, he noted that "in Every Part of the Country Where I have been[,] Your Unmeritd. Treatment of the Ship *Virginia* is Universally Condemn'd & I have found nothing to Impede our Load.g to you as Usual but the Great Price Given in the Country which has Induced many of your Friends to Sell." [8]

As we have seen through these past months, thoughtful Virginians were constantly examining their consciences to find either a substitute for slavery or a rationale that would let them believe that it was not only expedient but right and honorable. The foreign visitors who passed through the colony took remarkably similar views of what they saw. The Marquis de Chastellux, though noting that the slaves were "ill lodged, ill

[7] Ibid., July 22.
[8] *John Norton & Sons*, 382; Yorktown, Aug. 1.

clothed, and often overwhelmed with work," added that many owners treated "their Negroes with great humanity . . . and in general they seemed grieved at having slaves, and are constantly talking of abolishing slavery and of seeking other means of exploiting their lands." [9] Baroness von Riedesel declared that by and large Virginians did not treat their slaves well, though she too added that there were some good masters. "One can recognize them immediately," she observed, "because their slaves are well dressed and housed. These Negroes are very good servants, very faithful to their master, and very much attached to him. It is not surprising that the brutal type of masters have ill-disposed slaves." [1]

This distinction between the good and the bad master, and opinions of him in the eyes of his peers, was brought into unpleasant prominence in July through the controversy over the conduct of one Andrew Estave, who had severely beaten a fifteen-year-old Negro girl. So horrified and incensed were his neighbors and associates that Estave thought it necessary to publicly explain his actions—even though that explanation must have been intensely embarrassing and humiliating to himself and his family.

Since the 10th of February, 1775, when this wench came into my possession, she has eloped from my service no less than thirteen times, without the least shadow of provocation. For the three first times I gave her to the number of forty lashes, but all to no purpose. At last, seeing it was of no avail to correct her any more, I gave her entirely over to herself to see if this usage would have any effect on her stubborn nature; since which she has often run off, and been brought back to me, without receiving the least correction, although she had robbed me of two silver coffee spoons, in company with her husband, who had run off along with her. Since her last return she has continued with me for the space of fifteen days; during which time my little daughter, about three years of age, fell into a lingering disorder, the cause of which we

---

[9] Chastellux, *Travels in North America*, II, 439.
[1] *Baroness von Riedesel and the American Revolution*, 86.

could not discover, she continuing to cry incessantly. One day my negro woman found my child, together with this cruel and unnatural wretch, concealed behind my barn, among the bushes, with her thumb thrust into the private parts of my poor child. She being struck with a horror at the sight, ran in immediately to acquaint us. We accordingly found the little innocent all over bloody, and in a most terrible condition. During the confusion she [the Negro girl] took the opportunity of making her escape, and made to the palace. When brought from thence I gave her eighty lashes, well laid on, and afterwards applied to her back a handful of cold embers; for which I have been stigmatized with the epithets of cruel and inhuman; but I leave it to the impartial public, if, in this situation, I acted beyond the bounds of humany, in the extremity a father must be in upon seeing his innocent child used in this manner.[2]

Here, in a macabre little nutshell, are nested all the horrors and enigmas of slavery. There is no record of the public's reaction to Estave's explanation, but we may be sure that there were some who were still appalled and others who were surprised at his forbearance.

The unhappy lot of men who were forced to labor and suffer without reward caused Lord Dunmore constant concern—particularly as he was one of them. In his July 12 letter to Lord Dartmouth, Dunmore reminded his superior that the Virginia officers of the Crown derived their salaries from the duties on exported tobacco and on the tonnage of all vessels trading to the colony, both of which would be terminated at the beginning of September. "I have for near two years received little or no perquisites of my office," Dunmore complained, "as the collectors cannot be brought to accounts, but after the first of September I shall receive neither perquisites nor salary; I hope therefore your Lordship will acquaint me how I am to Subsist, if it be his Majesty's pleasure that his Governor remain here." He went on to say that since the departure of the *Fowey* he was in dire need of funds for the hire of a ship aboard which to live and

[2] *Virginia Gazette* (Pinkney), July 20.

to store his baggage and his servants. He had also to find a
vessel on which to house the hundred soldiers who were
promised from Florida. In case the Secretary of State should
have missed the point, Dunmore added that "I cannot but hope
that the inconvenience and distress wich I must necessarily go
thro' in this situation will be considered as proofs of my zeal for
his Majesty's service." [3]

It was obvious to Lord Dunmore that writing to London was
a mortally long-winded way of raising funds for needs that were
very present and very pressing. It seems probable, though the
evidence is scant, that he decided to resort to a more practical
method, and on an unrecorded date in the last week of July a
party of men from an unspecified man-of-war went ashore at
Hampton and helped themselves to £900 from the coffers of the
customhouse. By a quite remarkable coincidence, even before
news of this exploit reached Williamsburg, a body of willing
volunteers assembled and proceeded to the offices of the Receiver and Auditor General, the Postmaster, and the Naval
Officer of the Upper James River, where they seized £360,
£314 14s. 0d, and £1,000 respectively. The postmaster, incidentally, was John Dixon, of Dixon and Hunter's *Virginia
Gazette*, though discretion dictated that his paper made no more
of the incident than did his competitors.

At no point did Lord Dunmore report the Hampton seizure
to Lord Dartmouth, and it is possible that the rumor was false
and was used simply as an excuse for the patriots having dipped
their fingers into the Crown's purse. Pinkney's *Gazette* concluded its brief report of the blow and counterblow with the
statement that it was understood "that detachments are sent out
to secure all monies in the hands of the public officers throughout the colony, the people being fearful of its falling into the
hands of our enemies." [4] There was every likelihood that the
patriots' profit would be considerably increased before they were
through.

[3] Dunmore to Dartmouth, July 12; PRO,CO 5/1353.
[4] July 27.

In England, as the month ended, two travelers returned
from abroad. Captain Cook brought his *Resolution* into Plymouth on July 25 after completing his great voyage to the South
Seas, a journey whose length was almost three times the
equatorial circumference of the earth. The second traveler's
passage had been shorter, though the sight of England can have
been no more welcome. Captain Collins's *Magdelen* had brought
Lady Dunmore safely home, and the *Gentleman's Magazine* [5]
duly noted that she and her seven children arrived in London on
July 31. Neither it nor the London newspapers mentioned any
pregnancy.

[5] August 1775, p. 402.

[*VIII*]

AUGUST

It *was hot in Williamsburg in August, just*
as it had been through July, hot and humid. There had been no
rain since July 16, and then only scattered nocturnal thunder
showers in the night whose water had run straight off the hard
baked clay of the tobacco fields. Some promise of relief had been
offered on the night of the twenty-eighth, when the lightning
flashed throughout the dark hours, beginning in the north and
moving round to the east. Colonel Landon Carter had written in
his diary: "Perhaps, as the Electricians say, it ws unenubelated
explosions of the electrick fluid discharging itself, or, as we say
in common Parlans, heat flashes. It is thought to portend rain as
the same to the South does dry weather." [1] Carter's diary is a
valuable source of weather information, even if it does tend to be
contradictory; unfortunately it is very fragmentary and no
August entries survive. Consequently we do not know whether
the expected rain was forthcoming. But in any case it would
have taken a continuous wet spell to make much difference.

In town, those who went barefoot skipped nimbly along the
sandy streets keeping to the patches of shade, and householders
kept their front and back doors open to make the most of any
breeze. Houses were generally planned to locate both doors on
the same axis for this very purpose, with stairs rising from the
hall, helping to carry the draft upstairs—along with the dust

[1] Landon Carter, *Diary*, II, 932; July 30.

stirred up by every carriage and horseman that passed in the street outside.

None of the diarists and travelers complained of the flies, probably because they were such an integral part of life that they were accepted without comment; nor did mosquitoes attract much attention, though Fithian twice remarked on their absence from the Carter plantation at "Nomini Hall," and when one finally landed on him he was vastly incensed. Then, as now, mosquitoes were plentiful in the low-lying marshland areas of the colony, and anyone venturing into the swamps in the summer could expect little mercy. Most writers did comment on the ubiquitous ticks which could be relied on to mount any leg that ventured into long grass or assail any posterior that sat on a tree stump. Nicholas Cresswell was plagued with them during his travels through the forests of the back country, and he observed that "If they are not removed in a short time they grow like Ticks on a Dog." [2] Fithian also mentioned them on a number of occasions, and he believed that Fanny, his employer's daughter, had developed a fever as a result of having been bitten by seed ticks, the inflamed bites covering the child "like a distinct Small Pox." [3]

The summer bred all manner of unpleasant bugs, but, like the flies, they were so common that familiarity made them less offensive. Nevertheless if one wanted to keep one's room clean, it was thought a good idea to house a tortoise there who would live off the cockroaches. But history does not reveal how one kept the tortoise from being equally unattractive in his own way.

At this time of year there may have been some small advantages to living aboard ship, for the bugs were less varied, and there was many a breeze over the water that never cooled the land. Some of them may have blown through the open casements into the stern cabin of the sloop *Otter*, where Lord Dunmore was writing his first and only August dispatch to

[2] *Cresswell*, 79; May 26.
[3] Fithian, *Journal*, 171; Aug. 17, 1774.

London. It was not and could not be very encouraging in its content. The convention in Richmond had called for the raising of large numbers of troops and was about to issue £300,000 worth of paper money to pay for them. It had also prohibited the exportation of all provisions after August 3, thus going one better than the Continental Congress, which was not imposing such a restriction until September 10. The governor noted that this move had "given great disgust to many of their own party who had purchased great quantities of Grain which they meant to have exported" before the September deadline. The merchants of Norfolk, he added, had petitioned the convention for more time.

Lord Dunmore was able to report one item on the credit side, his reinforcements sent from St. Augustine on orders from General Gage had arrived the night before and were encamped at Gosport. He stated that they amounted to "about Seventy in number including Officers." [4] Pinkney's *Gazette*,[5] as did both other papers, quoted a report from Norfolk, placing the time of arrival a day earlier: "On Monday last arrived here from Saint Augustine about 60 soldiers, on board the sloop tender some time since belonging to Mr. Bowdoin, of the Eastern Shore. These with about 40 more, which are hourly expected, are to compose a bodyguard for his excellency the governor. . . . The troops above mentioned are under the command of a captain and two lieutenants; the ensign it is said, is on his way overland." None of the newspapers identified the regiment from which the men came, but it can have been no secret, for on August 4 the Norfolk loyalist James Parker wrote that they were part of the Fourteenth Regiment of Foot.[6] He too added that forty additional men were expected at any moment. But they failed to appear, having been detained in South Carolina.

Continuing his letter to the Secretary of State, Lord Dun-

[4] Dunmore to Dartmouth, "from Otter Sloop of War in Elizabeth River by Norfolk 2d August," PRO,CO 5/1353.

[5] Aug. 3.

[6] Parker to Steuart; CSP.

more pointed out with some truth that "this is a very small reinforcement considering the situation of this distracted Country." As he had earlier reported that the Richmond convention was calling for three thousand men for service in Tidewater, that fact should have been reasonably obvious to Lord Dartmouth. Dunmore went on to say, as he had before, that if only he could be supplied "with a few hundred more with Arms, Ammunition and the other requisites of War, and with full powers to Act that I could in a few Months reduce this Colony to perfect Submission." The governor would have been pleased to know that there was at least one Tory in the colony who agreed with him. A month earlier James Parker had declared that "If Ld D. had a little force he would soon cure them [the Richmond delegates] of Conventioning." [7] While there could be no question of defeating the patriots in the field, however disorganized they might still be, the reinforcement was good for morale. On the day of its arrival, Lord Dunmore went ashore at Gosport, a village across the Elizabeth river from Norfolk, and proceeded to review his new troops with all the aplomb of a Marlborough on the eve of Ramillies.

The arrival of the soldiers caused a deal of scurrying hither and thither among the patriot groups, and it was rumored that as soon as the additional forty men arrived, the entire force plus the marines from the men-of-war would march on Yorktown and then move up the peninsula toward Williamsburg. On August 4 Purdie's *Virginia Gazette* [8] defiantly declared that Lord Dunmore was likely to "pay us a visit in this city, although he cannot expect the same cordial reception as on former occasions, but will probably be received with *such illuminations* &c. as may make him forget his way to the palace." There is, however, no evidence that Dunmore had any such intentions. He was much too busy putting his own house—or ship—in order.

Knowing that he could not long continue to reside aboard the *Otter*, he had in mid-July impressed the Jamaica merchant

[7] Ibid., July 14.
[8] *Postcript.*

ship *William*, which he was now busily fitting out as his flagship, arming it with thirteen field guns, which he had probably seized at Hampton. The governor had assured the owners, John Brown and Company of Norfolk, that they would be handsomely reimbursed for the loss of their ship, but it is doubtful that they were very impressed.

Rumors of Lord Dunmore's aggressive intentions again increased when a brig arrived at Norfolk from Boston with seven officers aboard. They had been sent by General Gage to assist in the campaign—whatever it might be—and comprised two captains, a lieutenant, three ensigns, and a surgeon. It seems that their orders had been a little unclear, and they supposed that they were coming to command an existing loyalist force. "Some of them expressed great surprise, when, in answer to their enquiries, they were told there were no men raised here, as it seems they had been made to expect that government, as it is called, could raise troops at will." [9]

Concern about Lord Dunmore's intentions was blended with fear of that old black goblin, the rumor of an impending slave insurrection. It was not one whit allayed by Pinkney's *Gazette* [1] re-reporting a story circulating in England, but which had originated in Virginia, to the effect that the entire continent was in a state of dire apprehension. "Several insurrections have been attempted in different places," declared the report, "the planters are distressed beyond measure. Several of the conveniences, and even necessaries of life, are very scarce. The negroes, it is positively asserted, are almost naked; that, with some other disagreeable circumstances, it is imagined, stimulate them to such desperate attempts. In Yorktown, a strict patrol is kept every night, and any negro found in the street is confined till the next day. The like cautions are observed in other towns." [2]

Although there was in reality no fresh evidence of any organized Negro revolt, the number that was absconding in the

[9] *Virginia Gazette* (Purdie), Aug. 25.
[1] Aug. 10.
[2] *Virginia Gazette* (Dixon & Hunter), Aug. 5.

hope of gaining freedom aboard Dunmore's ships was causing the inhabitants of Norfolk county considerable concern. However, it is debatable whether they were as concerned over the swelling of Lord Dunmore's ranks as they were at the loss of their own valuable property. The exodus was apparently continuing regardless of Captain Macartney's assurances that "not the least encouragement should be shewn then."[3] Macartney had been wholly sincere in his belief that providing sanctuary for runaway slaves was a most improper procedure, a stand which had infuriated Lord Dunmore and delighted the slave-owning public. So pleased were the citizens of Norfolk that on July 28 a deputation of Common Councilors waited on both Macartney and Captain Squire of the *Otter* to present them "with the thanks of the Corporation, in discountenancing the runaway slaves that had made application for service on board."[4]

As August progressed the picture began to change, and Dunmore was learning that holds filled with Negroes were more of a liability than an asset. Whereas earlier owners applying to the governor for the return of their lost slaves had been roundly abused, by mid-month applicants were, in fact, getting them back. Captain Macartney, meanwhile, was sliding quickly down the popularity poll: "notwithstanding the very civil treatment he has met with since his arrival in Virginia, both at York and Norfolk, [he] lately took it into his head to write a very insolent letter to the mayor of Norfolk concerning town meeting, &c. which had a suitable reply."[5]

Macartney's fall from grace had resulted indirectly from the arrival of the St. Augustine troops at Gosport. No quarters had been available for either the officers or the men, and in remedying this oversight Lord Dunmore had requisitioned a house belonging to Gosport's leading merchant, Andrew Sprowle. The Norfolk Committee of Safety, always dutifully

[3] Ibid.
[4] *Virginia Gazette* (Purdie), Aug. 25.
[5] Dunmore to Graves, Sept. 12; PRO, Admiralty 1/485.

and joyfully hunting for defectors, decided that Sprowle had not been evicted, protesting, into the street but had actually agreed to permit the troops to occupy his house. Consequently he was ordered to appear before the committee to answer to that charge; whereupon Macartney sent a message to the mayor of Norfolk (conveniently named Paul Loyal) warning him that punitive action would follow if any harm came to Sprowle. At a public meeting held in Norfolk on August 21 Macartney was loudly assailed for having interfered in what the patriots considered to be a purely civil matter. But every cloud has some sort of a lining, and as a result of the Sprowle affair Macartney found himself being tossed into the welcoming arms and good graces of the governor. Lord Dunmore had come to the conclusion that Macartney's "imprudencies . . . proceeded more from a want of knowledge of Mankind than from any bad intention." [6] The timing was unfortunate, as Captain Montagu had already delivered Dunmore's letter to Admiral Graves calling for the recall and court-martial of Macartney, a letter that, as Montagu commented, could be relied on to break Macartney.

The presence of the governor and his forces in and around Norfolk put a heavy strain on the patriot committees, on the city government, and on the loyalist sympathizers who wanted to show their sympathy but were not sure whether to risk doing so. It seemed to be a game wherein all the players were likely to lose. There had been the case at the beginning of the month in which John Schaw of Gosport had decided to show where he stood (he happened to be beside Lord Dunmore at the time) and proceeded to point out to the troops a certain Alexander Main, who was wearing a patriot hunting shirt in the presence of his Lordship. Main turned out to be one of the fifers attached to a local volunteer company, and he was seized and imprisoned aboard the *Otter*. The Norfolk Committee of Safety let it be known that "Schaw had herein shewn himself a busy tool, and

[6] *Virginia Gazette* (Purdie), Aug. 11, postscript.

an enemy to American liberty, and as Such we advise every friend to his country to have no farther dealings or connexion with him." [7] If Schaw was anxious to be noticed, he had well succeeded, and Lord Dunmore appointed him "Deputy Commissioner for Supplying the Troops here with Provisions." For his activities in this role and in the Main affair, he was shortly thereafter grabbed by a patriot mob in the middle of Norfolk and "was beat and bruised in a most Cruel manner, and then had all his Cloathes torn from his back with an intention to have tarred and fethered him" [8] before friends could come to his rescue.

Alexander Main's contribution to history seems to have been confined to watching Lord Dunmore's parade in a provocative shirt, an exploit that might be deemed more foolhardy than useful. According to Purdie's *Virginia Gazette*,[9] he was released on August "after undergoing a strict examination by Lord Dunmore." [1] But what information the governor could have hoped to extract from a volunteer fifer is hard to imagine.

The affair of Messrs. Schaw and Main can be dismissed as ill-advised posturing on the part of an unlikable loyalist and a precocious patriot. As in all social and political upheavals the lunatic fringe always ignites first, and although its members are generally more tiresome than dangerous, their activities can sometimes maneuver the more responsible parties into unwanted confrontations. The activities of a certain Captain Phillips could conceivably have forced Lord Dunmore and the lower peninsula volunteer companies into such a position. Unfortunately I have been unable to find details of exactly what Phillips was planning (if anything), and therefore I can do no better than to quote the *Gazette*'s satirical commentary verbatim:

[7] Footnote to letter from Dunmore to the mayor of Norfolk, copy enclosed with Dunmore to Dartmouth of Oct. 5; PRO,CO 5/1353; n.d.

[8] Aug. 11, postscript.

[9] Ibid.

[1] Ibid.

In consequence of many false reports spread through the country of one Capt. Phillips having armed a number of men to assist in the destruction of our rights, we are well informed that offers of 500 or 1000 men have been made to march down, if it should be thought necessary. Phillips himself, it is currently said, was under such dreadful apprehensions, upon a report of a number of men being on their way to pay him a visit, that he betook himself to a swamp, where his fears alarmed him to that degree as to make him mistake the stumps and roots of trees for Indians, which his imagination, it is said, swelled to 500. After being in this delightful situation three days and nights, amid the musick of countless numbers of muskitoes, he ventured forth, but ah! (*quantum mutatus ab illo!*) so disfigured and deformed, by the stinging familiarities of his musical companions, that scarcely his own dog knew him. He immediately despatched letters of contrition, and promises of ammendment, to some gentlemen of the county; and it is probable another trip to the swamp will work in him a thorough reformation, and conviction of his folly.[2]

Rumors and counterrumors helped to keep the ale flowing in every Virginia tavern, and each night a few more honest Virginians would find that their characters had been drained of their virtues and left as empty as the bottles on the table. There was Anthony Warwick of Isle of Wight County, who was called before a neighborhood committee "on a suspicion of having violated the association." He wrote declining to appear unless assured of protection from assaults by people in his own county, and he added comments that were deemed to be abuse of the most scurrilous order. The content of the letter was imparted to the people involved, and as a result

a number of respectable inhabitants of Isle of Wight assembled, and seized the said Anthony Warwick and conveyed him to Smithfield, where they detained him some time, in order that a committee might determine in what manner he ought to be dealt with; but a sufficient number of members not attending, and the said Warwick not giving any satisfac-

[2] *Virginia Gazette* (Pinkney), Aug. 24.

tory reason for his illiberal abuse, the populace very deliberately led him to the stocks, and having prepared him for the
purpose, gave him a fashionable suit of *tar and feathers*,
being the most proper badge of distinction for men of his
complexion. They then mounted him on his horse, and drove
him out of town, through a shower of eggs, the smell of
which, our correspondent informs us, seemed to have a
material effect upon the delicate constitution of this *motleyed*
gentleman.[3]

This victory over the enemy must have been most satisfying
for "the respectable inhabitants" of Isle of Wight, and no doubt
the humor of the thing obscured the minuscule detail that no one
had established that Mr. Warwick had, in fact, committed any
violation. It is quite possible that he had, but if this was the sort
of justice one could expect in the new, free America, there might
be something to be said for British bondage.

It would be a mistake to suppose that this treatment of the
alleged opposition was confined to the Southern colonies; far
from it. The need for demonstrative patriotism transcended all
barriers of geography, race, creed, color, or sex. Later, in
Boston, when an offending civil officer could not be brought to
patriot justice, his wife and daughter were stripped, tarred and
feathered, and driven through the city.

Keeping pace in Virginia with the rumors of local indiscre-
tions were those of victories and defeats (the interpretation
depending on one's point of view) to northward. Many of the
stories were first printed in the London papers, then shipped
back to Virginia and reprinted in the *Gazettes*. But once having
been lifted from the printed page and argued over in the
taverns, even the most lifeless of three-month-old rumors could
be miraculously resurrected. A story circulating on the floor of
the Royal Exchange in London on June 15, reporting that
50,000 patriot troops had surrounded Boston, saved the women
and children, and then burned the city, was printed in the

[3] Dixon & Hunter.

August 19 issue of the *Virginia Gazette*,[4] spruced up and ready to be passed around again. Not only was Boston in ashes, but General Gage and his entire army had been forced to lay down their arms. The same *Gazette* also offered other provocative reports from a source nearer at hand:

> *August* 7. We are credibly informed that General *Burgoyne* has lately shewn every appearance of a deep seated *melancholy*, is continually walking the streets of Boston with his arms folded across his breast, and talking to himself.
>
> We are also credibly informed that General Gage and Admiral Graves have publicly quarrelled; Admiral Graves having told Gage it was a cowardly action to burn Charlestown. Gage sharply replied, he should not consult him in such matters.
>
> General Gage, it is said, has resigned the command of the troops to General Howe.

There could have been seeds of truth in all three items. Burgoyne was not only an able soldier but also a playwright, actor, and intense admirer of himself, all of which elements may have provoked a melancholy visage at so frustrating a stage in the game. General Gage and Admiral Graves were indeed at loggerheads, but the report was premature in stating that Gage had resigned in favor of Howe. On the contrary, on August 2, in London, a commission received final approval appointing Gage commander in chief over all North America. The change of command was still more than a month away.

Readers of Pinkney's *Gazette* [5] were treated to more sensational revelations stemming from a report from Cambridge, Massachusetts, of July 27: "It is said general Burgoyne is *delirious about half his time*, and that general Gage is often *out of his head*. Whether or not it is the same *distemper* that *infects* both is not certainly known."

Even more colorful were the so-called first-hand reports

[4] Aug. 17.
[5] Dixon & Hunter, Aug. 12.

from London, which brought such tales of chaos and collapse
that only a Gibbon could do them justice. News of the British
defeats at Lexington and Concord were received in the city with
general rejoicing, and many more influential people were now
openly supporting the American cause. News was received at
Portsmouth, New Hampshire, that "there has been the largest
mob in London that ever was known, who surrounded the
Parliament House, and demanded an immediate repeal of all
American acts, or they would pull down the House; on which
Lord North looked out of the window, and said, if they would
disperse, no more troops should embark till they heard from
Boston again." On the same page of the *Virginia Gazette* [6] was
carried a New York report also noting great disturbances in
England but adding that the parliament building *had* been
pulled down and that Lord North had fled to France. The reins
of government were now in the hands of America's champions,
Edmund Burke and the Englishman's Patrick Henry, John
Wilkes, Lord Mayor of London. Another source had it that
Wilkes and the City Corporation had agreed to authorize the
training of the London militia "for the preservation of their own
liberty, as well as that of America." [7] The same report added
that Lord North's government was sending increases of pay to
the troops at Boston and that the governor of Canada was
ordered to attack across the American frontiers. Elsewhere on
the same page the flight of Lord North was again reported, and
all the troops were to be recalled from Boston. You paid your
money and you took your choice. Stocks had plunged ten per
cent, mobs were roaming the London streets, the palace was
besieged, and the King had fled to Kew.

All these stories, however improbable, helped to boost
patriot morale; so, too, did the ever-persistent rumors of foreign
intervention. However the more sober patriot leaders may have
wondered whether the enemies of England might not later be
theirs. For more than two hundred years the threat that "the

[6] *Virginia Gazette* (Pinkney), Aug. 17.
[7] *Virginia Gazette* (Dixon & Hunter), Aug. 12.

Spaniards will get you" had been enough to make the most contrary child eat his porridge. The possibility of a Spanish invasion had been of as much concern to the Jamestown colonists as the Indians. The same largely imaginary threat persisted still in South Carolina and Georgia, even though the Spaniards had surrendered their fortress, the Castillo de San Marcos, along with the rest of Florida in 1763.

Catholic Spain and a free America would make most unlikely bedfellows, and the news that the Pretender had gone there from Italy should have given as much cause for concern in America as it did in England. The report of his journey was contained in a letter from an English merchant of Leghorn to another in London, who added that the Spanish armament "preparing with such diligence, will surprise all Europe when its destination is known. It is no wonder your American Quixotism, as the phrase is, should have put schemes into the heads of some of the great powers, which they otherwise would never have thought of." [8]

Reports of the vast size of the Spanish armada were reaching England from all quarters, each more hair-raising than the last. A dispatch from Barcelona spoke of 150 transports onto which were boarding three battalions of Spanish guards, three of Walloon guards, each with a complement of 700 men; in addition there were two battalions from the Aragon regiment, two from the Irish regiment, plus battalions of grenadiers, cavalry, and dragoons. The convoy was planning to rendezvous with others at Carthagena; but, ended the report; "We are totally ignorant of the destination of this armament." Other accounts gave the fleet a total of "500 sail of transports, 8 ships of the line, 3 frigates, and 3 fire-ships, with 18,000 foot, and 1000 horse, and that they were seen standing to the westward but their destination not known. . . ." [9]

It seems fantastic that so vast a punitive force could have been put together over a considerable period of time without its

[8] Ibid.
[9] Ibid.

purpose being revealed. But if British intelligence did know, it too managed to keep the secret remarkably well. Lord Rochford assured the House of Lords that merchants in Spain were not worried that the preparation were being made against England. But, a London newspaper contradicted, saying: "it is but right to inform the public, that a very intelligent English merchant has written several times to his correspondent in London, in the most positive terms, that there is no doubt that the Spaniards intend to go to war with us. He says, 'that throughout the Spanish nation, particularly among the sailors, there is an eager wish, and strong expectation, for a war with England.'" [1]

There were some who were equally convinced that the Spaniards' intention was to thrash the Moors and Algerians for having laid siege to the Spanish fortress of Melilla on the North African coast. Others were certain that Florida and the Carribean Islands were due for a visit, while yet another group of experts knew that Portugal was the target. A May 26 report from London announced that the Spanish king had conscripted one man in six out of his entire population and that two armies were being assembled, one for use in Europe and the other in America.

The same source, published in Pinkney's *Gazette* went on to argue with itself, saying: "Notwithstanding all conjectures to the contrary, the armaments making by the Spaniards, if there be any truth in the accounts of them, can never be destined against Gibralter or Jamaica. Six thousand horses can neither be deemed proper or necessary to traverse the Woods and Gullies of the latter, much less will they be suited to clamber the rocks of Gibralter. Ireland, beyond dispute, if they have any designs against the British crown, must be the place. . . ."

If this were true, the danger to England was at this moment greater than it had been in 1588. She had no Drake, Frobisher, or Hawkins nor any great advantage of maneuverability over the enemy at sea. Besides, Britain's military defenses were now

[1] Aug. 10.

alarmingly depleted by her commitments in America. If Spain was, in truth, arming against England, now would be the time to strike. Of course, "now," as far as Virginia was concerned, was already two months into history. When these alarming reports were being read in Williamsburg the blow had undoubtedly long since fallen. It was not beyond the realms of possibility that the white standard of Spain had been flying over St. James's Palace for at least a month—in which case Lexington, Bunker Hill, the trials of Dunmore, and the oratory of Henry had all been wasted effort.

Had the Spanish armada headed northward, the glory of Britain might have been eclipsed in the eighteenth rather than in the twentieth century. But instead the fleet sailed to the south and on July 2 appeared off the Bay of Algiers; it was seen to be vastly larger than previous reports had led the world to believe. There were seven ships of the line, eight of 40 guns, and thirty-two frigates, 19,000 seamen and 28,000 infantry and cavalry, the ships being commanded by Admiral Don Pedro Castejoin and the army under General Alexander O'Reilly, who six years earlier had been the Spanish commander at New Orleans.

It was O'Reilly's plan that he should not engage the enemy until his entire force had landed. Such reticence was particularly desirable in view of the impressive array of Moors that was drawn up to meet him. But the first division to go ashore was so anxious to get to grips with the enemy that they rushed headlong into battle, ignoring the cover provided for them by the guns of their fleet. The result was total disaster; thirteen hours of carnage ensued, with the Spaniards finally being driven back into the sea with a loss of 800 dead and 2,000 wounded. The *Annual Register* [2] noted that "Some foreign accounts state the loss at double that number, which, considering the length of the engagement, the fury of the combatants, and the number of officers of rank who were killed or wounded, does not appear improbable." The *Register* concluded by describing the entire

[2] *Annual Register, 1775,* "History of Europe," 146.

expedition as "amongst the most disgraceful in its event, as well
as the most formidable in its preparations, of any in the present
age." Afterwards the blame was being laid in all directions: the
first division disobeyed orders, the stores and provisions should
not have been landed, and the marines were so frightened of
falling into the hands of the Moors that they would not approach
the shore. There seems to have been some support for the
marines' fears, if not for their conduct, as the Moors later
burned 600 wounded prisoners. But the largest brickbats were
reserved for General O'Reilly, whose appointment as commander had been cause for jealousy before the attack and who
was now condemned as an incompetent foreigner. The Spanish
military aristocracy wanted to offer him as a sacrifice to their
wounded national honor, and as solace to the shades of their
dead friends. Commented the *Annual Register*:[3] "This is the
usual ebullition of national vanity, which will ever seek some
foreign object of resentment, on which, if possible, to heap its
own disgrace." However King Charles III of Spain stood by
O'Reilly, and, although he had no alternative but to remove him
from military command, O'Reilly was given the quiet but
lucrative governorship of the province of Andalusia. Thus, as
far as England was concerned, the ghost of the Spanish armada
was laid to rest.

But there were still the French. What they were up to was
anybody's guess, and everybody was trying. There were as
many French experts as there had been of the Spanish affair; but
on one point they were all agreed—whatever France had in
mind, it could not be good for Britannia. Reports still persisted
that armaments were being assembled at Brest and other
harbors, and there could be very little purpose to such preparations if they were not directed toward England. Nevertheless the
papers also reported that "the French Court has repeated the
most solumn assurances that they have not any hostile designs
against this kingdom." But few Englishmen would have been

---

[3] Ibid.

prepared to bet a counterfeit farthing on the word of a Frenchman. The very same issue of the *Virginia Gazette* [4] that printed these assurances also carried the statement that "It is affirmed that the riots in France are much exaggerated with a view to draw off the attention of our Court from the very formidable armament now going on at Brest, Rochfort, and Toulon." On top of that it was rumored that the King of Prussia had recently been in Paris incognito and after three days had disappeared. Somebody had to be up to something.

Apart from her problems of substantial popular opposition to her American policy, Britain was also having trouble in the very groin of her endeavors, in the dockyards that built and fitted her ships. The shipwright's pay had long been a source of discontent, but tradition had it that the men could augment their pay with "chips," pieces of scrap wood which they could take home as perquisites. But as Britain's forests dwindled and wood became more valuable, it was decided that the men were taking too much home and that some were deliberately mutilating good pieces to make them eligible as "chips." Consequently it was decided to stop this practice and instead to give the men a small increase in salary. The next step was to establish rates of pay for piecework in the hope of encouraging those who wanted more money to work harder, a policy that had been found effective in private yards, but which had not before been tried in the royal docks. But the shipwrights took a very dim view of this; they were not in the least interested in more pay for more work; what they wanted was more pay for less work. They therefore went on strike and refused to return unless piecework was abolished.

The navy board told the men that the piecework policy was adopted to enable them to earn more money, and if they did not like it the proposal would be dropped. But the course of management and labor relations ran no smoother then than it does today; the men still did not go back to work, but bound

[4] Dixon & Hunter, Aug. 12.

themselves by oath to stay out until their wages were raised from 2s. 1d., to a half crown (or 2s. 6d) a day. Some did go back, notably at the Woolwich yard, but the strikers attacked the blacklegs and started a riot, which had to be put down with troops. "At Plymouth they had the cruelty to run a pole under the legs of some of the people who had returned to their duty, and after hoisting them up on their shoulders, conveyed them, in that painful state, through the streets." [5]

The dockyard troubles were not confined to the navy yards, but were apt to break out anywhere where two or three agitators could gather together. A gang of sailors rigging a ship at Liverpool claimed that the owners had underpaid them, and they went aboard again and demolished the lot. A party of constables seized nine of the men and hauled them off to gaol, whereupon some two thousand were whipped into a mob, which proceeded to break every window in the prison. The Riot Act was read, but to no purpose, and the crowd threatened to tear the building apart. The constables, unable to defend the prison, released the sailors, and the mob marched off in triumph, terrorizing the town far into the night. A few days later another mob of sailors (probably the same ones), demonstrating against export regulations that damaged the slave trade and so put them out of work, threatened to destroy the whole of Liverpool. Armed with cannon they proceeded to open fire, but were eventually dispersed by a troop of light cavalry summoned from Manchester. There was, all in all, little tranquillity on the home front.

The search for the new ultimate weapon was a quest that was always diligently pursued at times like these. Patrick Ferguson was working on a rifle that loaded at the breach instead of at the muzzle, and on June 12, according to the *Virginia Gazette*,[6] a new cannon was demonstrated at the royal arsenal at Woolwich, two of them firing fifty-nine shots in as many seconds. This remarkable performance was witnessed

[5] *Gentleman's Magazine* (1775), 389.
[6] Dixon & Hunter, Aug. 12.

by Lord Townsend, Master General of the Ordnance, and by
General Sir Jeffrey Amherst, who had commanded against the
French in North America in 1758 and who had subsequently
been appointed Governor General of British North America.
On August 19 Sir Jeffrey almost came to grief through an un-
intentional demonstration of a much less sophisticated weapon:

> The master of the Rose and Crown, the corner of Downing-
> street, Westminster, intending to get cleaned an old musket,
> which had been a long time loaded for the security of his
> house, drew out the slugs, as he thought, and gave it to a man
> to fire off the powder, which the man did; but there being a
> slug left in the gun, on firing it, it went into the dining room
> of Sir Jeffrey Amherst, which is almost opposite; took with it
> the glass of the window, passed over Sir Jeffrey's head as he
> sat writing, and after striking against the opposite side of the
> room, fell to the floor. Happily Sir Jeffrey had left the
> window about five minutes, or he would have been shot.[7]

The danger of idiots playing about with guns was frequently demonstrated in Virginia during these summer months,
as new recruits to the patriot cause practiced their arms drill and
their marksmanship. In Middlesex County a small posse was
gathering to hunt for three Negroes who had robbed a local
widow, and while they waited for their friends to assemble, early
arrivals amused themselves by going through the manual exercise. Just as they got to the point of presenting their muskets
to fire, one of their friends arrived and found himself with four
or five guns pointed at him. So, just for fun, he pointed his
musket at them and, also just for fun, pulled the trigger. The gun
turned out to be loaded, and two men were killed.

The lowland Virginia volunteers and militia were armed
with whatever muskets, fowling pieces, or other weapons that
happened to be available, but the mountain men from the
frontiers generally owned Pennsylvania rifles, the finest weapons on the North American continent. Nothing the British had
could match them except, later, Major Ferguson's breach-

[7] *Annual Register, 1775*, "Chronicle," 148; Aug. 19.

loading rifle, which ironically, would never be issued in any quantity. The volunteer riflemen came down from the frontier counties, marching through Maryland on their way to join Washington's army in Massachusetts. Stopping at the town of Frederick on August 1, Captain Michael Cressap's company of 130 men were pleased to demonstrate their marksmanship:

A clapboard with a mark the size of a dollar was set up; they began to fire off hand, and the bystanders were surprised, few shots being made that were not close to or in the paper; when they had shot for a time in this way, some lay on their backs, some on their breast or side, others ran 20 or 30 steps and firing, appeared to be equally certain of their mark. . . . A young man took up the board in his hand, not by the end but by the side, and holding it up, his brother walked to the distance and very coolly shot into the white; laying down his rifle, he took the board, and holding it as it was held before, the second brother shot as the former had done. . . . One of the men took the board, and placing it between his legs, stood with his back to the tree, while another drove the center.

The bystander who recorded this exhibition, asked: "What would a regular army, of considerable strength in the forests of America do with a 1000 of these men?" [8] What, indeed?

John Harrower told much the same story of George Washington's experiences in recruiting frontier riflemen. He had called for 500, but so many volunteered that he decided to take only the better shots; to test them, Washington set a board a foot square at a distance of 150 yards and drew a life-size nose in chalk in the center of it. Those marksmen who came closest to it were to make up the force. But after the first forty or fifty had tried their luck, the nose had been blown clean out of the target, and it was not long before the rest of the board was splintered to pieces. Experience would show that the frontiersmen were effective at even greater distances; while hitting a man-sized target at 75 to 100 yards was about the best that could be expected from the average, musket-toting Redcoat. The British

[8] *Virginia Gazette* (Dixon & Hunter), Sept. 7.

army was almost entirely armed with the regulation "Brown Bess," which had remained essentially the same since 1690, though its performance varied in some degree owing to the fact that the parts were purchased by contract—often foreign contract. However, the musket had one great advantage: it alone was fitted with a bayonet; and as had been painfully demonstrated at Bunker Hill, you cannot halt a bayonet charge with swinging gunstocks.

The motley collections of arms available to the Continental army and to the militia companies was a matter of concern to the congress, and in the session of July 18 it was resolved "That it be recommended to the makers of arms for the use of the militia, that they make good substantial muskets, with barrels three feet and a half in length, that will carry an ounce ball, and fitted with a good bayonet and steel ramrod, and that the making of such arms be encouraged in these united colonies." [9]

The British government had on August 23 placed an embargo on the shipment of arms and ammunition to the colonies in the hope of capitalizing on their supposed lack of preparedness to wage war. Not suprisingly, therefore, a considerable display of Ministerial pyrotechnics occurred when a report reached London claiming that a ship bound for America had been apprehended in the Bristol Channel and found to be carrying 30,000 muskets. Six days later, however, the report was declared to be untrue.

The British and colonial lack of enthusiasm for the improvement of firearms in the eighteenth century is hard to explain. The Pennsylvania rifle, though slower to load, was obviously an improvement over the smooth-bore musket, and one might reasonably expect that everyone would have wanted it. Similarly, Ferguson's breach-loader so greatly increased the speed of loading that one would suppose that the army that equipped its men with it would have the edge over any ramrodding opponent —yet it would never be at all widely distributed. It is curious,

[9] Ibid., Aug. 5.

too, that the bow and arrow had been totally dropped, for the
English longbow had a killing range of more than 200 yards
and could be shot five or six times while a musket was being
loaded and fired once. It had no springs, hammer, or frizzen to
break, could not misfire, and was not dependent on the availa-
bility of lead or dry gunpowder. The Indian bow naturally had
these advantages, but it was much smaller than the traditional
English longbow and so had nothing like the range.

The Indians of Tidewater played virtually no part in the
events of 1775, for they had long since been confined to
reservations; their number had been more than decimated, and
their military prowess had withered away. On the frontiers,
however, it was a very different story, and both sides were
making strenuous efforts to win Indian support. On August 12
Nicholas Cresswell was on his way to Fort Pitt, when he met an
envoy sent by the Virginia convention to encourage the Indian
leaders to assemble there on September 10 and to throw in their
lot with the patriots. The ambassador, Captain James Wood,
reported that he had been preceded by an English officer and a
Frenchman from Detroit, who "had been at all the Indian towns
to persuade the Indians not to go to any Treaty held by the
Colonists." [1] Wood claimed, however, that his own eloquence
had prevailed and that the Indians intended to appear on the
chosen date. But when his report reached Richmond some days
later, it was not quite as optimistic as Cresswell might have
supposed; it told the convention that "the Mingo, Wyindot, and
Shawanese tribes of Indians appear to be friendly and have
promised to attend the treaty at Pittsburg, the 10th of next
month." But it went on to admit that "many of the more
western and south western tribes seem determined to take up
the hatchet against us." [2] There was reason for concern in the
north too, though the danger did not immediately threaten the
colonists of Virginia or Pennsylvania. A report from Ports-

[1] *Cresswell*, 100; Aug. 12.
[2] *Virginia Gazette* (Dixon & Hunter), Aug. 26.

mouth, New Hampshire, was reprinted in the *Virginia Gazette* ³ of August 3:

> WE have the most certain intelligence that the Indians of the Caghnawaga tribe have taken their children from Dartmouth college, from which there is great reason to fear some attack upon our back settlements will shortly be commenced.
>
> We also hear that governor Carlton of Quebec is endeavouring to procure, and has had conferences with Indians 1500 miles back of that city. He has made them great offers to take up arms against the English colonies.

One tends to think of all Indians as being suspicious of any and every white man and that any relationships between the two were simply matters of expediency. To those of us who are not students of Indian history and life it comes as something of a surprise to find that at the individual level those relationships could become remarkably intimate. Nicholas Cresswell enjoyed a memorable demonstration on August 26. After leaving Fort Pitt and pushing on into Indian country he became lost just before dusk, which was, of course, a most inopportune moment. Fortunately, however, he soon came upon three Indian women and a young boy who were encamped for the night. He could not speak their language nor they his, but the youngest of the women unsaddled his horse and the eldest invited him to share their supper of dried venison and bear's oil. Later, when it came time to sleep, the youngest woman made it clear to Cresswell that she was prepared and anxious to carry hospitality even further. He later noted in his journal that "She was young, handsome, and healthy. Fine regular features and fine eyes, had she not painted them with red before she came to bed." ⁴ It was not the first time that Cresswell had been thus entertained, and, having lived for some months now among frontier gentry, it is unlikely that any liaison would have surprised him.

Reward notices for missing slaves provided many references

³ Pinkney.
⁴ *Cresswell*, 105; Aug. 26.

to mulattoes, and there is evidence that even in the more proper society of Tidewater the less fastidious owners were not averse to bedding with their female slaves. However it is generally believed that the majority of halfbreeds were the offspring of white male servants and Negro women—and vice versa. Although miscegenation was illegal, it seems to have been less frowned upon than extramarital fun between whites, the latter having become a very real problem in the previous century, when there were more indentured white servants than black slaves. The objections were more economic than moral, and they arose in part from masters' irritation at having their expensive investments put out of commission for at least a month and in part from the fact that bastard, white children were likely to become a charge on the parish in which they were found. Numerous punishments were meted out to offenders, both to the men and women, though the women usually got the worst of it. The man, for example, might be ordered to go before his parish congregation and confess his sin, while the woman involved in the same affair received up to thirty lashes across her bared back. Bedding with slaves was an entirely different kettle of fish; it was true that the woman might be put out of service for a while, but the child became the property of the owner and thus a financial asset to the estate.

The desire to possess has been uppermost in man's mind ever since he called the first eolith his own; and along with this urge has grown the fascination of buried or sunken treasure. The pursuit of riches and relics from the water was a subject for some popular interest in the summer of 1775. Three attempts had been made to search the bed of the river Tiber for Roman antiquities, and late in August the last was abandoned without result, even though, as the *Annual Register* noted, the Italians had been using an English chain-pump which "did for its part wonders, in throwing out the water; but seems all the pumps in the navy would not answer the purpose, as the water leaked in as fast as it was thrown out." The *Register* went on to suggest

that the project should have been equipped with Halley's diving
bell, a sideline of the celebrated astronomer Edmund Halley,
which he had presented to the Royal Society in a paper read
fifty-nine years earlier. "The leakage, which has hitherto proved
so fatal, is in all probability from the bottom," observed the
Annual Register. "Now, Dr. Halley's diving bell may be cleared
of water within a very small way of its lower rim, and this lower
rim brought so close to the bottom, if any way even, as to afford
the workmen the same opportunity of digging, &c. which they
would have in a piece of ground overflowed with water to a
small depth. Nay, the bell may be lowered, with the same
advantages, in pursuit of treasure, into the hole itself, let it be
ever so deep, if made large enough for that purpose." [5] Earlier
in August the same source reported another possible application
for the diving bell. The ship *Two Sisters* of Bristol had arrived
at Dominica, and in unloading a large chest into a boat to send it
ashore the crew had let it slip into the water, whereupon it sank
—which was only to be expected, as the chest contained £4,000
in Portuguese gold. The treasure was lying (as it may still be) in
ten fathoms of water, and the *Register* added: "We insert this,
as some of our ingenious readers might possibly hit upon some
method of recovering it." [6]

Devices for the recovery of treasure from the sea still
engage the attentions of the students of greed, just as the
agencies of the law seek new methods of crime detection. One
such eighteenth-century success in the war against disorganized
crime occurred on August 3 and became the *Gentleman's
Magazine's* [7] story of the day. It was reported like this:

Lambert Reading, the principal in the robbery at Copped-hall
[a country seat in western Essex], was tried for the same at
the assizes at Chelmsford, convicted, and ordered for execution on the Saturday following. The villains had engaged a

[5] "Chronicle," 150; Aug. 29.
[6] Ibid., 143; Aug. 2.
[7] P. 403.

hackney-coachman to be of their party: and they were discovered by the sagacity of a magistrate, who, observing a hackney-coach pass through Stratford at an unusual hour, with the blinds up, had the presence of mind to take the number; and, when he heard of the robbery at Copped-hall, sent it in a letter to Justice Fielding, whose men, having that clue, soon traced it to the bottom. They found Reading at a house he had just taken in Brick-lane, in bed with a woman who passed for his wife, surrounded with loaded pistols, hangers, picklock keys, dark lanthorns, and, in short, the whole apparatus of a first-rate house-breaker: yet, though there were ten pistols, he had not the heart to make use of one of them. Here they found three sackfuls of plate, containing all that was taken from Copped-hall.

It is conceivable that this was the first time in recorded history that criminals were undone through a pedestrian spotting their vehicle's license number.

In Virginia, another piece of detective work was less tidily concluded. On Saturday, August 19, at daybreak "a gentleman of credit . . . discovered a man of war's barge in the college landing creek, with eight men on board, one of which was dressed in red, and had all the appearance of a certain lord. The oars were all muffled, and the people seemed in the greatest hurry to get away"—to which Pinkney's *Gazette* added the warning: "*Beware*, my penetrating *lord*, *lest, one day or other, you pay dear for your curiosity!*" [8] It is hard to imagine what in the world Lord Dunmore could have been doing at College Landing, for its approach road led only to Williamsburg, and it is inconceivable that he would have ventured into town so lightly protected, no matter how valid the reason for going there. Just as College Creek provided the water approach to Williamsburg from the James river, so Queen's Creek did the same from the York, and it was on the latter that Dunmore's "Porto Bello" lay. Therefore there can be no question of his trying to get to the farm. There is no reference in the governor's papers to any

[8] *Virginia Gazette* (Pinkney), Aug. 17. N.B.: Although dated Aug. 17, the entry refers to an event occurring two days later.

College Creek sortie, nor is there any confirmation that a man-of-war was standing off the creek mouth at this date. Had the ship been there it is almost certain that its presence would have caused all manner of excitement in Williamsburg. If there were no man-of-war, then the barge would have had to have rowed all the way up the James, a journey that would have taken all night and probably half the previous day as well. All in all, it would seem that the *Gazette*'s informant had left either his glasses or his veracity at home.

By the end of the month Lord Dunmore's position was somewhat more comfortable and secure. The ship *William* had been converted into a suitable flagship, the *Otter* under Captain Squire had shown itself to be a small but well-manned and maneuverable vessel, Captain Macartney had fallen into line and his *Mercury* could be relied on to do its duty. In addition, Dunmore had seized two other valuable ships from Norfolk merchants, the frigate *Eilbeck*, belonging to Eilbeck, Ross and Company, and a brig owned by Mr. Daniel Barraud. Purdie's *Gazette* [9] described the *Eilbeck* as "a fine new ship lately launched, frigate built, and pierced for 22 guns." However the ship was not yet rigged, and the Norfolk committee ordered the owners to refrain from handing over the sails and rigging. We may suppose that they accepted this directive without argument, for although they were loyalists, they can have had little desire to see Lord Dunmore go off with their handsome new ship. It was a large vessel by Virginia standards, with a capacity of 400 tons, and was already engaged to transport a considerable cargo of tobacco. When Eilbeck and Ross complained to the governor, he told them that he was chartering the ship and that they would be paid, though he could not tell them exactly when or with what. The ship, and a number of others, were needed for the King's service, and that was that. Exactly what these ships' duties would be was not disclosed, but the *Virginia Gazette* [1] speculated that they were "to be fitted up and manned, in order

[9] Aug. 25.
[1] Dixon & Hunter, Aug. 26.

to assist the men of war and tenders in committing infernal depredations in the rivers, and on the coast." This was in fact pretty much what Lord Dunmore had in mind, although, in his view, that was not the best way of putting it.

At the same time that the governor was preparing for a war, a letter was on its way from London giving the King's permission for him to abandon the endeavor should his position become untenable. But this in no way indicated that King George found the war too indigestible to continue; on the contrary, he slammed another bar across the door of conciliation by issuing a proclamation declaring the Americans to be rebels and adding that "such Rebellion hath been much promoted by the traiterous correspondence, councels, and comfort, of divers wicked and desperate persons within this realm." From then on, all British subjects "within this realm, and the dominions thereunto belonging" were bound by law to report as traitors all those whom they knew to be aiding and abetting the American rebels.[2]

The proclamation was issued without any storm of protest from the Opposition, even though it was privately considered to be a further "stretch of power."[3] But when it was read in public American sympathizers demonstrated with boos, hissing, and catcalls. The City of London's violently radical Lord Mayor, John Wilkes (whose activities could themselves be construed as seditious), refused to permit the proclamation to be dignified with the ceremony usual to such occasions. Thus, while it was read by the heralds attended by appropriate legal and civic officers, outside the City at Palace Yard, Westminster, and Temple Bar, the reading at the Royal Exchange was by the common crier accompanied by a single sheriff's officer, neither of whom would Wilkes permit to be mounted. Neither he, the mace-bearer, nor the sheriffs attended—leaving no doubt in anyone's mind where the leaders of the City of London stood,

[2] *Gentleman's Magazine* (1775), 405; Aug. 23.

[3] Hampden, *Journal*, 202; quoting Horace Walpole, *A Journal of the Reign of King George III, 1771–1783* (London, 1859), I, 500; Aug. 23.

proclamation or no proclamation. But just as the radicals in America made the most noise, so, too, did their supporters in London. Although the Exchange piazza and the streets and alleys leading to it were filled with disgruntled merchants, shouting agitators, idle apprentices, and tavern ruffians, it did not follow that the entire population supported them. Far from it; most of the ordinary people who had no financial involvement with the colonies cared little as to how, or in whose favor, the American mess was resolved—as long as it *was*, before they or their loved ones were caught up in it.

There was a goodly number of people in Virginia too who cared little for politics and simply wanted to live in peace, but they were already enmeshed, and life would never be quite the same again. Nevertheless there was no point in throwing away the wheel and reverting to savagery just because a war had to be fought, particularly if one happened to be in the business of imparting social graces to the first of the D.A.R. Mrs. Sarah Hallam, the long-abandoned wife of actor Lewis Hallam, Jr., had been making both ends come passably close together by keeping a boarding house; she now decided to further improve her lot by opening a dancing school. Throughout August she advertised in the *Gazette* as follows:

> Williamsburg, *August* 17, 1775
> The subscriber begs leave to inform the public that she intends to open a DANCING SCHOOL, on *Friday* the 25th instant, for young ladies; she therefore hopes the gentlemen and ladies will be kind enough to favor her with their daughters. She flatters herself she shall be able to give entire satisfaction, as no care or pains on her part will be wanting. Her days for teaching (every week) are *Friday* and *Saturday*. The price; TWENTY SHILLINGS entrance, and FOUR POUNDS a year. The school will be kept at Mrs. Brovet Pasteur's.
> SARAH HALLAM

The frequent appearance of this innocuous advertisement was finally too much for one patriotic reader, who seized his quill and wrote across the bottom: "We are now engag.d in a War—Damm!" [4]

But although the sounds of drums were growing ever louder in the wings, most of the players were still involved primarily in the small dramas, comedies, and tragedies of everyday living. For John Harrower August 31 was so mundane that it did not merit an entry in his journal, while it found Nicholas Cresswell trading his merchandise for furs in the Indian town of Coashoskis. He was, he noted, doing everything he could to make himself agreeable to the inhabitants, but was making his squaw uneasy by writing too much. Thousands of other gentlemen, merchants, servants, and slaves wrote nothing (or nothing that has survived) and simply passed the day going about their business and wishing that it were not quite so hot and humid.

There had been rain off and on for the past five days, sometimes continuing through the nights, and Williamsburg, which had been parched and choking with dust earlier in the month, was now dripping and steaming. The sweet smell of damp hung in the curtains and closets, and green mold bloomed overnight on the covers of books and dulled the varnish on paintings. It was all very familiar but none the less unpleasant. For those who could read, Pinkney's *Gazette* [5] wryly offered a cooling moment, though it is doubtful whether his perspiring typesetter was particularly amused as, laboriously and sticky-fingered, he set up the galley for this week's "Poet's Corner":

When the trees are all bare, not a leaf to be seen,
    And the meadows their beauties have lost,
When all nature's disrob'd of her mantle of green,
    And the streams are fast bound with the frost.

While the peasant, inactive, stands shiv'ring with cold,
    As bleak the winds northerly blow,
And the innocent flocks run for ease to the fold,
    With their fleeces besprinkled with snow.

[4] *Virginia Gazette* (Pinkney), Aug. 24.
[5] Aug. 31.

In the yard, where the cattle are fodder'd with straw,
    And they send forth their breath like a stream,
And the neat looking dairy maid sees she must thaw
    Flakes of ice that she finds in the cream.

When the lads and the lasses, for company join'd
    In a crowd round the embers are met,
Talk of fairies and witches that ride on the wind,
    And ghosts, till they're all in a sweat.

Heaven grant, in this season, it may be my lot,
    With a nymph whom I love and admire;
While the icicles hang from the eve of my cot,
    I may thither in safety retire.

Where, in neatness and quiet, and free from surprise,
    We may live, and no hardships endure,
Nor feel any turbulent passions arise
    But such as each other can cure.

To the native-born Virginian this was no more than a poem on winter, which unkindly served to make the summer seem even hotter. But to English indentured servants, parted from their families, and convicts who hoped one day to go home, it banked memories as high as the snow. For many of them that day would never come; but they could remember, and they could dream.

Masters and servants alike knew full well that life in the eighteenth century could be soon over, and therefore what joys could be wrested from each day should be savored to the full. On August 31 the barometer needle was falling fast; there would be a change in the weather, and that was something to be thankful for—or so they thought.

[IX]

SEPTEMBER

By *the morning of Saturday, September 2,*
the rains and occasional squalls of the previous days had
developed into a gale of gradually increasing intensity.
Weather-wise overseers watched the racing clouds with fore-
boding and cursed the rows of bowing tobacco and unharvested
corn for having been too damned slow to ripen. It had rained all
night over most of the Virginia lowlands; high winds were
tearing at the rigging of every ship from Cape Fear to the
Potomac, and gusts lifted tiles from roofs as far north as
Philadelphia. From time to time through the morning the rain
eased off and allowed the sun to tease the inexperienced with an
occasional encouraging shaft. But few landowners were deceived, and they loudly urged their hands to redouble their
efforts to tie down everything portable and to herd all livestock
under cover. It was shortly after noon that the first hurricane-
force winds hit Norfolk, driving the tide up over the wharfs and
into the warehouses. By 3:30 (according to Landon Carter's
watch) the storm had reached his home at "Sabine Hall" in
Richmond County. John Harrower was riding home from
Fredericksburg when the great wind struck, and he called it
"one of the hardest gales of wind & rain I have seen since I have
been in the Country." [1] The *Norfolk Intelligencer* went further
and declared it to be one of the worst "within the memory of
man." [2] All through Tidewater, trees were being torn up by the

[1] *Harrower*, 113; Sept. 2.
[2] *Virginia Gazette, or Norfolk Intelligencer*, Sept. 6.

roots and hurled through fences, shingles were stripping from roofs and flung across streets and yards with the force of chain shot. In Charles City County a homestead was demolished, killing a seven-week-old baby and so injuring the mother and another child that doctors despaired for their lives.

The wind was, as Col. Carter said, largely "from N to NE and sometimes to NW," with seemingly unbroken sheets of rain lashing the houses and finding the weaknesses in every one of them. Wrote Colonel Carter in his diary: "It has no[w] struck 6, and I wish I could say there was any signs of it abatg." Watching the water pooling under the front door and running down the walls below badly fitting windows, he added: "If the window sand bags or some such thing had been thought of before night this leaking might in a great measure been prevented." [3] But it was much worse for those at sea.

Governor Martin aboard the *Cruiser* off Cape Fear was engulfed in a wave of spray, and weeks later friends in Norfolk were still wondering whether he had survived. Some thirty-seven ships were lost or badly damaged in North Carolina, and on September 22 the hulls of two of them, the *Minerva* and the *Hibernia*, would be offered for sale where they lay "on the Beech, within 10 miles of Currituck." [4] At least twenty-four vessels were driven ashore at Norfolk and on the shoals in Hampton Roads, including Captain Macartney's *Mercury*, which ended up on her beam in two feet of water. The ship's log graphically reported the crew's efforts to batten it down for the blow and described the mounting winds as they increased from gale force at 9:30 in the morning to hurricane velocity by the afternoon. At 5:00 P.M. the *Mercury* was dragging her anchors and being driven up into the Elizabeth river. A sheet anchor was put out but failed to hold her into the wind, and she was soon driven hard aground on Portsmouth Point. The crew struggled in the blinding rain to move some of the port side guns to starboard in an effort to straighten the ship, but even this and

[3] Landon Carter, *Diary*, II, 935, Sept. 2.
[4] *Norfolk Intelligencer*, Sept. 20.

the rising tide could not combat the force of the wind. At 8:00
P.M., with night already upon them, the capstan crew tried to
bring the ship upright by hauling in on the bow anchor. More
guns were moved to starboard and the longboat was hoisted up
into the starboard yard tackles, but the sea was now breaking
right over the vessel and none of these maneuvers had the
slightest affect. Shortly after eight o'clock the seams began to
spring, and there was every chance that the *Mercury* was about
to go to pieces. In an effort to lighten her and to prevent the
sliding casks from breaching the hull, the bulk of the ship's
stores were heaved over the side. This included 2,100 pounds of
bread, 930 gallons of beer, 216 gallons of rum, and eight-
hooped cask containing 130 pieces of beef, another with 230
slabs of pork, eight firkins holding 620 pounds of butter, plus
miscellaneous large barrels and 207 iron hoops. By midnight
the worst was over; although the *Mercury* and her 160-man
crew were in sorry shape, she was still in one piece, and it was
with an almost audible note of relief that the log ended by
observing that when the tide fell there was only three feet of
water left inside the ship.

Many others were even less fortunate and were "irrecover-
ably gone." [5] The storm had come at the worst possible
moment, because, as the Norfolk paper pointed out, "at this
time . . . many vessels had taken on board part of their cargo,
and the remainder were afloat, and would have been ready for
sea before the tenth of this month." [6] A sloop tender used by
Lord Dunmore to patrol the bay was driven ashore near
Hampton with Captain Squire aboard and was almost immediately burned by the inhabitants. The unhappy captain escaped
dripping into the woods, where he hid until the wind dropped,
and he was later able to borrow a Negro's canoe and paddle
back to the *Otter*. Most of the remaining eight-man crew was
captured by villagers, along with six swivel guns, a seine, and
various other valuable pieces of equipment. As for Lord Dun-

[5] *Virginia Gazette* (Pinkney), Sept. 7.
[6] *Norfolk Intelligencer*, Sept. 6.

more, one newspaper reported that in the confusion he fell overboard "and was severely ducked." However there seems to be no confirmation for the story, and it was probably concocted to serve as a peg for the tag line: *"those who are born to be* H----D *will never be* DROWNED." [7]

As the winds abated early on Sunday morning, patriots and loyalists alike gave thanks to their God and went to bed. But as soon as the first streaks of a gray dawn showed in the east, they were up and preparing to survey the wreckage. The governor's *William* had escaped undamaged, as also had the *Otter;* but the *Mercury* remained heeled over and hard aground, and scores of small craft had been either tossed into fields or broken to pieces against the Norfolk wharfs. The harbor was abob with kegs, boxes, splintered timbers, and shredded canvas. "We are informed," announced the *Gazette*, "that the devastation at Norfolk is inexpressible." [8] The same description was applicable to most of the harbors along the coast, and for weeks to come ships reaching port would bring tales of disasters and astonishing escapes. The sloop *Joseph*, bound from St. Eustatius to Philadelphia, had lost a mast in the storm; on Sunday she sighted "a brig with a white stern, and plain quarter pieces, which had been overset in the gale, and was then swimming with only her stern out of the water." [9]

Ashore, the destruction was equally appalling: roofs torn off, chimneys blown down, and mill dams broken and swept away. But more serious in the long run was the irreparable damage to the season's crops. Colonel Carter found his "fodder all gone[,] corn quite flat, tobacco leaves all broke off and drove about, all the fences down everywhere. In short one general destruction except my houses People and cattle." [1] Even those

---

[7] *Virginia Gazette* (Pinkney), Sept. 14.

[8] Ibid., Sept. 6.

[9] Ibid., Sept. 28.

[1] Landon Carter, *Diary*, II, 935; Sept. 3. Retaining abbreviations and punctuation of the Greene transcript.

whose tobacco was ready for shipping did not necessarily escape:

To be SOLD to the highest bidder, for ready money, on monday *the* 16th *of* October, *at* York,

FIVE hogsheads of TOBACCO, saved out of 14 delivered to mr. *Edward Hughes's* man *Isaac*, to be put on board the *Prospect*, capt. *Norwood*, but drove on shore, and damaged in the late storm.

JAMES MILLS, & co.[2]

It would appear that the storm continued on a northeasterly course, which brought it off St. Johns, Newfoundland, on September 11, where "the sea rose on a sudden 30 feet; above seven hundred boats, with all the people belonging thereto, were lost, as also eleven ships with most of their crews. Even on shore they severely felt its effects, by the destruction of numbers of people; and for some days after, in drawing the nets ashore, they often found twenty or thirty dead bodies in them; a most shocking spectacle!"[3]

In England too September was one of the wildest in living memory, beginning on the fifth with violent storms of rain accompanied by tremendous bolts of lightning, one of which struck a Gloucestershire wagon loaded with barley and killed all five horses pulling it. The Cherwell and Isis rivers overflowed and flooded wide stretches of valley pasture including the parish of St. Thomas, where the inhabitants were driven to the second floors of their houses, from which vantage point they could watch their furniture floating down the street. Then, on September 8, much of the south of England, South Wales, and part of the Midlands were shaken by an earthquake. "Though not attended with any desultory noise, many both in bed and out, and in the upper and lower rooms of their houses, were effected with a violent horizontal agitation or percussion, especially those in bed and above stairs."[4] On the twentieth another violent

[2] *Virginia Gazette* (Purdie), Sept. 29.

[3] *Annual Register, 1775*, "Chronicle," 157; Sept. 11.

[4] Ibid., pp. 155–6.

storm broke over the Oxfordshire area, and lightning struck a house in Oxford itself, stripping a yard square swath of plaster from a garret ceiling without so much as charring the timbers and laths. The next morning, in Yorkshire, the daughter of Mr. Car of Leeds was less fortunate; she was struck dead by a bolt of lightning, which entered down the chimney and went out through a window.

Had not this been an enlightened age, both British and American leaders might have looked upon these natural pyro-technics as omens of terrible disasters to come. Indeed, in Virginia, there would have been substance to such a belief, for the great hurricane did materially affect the course of the future. The burning of Captain Squire's wrecked tender provoked a stiffening of the positions adopted by both sides and led ulti-mately to the colony's first battle of the war.

It seems that four of the tender's crew were taken before the Hampton committee for questioning: George Gray, the gunner; Mr. Ruth, the pilot; and Archibald Campbell and Angus Fisher, two seamen who had been impressed from the merchant ship *Thomas*. These sailors, both presumably Scotsmen and neither able to write his name, testified that in addition to the white crew the tender also carried three Negroes and a mulatto named Joe Harris, who was believed to be the property of Mr. Henry King of Hampton. Two of the Negroes, Aaron and Johnny, were apprehended on the Sunday morning and later returned to their owner, Wilson Miles Cary—who thus discovered that the hurricane had not been an entirely ill wind. On September 8 he wrote an open letter to the paper to express his warmest thanks to Captain Squire "for his very kind and hospitable treatment of my two slaves. . . . The publick may be informed, that upon notice given me that they were on board, I . . . obtained leave to search for them; but as the captain had taken them on a cruise, they were not to be found." [5] Two days later they were washed ashore in the hull of the wrecked tender.

From Lord Dunmore's point of view the loss of the tender

[5] *Virginia Gazette* (Purdie), *Supplement*, Sept. 8.

was distinctly regrettable, but the loss of Captain Squire would
have been disastrous. He must therefore have breathed a deep
sigh of relief when the castaway captain came paddling back in
his borrowed canoe. Squire, of course, was not in the least
amused, and he made it very clear to the people of Hampton that
anything they might have heard about the English being good
losers and splendid sportsmen did not apply in this instance. It
is not clear whether he was unaware that his boat had been
burned or whether he was just being difficult, but he wrote a
terse letter to the Hampton committee demanding "that the
king's sloop, with all the stores belonging to her, be immediately returned; or the people of Hampton, who committed
the outrage of stealing the stores, must be answerable for the
consequences." Appended to the letter was his list of the
missing items: "6 swivels, 5 muskets, 5 cutlasses, 2 powder
horns, 2 cartouch boxes, 36 swivel shot, 1 seine and rope, an
anchor and grapnel, with two cables and hawser, 1 boat's
awning, 1 iron stove, with some lead." [6]

The letter was dated September 10, and on the sixteenth it
produced a reply from the Hampton committee that did nothing
to improve Squire's disposition. The committee took the position
that the sloop "was not in his majesty's service, as we are well
assured that you were on a pillaging or pleasuring party; and
although it gives us pain to use indelicate expressions, yet the
treatment received from you calls for a state of the facts in the
simple language of truth, however hard it may sound." [7] It was
contended that the vessel was privately owned and actually
belonged to Lieutenant Collins, commander of the *Magdalen*.
The truth of the matter was that she had been seized by Collins
earlier in the year, had been condemned by the Court of
Admiralty and offered for public sale. Patriot committees let it
be known that any purchaser would be considered an enemy of
the people; consequently the sloop was still without a buyer
when Collins was ordered home to England. Lord Dunmore

[6] Ibid., Sept. 15.
[7] Ibid., Sept. 22.

then took charge of this and another tender acquired in the same manner, and used both for inshore patrolling.

The Hampton committee went on to claim that "neither the vessel or stores were seized by the inhabitants" but had in fact been presented as a gift to a certain Mr. Finn, who had given Squire and his crew shelter on the night of the hurricane. Adding insult to injury, the committee members suggested that the vessel had been abandoned without cause. They were satisfied that they could not legally be accused of robbing the ship, and with splendid magnanimity they offered to see that the stores were duly restored—on certain conditions. They required that the King's ships should cease molesting boats and persons passing to and from the town, that all boats currently detained should be returned, and that all slaves then in sanctuary aboard the various ships should be returned to their rightful owners. In this clause the mulatto Joseph Harris was specifically named, indicating that he, like Captain Squire, had been able to make his way back to the *Otter* undetected.

It is highly unlikely that the Hampton committeemen expected any of their demands to be met; they were simply bolstering their own morale by wringing some of the water out of the lion's tail. They knew full well that it would take time for Lord Dunmore to repair his storm-damaged ships and there was little likelihood that he would attempt any major military effort for quite some while. Besides, they had a hundred militiamen standing to arms and eager for something to do.

Throughout this period Captain Squire worked out his irritation by effectively bottling up the harbor of Hampton and preventing any traffic between it and Norfolk. At some date prior to September 15 he seized three passage boats (rental ferryboats) with their Negro crews in reprisal for the loss of his tender; noted the *Gazette*, "which boats and negroes, it is likely, he intends taking into the *king's service*, to send out a-pirating for hogs, fowls, &c.—A very pretty occupation for the captain of one of his majesty's ships of war!" [8]

[8] *Virginia Gazette* (Purdie), *Supplement*, Sept. 15.

From another passage boat intercepted on the night of September 17 was seized an unidentified man coming from the eastern shore whom Squire reported to Lord Dunmore as being "a great Rascal." The man had been seen at Yorktown and at Hampton "raising men to fight against the King," and "was always in Company with one Trotter, who was present in Robbing your Palace of the Arms." [9] Squire pressed the man into service aboard the *Otter* (though he must have been a doubtful asset to the crew) and made Lord Dunmore a present of his horse and saddle. A few days later the packet boat from Richmond was boarded in Norfolk harbor just after the passengers went ashore. According to a *Virginia Gazette* [1] report, their baggage was rifled and robbed of a slab of bacon, one pig, two hunting shirts, a tomahawk, two fowling pieces, and a silver-hilted sword.

On another occasion a vessel carrying a Mr. Joseph Middleton, of Annapolis, and his family was seized, the Middletons being put ashore and the boat and its contents carried off. Mr. Middleton claimed that he was simply visiting relatives in Norfolk—although his lost possessions included seven swivel guns and a musket. Middleton subsequently went aboard the man-of-war and demanded the return of his goods, whereupon "the *valiant captain*, with the usual insolence of the *small gentry* in the navy, *damn'd him for a rebel*, and said, had it not been for his wife and children, he would have sent him to Boston *in irons*, pointing to some that were lying upon deck." [2]

The ship involved in the Middleton affair was not Captain Squire's *Otter*, but a somewhat embarrassing newcomer, the *Kingfisher*, which had arrived from Boston on about September 15. This was the ship sent by Admiral Graves in response to Lord Dunmore's complaints regarding Captain Macartney's initially liberal approach to the Virginians. But two months

[9] Squire to Dunmore, Sept. 18; "Aspinwall Papers," MHS *Collections*, 4th ser., X, 750.

[1] Purdie, Sept. 29.

[2] Ibid.

almost to the day had now elapsed, and Macartney had done his duty well—so well that, as we have seen, he had earned the ultimate accolade of being attacked in the newspapers. But neither Macartney's record nor Lord Dunmore's change of heart made the slightest difference to the fact that *Kingfisher's* captain's orders were to arrest Macartney and to send him to Boston, aboard his own ship, which would be commanded by Lieutenant Graham. The latter had come down in the *Kingfisher* for that purpose. However, there was one small snag— Macartney's *Mercury* was still fast in the mud, and was not about to leave for Boston or anywhere else.

The presence of the *Mercury* lying like a stranded whale in full view of the citizenry of Norfolk aroused violent passions in the breasts of the more violent and passionate patriots. One of them, calling himself "THOUSANDS," vented his spleen in a fusillade of ink, most of which landed in the eye of the unfortunate mayor of Norfolk.

Mr. PINKNEY,

If you can, please to inform us why the Mercury man of war, which has so long been the terror of Norfolk, and a refuge to our slaves, is not yet burnt, notwithstanding she has been ten days and upwards upon her broadside. We, sir, who live at a distance are at a loss to account for the strange remissness of the inhabitants of Norfolk in neglecting to seize the opportunity which Heaven has kindly thrown in their way. Surely the interest of the mayor, who, from his letters to Macartney, seems to prefer the friendship of that deceitful enemy to the welfare of the town over which he presides, must have prevented the noble rage of the citizens from bursting forth in vengeance upon that accursed vessel, which they now have in their power to sacrifice for the captain's bloody threats to destroy their town. We can by no means attribute the omission to a partiality in the inhabitants of Norfolk to the avowed enemies of our country; nor can we suppose them so far destitute of courage as to be afraid to make the attempt. But let the cause be what it will, we do inform them, through the channel of your intelligence, that unless they immediately perform this act, so ardently wished for by their countrymen, and so easily to be effected, that THOUSANDS are resolved to burn the devoted vessel, even if the consequences of it should be the total ruin of Norfolk.[3]

It says much for the integrity of *Gazette* publisher Pinkney that he defended the mayor and explained that the *Mercury* was constantly protected by the guns of Lord Dunmore's other ships, and that any attempt on her would probably have resulted in the bombardment of Norfolk. In addition, Pinkney came to the defense of Captain Macartney, blaming Dunmore for the captain's attitude, which he described as "*something* of the usual disposition of the king's officers." [4] However, the attitude to which Pinkney referred was simply that of an officer doing his duty, and we may reasonably suppose that Macartney would have done it without any prompting from the governor.

The incident, already touched on, that had so provoked the patriotic wrath had been Captain Macartney's response to the Norfolk committee's demand that Andrew Sprowle should be called to account for his alleged harboring of Dunmore's troops at Gosport. Macartney had written to Paul Loyal, the mayor of Norfolk, reminding him that as senior British officer it was his duty to protect both the King's governor and all his loyal subjects. "This is my duty," he wrote, "and I should wish it to be known that my duty and inclination go hand in hand. The same principles which have induced me not to harbour the slaves of any individual in this province will operate with me to protect the property of all loyal subjects." To this end he declared his intention to "place his Majesty's ship under my command abreast of the town; and I must assure you, that, notwithstanding I shall feel the utmost pain and reluctance in being compelled to use violent measures to preserve the persons and properties of his Majesty's subjects. . . ." [5]

This firm stand on Macartney's part does not in any way suggest that he had abandoned the principles which he had

[3] *Virginia Gazette* (Pinkney), Sept. 21.

[4] Ibid.

[5] *Virginia Gazette* (Dixon & Hunter), Sept. 2.

displayed so openly on his arrival. He was undoubtedly wiser now, but not weaker, and at no time could there have been any doubt in his mind as to where his duty lay. Some patriots may not have been sufficiently acquainted with honor and principle, or with the conduct befitting an officer and a gentleman, and they may have mistaken them for an infirmness of purpose on Macartney's part. It was doubtless these same people who had applauded him earlier who were so loud in condemning him now that they discovered their error.

While it is clear that Macartney would have fired on Norfolk if he had to, there is no evidence that he took part in the looting of passage boats, the robbing of chicken-yards, and the other punitive efforts sanctioned by Lord Dunmore and apparently executed with some verve by Captain Squire and his tenders. Macartney's objection to the harboring of runaway slaves had been clear all along and had not been withdrawn when he wrote to the mayor of Norfolk. This stand could not have endeared him to the governor or to Squire, both of whom, as we have seen, continued to look upon slave support as a valuable reinforcement. It is not known whether Lord Dunmore informed Macartney of the content of his letter to Admiral Graves at the outset, or whether the arrival of the *Kingfisher* and the orders for his arrest came as a surprise. The latter would seem to have been the more probable, for the governor knew that he would have to work with and rely on Macartney for some weeks; there would have been nothing to gain and everything to lose by revealing that the officer was holding his command on borrowed time. Besides, Dunmore could not be sure that Admiral Graves would recall Macartney. All in all, it seems likely that Macartney was astonished when the *Kingfisher* hove in sight and positively flabbergasted when he discovered the reason for its arrival. His opinion of Lord Dunmore at the moment of that discovery must have been quite low.

There was no attempt at further concealment, and we may suppose that the *Kingfisher*'s commander presented Admiral

Graves's orders to Lord Dunmore immediately on arrival and that their content was equally quickly imparted to Captain Macartney. As usual the patriot spy machinery was well oiled, and the news of Macartney's downfall appeared in a supplement to Purdie's *Virginia Gazette* [6] within two or three days of the *Kingfisher*'s arrival. The paper correctly reported that Lieutenant Graham was to take command of the *Mercury* and that Macartney had been "put under arrest (for disobedience of orders, it is said) and is to be sent to Boston, to be tried by a court-martial."

An uneasy ten days were to elapse before the *Mercury* would be afloat again and ready for sea, and during that time Macartney was presumably held under arrest aboard the *Kingfisher*. Despite the exhortations of "THOUSANDS," no one made any effort to burn the *Mercury* or to interfere with her refitting. However the *Gentleman's Magazine* [7] later informed its English readers that following the September 2 hurricane "The Mercury man of war was driven ashore, and left in two feet of water, and has since been burnt by the populace," presumably having confused it with Captain Squire's tender.

By September 23 work on the *Mercury* had been completed, and she was on her way to Boston, thus removing the unhappy Captain Macartney from the Virginia scene. On this score Lord Dunmore was well content; it was true that the *Kingfisher* was smaller than the *Mercury* by eight guns, but it had the distinct advantage of being commanded by Captain James Montagu, brother of the governor's good friend George Montagu, captain of the *Fowey*. Montagu's ship was a sloop, as was the *Otter*, and the command of Lord Dunmore's little fleet fell on the senior officer, who happened to be *Otter's* Captain Squire. Admiral Graves pointed this out to Dunmore adding: "I shall be happy to know that he zealously endeavours to exert his utmost for the good of His Majesty's Service, and is acceptable to your

[6] Sept. 15.
[7] P. 494.

Lordship." [8] There was, of course, no doubt that he was.

On reviewing his position Lord Dunmore found that he had suffered no great or permanent losses as a result of the hurricane. The *Mercury* had been repaired and replaced, and all his troops and their equipment had come through uncomfortable but unscathed. The colonists, on the other hand, had lost much of their year's crop income, as well as the fodder that would be needed to carry their livestock through the winter.

The governor's military strength at this time was estimated by historian Burk as comprising "two companies of the 14th regiment, just arrived from the West Indies, where they had been trained to hunt Caribbs, about one hundred negroes, and from twenty to thirty tory volunteers." [9] A correspondent writing for the September 21 issue of the *Virginia Gazette* [1] spoke of reinforcements from St. Augustine as having been "taken" by the "brave Carolinians," the result of a rumor circulating in Norfolk that the rest of Dunmore's force had been seized on the high seas and carried to Charleston. They were, the writer added sarcastically, to have been used to augment "the sixty men who have been so very formidable to the towns of Norfolk, Portsmouth, and Gosport. What might have been the consequence had they arrived!" A week earlier Purdie's *Gazette* [2] had reported that "Lord Dunmore has received another reinforcement from St. Augustine, of no less than between 20 and 30 effective men, and soon expects to have his army augmented to 500; with which, we hear, he intends to take possession of his palace in this city, that he lately abandoned—*if not prevented by those he terms rebels*." Then, on September 23, a third *Gazette* [3] informed the public that "The number of regulars with Lord Dunmore, which lately composed the garri-

[8] Graves to Dunmore, Aug. 7; "Aspinwall Papers," MHS *Collections*, 4th ser., X, 753.

[9] *History of Virginia*, III, 431.

[1] Pinkney.

[2] Sept. 15.

[3] Dixon & Hunter, Sept. 23.

son of St. Augustine (being part of the 14th regiment, under command of Lieutenant Colonel William Dalrymple) does not exceed 80 effective men; the other part we have reason to believe is at Boston, where, in all probability, their assistance is, or will be, so absolutely requisite, that we need not be under any apprehension *they* will be sent to this colony." As usual, you paid your money and you took your choice; but on the basis of available evidence it would seem that a total of eighty men, plus their officers, was a fair estimate of Lord Dunmore's strength. It was far from spectacular, and his Lordship continued to plague General Gage and to badger Governor Tonyn of East Florida for more men, bedding, arms, and ammunition—supplies the latter could ill afford to release.

Although Lord Dunmore could find some satisfaction in the size of his fleet and the fact that his eighty regulars could put on an adequate show of strength as long as they avoided a pitched battle, his lack of instructions (preferably laced with encouragement and congratulations) was steadily eroding his morale. On September 24 he received Lord Dartmouth's dispatch Number 20, dated May 30, but it contained little besides now-useless directives regarding the position of the western frontier of Virginia and Pennsylvania. This letter had been brought over by the son of Thomas Nelson, president of the council, but it had not been delivered. On September 5 Lord Dunmore demanded that he receive it "with all possible dispatch" [4]—he got it nearly three weeks later, after it had been opened and read. Two and a half months later he would refer again to this letter in writing to Lord Dartmouth saying: "I have so often prayed to be instructed in the Crown's desired course of action for many months past, but not one line have I had the Honor to receive from your Lordship since yours of the 30th of May." [5] In September he admitted that he waited "with great impatience for a full answer to my former letters Nos. 26, 27, 28, 29 and

[4] Copy of letter from Dunmore to Thomas Nelson, Sept. 5, enclosed with Dunmore to Dartmouth, Sept. 24; PRO,CO 5/1353.

[5] Dunmore to Dartmouth, Dec. 6; ibid.

30 which I trust in God will relieve me from the very disagreeable Situation I now find myself in, Surrounded with Enemies, and Seeing them every day grow more formidable both as to Numbers and discipline." [6]

The Secretary of State had the whole of America in his lap, and it was hardly surprising that he did not have time to indulge in a voluminous correspondence with his man in Virginia. Nevertheless there *were* three missing letters: Number 21 told Dunmore that he could rely on General Gage for a small body of troops and that 2,000 stand of arms were on their way from England. Number 22 amended the quantity of arms to 3,000 stand, but then took an unspecified number away by telling Dunmore that he should supply Governor Martin of North Carolina with "such a portion of them as he shall want, and your Lordship may be able to spare him." [7] Dispatch Number 23 was that of August 2, wherein Lord Dartmouth gave Dunmore leave to return to England if his position should become untenable. In this eventuality the governor was instructed to deliver an enclosed commission to Receiver General Corbin to administer the government during his absence. If the missive had been shipped almost immediately after it was written it could have reached America in the first days of September; but there is no knowing whether it was delayed, landed into enemy hands, lost in the hurricane, or seized at sea. But it is a curious coincidence that Purdie's *Virginia Gazette* of September 8 was able to print the following story:

It is reported, and generally believed, that LORD DUNMORE is called home, with what view we have not yet learned, but probably it is to render an account of his *sagacious* and *spirited* conduct in Virginia; which can hardly fail to attract the *admiration* of Lord North and the Butonian juncto, so as to have his *eminent* services recompensed with some higher department in the state, perhaps Lord Dartmouth's. His lordship has this satisfaction upon his departure, that he will

[6] Ibid., Sept. 24.
[7] Dartmouth to Dunmore, July 12; PRO,CO 5/1375.

leave the colony with the *universal consent* of the inhabitants, of all ranks and denominations.

Thus there might be some grounds for supposing that the content of Lord Dartmouth's dispatch Number 23 was known to the patriots and that a garbled version reached the press. By another and undoubtedly genuine coincidence Richard Corbin, whom Lord Dartmouth had authorized to replace Dunmore, chose this time to leave the colony to attend to business matters in England. Corbin had written to Lord Dunmore on August 10, explaining his desire to leave and seeking his approval. The governor did not receive it until much later, and he replied on September 5, giving his blessing and showing that even at this late date he was still hoping for an amicable reconciliation between Virginia and the Crown. "I think," he wrote, "that if there is but a chance that y'r going can be of the smallest service to this y'r native land nothing ought to prevent you, and if my concurrence is necessary, you have it with all my heart and from my soul, wishing that you can be the means of reconciling these very unfortunate differences between 2 countries whose mutual advantage is to be firmly united." [8] This letter was written on thick, gilt-edged yellow paper, folded and sealed within another sheet of the same, and addressed to Corbin. It was then enclosed in yet another sealed sheet and directed to merchant William Prentis of Williamsburg, with instructions to see that it was safely delivered.

Another friend of the Crown chose this same time to depart; Attorney General John Randolph, who had delayed his departure through the summer, now found life in Virginia increasingly hazardous. In June Lord Dunmore had proposed to Lord Dartmouth that Randolph should be given a pension; now he wrote again approving his departure, saying that "he together with his Family after having suffered the grossest insults and being threatened with the loss of their lives and having their House and every thing they have destroyed, are by my advice

[8] Dunmore to Corbin, "Off Norfolk on bd. the William Sept. 5, 1775"; *VMHB*, III, No. 3 (Jan. 1896), 314–5.

and approbation determined to go to England knowing they could not live any longer here, with much difficulty they have been persuaded to go." [9] This letter, dated September 24, was to be delivered personally by Randolph to Lord Dartmouth. He was presumably also the carrier for the governor's official dispatch of the same date.

John Randolph's intended departure had been no secret, for on August 25 he gave notice that he had conveyed his estate, "both real and personal, to *Peyton Randolph, John Blair,* and *James Cocke,* esqrs. who are authorized to sell the same." [1] He went on to explain that he proposed to leave the colony for a few months and that Mr. Blair would handle his duties as Attorney General in his absence. It is obvious, of course, that he and the readers of his statement all knew that the length of that absence would be dependent on the outcome of the Anglo-American struggle. Political seers in Williamsburg could draw simple conclusions from the fact that Randolph had decided to sell up everything he owned in Virginia.

In Lord Dartmouth's undelivered letter of July 12 he had expressed the hope that Dunmore would have been able to raise a sufficient force "from among the Indians, Negroes & other Persons," [2] to hold his own. But the Negroes would have to be housed and fed, and it was dubious whether they could be disciplined into a fighting unit. The "other Persons" were an equally doubtful quantity, both as to numbers and fortitude. According to historian Burk, no more than thirty volunteers had yet appeared. Patriots thought that Norfolk and the neighboring communities were thick with Tories; but, if they were, they were not in a hurry to reveal themselves. It seemed more likely that Norfolk's inhabitants' reluctance to burn the navy ships or to oppose Captain Squire's raiding parties was prompted more by a desire for a quiet life than a yearning to do battle in the King's name. However there was the possibility that they were

[9] Dunmore to Dartmouth (private), Sept. 24; PRO,CO 5/1353.
[1] *Virginia Gazette* (Purdie), Sept. 1.
[2] PRO,CO 5/1375.

waiting only for a single unifying call to arms. There were,
apparently, those who believed this to be the case. Wrote Lord
Dunmore to the Secretary of State: "I have been strongly
solicited by a great Number of Gentlemen well disposed to His
Majesty's Government to Erect the King's Standard, and that
they and thousands more they are pursuaded would flock to it
immediately." ³ But Dunmore demurred, ostensibly on the
grounds that he did not have the arms or ammunition to equip
such an army, but possibly because he feared to take the risk. If
he raised the standard and only a handful rallied to it, it would
be an enormous psychological victory for the rebels and an
equally mortifying defeat for his own supporters. There was
still no battle smoke to hang in the Virginia air, but a call to
arms would certainly produce it. It was better to wait, and hope
for regular reinforcements.

But if the Negroes and local Tories were not to be the
answer to a Dunmore's prayer, there were still the Indians.
While they were too far away to directly affect the affairs of
Tidewater, they could be of inestimable value on the western
frontier in dividing the patriots' efforts and attentions. Newspaper reports of what the Indians would or would not do continued
to bemuse the public, and even the British and American
military leaders were unable to gauge the dangers or benefits of
Indian involvement—except perhaps Lord Dunmore, who was
convinced that he held a privileged place in the hearts of the
Indians of the Virginia frontier. His king of trumps was his old
frontier agent and admirer, John Connolly, who had left Fort
Pitt (Fort Dunmore) on July 25 and had ridden to Williamsburg without being challenged, and from thence to Norfolk and
to Lord Dunmore's ship *William*. The news he brought was
immensely encouraging, and the ideas he proposed were equally
exciting. He assured the governor that the Ohio Indians were
agreed to stand firm for the Crown, and Dunmore later reported
to Lord Dartmouth that "whatever the Virginians might say to
them, unless it came from me, they would receive it at one Ear,

³ Dunmore to Dartmouth, Oct. 5; PRO,CO 5/1353.

and let it out at the other, and that they were ready to aid in whatever manner I should direct them." [4] Connolly's proposal was that he should go to Canada with a warrant to raise a regiment which he would bring down from Detroit to Fort Pitt, raising Indian support as he went. With the army thus assembled, he would be able to march into Virginia through the Cumberland Narrows and create all manner of havoc. Connolly and Lord Dunmore discussed this satisfying prospect over many a glass of wine, and it grew more intriguing with each repetition. The *Virginia Gazette* [5] of September 2 reported that on the previous Sunday Connolly had set out for Boston aboard one of Dunmore's tenders. What the paper did not say was that he was instructed to lay his plan before General Gage and, hopefully, to obtain a commission to raise the Canadian regiment. By this time, of course, Connolly's idea had been transformed into Lord Dunmore's grand design.

Meanwhile, back on the frontier, the Virginia convention's stab at Indian diplomacy was getting off to a shaky start. Fort Pitt was full of commissioners, delegates from the convention, and members of congress, but very few Indians. Our correspondent on the scene was the unmistakably biased Nicholas Cresswell, complete with bugs, squaw, and trade goods. The gathering had been scheduled to start on September 10; Cresswell arrived on the fourteenth and noted that the commissioners had already been waiting a week. On September 19 he wrote in his diary: "No news of the Indians, the Commissioners are afraid they will not come at all." [6] As the days dragged by, the Virginians and Pennsylvanians passed the time stirring the old animosities that existed between them, prompting Cresswell to note on September 24 that there was "Nothing but quarrelling and fighting in every part of the town." [7] Fortunately for the survival of this peace mission the Shawnee and Delaware

[4] Dunmore to Dartmouth, Sept. 24; ibid.
[5] Dixon & Hunter.
[6] *Cresswell*, 114.
[7] Ibid., 115.

Indians arrived before the commissioners, aides, and retainers had stuck their olive branches in each other's eyes. Along with the two major tribal envoys came Chief Shaganaba of the Ottawa Indians, who admitted that the British at Detroit had led him to believe that he could not trust the commissioners. However he was pleased to say that he had been handsomely treated by the patriots and that he was glad to give his hand in friendship. He did not actually say that he would urge his tribe to take the patriots' part against the King; but had Connolly heard his speech he might have lost a little of his enthusiasm for his Canadian mission.

Diplomacy was not a game that only the white man could play; the Indians were equally adept at it and well knew that the honeyed word could be as valuable as the knife. It could win time for the Indian, bring him bribes thinly disguised as gifts, and enable him to read his adversary's mind while ostensibly listening to his talk. For all these advantages he need give very little beyond the fortitude to suffer his hosts' patronizing and their often tiresome desire to play at being Indians.

It was important to the patriots that their less belligerent colonist neighbors should be frequently reassured as to the intentions of the Indians. Thus we find the *Virginia Gazette* [8] of September 1 putting a month-old Massachusetts report on its front page stating that "the Canadians and Indians cannot be persuaded by governor Carleton to join his forces, but are determined to remain neuter." In truth, however, John Connolly was right in reporting to Lord Dunmore that the majority of the frontier tribes, the Shawnee, Delaware, Ottawa, Cherokee, Chippewa, and Miami, had little love for the colonial settlers and saw them only as barbarians anxious to destroy their cultures and to rob them of their lands. The British military and trading posts were, by comparison, havens of friendship, just as the French posts had been before them. Lieutenant Colonel Henry Hamilton, commander of the fort at Detroit, was the British father figure who gave the Indians the weapons and

[8] Purdie.

supplies they needed to defend themselves from the frontiersmen of Kentucky, Virginia, and Pennsylvania. There was
very little doubt that, regardless of the treaties the Indians
might attend, they would ultimately side with the Crown. It has
been suggested from time to time that had they backed the
patriots their subsequent history might have been less melancholy. But the fact remains that the Americans were bent on
pushing westward and they could not do so without violating the
sovereignty of the tribes in their path. The rights so loudly
championed as inherent in the Constitution today did not extend
to the Indians, even during the lifetime of its framers. There is
some irony to be found in the fact that at a moment when the
fate of the Virginia colony hung in a none too certain balance,
the only directive the governor received was to ensure the
stabilization of a frontier that was far from his reach and that
was intended to preserve the liberty of the Indians from those
Sons of Liberty, the Virginia and Pennsylvania frontiersmen.

To the colonists the well-being of the Indians was of the
smallest consideration, now or at any other time. All that was
necessary was to woo them just ardently enough to keep them
from siding with the British. They could hardly be expected to
understand the philosophy of the patriot cause, nor did they
share the bond of suffering that soulless Ministerialists had
inflicted on the colonists. There was no need, therefore, to think
in terms of permitting the Indians to share in the rights and
freedoms to be enjoyed when the British yoke was cast aside. It
is doubtful whether the average patriot colonist of Tidewater
gave them much thought; he was a great deal more concerned
with the doubtful quantities in his midst—such as the prosperous merchant John Greenhow. This gentleman's prosperity was
built on his business acumen, and as many Williamsburg
citizens claimed to have been fleeced by him it was hardly
surprising that his popularity was small. His home on Duke
of Gloucester Street was as large as that of many a Virginia
plantation owner, and in addition he owned the house next door
and the brick office behind it. All this was the very visible

product of the general store, which Greenhow kept immediately
adjacent to his home and from which he had the gall to sell
liquor to Negroes—even on a Sunday. Before the current
unpleasantness this was the sort of charge that was leveled
against him; but now the attacks could be elevated to a much
more altruistic plane, though the assailant would, if possible,
still prefer to hide, chicken-hearted, behind the mask of a
pseudonym. In the September 14 issue of the *Virginia Gazette* [9]
"Galba" called on the Williamsburg Committee to set up a
popular tribunal to investigate profiteering. "I would recommend it to this committee," he wrote, "to take cognizance of a
certain JOHN GREENHOW in this city; who seems to prefer the
interest of his *pocket* to that of his country. It can be proved by
many that he sells a number of articles at an advanced price, of
at least 200 *per cent.* to wit, 20d. nails at 18s. 9d. per thousand,
which cost about 6s. 4d. flake white, at 5s. per pound, which
cost between 16 and 18d. sterling, yellow oker at 15d. per
pound, which cost 3d. sterling, and lake at 6£. per pound,
which cost about 40s. &c. &c. Is this sufferable?" Galba
demanded: "I call upon you, by the trust reposed in you, to drag
forth this JEW, in answer to those charges, and let him clear
himself if he can." It does seem likely that Greenhow was
overcharging, but there is no evidence that he was of the Jewish
race. The epithet appears in an eighteenth-century dictionary of
the "Canting Words and Terms, both ancient and modern, used
by Beggars, Gypsies, Cheats, House-Breaker, Shop-Lifters,
Foot-Pads, Highway-men, &c.," where it is given to mean "any
over reaching Dealer, or hard, sharp fellow. *He treated me like
a Jew:* He used me very barbarously." [1] Presumably John
Greenhow had used the patriotic Galba somewhat barbarously.
Nevertheless, Greenhow's loyalty to the American cause can
hardly have been in doubt: his son, Robert, was a member of the
boy volunteer company and had been one of those who had
raided the public magazine earlier in the year. The shooting war

[9] Pinkney.
[1] Bailey, *Dictionary*, Appendix.

may not yet have started in Virginia, but it was already possible to be shot in the back by one's own side—if only with verbal bullets.

Bullets of the same caliber were getting through the armor of Lord Dunmore and his naval friends, and as the month progressed their irritation mounted. Captain Squire made the mistake of writing to the publisher of the *Norfolk Intelligencer* and letting him know that his barbs were smarting. This was manna from heaven for publisher John Hunter Holt, who promptly printed Squire's note. Other papers also picked up the story, adding their own embellishments. Pinkney's *Virginia Gazette* [2] informed its patrons that

> The *little hornet* (alias *Master Squire*) lately sent the follow-ing *courageous* letter to Mr. Holt, printer of the Norfolk Intelligencer. As it is one of those *great* productions which never fail to characterize a genius of the *first* magnitude, we, in justice to that *illustrious* captain, present it *verbatim* to our readers.
>
> Otter Sloop, Norfolk river, September 9, 1775
>
> To the Printer of the Norfolk Intelligencer
>
> *Sir,*
> You have in many papers lately taken the freedom to mention my name, and thereto added many falsities. I now declare, if I am ever again mentioned therein, with reflections on my character, I will most assuredly seize your person, and take you on board the Otter. I am, &c.
>
> MATTHEW SQUIRE

Mr. Holt was not to be intimidated, and he continued to attack the readily assailable exploits of the governor and his officers. Dunmore, in his wrath, referred to the paper as "The Public press of the little dirty Borough of Norfolk" and accused it of being "wholelly employed in exciting in the minds of all Ranks of People the Spirit of Sedition and Rebellion by the grossest misrepresentation of facts both public and private." [3]

[2] Sept. 14.
[3] Dunmore to Dartmouth, Oct. 5; PRO,CO 5/1353.

At about two o'clock on the afternoon of Saturday, September 30, he sent a small party of some fifteen men ashore at the county wharf, who marched up the main street of Norfolk to the printing office and proceeded to seize all the type, ink, and paper, as well as part of the press and two workmen, one of whom was the bookbinder. But if the soldiers hoped to capture Mr. Holt they were disappointed, though one report had it that he remained hidden in the building throughout the raid. A crowd of two or three hundred gathered to watch this violation of the freedom of the press, but nobody seemed inclined to do anything about it. A few patriots called on the drums to be beaten through the city to summon the volunteers to arms, but they were all either out of town for the week end or suffering from some auricular ailment. Few, if any, turned out, and Dunmore's men made their way back to the wharf with their prisoners and booty without any interference. After loading their boats the soldiers gave three rousing huzzas, "in which they were joined by a crowd of negroes," [4] who were presumably hanging about with nothing better to do—a somewhat disconcerting image to be accepted by a twentieth century in which it is popularly supposed that slaves lived only to work, breed, and die.

Anyone having the temerity to ask the soldiers what was going on was informed that the materials were being seized because the rebels had already robbed the press of its freedom, and, as the Norfolk paper could no longer give the people the truth, the governor proposed to do the job himself. One writer commented that this would be impossible, as he thought the soldiers had taken neither ink nor either of the compositors. He added, however, that he thought that there was already a printer on board the *Otter*. But whether or not his Lordship was capable of putting out a paper, the *Virginia Gazettes* had a fine time at the expense of the very idea. Purdie announced that a breathless public might "soon expect to see the GOSPORT CHRONICLE *published by authority*, which it is said is to contain, occasion-

4 *Virginia Gazette* (Purdie), *Supplement*, Oct. 5.

ally, the commentaries of a certain *illustrious chief's* wars in *Vandalia*, some *curious anecdotes*, *diverting stories*, and a number of other valuable and interesting particulars, which no doubt will ensure this *new publication* a very extensive circuit, and consequently redound to the *credit* and *interest* of its noble *proprietor*." [5]

Pinkney's *Gazette* [6] reported that when the officials of Norfolk complained at the loss of their paper, Lord Dunmore replied that they were really losing nothing as the new floating printing office would be most happy to print any copy they cared to send it. "But here, too," added the *Gazette*, "his lordship may fail, as it is reported he did in a certain other duty, though probably, by sending for his *Minden hero* (his old *speech-writer* &c.&c.) he may procure some aid:—Suppose, then, Foy to be his *foreman*, would not Squire make an excellent *printer's devil?*"

The seizure of Mr. Holt's printing equipment may have removed a thorn, but the operation created an infection which quickly seated itself elsewhere. Other publishers indignantly condemned Dunmore's action as wanton, cruel, unjust, and oppressive. The public was equally incensed, regardless of whether or not they happened to read Holt's paper. The newspapers then were more important than they are today, for they were the only means of mass communication, and in Virginia, where plantation life created innumerable semi-isolated islands of civilization, the arrival of the paper was a major event. Not only did it bring news of happenings in England and the sister colonies, it provided important information regarding the arrival and departure of ships, the new services and commodities to be purchased in the towns, notices of the capture of runaway slaves, and announcements of forthcoming auctions —which were usually inserted weeks in advance to enable would-be purchasers to get to the sale. We have been looking at examples of these newspaper contributions all through the year, but seeing them largely as documentary evidence of the events

[5] *Supplement*, Oct. 6.
[6] Oct. 5.

of 1775. Let us now look at more of them in all their diversity, thinking of them in terms of a newspaper's contribution to the life of its time, to the fears, hopes, interests, arguments, discussions, and particularly the humors of September 1775.

If one's own trade was not going well, there was an opportunity to rent a tavern in Fredericksburg; it would be hard work, but profitable, and many a distinguished craftsman had taken to it. There had been goldsmith John Coke, of Williamsburg, who worked his metals and operated a tavern on the same location and at the same time. Anthony Hay had been a well-known cabinetmaker but became distinctly more popular when he gave it up to become landlord of Williamsburg's famed Raleigh Tavern. Purdie's September 15 *Virginia Gazette* now offered a splendid opportunity to follow in their footsteps. Of course Fredericksburg was not Williamsburg, and the times were not good for business; but travelers had to eat and tavern keeping might be a better bet than many another trade. The building was, so the advertisement said, well situated in the center of the town and "has been long accustomed by the first gentlemen of this and the neighboring colonies. It is large and commodious, there are all convenient outhouses, including a storehouse on the main street, an exceeding good garden, a well of fine water within a few steps of the door, a billard table, &c.&c." The etceteras, so the ad went on to explain, included the stock of liquor consisting of "best *Madeira* wine, old arrack, port wine, and spirits."

Anyone with a need for horses should make the trip to Stratford on October 10, for on that day the famous Dotterel and many of his colts and fillies would be sold. This was the same great horse from the estate of Philip Ludwell Lee that had failed to find a buyer back in March. Again potential customers were reminded that this horse was "greatly distinguished on the turf in *England*, and in high estimation in this country for getting foals of beauty and form" [7] and that his pedigree would be exhibited on the day of the sale. Poor Dotterel—his past

[7] *Virginia Gazette* (Purdie), Sept. 29.

prowess would ensure him his place in the annals of Newmar-
ket, but it was of little worth in Virginia on the eve of
revolution.

If you, the newspaper reader, were in the market for neither
a tavern nor a race horse, perhaps you suffered from that
ubiquitous disease which every nationality tried to blame on
someone else: the Spaniard's *sarva des Indias*, the Frenchman's
mal de Naples, and the Englishman's French pox. If so, a great
new remedy was at hand. "EVERY MAN HIS OWN DOCTOR,"
ran the headline, "particularly in a certain Disorder, be their
case ever so deplorable, by the use of Dr. KEYSER's celebrated
PILLS." These little gems had proved themselves to be successful "beyond all other Inventions of human Subtlety." Furthermore, "The Patient is most effectually cured without any
inconvenience to himself, or being exposed to the Shame or
Confusion of his Disorder being known to the nicest Observer."
So impressed had King George been with this boon to lechery
that he had "established a Hospital where these Pills alone are
administered, and from whence seven Thousand Soldiers have
been in a short Time dismissed, perfectly restored to health."
Not only could Dr. Keyser's pills make clean soldiers, they
could also cure "dropsical Disorders, the Gravel, Palsey, Apo-
plexy, White Swellings, Stiff Joints, and the Asthma," as well
as "that Disorder, hitherto almost insuperable to Medicine,
called the Yaws." One might naïvely suppose that these obviously potent pills were obtainable only from the family
physician. But not at all; they were to be had solely from
Messrs. Dixon and Hunter, "the Printers of this Paper, who
have got a fresh Parcel lately from PARIS, in Boxes of 10s. 20s.
and 40s. each." [8] Here, then, was a contribution to the public
welfare that is not to be obtained from a newspaper office even
today.

The same publishers catered not only to the maladies of its
readers, they also concerned themselves with the public's funny
bone, not in a humor section on a back page but in the main

[8] Sept. 23.

columns jammed between items of the gravest portent. In the
same column that provided Virginians with news from Ticonderoga and a report of a guardsman who hanged himself in Mr.
Hecknill's yard in London rather than serve in America, we find
the following account of a tanner's good fortune:

Saturday, May 20, a tanner who lives within twenty miles of
Hutchin Back-street, near Baldock, returning late from his
work, found his wife was gone to bed, but had forgot to lock
the door. The husband blundering in the dark, just gave time
to another, who had supplied his place, to get under the bed.
The husband had put off his clothes, and was getting also into
bed, when his wife complained she was exceedingly ill, and
should be glad of some anniseed water, but feared the public
houses were all shut up, except the Sun inn, which was at the
greatest distance. The honest man put on his clothes, and
went to the Sun, where, putting his hand into his pocket for a
shilling to pay for the water, the waiter returned it him,
telling him he could not change his guinea. The man, amazed
to hear mention of a guinea (as knowing he had but a few
shillings) hastily put his hand again into his pocket, and
pulling out nine more, with a ten pound bank note, and on
farther examination found he had got a new pair of breeches,
and a fine watch. Comprehending the whole then in an
instant, he observed, with the coolness of a philosopher, that
the affair was over before this, and what was done could not
be undone; as his wife, therefore, had been so industrious in
putting him into so much ready money, he would have a
bottle of wine first, and then carry her the anniseed water.
The tanner had the breeches cried on Tuesday in the open
market, but has not yet found an owner.[9]

Dixon and Hunter were more prone to inserting curiosities
than were either Purdie or Pinkney, and it was the same firm
that offered its readers three matrimonial oddities for September. The first told of a marriage at Mile End near London,
between a bridegroom of seventy-two and a girl of nineteen.
"The former was attended to church by four young maidens,
and the bride by the same number of young men; but when the

[9] *Virginia Gazette* (Dixon & Hunter), Sept. 2.

company became to separate, it was discovered the bride had
eloped with one of the bridemen, and about 700£ in cash and
jewels of her unfortunate spouse." [1] The second item was in the
same vein, though the crime involved was purely social. "A few
days ago a widow Lady of Lambeth, who is upwards of 60 years
of age, was married to her footman, a young fellow of 23. The
above Lady has seven daughters." [2] The third account related to
a presumably terminated marriage at Coventry, where a husband circulated a handbill describing his lost wife. "She is about
five feet four inches and a half high, fresh coloured, brown hair,
is full eyed, has a wart on her right breast, had on, when she
went away from her honest husband, a dark flowered cotton
gown, a white hat and ribands, a light brown shalloon quilt,
leather pumps, and plated buckles, soft solder, has tight clean
legs and garters below knee." [3] Neither this nor subsequent
issues of the *Gazette* revealed whether the honest but ungallant
husband's ploy proved successful.

For those who found none of these items amusing there was
offered what the *Gazette* termed "An instance of wit in low
life." The story concerned "a smith not far from Whitecross-
street [London], having frequently pawned his hammers, vices,
&c. at length his wife sold them while he was getting drunk; on
which a cobler said, that 'Dick—was now an *honest* fellow, for
his wife had disposed of his vices,' " On the strength of this effort
social historians might be prompted to deduce that in "low life"
wit came as small as the purses. The same issue of the *Virginia
Gazette* [4] provided a whimsical comment on that most unfunny
of subjects, the affair at Lexington, reporting that the author of
an improbable work entitled *Musical Travels through Germany*
"imputes the advantages gained by the Bostonians over the
troops of General Gage to those inspiring notes so generally
known by the name of *Yanky Doodle;* and by no means wonders

[1] Ibid., Sept. 16.
[2] Ibid.
[3] Ibid., Sept. 23.
[4] Ibid.

that the detachment headed by Lord Percy was unsuccessful, considering that they marched to the tune of *Room for Cuckolds*."

Earlier in the summer Dixon & Hunter had instructed the public in the etymology of the word "Yankee." [5] A correspondent had assured them that it derived from a tribe of Indians known as the Yankoos, meaning invincible, who fought hard against the New Englanders during the early years of colonization. After the tribe had been subdued "The remains of this nation (agreeable to the Indian custom) transferred their name to their conquerors. For a while they were called Yankoos; but from a corruption common to names in all languages, they got, through time, the name of Yankees; a name which we hope will soon be equal to that of a Roman, or an *ancient* Englishman."

All the Virginia papers followed the dictum that no opportunity, however small, should be missed to take a swipe at the Englishmen of 1775. If they could, at the same time, be made into figures of fun, so much the better, and few finer vehicles could be hoped for than the affair of Lord Dunmore and the mullet fishermen. It went like this:

A certain sloop of war, not a 100 miles distant, was lately kept in constant alarm a whole night, with her matches burning, tomkins out, guns loaded with grape shot, and all hands at their quarters, till day-light discovered the formidable enemy, which had caused such terrible apprehensions, to be only one of the neighbours with his negroes catching mullets! A certain governor, it is said, was in all haste sent for, to assist with his sage advice at the council of war that was held on this mighty occasion.[6]

The comic and satirical anecdotes were scattered so haphazardly through the papers that it was often extremely difficult to determine whether actual events were being amusingly reported or whether they were simply apocryphal pegs on which to hang

[5] Ibid., June 10.
[6] Ibid., Sept. 2.

a funny line. There were no professional reporters to gather the news; the publishers relied on the tales of travelers, reports carried by ships' captains, private letters, and, most important of all, the columns of other newspapers. But as far as local news was concerned, the Virginia papers realized their obligation to pass on the news more or less as it happened, though it might take two different publishers to give the reader the whole of any one story. Thus Purdie reported on September 2 that Messrs. Peyton Randolph, Thomas Nelson, George Wythe, and their respective wives had left Williamsburg en route to the congress at Philadelphia; but one would have to read Pinkney on September 14 to discover that the carriage of Randolph and Nelson had come to grief just after they crossed into Maryland. That was not the end of it, for having borrowed another from a nearby resident "through the unskillfulness of the driver, as is supposed, it run against a tree, and was entirely demolished." Neither passenger seemed to have been hurt, but the correspondent did not know how they continued their journey, only that they parted company at that point. No mention was made of their wives. The obvious course might have been to look for the end of the saga in the pages of Dixon and Hunter. But it would have been wasted effort, for they failed to report the story at all.

Peyton Randolph's coaching accident was not the only major story to escape Dixon and Hunter. Neither they nor, for that matter, their competitors ever revealed to their readers that the Great Seal of the colony, which had been in the Capitol when Lord Dunmore left Williamsburg, had now been stolen. Indeed, the loss was apparently mentioned by no one for eleven years, until the man who stole it proudly informed the British government that he had done so. The man, Adam Allen, a Williamsburg stocking maker, did not consider himself a thief but rather an agent of Lord Dunmore on "secret service," [7] and he said that it was at his Lordship's instigation that he stole the seal. Applying to the commissioners appointed to inquire into the claims of loyalists, he inserted in the section marked "List of

[7] Allen's widow's pension claim, Oct. 14, 1823; PRO, WO 42/59, 3.

Services Suffering & Losses" the information that his services
included "getting the Great Seal of the Collony of Virginia out
of the hands of the Rebels after they had been upwards of a
Month in their possession." [8] It is immaterial that the patriots
must have had the seal for more than two months; but it is
significant that Allen gave the name of Lord Dunmore as being
one who would vouch for the validity of his claim. No one knows
what became of the seal, for Dunmore seems to have made no
report of its recovery. As for Allen, he remained in Williamsburg apparently undetected after the September snatch, though
he would later be discovered to be inimical and would be tarred
and feathered in Fredericksburg.

Due to be more immediately unhappy was Lord William
Campbell, the only-recently appointed governor of South Carolina. At the end of the month he found it necessary to leave
Charleston and to take refuge aboard the *Tamar* man-of-war, a
fourteen-gun sloop in such poor condition that Admiral Graves
had planned to withdraw her from service. Like the Williamsburg burgesses, the Charleston committee wrote asking the
governor to return, and, like Dunmore, Campbell declined. On
September 30 he replied, saying that the committee had no legal
authority and that he considered its existence an "actual and
open rebellion against their Sovereign." He would never return
to Charleston, he declared, until he was able to "support the
King's authority, and protect his faithful and loyal subjects." [9]

Thus the British government began its American autumn
with its control of three Southern colonies extending no further
than the gunwales of a warship.

[8] The Memorial of Adam Allen, Fredericktown, New Brunswick,
March 1, 1786; PRO,AO 13/80, *Loyalist Claims*, 1776–1802.

[9] *American Archives*, 4th ser., III, 846.

[X]

OCTOBER

"Norfolk is at present a very insecure place
for the life or property of any individual," declared Purdie's
Gazette.[1] There was doubtless a good deal of truth in this,
though it is debatable whether it was the patriot or the loyalist
who was in the greater danger. The patriots could have derived
little comfort from the feeble response to the call to arms during
the printing office raid, and many of them decided to move out.
A somewhat melodramatic correspondent writing to a friend in
Williamsburg on October 1 described the melancholy "cries of
the women and children in the streets" and reported that most
families were leaving; "the carts have been going all this day." [2]
At the same time there were other citizens who were leaving for
the opposite reason.

Colonel Joseph Hutchings, one of the more vociferous local
patriots, was heard to swear "and several times repeat, in the
hearing of Women, Children & the nigroes as they past him,
that that very night he would make Sure to Drive the scoundrels
out of Town that would not take up arms." A certain Mrs. Ross
of Norfolk testified that Hutchings had threatened "to set fire to
the Town and burn the scoundrels Out of it." The poor woman
"was frighten'd almost to death at hearing of it, and hastening
to Abandon her house & her business." [3] This would seem to

[1] *Supplement*, Oct. 6.
[2] Ibid.
[3] Copy of a letter from Alexander Gordon to the Norfolk Common
Council, Oct. 2, enclosed with Dunmore to Dartmouth, Oct. 5; PRO,CO
5/1353.

have been the first threat by either side to burn Norfolk, and it is significant that it came from a patriot leader.

The affair of the printing office seizure had an effect that far outstripped Lord Dunmore's expectations; indeed, there is little reason to suppose that he thought any further than his desire to put the *Norfolk Intelligencer* out of business. But the failure of patriotic citizens to prevent the raid caused as great an outrage and uproar as the confiscation itself. From far and wide infuriated Virginians seized their quills and wrote scathing letters to newspapers and friends. Paul Loyal, Norfolk's mayor, did his best to salvage the image of his borough by immediately sending a courageous missive to the governor calling his action "illegal and riotous" and declaring that it, together with a stray musket ball fired from the *Kingfisher* on the previous day, had scared the town out of its wits. The address went on to claim that the mayor and Common Council had been active in preserving the peace of the town, but that if "the inhabitants had been disposed to repel insult, that they were sufficiently able either to have cut off, or taken prisoners, the small party that came on shore." [4] The piece ended by calling on Dunmore to play fair with these good people and give them back their printing press.

To this his Lordship replied that he had watched the raid and that he was satisfied that the exploit had done the townspeople a signal service by scotching the printed viper that was pouring its poison into their midst. As for the musket shot, he assured the mayor that it had been an accident and that it would not occur again. "But with regard to your having ever preserved the peace in your town," Dunmore added, "there is recent proof to the contrary. As to your not repelling the insult, as you call it, or taking prisoners, the small party that was on shore, *I impute it* to some other reason (from your drums beating to arms during the greatest part of the time the party was on shore) than to your peaceable intentions." This well-aimed barb landed squarely in the underbelly of Norfolk's honor and remained

---

[4] Copy of Loyal's address enclosed with the above.

there for all to see. On October 13 Purdie published both
Loyal's address and Lord Dunmore's reply in full, and there is
little doubt that Norfolk was the loser. He also printed a lengthy
tirade directed at Dunmore by someone signing himself "C,"
who accused the governor of having "robbed forcibly two men
of their freedom, without a hearing or trial," and of having
"deprived the publick of a *free press*, the property of a *free man*,
one of the criterions of a happy constitution."

The anonymous Mr. "C" went on with great bravura to
accuse Dunmore of silencing Holt's paper not for the good of the
colony but out of personal pique:

> I was really at a loss to discover what act of the unhappy
> printer had rendered him so obnoxious to you, until I looked
> into the Norfolk gazette of the preceding week, and there I
> found your *genealogy* described, which I confess reflects little
> honour on your family; yet, as we presume it to be truth, the
> recital could not justly subject the bare retailer to such
> violence and oppression. The disgrace of your ancestors could
> have little affected you, had *your character* been free from
> *guilt;* but when the *blood flows contaminated*, it is not
> difficult to investigate the rise and cause of *perfidy*.

Unfortunately the extant file of Holt's *Virginia Gazette, or the
Norfolk Intelligencer* ends with the issue of September 20, and
therefore we can only guess at the content of the Dunmore geneal-
ogy in the September 27 edition. It is likely, however, that it
dwelt on his father's involvement in the 1745 Jacobite Rebellion
and perhaps upon a more than academic family interest in
Roman Catholicism—as damnable a suggestion as one could
make at that time. "C's" charge that the paper was suppressed
because of this makes sense, for Holt's sheet had hitherto been
no more anti-Ministerial or anti-Dunmore than the three Williamsburg *Gazettes*. Therefore the removal of one would not
silence the others; on the contrary it would be liable to make
them all the more vociferous. Captain Squire had previously
threatened Holt, and it seems probable that when Lord Dunmore saw the September 27 issue the two men decided that they

had taken enough. It is significant that Holt's personal attacks were not mentioned in Dunmore's report to Lord Dartmouth, instead he referred only to the poisoning of the minds of the people and his need for printing machinery.

If, as is hardly likely, the governor had some idea that the suppression of Holt would frighten Williamsburg editors into a more seemly respect for his person, he was sadly mistaken. On October 19 Pinkney came out with his most scurrilous blast to date, a speech by "Cato" reminding the people of Virginia of the iniquities of their governor. Having hauled over all the events of the past months the writer produced a new and succulent charge:

> But how will your breasts glow with just resentment, and honest indignation, when I tell you he had dared offer violence to the chastity of a poor innocent girl? This unhappy victim to his lawless lust, whose beauty had stricken him, was by him, or by some of his minions, torn from the poorhouse in Norfolk, from the few friends which poverty could procure her, carried on board his ship, and forced to become an instrument of pleasure to him who had degraded himself far beneath the most grovelling of the brute creation.

Thus did his Lordship appear as the precursor of the standard villain of Victorian melodrama, a monstrous bridge between Cawdor and Corder to be hissed and booed on every entrance.

This was only the beginning, for, according to "Cato," the frail defenseless child was kept aboard ship until an unidentified father, "that notorious pander of his brutal passions, by the prostitution of his own offspring, supplied him [Dunmore] with more charming objects; for on their arrival this unhappy girl was dismissed, and thrown upon the world, robbed of all she held most dear, of all on which she relied for a future reputable subsistence." One can almost hear the violins and see the paper snow fluttering over her shoulders.

But "Cato" 's purpose was not simply to paint a black cloak and a twirly moustache on the portrait of Lord Dunmore: "Ye inhabitants of Norfolk! why were ye passive here," he demanded. "Why suffer such an outrage to go unpunished? Could none be found among you animated with the noble spirit of old VIRGINIUS?" Then turning to every clean-living and honorable rebel in the land, he charged: "To let the sword, therefore, remain a moment longer within the scabbard, will be criminal. . . . Give vent, then, to every sentiment of revenge; let it, like the obstructed torrent, burst forth with gathered fury; let it sweep off, and bury in eternal oblivion, that more than Tartarean monster of impiety . . . [so] that the future daughters of Virginia may never blush to hear, that there was a time when one of their sisters could so shamefully depart from the amiable characteristic applied to the fair sex in general, but more particularly to them." The fetal honor of the Colonial Dames, the First Families of Virginia, and the D.A.R. was at stake. Its defense, according to "Cato," might "cost either the partial or total destruction of one of our seaport towns," but, he assured his readers, "the inhabitants of it are ready to see it sacrificed when the general good requires it." There were undoubtedly a goodly number of Norfolk citizens who disagreed with him, but that was of small concern. "While we can," he went on, "with the loss of the lives of but few of our countrymen, and with the destruction of only part of the property of a few others, let us sacrifice the whole infernal crew to the guardian deities of American liberty, and to those of Virginian chastity." [5]

There seems to be no extant confirmation of "Cato"'s charges, though Lord Dunmore's career in New York and Prevost's mention of a mistress in Williamsburg leaves room to suppose that he may not have found memories of marital life sufficiently satisfying. But true or not, "Cato"'s was the most unrestrained newspaper attack yet made on him. Meanwhile John Holt was busily girding himself for a return to the fray. On October 13 he published an advertisement announcing that he was acquiring new printing equipment and would shortly be returning to his chosen task of keeping his countrymen apprised of "the machinations and black designs of their common

[5] *Virginia Gazette* (Pinkney), *Supplement*, Oct. 19.

enemy." He hoped to establish himself close to Norfolk so that he could again keep an eye on "the gentlemen of the Army and Navy" [6] and sound the alarm whenever danger approached. On the twentieth, still having no paper of his own, Holt inserted an open letter in Purdie's *Virginia Gazette*, presenting his compliments to Lord Dunmore and begging leave "*to inform him that he has as a partial retaliation for the loss he has sustained by his lordship's seizure of his types, and other effects, taken possession of several of his lordship's horses.*" [7] They were presumably taken either from the palace park at Williamsburg or from the Dunmore farm at "Porto Bello" and had doubtless already been written off by the governor.

The cauldron was rapidly coming to the boil as each side stoked the fires of escalation. Patrick Henry, commander in chief of the Virginia forces, was encamped at Williamsburg with the first nine companies of his newly recruited army, and more men were expected to assemble during the month. On October 5 Dunmore reported to Lord Dartmouth that guns seized from the government were being mounted on field carriages in Williamsburg and that great quantities of iron balls were being cast for them. "They have just now received," he said, "by Land from Baltimore in Maryland three and twenty hundred Weight of Gunpowder which they got from the West Indies; the Men of War have three tenders out now cruising for two Schooners and a Sloop that I have intelligence of that are expected from the same quarter with powder, two of which are bound to Baltimore, the other for this Colony." [8]

Ten days later Edmund Pendleton in Williamsburg wrote to Richard Henry Lee in Philadelphia confirming the governor's intelligence report. "Had we arms and ammunition, it would give vigour to our measures," he wrote. "We hourly hoped to hear of the arrival of the necessaries, but now fear we shall be defeated. A villian has given Lord *Dunmore* information of it,

[6] *Virginia Gazette* (Purdie), Oct. 13.

[7] Ibid., Oct. 20.

[8] Dunmore to Dartmouth, Oct. 5; PRO,CO 5/1353.

and he has six or seven tenders flying out for it about the capes." [9]

While his tenders waited for the ammunition ships, Lord Dunmore made an abortive attempt to seize existing rebel supplies recently assembled at Kemp's Landing, some ten miles southeast of Norfolk. On Tuesday, October 17, the governor, at the head of a force of what was claimed to be about 140 men, descended on the village, where he met with very little resistance. They broke open a blacksmith's shop and destroyed fifty muskets which were waiting to be repaired. But the chief prize, the powder, had already been removed to safety by the patriots. Four privates and two officers of militia fared less well and were captured, causing considerable speculation as to how this could have come about. In a supplement dated October 20, Alexander Purdie reported that "*It appears, from the examination of a gentleman on oath that the account published in* Hunter *and* Dixon's *paper, of Mr. Mathews's being taken by Lord Dunmore at the head of a company of minutemen, is much misrepresented, the said Mathews having been surprised by the enemy in the night, alone, and unarmed.*" The correction would have been very helpful were it not for the fact that the Dixon and Hunter paper said only that Mathews was "of the Norfolk minute-men" and that it did not know how he came to be taken. That paper is dated October 21, a day later than Purdie's supplement, demonstrating once again that the papers did not necessarily come out on the dates printed on their mastheads.

Lord Dunmore's account of the Kemp's Landing raid was rather different from that given in the newspapers. He gave no indication that a consignment of powder was his principal target; instead he said he was looking for artillery, which he was informed the patriots were assembling. He admitted that he did not find them, but claimed to have seized some small arms and ammunition. As for the minutemen, he stated that the rebels "had collected about 200 of their Shirtmen, who all fled to the

[9] *American Archives*, 4th ser., III, 1067; Oct. 15.

woods." [1] A British marine aboard the *Otter* wrote his own
hearsay account of the sortie and in it left no doubt that the
capture of the elusive powder had been the object of the
exercise. He claimed that there were supposed to be 250 rebels
guarding it, but "nothing of them was to be seen, and our men
all went out in full expectation of a smart resistance." After a
small quote from *Hudibras* the literary marine declaimed: "Oh
tell it not in *Gath* nor Publish it not in *Askalon*, that 200
Virginian troops run away from scarce 90 Regulars." The latter
figure differs markedly from that of the newspapers but more
closely parallels Lord Dunmore's figure mentioned in his report
of a previous foray on October 15, at which time he stated that
he landed "between 70 and 80 Men (which was all we could
spare to take with us)." The marine's account of the patriots'
absence also tallied well with the governor's report: "We were
informed by the inhabitants [of Kemp's Landing]," he wrote,
"that the Powder, was removed the night before, but that half
an hour before we arrived, there was 250, of their troops
exercising, who marched away on our approach thus ending the
expedition so much to the honor of the Regulars, and so
disgracefull to the Buskins." [2]

Beesly Joel, the marine, gave the date of the Kemp's
Landing raid as the fifteenth, but he was certainly in error, for
on that night Lord Dunmore reported that he "marched about a
mile and a half up the Country, where we destroyed 17 pieces of
Ordinance and brought off two more that the Rebels had carried
from the Town of Norfolk, and concealed there." On the
nineteenth his men went out again and brought back six guns
after destroying ten others; two nights later they grabbed six
more and on the twenty-first made the largest haul of the series,
bringing home ten guns, more than fifty small arms "and a
great quantity of Ball of all Sorts and Sizes." [3] This was,

[1] Dunmore to Dartmouth, Oct. 22; PRO,CO 5/1353.
[2] Beesly Joel to Joseph Wright, Oct. 25; *RCHP*, I, 98–99.
[3] Dunmore to Dartmouth, Oct. 22; PRO,CO 5/1353.

Dunmore deduced, the sum of the remaining rebel military stores in the area. He added that, in all, seven prisoners were taken, among them Captain Mathews and delegate Robinson, a brace of superior game. The manner in which these birds were downed was described for us by our old Tory friend from Norfolk, James Parker, who can always be relied on to supply colorful touches which may or may not be of his own invention.

It seems that the Princess Anne County minutemen under the command of Colonel Joseph Hutchings (the arson-minded patriot who wanted to burn Norfolk) were bracing themselves in preparation to offer the governor battle, but were surprised by Dunmore's arrival at Kemp's Landing before they were ready. When news of the British approach reached the assembled warriors, the officers held a short council of war and decided not to fight. Captain Mathews therefore gave the order to disperse— which the men did with "instantaineous exactness" except for Colonel Hutchings, who, Parker recorded with some delight, "for joy of the approaching action had made rather too free with the bottle, he got however as far as the back road & fell, a Town Butcher driving some Cattle . . . trail'd him into the Woods & Covered him with trash by which he escaped." According to Parker, only the officer prisoners were held by Lord Dunmore, these being "a Capt Mathews a Barbadian who is a Capt of Minute men, & Wm Robinson . . . a Delegate & an Officer in the Same Service. Poor Robinson went up to them [the British soldiers] Drunk when in one of the Stores, declaring he wd allow no such doings while he had the honour to be a Delegate." Parker added: "It is Suspected that Mathews has turned Kings evidence; for the Marines have found all the Cannon that was Missing & Several others, also Colours, Drums Since he went on board[,] also 37 Cases of Gin. The Cannon Now taken & destroyed amount exactly to John Wilkes favourite Number"— a reference to the forty-fifth issue of the *North Briton*, in which the radical Wilkes had attacked Lord Bute and the Treaty of Paris, and so first earned his political spurs. "Such are the proceedings in this place," Parker concluded, "& tho' Purdies Gazette may Say otherwase, this Account is the truth." [4]

The most authoritative evidence should have come from Captain Samuel Leslie commanding the detachment of the Fourteenth Infantry Regiment at Gosport, who wrote to General Howe on November 1. In his report he identified the raiding party sent to Kemp's Landing as comprising: "Captain Cooper, Lieutenants Batut, Lawrie, and Leslie, Ensigns Wool, Boys, Ogle, and Lindsay, three Sergeants, and seventy rank and file, [and himself] of the Fourteenth Regiment, Lieutenant Allen, one Sergeant, and twenty marines, some young gentlemen of the Navy, and ten or twelve seamen," [5] a total of about 125. This figure was larger than other loyalist reports and only a few short of the figure given in the newspapers.

Lord Dunmore's account of the sorties on October 15, 17, 19, and 21 begin with "I" and continue with "we," suggesting that he had taken an active part in each of them. But Captain Leslie suggests otherwise. He gives the date of the first effort as October 12, not 15, and describes the party under his command as comprising "Lieutenant Lawrie, two Sergeants, and forty rank and file, of the Fourteenth Regiment. . . . Lord Dunmore accompanied us upon this expedition." He made no mention of the governor's presence in subsequent musters. He did not contend that the visit to Kemp's Landing was specifically in pursuit of gunpowder, but said only that they had heard that there was there a "great quantity of artillery, small-arms, and all sorts of ammunition" and tabled his haul as comprising "nothing but a good many small-arms, musket locks, a little powder and ball, two drums, and a quantity of buckshot." As an assault on the patriot's military stores, no matter how you sliced it, the project had not been much of a success. Nevertheless Leslie went on to state that since his detachment's arrival his men had seized or destroyed at least seventy-seven pieces of ordnance "without the smallest opposi-

[4] Parker to Steuart, Oct. 29; CSP.

[5] *American Archives*, 4th ser., III, 1716.

tion, which is proof that it would not require a very large force to subdue this Colony." [6]

The detachment under Leslie in mid-October amounted to four captains, three lieutenants, four ensigns, one adjutant, a surgeon's mate, four sergeants, four corporals, five drummers and fifers (four of them sick) and seventy-nine privates, four of whom were also sick. On October 14 one of the senior officers, Captain William Blackett, died and was buried at Portsmouth with full military honors; in attendance, according to an obviously reliable report, were "his lordship, the gentlemen of the navy, and 91 men rank and file, besides Officers, which it seemed composed the whole corps under lord Dunmore's command at that time. Four of the soldiers were so feeble, occasioned by sickness, that they could not carry their arms." [7] We know very little about Captain Blackett beyond a comment by a brother officer when writing to the commander of the Boston contingent of the regiment: "I have forgot all this time to condole with you on the death of your good friend, and quondam Captain, Blackett, who drank his last dram, and resigned his breath on the 12th of October. They say he was a most miserable object before he died. I think you have been in tolerable good fortune this year to get quit of him. . . ." [8]

The writer of this none too charitable epitaph was Captain Charles Fordyce, who arrived at Norfolk with reinforcements from St. Augustine on October 20. It was not by any means as large a force as Dunmore hoped for, comprising only "Lieutenants Napier and Wallace, three Sergeants, three Corporals, two Drummers, and fifty-five private men," [9] plus a handful of noncommissioned officers on their way to join their companies at Boston. The equipment and supplies that Fordyce brought with him were hardly adequate, as Governor Tonyn of East Florida

[6] Ibid.

[7] *Virginia Gazette* (Purdie), *Supplement*, Oct. 20.

[8] Captain Fordyce to Captain Urquhart, Dec. 1; *American Archives*, 4th ser., IV, 349.

[9] Captain Leslie to General Howe, Nov. 1; ibid., III, 1717.

had objected to the further reduction of his arsenal and had specifically instructed the barracksmaster at St. Augustine that supplies of provisions and blankets were to be limited.

There seems to have been some displeasure both north and southward regarding Lord Dunmore's constant and wearisome demands for troops. Governor Tonyn thought he was being emasculated and left wide open to attack by Spanish, French, Dutch or any rebel adventurer who might take a fancy to the Florida peninsula. In Boston, Major General James Grant was sure that Dunmore was making his demands without authority, thus prompting an explanation from St. Augustine: "you are mistaken in regard to Lord Dunmore's sending for [the men] without authority. The first detachment of Captain Leslie and sixty men and the Providence company, was a positive order from General Gage; the detachment of sixty which goes now was also a positive order of the General's; and the last order says that, if Lord Dunmore makes a requisition of the rest of the regiment, it is to go upon the arrival of the three companies of the Sixteenth." [1]

Captain Leslie's comment that it would take only a small force to quell the Virginia rebels was the same as that voiced by most loyalists from the outset and by Lord Dunmore himself. On September 26 General Howe had received instructions from London giving him command of the British armies in America in the absence of General Gage, who was returning to England, ostensibly for consultations. One of the first letters to Howe from Lord Dartmouth commented on Dunmore's contention that he could put down the rebellion with a mere two or three hundred men. "I will confess," wrote Dartmouth, "that it appeared to me, at the first view of the propositions made by Lord Dunmore and Governour Martin, that they were too sanguine in their expectations; but later advices confirm what they represented of the temper and disposition of the people, and there is good ground to believe that the appearance of a

[1] Frederick George Mulcaster to General Grant, Oct. 3; ibid., IV, 330.

respectable force to the southward, under the command of an able and discreet officer, will have the effect to restore order and Government in those four Provinces." He was referring to Virginia, Georgia, and the Carolinas, and he informed Howe that the King had ordered five regiments of infantry to be made ready for the expedition. They were to be the Fifteenth, Thirty-seventh, Fifty-third, Fifty-fourth, and Fifty-seventh, and were to embark at Cork on or before December 1. They would be augmented by two companies of artillery already in America and were to proceed "under convoy of a proper naval force, to Cape Fear River, at which place there is good ground to hope they will be immediately joined by the Highland emigrants settled in that neighbourhood, whose assistance Governour Martin says we may depend on." Dartmouth went on to inform Howe that it was the King's pleasure that the force should be under the command of one of the generals already on duty under him and that the chosen officer "do immediately proceed in a ship of war to Cape Fear River. . . ."[2] Ironically Lord Dunmore's counsel was at last being heeded, but when relief came he was to be bypassed in favor of opening the campaign in North Carolina.

In Virginia, meanwhile, loyalist morale had risen considerably as the result of the governor's punitive measures against the rebel ordnance. There was reason to hope that the remainder of the Fourteenth Regiment would soon arrive from St. Augustine and from Boston, and that when it did Lord Dunmore would have strength enough to frighten the rebel minutemen to death even if he could not catch them. Beesly Joel wrote home from the *Otter* declaring that he was in "the most agreeable situation imaginable" and wanted only that his mother should send him some money, and that a friend should find him "a neat collection of Prints a few old magazines, and a goodly collection of hair Pencills"[3]—these last were artists' paint brushes. It took all sorts to make up a ship's company.

[2] Dartmouth to Howe, Oct. 22; ibid., III, 1135.
[3] *RCHP*, I, 98–99; Oct. 25.

In Williamsburg the Capitol dutifully opened its doors for the scheduled meeting of the assembly on October 12. To nobody's surprise only thirty-seven burgesses appeared, not enough to proceed with business, and they formally adjourned themselves until March 1, 1776. The attendance of the thirty-seven was merely a formality serving to pour a few drops of oil on the rusting machinery of colonial government for the benefit of those who believed that reconciliation was still possible and desirable.

Immediately beneath Purdie's account of the assembly's adjournment was inserted an extract from a letter written by an unnamed Virginia delegate to the congress in Philadelphia. "We have hopes here," it said, "of an accommodation with Great Britain. . . . The ministry themselves agree that IT MUST BE MADE UP, and will in all probability TAKE HOLD of the OFFER MADE THEM by the CONGRESS in their petition." [4] But the *Gazette*'s next item gave little encouragement to the doves in Virginia. "We hear that lord Dunmore has just received a reinforcement of soldiers from St. Augustine, to complete his corps of *banditti* to the number of 500; and that, by and by, he expects five regiments of the *same sort of trumpery* from England, with which, no doubt, he expects to perform deeds *worthy of his noble ancestors*."

This entire item, quite apart from its obvious reminder of Dunmore's bellicose intentions, is a most disturbing piece of intelligence, one which might suggest that Hecate herself had been hired as a *Virginia Gazette* reporter. There is no evidence that a reinforcement had arrived from St. Augustine on or about October 13. Captain Fordyce and his men would not reach Gosport until October 20; and what of the five regiments from England? Lord Dartmouth did not sit down in Whitehall to write those instructions to General Howe until October 22. Where then did Purdie obtain this astonishingly prophetic information? One can only suppose that news of Fordyce's approach preceded him and that rumors of the Ministry's plan

[4] *Virginia Gazette* (Purdie), Oct. 13.

for a southern campaign had been circulating in London long before the King gave it his approval.

The *Gazette*'s contention that Lord Dunmore's forces amounted in all to some five hundred men was undoubtedly an exaggeration, even if one included all the seamen, loyalist volunteers, and Negroes. Nevertheless five hundred was not an unbeatable number, and the patriots already had more than that assembled at Williamsburg, with prospects for the imminent arrival of additional riflemen. The increase in Tory morale was certainly not offset by any proportionate decrease of enthusiasm among the patriots. On the contrary they were anxiously awaiting an opportunity to engage the British forces. It was true that the Princess Anne County people had not put up much of a showing, but that could be readily explained on the grounds that they *were* Princess Anne County people. There had been considerable support among convention delegates for abandoning the whole coastal region in the belief that it was both strategically impossible to defend and riddled with Tories. Eventually, however, John Page of "Rosewell," the leader of the advocates for a firm defense of the lowlands, prevailed over the backcountry boys. But while the debate over this fundamental decision was going on, the military leaders in Williamsburg were unable to do anything but wait.

Dunmore and Squire had focused much of their attention on the little port of Hampton, for it lay just across the roads from Norfolk and provided the Williamsburg patriots with a strategic access to the Chesapeake Bay and the open sea. It was also the seat of the customs office for the district of the Lower James River. The governor had ordered the office moved to the comparative safety of Norfolk, but Wilson Miles Cary, the naval officer, informed Dunmore that he was "an officer belonging to the Country and not to the Crown" and that he had no intention of leaving Hampton. Reporting to Lord Dartmouth, Dunmore noted that on October 21, "Mr. Mitchell the Collector with his books and papers made his escape in the Night and arrived here yesterday in the Morning," adding ". . . Mr.

Bradley the Comptroller I expect will come if he can make his escape, if Mr. Cary or his Deputy does not come I shall appoint another in his place." [5] At this point in the game, the loss of the customs house and its naval officer did not matter very much, for they had long since ceased to be of service to the Crown. But for Dunmore, Cary's rejection forced the thorn of Hampton further into his side. There had been reason to expect that he would eventually goad himself into an assault on the town, and in response to threats of this nature the King and Queen County company of minutemen, under the command of Captain George Lyne, had been sent down from Williamsburg on October 7 to do garrison duty. They relieved some of the local volunteers and militia and brought the total of men under arms in the town to about four hundred.

Burk, in his *History of Virginia*, wrote that "it was now considered on all hands, that in the first encounter with the British, something worthy of the American character should be atcheived, which like the battle of Lexington, would act as an example, and inspire the enemy with apprehension and respect." [6] It seemed likely that Hampton would become the South's Lexington.

The town was L-shaped, with about thirty buildings or blocks of buildings along two streets, one leading southwest and joining the Back River Road to Yorktown and the Great Warwick Road to Williamsburg. The second street ran down to a jetty extending out into Hampton Creek, giving the inhabitants a clear view into Hampton Roads. The church stood at the junction of the two streets in, as it were, the heel of the "L." To the north and east of the town was its principal source of livelihood, the shipyard. This, however, was not visible from the Roads, as it lay in a bend of the creek behind a promontory known as Little Scotland, on which the patriots had built an entrenchment commanding the mouth. The creek itself provided some natural obstacles in the form of shoals, which, though not

[5] Dunmore to Dartmouth, Oct. 22; PRO,CO 5/1353.
[6] Vol. III, p. 433.

making the approach dangerous, did require that one kept one's mind on the business of navigation. To these had been added a string of scuttled boats, which further narrowed the channel. The creek's mouth was about a third of a mile in width, but was, at best, navigable across only half of it. Although in sight of the mouth, Hampton lay about a mile and a half from it, safe from anything but the "greater random" range of any ship that feared to enter the bottleneck of the creek.

Because all the road approaches to the town came from the west and because it was protected by the wide Hampton Creek to the east, it was reasonable to expect that any attack would be launched from the rear, following a landing to the southwest, probably somewhere between Hampton Creek and Salt Creek. But just as these considerations protected the town from an actual assault from the east, the creek could not keep it out of gunshot if Dunmore should take the trouble to cross a stretch of inhospitable marshes and set up his cannon on the east bank. Furthermore, the creek would serve also to prevent patriot troops from moving in to dislodge him.

On the night of October 25 one of Captain Squire's raiding parties did go ashore at Mill Creek east of Hampton and proceeded to loot a number of houses. News of this sortie did not reach the minutemen at Hampton until dawn, whereupon they looked down Hampton Creek and saw the British tenders lying in the channel. It was presumed that they had taken up that position to prevent the patriots from sinking any more obstacles across it. Captain Lyne immediately mounted his horse and rode off around the west arms of the creek to take a closer look at whatever it was that the British were doing. He left instructions with his lieutenant, Mr. Smith, that he was to follow with thirty men. Unfortunately the details of this affair are not sufficiently specific for either the patriot or British movements to be plotted with complete accuracy. But it would seem that Captain Lyne rode to the point on the west bank of the mouth where a windmill stood, and that he found the British tenders lying in the T-shaped channel behind the outer sand bar. As soon as

Lieutenant Smith arrived with his thirty men, two quick volleys
of musketry came their way from the tenders. Lyne replied with
a single rifle shot and got back in return a four-pound ball, the
beginning of a cannonade which went on for about an hour.
Lyne was soon reinforced by another twenty-five men, who
blazed away with a will, eventually causing the nearest of the
tenders to withdraw out of range. Although the riflemen were
able to force the British to keep their heads down, the majority
of the militia were armed only with muskets, whose fire fell
badly short. At no time were the vessels within 300 yards of the
shore, and so the first pitched battle of the Revolution in
Virginia turned out to be full of sound and fury, signifying very
little. After the gunfire ended Captain Lyne waited around for
something to happen, and when nothing did, he undertook a
very obvious retreat in the hope of encouraging the British to
land and give chase. But still nothing happened, and finally
around five o'clock in the afternoon Lyne gave up and marched
back to Hampton, whereupon men from the tenders promptly
went ashore and burned the house of a Mr. Edward Cooper.

A request for help reached Edmund Pendleton in Williamsburg shortly before midnight, and he immediately ordered
William Woodford, colonel of the colony's Second Regiment, to
take a company of Culpeper County riflemen and proceed
immediately to the relief of Hampton. Historian Burk puts the
arrival of the request for aid at midnight in one reference and
9:00 P.M. in another, but, no matter which was correct,
Woodford had to move quickly if he was to prevent the
destruction of the town. The distance was about thirty miles
from Williamsburg, and, according to Burk, "it rained incessantly the whole night." [7] Nevertheless, riding "without any
other incumbrance than their provisions and blankets," [8] the
detachment reached Hampton by 7:30 A.M.—the town was still
there, and so were Captain Lyne and his men.

The British had spent the night cutting their way through

[7] *History of Virginia*, IV, 64.
[8] Ibid., III, 433.

the bowsprits of the vessels sunk in the creek channel, and half an hour after Woodford's arrival, making use of the high water, five tenders "to wit, a large schooner, 2 sloops, and 2 pilot boats, passed the passage they had cleared and drew up a-breast of the town." [9] The schooner was commanded by Captain Squire, who ordered his gunners to open fire. Three rousing cheers emanated from the five ships, followed immediately by a barrage of balls, double-head, and grape shot, which crashed into the houses beside the quay and enfiladed down the length of the main street. Clouds of dust and smoke rose over the little town, and chickens flew cackling off in all directions, but no one was hurt. Nevertheless, the first blast was enough to cause the less courageous elements to contend that the town could not be defended, claiming that, with the street raked by Squire's cannon, the fire could not be returned. Woodford disagreed.

After quickly taking stock of his position, Woodford sent Lieutenant Bulford with the Culpeper riflemen and the local militia to man one side of the street, while another local company under Captain Nicholas took the other. Captain Lyne and his King and Queen County minutemen were ordered to the crossroads west of the town to guard against surprise from the rear. Meanwhile Squire's cannonade continued with vigor, as the patriots scuttled from house to house to take up their positions. For the gunners aboard the tenders, this was a splendid opportunity to practice, and all concerned remained in the best of spirits, until carefully aimed bullets began to splinter the timbers around their heads. Woodford's riflemen were in position and were following their orders to fire only at specific targets. So accurate was their shooting that Squire's men had the greatest difficulty in loading the cannon without exposing inviting areas of their anatomy. Slowly the fire from the ships slackened. Realizing that he was being outgunned by Woodford's rifles, Squire reluctantly gave the order to slip cables and retire. He soon discovered that that was easier said than done, for as Burk recorded later, "No man could stand at the helm in

[9] *Virginia Gazette* (Pinkney), Nov. 2.

safety; if the men went aloft to hand the sails, they were immediately singled out."[1] One of the tenders, the *Hawke*, commanded by Lieutenant Wright, was unable to get under way and drifted ashore into a hail of bullets. The crew, according to one report, had decided not to play any more and had retired to the comparative safety of the hold. Wright was shot through the knee but managed to leap overboard and swim away, along with one of the Negroes, but a boarding party seized the rest of the crew, among them the master gunner, seven men, three of whom were wounded (two mortally), one white woman, and two Negroes. As well as the ship, the prize included six swivel guns, seven muskets, several pistols, a sword, and various papers belonging to Lieutenant Wright.

In an effort to enlarge his victory, Woodford hastily dispatched a contingent to Captain Lyne's earlier vantage point at the mouth of the creek in the hope of taking a further toll as the four tenders felt their way out. But on hearing that British troops were moving on Hampton from the rear, the party was halted and was brought back before reaching the point. By the time the patriots had assured themselves that the rumor was false, Squire's tenders were safely out and away.

The confrontation at Hampton was no Lexington in the South, but it was, to use Burk's words, "something worthy of the American character," and it might reasonably have been claimed to have inspired the enemy "with apprehension and respect." The victory was certainly a splendid boost for patriot morale, of that there can be no doubt. On the other hand, the loss of one small tender and Squire's retreat did not in themselves represent a military disaster for the British. The outcome was more embarrassing than damaging, though for Captain Squire himself, it may have been both. On November 3, Purdie's *Virginia Gazette* carried the following open letter:

The rifle-men and soldiers of Hampton desire their compliments to capt. Squire and his squadron, and wish to know

[1] *History of Virginia*, III, 433.

how they approve the reception they met with last friday. Should he incline to renew his visit, they will be glad to see him; otherwise, in point of complaisance, they will be under the necessity of returning the visit. If he cannot find the *ear* that was cut of, they hope he will wear a *wig* to hide the mark; for perhaps it may not be necessary that all should know *chance* had effected that which *the laws* ought to have done.

This seems to be the only reference to Squire having lost an ear in the engagement, and it is entirely possible that the story was circulated simply as a joke on which to hang the point that Squire *deserved* to have his ears cut off.

Whether or not Squire's lost ear was wishful thinking, there was not the smallest fiction in the reports that American riflemen had outshot British muskets and cannon. In the same issue of the *Gazette* it was noted that in the course of the Hampton affair a rifleman had killed from a distance of 400 yards, to which was added the editorial comment: "Take care, ministerial troops." The remarkable accuracy and range of the Virginians' rifles did not come as a surprise to Lord Dunmore, and he had been taking care for some time. In his letter to Richard Henry Lee of October 15, Edmund Pendleton noted that "Lord Dunmore, it is said, is much afraid of the riflemen, and has all his vessels caulked up on the sides, above men's height." [2] As a purely defensive measure this was certainly a wise precaution, but it was of small help if one wished to sail the ships or return the fire—as the Hampton fiasco had eloquently demonstrated.

If Dunmore feared the precision of rebel rifles, the patriots were concerned to some small degree over the rumors that the British were using split bullets, which spread after leaving the barrel, tearing large and jagged holes in their targets. Previously the English papers had accused the Americans of loading "their rifle-barrel guns with a ball slit almost in four quarters, which when fired out of those guns breaks into four

[2] *American Archives*, 4th ser., III, 1067.

pieces, and generally does great execution." [3] More than a century later a Captain Clay on the staff of the ammunition factory at Dum-dum in India would make his contribution to history by "inventing" much the same thing.

The question of who was or was not using split bullets was of small concern to Lord Dunmore; much more important was the problem of limiting the rebels' ability to propel any sort of ball, round or split. Only by cutting off the patriots' supplies of gunpowder could he hope to even the odds. The raids on Kemp's Landing and other suspected arsenals had yielded plenty of weapons but very little powder. It was apparent that Captain Squire's blockade was not entirely effective, but just how much was getting through was, and still is, undetermined. Earlier in the month Dunmore had seized a letter being carried by four Negroes in a small boat out of Portsmouth—a letter that revealed that John Goodrich of Norfolk was expecting two smuggling sloops to unload their cargoes at some point on the seacoast of Princess Anne County. John Goodrich, Jr., and Robert Shedden, the writer of the letter, were seized and taken on board the *Otter*. According to James Parker: "Shedden immediately confessed to his Ldshp. that he knew his brothers in Law were concerned in a Smuggling adventure of dry goods, that he had as was natural advised them, & wrote that letter, how to escape but that he was unconcerned, & entirely ignorant of any Ammunition being on board." [4] Nevertheless, the fact remained that there *had* been ammunition on board and, according to an unidentified patriot in Alexandria, Goodrich had brought in "one hundred and fifty barrels of gunpowder, and land[ed] the same safely, without asking his Lordship's consent," [5] thus earning his eldest son a set of irons and accommodation in the hold of one of the governor's ships.

The patriots of neighboring North Carolina had also come into a small but satisfying legacy of ammunition—by courtesy of

[3] *Virginia Gazette* (Purdie), Oct. 20.
[4] Parker to Steuart, Oct. 29; CSP.
[5] *American Archives*, 4th ser., III, 1193.

Governor Martin. The *Virginia Gazette* [6] of October 21 delightedly reported "the discovery of the grand repository and dark
depositum of Governor Martin's infernal magazine, which, with
cool deliberation, he intended to deal out in missive weapons of
death to the good people of this province." It went on to explain
that

> In the palace garden, and under a fine bed of cabbages, was
> discovered and dug up, a barrel containing about three
> bushels of gunpowder; in the palace cellar was also dug up
> two quarter casks of the same commodity, the casks quite
> new, and marked R. B. In the palace garden was also dug up
> about 1000 weight of musket balls, lately cast, about 500
> weight of iron swivel balls, a large quantity of small shot,
> lead, iron worms for the cannon, with swabbs, rammers,
> artillery boxes, matches, and the whole apparatus for his park
> of artillery.

The report concluded by saying that the cannon had been spiked
when Martin fled from the palace and that the culprit would
eventually be caught and brought to account, as also would the
villain who had supplied the governor with the ammunition in
the first place.

Governor Martin had at least tried hard to prevent his arms
from falling into the hands of the rebels, but Governor Campbell of South Carolina seemed to have done very little. General
James Grant received a letter from a correspondent in St.
Augustine telling him that "The guns at Fort Johnston were
thrown over the parapet by the *Tamar's* people, but what could
possess them not to destroy the carriages and knock off a
trunnion I cannot conceive; they might at least have thought of
spiking them, but Thornborough [commanding the *Tamar*] is
old, and unfit for service. It is very well to send such men in
time of peace to a hot country, for the chance of a vacancy; but
in time of rebellion, surely active officers should be employed." [7]

[6] Dixon & Hunter.

[7] Frederick George Mulcaster to General Grant, Oct. 3; *American
Archives*, 4th ser., IV, 330.

Governor Campbell, incidentally, was still in residence aboard the leaking *Tamar* at the end of October, regardless of the fact that Admiral Graves had written to him in August agreeing with Captain Thornborough that the ship could not remain "any longer in the Service without the greatest Risque." [8] To the list of ships honored by the presence of royal governors was next added the packet *Halifax*. Early in October Governor Tryon of New York heard it rumored that the congress in Philadelphia was advocating the seizure of his government and his person, and on the fourteenth he wrote to Mayor Whitehead Hicks of New York telling him that his duty would not permit him to remain any longer on shore unless he received positive assurances that he would be protected. These were not forthcoming, or at least were not sufficiently reassuring, and Tryon duly took to the water, where he announced he would "be ready to do such business of the Country as the situation of the times will permit." [9]

None of these floating plenipotentiaries were nearly as effective as Lord Dunmore in his efforts to keep his finger on the pulse, or his sword at the throat, of his colony. Dunmore might have lost a skirmish, but as far as Virginians were concerned he was a very real antagonist capable of appearing miraculously out of the night and descending like the demon Behemoth to ravage and destroy. On October 23 Nicholas Cresswell, who was now in Alexandria, heard it rumored that the governor was on his way up the Potomac with a force of four thousand men to attack the town. Added Cresswell: "I am determined to get on board the King's Ship as soon as possible." [1] The inhabitants of Alexandria busied themselves packing up their favorite belongings ready for flight, and some even left the town before it was learned that his Lordship was engaged elsewhere.

An assault on Norfolk by the troops assembling at Williamsburg had been under discussion before the successful test

[8] Graves to Campbell, Aug. 22; *Naval Documents of the American Revolution*, I, 1203.

[9] Tryon to Hicks, Oct. 19; *American Archives*, 4th ser. III, 1053.

[1] *Cresswell*, 127.

of arms at Hampton. Now, with that behind them, it seemed the moment to cross the James and prepare for the attack. Consequently at the end of the month there was a deal of activity around the ferries at Jamestown and at Burwell's Landing, a few miles further down river. None of it escaped the attention of Lord Dunmore, who sent a "small squadron" [2] up the James with instructions to fire at anything that moved. There was a chance that it would encounter an armed packet boat belonging to Colonel Hutchings of Norfolk, which Parker reported as being "filled up with 6 swivels & 20 Rifle men," [3] but it had either departed upstream or was hiding in one of the creeks. The ships did, however, manage to raise a modicum of opposition when they appeared off Jamestown Island, exchanging bangs with a party of riflemen, though to no purpose. According to Pinkney's *Gazette*, the riflemen were not found at Jamestown, but were sent there after word was received in Williamsburg that at least nine shots had been heard from the direction of the river. According to the patriots, about twenty-six shots were fired from the swivel guns of two tenders, none of them doing any damage, save for one ball, which struck the ferry house.[4] Dixon and Hunter put the score a little higher, allowing that "two or three small balls" [5] went through the building. But no matter which report we accept, the fact remains that Dunmore's gunners were clearly in need of the practice.

We do not know exactly what the commander's orders contained; it is possible that they were not specific, requiring him only to harass the enemy wherever it could be found. On the other hand, they may have included instructions to land and accomplish some very definite and hazardous task—so accounting for the rumored presence of a small party of shadowy and silent figures hurrying through James City County toward Williamsburg as the last dark minutes of October ticked away.

[2] *Virginia Gazette* (Purdie), Nov. 3.
[3] Parker to Steuart, Oct. 29; CSP.
[4] *Virginia Gazette* (Pinkney), Nov. 2.
[5] *Virginia Gazette* (Dixon & Hunter), Nov. 4.

[XI]

NOVEMBER

T*he stationing of Lord Dunsmore's ships* within ten miles of Williamsburg undoubtedly ensured that the guards at the magazine and other posted areas were more than normally vigilant—"jumpy" might have been a better word. Second only in importance to the magazine was the public treasury, a building that has not been positively identified but that may have stood adjacent to the house of Treasurer Nicholas to the southwest of the market square. Behind the house site a draw runs down to a broader bottom, leading, in turn, to College Creek and thence to the James river at Archer's Hope. Up such a draw "a little below the treasury office"[1] guards thought they saw four men moving. It was then between 1 and 2 A.M. on November 1, and just about time for the guard to be changed, but as no one was expected to approach from that direction, they duly challenged whoever it was they thought they saw, and getting no reply, blazed bravely away into the darkness. According to Pinkney's *Virginia Gazette*,[2] the rascals returned the fire and then withdrew. The report concluded by saying that: "We understand the villains have been industriously pursued, but without any effect," to which a reader added in ink "a silly story."

Just how silly the story was we cannot tell; but we do know that it bore small resemblance to Purdie's account of the same

[1] *Virginia Gazette* (Pinkney), Nov. 2.
[2] Ibid.

affair. Both were agreed, however, that it was a dark night, though Purdie adds that it was also a wet one, conditions that do not make for congenial or efficient guarding. Nevertheless a sentry at the treasury thought he spotted something or somebody move, and, after challenging it or him, he fired one shot. There was no response; so the man hung his blanket over some palings as a decoy and took up a position to one side, waiting for an opportunity to fire at the flash of any assailant's gun. Nothing happened for half an hour, and then a single shot fired from behind the treasury splintered a paling commendably close to the blanket. The sentry discharged his musket as planned, but failed to score. However, the noise of the two shots roused the captain of the guard at the magazine (the single shot fired half an hour earlier presumably had not), who sallied forth with a small detachment "to endeavour to intercept the villains upon their retreat, and it is said saw three men, at whom he fired, without success, it being exceedingly dark." The next morning pursuit parties were sent out to scour the countryside, but they found no trace of the supposed raiders beyond a dubious report that "two or three men, in blue jackets, had been seen earlier that morning, near the creek, by some negroes." Nevertheless Purdie did not hesitate to play the story for all it was worth, and probably a good deal more.

"It has been suspected," he declared, "that capt. Montagu himself was the person, and that his design was to attempt to destroy the magazine or treasury; and that his madness and folly made him return the sentinal's fire. Whoever he was, he had a narrow escape." [3] Narrow or not, he had a good four hours' start over his pursuers and could have been back aboard his ship almost before they set out from Williamsburg. The entire business, be it by courtesy of Purdie or Pinkney, seems extraordinarily improbable, and the contemporary reader who dubbed it "a silly story" may well have known what we can only surmise—that it hatched from an egg conceived by the union of a dark night and a windy sentry.

[3] *Virginia Gazette* (Purdie), Nov. 3.

There is no evidence that Captain Montagu was aboard either of the tenders, and it is even more improbable that, had he been, he would have led so small and inept a sortie into the heart of the enemy camp. We do not know how long the two vessels remained off Jamestown, but it seems likely that they withdrew before the week was out. The number of smaller ships in Lord Dunmore's fleet at this time is uncertain, but it is apparent that if he was to maintain a grip on the Atlantic coast of the Eastern Shore region, the Chesapeake Bay, and the shipping lanes from the West Indies and the Southern colonies, every inch of sail had to be deployed to maximum advantage. Therefore, if the Jamestown venture was achieving nothing and there were no signs of the rebels preparing for an immediate crossing, the tenders might have been deemed to be better employed elsewhere.

Much more successful in its mission was the single tender cruising off Ocracoke on the Outer Banks of North Carolina. On November 1 it spotted a sloop from Martinique heading northward, and after giving chase, boarded her to find the crew frantically trying to dispose of the cargo. A quantity of coffee had already been thrown overboard and so, too, had 570 pounds of gunpowder. The rest of the cargo comprised casks of rum, which the captain had ordered breached; he was caught trying to pump it out of the bilge. The loss of the cargo was regrettable, but at least it did not get through to the rebels. The tender had better luck with the brig *Adonis* from Jamaica, which followed the same route on the same day. It was taken intact with its cargo of "2,000 bushels of salt; 46 casks of molasses; 37 casks of rum; 10 barrels of lime; 1 bag ginger; 65 pieces of Irish linen; 24 bolts of osnaburgs; 53 flannel waistcoats; 93 pairs of shoes; 12 cruppers; 36 girths; 69 round hats" [4]—but no gunpowder. The brig's destination is not recorded, but the presence of Irish linens suggest that it was a

[4] Montagu to Graves, from "Kingfisher off Jamestown, Virginia," Nov. 14; *American Archives*, 4th ser., IV, 343.

smuggler intent on defying the American ban on British imports.

Lord Dunmore had the matter of who was importing what very much on his mind as November began, the last day of the previous month having been devoted to his attempt to sort out the tortuous dealings and adventures of the Goodrich family, at least one of whom was confined aboard the *Otter*. His problem had been to decide which side they were on and how best to exploit the information his interrogation had extracted from them. The sequence began, as you may recall, with the landing of a large quantity of gunpowder, which slipped through Dunmore's fingers, and the subsequent interception of a letter from Robert Shedden to his father-in-law, John Goodrich—a letter hinting at the family's involvement in all kinds of nocturnal traffic. The smuggler, like the highwayman and the outlaw, has acquired a largely undeserved cloak of romance and heroism, and Shedden's letter fits splendidly into the mold. The head of the family, John Goodrich, Sr., who owned a plantation in Nansemond County, had been waiting on the seacoast for the return of the sloop *Fanny*, commanded by his son Bartlett, which was bringing an illicit cargo from the West Indies. Another son, William, had skippered the vessel that had brought the offending powder and had subsequently made his way to Williamsburg to report his arrival in North Carolina. In the letter, William is referred to as Billie, and the third brother, John, Jr., as Johnie. Other names were indicated by initials only, but the missing letters were added as footnotes when Lord Dunmore sent a copy to England; here they are inserted in brackets. The document bears no date other than "Sunday 8 O'clock," but it was in all probability October 15.

Sir

Johnie came up yesterday and Set off about 2 O'Clock this Morning for Nansemond—T H Boat [Thomas Harbart's boat] could not find the way in, and got safe up here—Johnie hired a Vessel, which would sail this day, Morris would be in

time to prevent any other Vessel Returning except the long
Splice with Salt from Turks Island which is much wanted—
Johnie has placed Several Boats for to look out—I have not
heard from Nansemond Since Billie went up, but no doubt
the business is done—J:° Webb set of to Secure the papers
&c. and to push the Sloop out. The F [The Fanny coming
from St. Eustatius] must now be at Sea 10 or 11 days—
Bartlett's Letters is not yet come to hand—The Sloop Sailed
this day fortnight and has a considerable Value in Course
Linens a Board which Billie seemed Resolute to have Secured, I begt him to get W. C. [Willis Cooper] to undertake
it and not be seen himself in S--[Suffolk] as it might be a
means of discovering what Course to Steare—Receive your
Shirt &c. by Jupiter who goes to conduct Greenock and
Luckie—I wish you may be so luckie as to get a Sight of the
F— to Secure her and the letters a Shore to dissapoint the
many Malicious Enemys you have, who have made themselves busie for your destruction—Every thing remains quite
here at present, take care of yourself which is the only
uneasiness we have now.—

I am
Sir
Your Most Obedt. Servt.
Robert Shedden [5]

Even after Lord Dunmore had filled in some of the missing
words a number of questions remain unanswered, and the
following interpretation may or may not be the right one. John,
Jr., hired a ship in Virginia to be sailed by Morris to the West
Indies to warn other Goodrich vessels not to return while Lord
Dunmore's tenders were patrolling off North Carolina. But
Morris would not be in time to prevent the vessel *Long Splice*
from leaving Turk Island with its cargo of salt, and if he fell in
with it enroute he should let it continue, the salt being much
needed for curing food supplies. John, Jr., had sent out several
small boats to look for the *Long Splice* and any other Goodrich
vessels already homeward bound, to warn them of the hazards

[5] Copy enclosed with Dunmore to Dartmouth, Dec. 6; PRO,CO
5/1353.

that lay ahead. Shedden had not heard from the Nansemond plantation since William went up to Williamsburg to finish his business with the patriots. Meanwhile, John Webb had been sent down to North Carolina to refloat William's ship after unloading the gunpowder. Bartlett Goodrich, the third brother, was bringing, or sending, the *Fanny* home with a cargo of dry goods from the Dutch Island of St. Eustatius. It is not clear whether this same cargo is referred to in the next section and why William should have had to go to the town of Suffolk on the Nansemond river to deal with it. John Goodrich's shirt is also something of an enigma; taken at face value it would seem that Shedden received the shirt from the slave Jupiter, who was on his way to collect two children(?) named Greenock and Luckie. But as we are dealing with a secret message passing between very devious people, it is possible that the sentence meant something entirely different.

The *Fanny* did eventually arrive but later fell foul, not of Lord Dunmore but of the patriots, who set up a committee to look into the Goodrich affairs and, having done so, promptly branded them enemies of the people. While William was in the West Indies looking for gunpowder for his patriot customers, he met a small English Guinea ship from Antigua from which he purchased 1,600 pounds of powder. He also bought £291 16s. 10d. worth of British textiles and other merchandise from the same vessel, which he passed to his brother Bartlett to be shipped home on their own account. It was for this reason that Robert Shedden found William so concerned over the safe landing of the *Fanny*'s cargo. The patriot committee found that the goods came originally from Liverpool and included "checks, cottons, ginghams, striped Holland, jeans, Scotch thread, printed linens, Irish linens, white lead, and linseed oil." [6] They had all been packed, or rather, hidden in rum casks and shipped to the Potomac addressed to John Goodrich and Company, and were then offered for sale by John Goodrich, Jr., who knew full

[6] Report to the Virginia convention in Williamsburg, Jan. 13, 1776; *American Archives*, 4th ser., IV, 122.

well that they were of British origin and subject to the embargo. The committee also reported that there "appeared to be several erasures in the invoice of the said Goods, intended to conceal the place from whence they were originally imported, particularly the words *Liverpool* and *Antigua*, which are yet legible—the latter having been altered and *St. Eustatia* inserted; the words *Scotch* and *Irish* erased, and the word *Dutch* inserted."

According to Lord Dunmore's official report on the very involved affair, he arrested Shedden and John Goodrich, Jr., immediately on reading the former's letter. From his interrogation of the two men, the governor claimed to have learned of the arrival of William and his powder; whereupon, Dunmore declared, "I took every Step in my power to intercept it, but my want of force prevented my effecting it." [7] However, it would appear that the powder was already in patriot hands before Dunmore learned of its existence. The governor could not find that Shedden was actually implicated in the powder business, and decided that he had written the letter only to "prevent as far as lay in his power the Ruin his friends had involved themselves in." Shedden was accordingly released, and a few days later he returned with a letter from John Goodrich, Sr., begging for an audience and declaring "his Sincere repentence of what was past and his earnest Desire of returning to his Duty." [8] This was quickly granted, and Goodrich duly presented himself and gave every indication of being a man who was prepared to go to any lengths to prove his loyalty to the Crown. He even offered to surrender his son, William, into Dunmore's hands by instructing him to be at a certain place where he could be readily apprehended. This Dunmore accepted, and William was shortly added to the bag.

A copy of William's sworn statement was sent to Lord Dartmouth, and from it we can piece together most of the gunpowder story. He had been introduced to Treasurer Robert Carter Nicholas by another Norfolk merchant, Thomas Newton,

[7] Dunmore to Secretary of State, Jan. 4, 1776; PRO,CO 5/1353.
[8] Ibid.

as a man who might undertake a difficult mission on behalf of the colony. It was, he was told, to obtain a large supply of powder to be purchased in any of the French, Dutch or other islands of the West Indies. The necessary money would be derived from bills of exchange to the value of £5,000 to be drawn on Messrs. Norton and Sons of London—the same company that was then being damned in Gloucester and elsewhere as inimical to the cause.

Goodrich demurred and asked whether the venture might not endanger his life, whereupon both Nicholas and Newton quickly reassured him. The very worst that could happen, they said, would be the confiscation of his ship, a minor consideration in view of the profit he would make from the handling of this business. It all sounded very attractive, and approximately a month later, on July 15, William hauled his anchor and set out. But the mission soon proved more difficult than he had been led to expect, for gunpowder was hard to come by, and instead of making one neat purchase he had to sail from island to island picking it up in small quantities wherever he could. He had also to transform his bills of exchange into ready cash to handle these small purchases and for the benefit of those who did not relish swapping good powder for doubtful paper. It all took considerable time, and even when he had explored every possible source, he found himself with only between four and five thousand pounds of powder and a large percentage of his money still unspent. Goodrich decided to return with what he had, and to leave the rest of the bills of exchange with Isaac Van Dam, a Dutch merchant of St. Eustatius, who had been responsible for collecting much of the existing cargo. The sum left over amounted to £3762 11s 0d in West Indian currency— enough to buy a very large quantity of gunpowder. Van Dam told Goodrich that, given time, he could produce the required amount and proposed sending £2,000 of the money in sterling to Bordeaux, where powder could be easily obtained and equally readily shipped to St. Eustatius.

Goodrich agreed and left the island on October 1, arriving

at "Ochrococh" in North Carolina on the ninth. This was presumably Ocracoke on the Outer Banks below Cape Hatteras, where Edward "Blackbeard" Teach had met his match fifty-seven years earlier. Now it served as a haven for blockade-runners, who could sneak into the inlet below the treacherous Diamond Shoals, which so successfully discouraged British tenders from venturing in-shore around the cape. Leaving his ship and traveling overland, Goodrich hurried to Williamsburg and reported to Nicholas, who "seemed very well Satisfied." On his way back "he met the greatest part, if not the whole of the Gun Powder in two Waggons, escorted by a Number of Armed Men who were conveying it up the Country." That, as far as William knew, was the end of the story—or, as his written statement put it: "And further this deponent sayeth not." [9]

There could really have been little doubt that William Goodrich had acted in a manner unbefitting a loyal subject of the Crown. Slightly more difficult to determine—though not much—was the degree of the involvement of papa Goodrich and the other sons, John, Jr., and Bartlett. The latter was not available for questioning and was either aboard the *Fanny* or more probably still in the West Indies handling that end of the family business. Dunmore was not blind, and having failed to capture the offending powder, his critical faculties must have been more sensitive than usual. It is almost certain, therefore, that he saw the Goodrich family for what it was, a pack of scoundrels who would sacrifice their honor, their King, or even a son, if there was profit in it. John Goodrich, Sr., admitted as much when he tried to excuse himself by saying "that he and his Son had no other motive for engaging in this business but the prospect of a good freight for their Vessel." [1] The governor must have been sorely tempted to make an example of them; but John, Sr., had made an attractive proposition which, to be

[9] Deposition of William Goodrich, Oct. 31, enclosed with Dunmore to Dartmouth, Dec. 6; PRO,CO 5/1353.
[1] Dunmore to Secretary of State, Jan. 4, 1776; ibid.

consummated, required the wholehearted cooperation of the family. He knew, and Dunmore knew, that that would not be nurtured by an introduction to the cat, by keelhauling, or suspending Goodriches from the yardarm.

The proposal was that he, John Goodrich, Sr., should go down to St. Eustatius and bring back the balance of the money still in the hands of Van Dam, either in bills or in powder, and turn it over to Lord Dunmore. As security for his good faith, John offered to leave his son William in his Lordship's hands. However, the governor decided that the offer was proof enough and so released William on November 1. He made no mention of the fate of John, Jr., but, according to the patriot committee which later examined the Goodrich activities, he was released into the custody of his father with instructions to report on board every tenth day.

Before he sailed, Lord Dunmore provided John, Sr., with a letter of authority declaring that he knew "the bearer John Goodrich to be well disposed to his Majesty's Service, and likewise connected with the persons who have lodged the money in the aforesaid Islands." [2] Dunmore also sent him a brief personal message saying: "I would wish you to bring Arms or Powder if equally convenient rather than the Money, wishing you a good Voyage and quick return." [3] On this amicable note his Lordship sat back to wait for his shipment of free gunpowder. But he was without doubt one of the unluckiest of men, for no matter how well he planned, something unforeseen invariably went wrong.

Goodrich had sailed only a very short distance (no further than Hatteras at most) when he fell in with one of the *Kingfisher*'s tenders. Its master, Mr. Jones, boarded the Goodrich vessel, and, as Lord Dunmore later reported, "he did, without paying the least regard to my Pass for which he says he

---

[2] Dunmore "To all Persons whom it may Concern," Oct. 31, enclosed in Dunmore to Dartmouth, Dec. 6; ibid.

[3] Ibid., n.d.

had his Captains orders, Seize Mr. Goodrich and his Vessel and
after detaining them many days, brought them in here." [4] We
may suppose that the governor was at pains to acquaint Mr.
Jones with the magnitude of his mistake. The unfortunate
master's excuses are not recorded, but it is entirely reasonable
that he was aware that the Goodrich family was habitually up to
no good, and so could not believe that this particular piece of
chicanery was being undertaken in the King's name.

Lord Dunmore was furious, not only because his pass had
been ignored but also because he feared that the delay would
have given the patriots time to learn of his plan and so to send
their own ship on the same mission. If such were the case, they
would already have enjoyed a considerable head start, so
Dunmore hastily provided William Goodrich with one of the
Otter's tenders and sent him off in hot pursuit. In fact, however,
the patriots had not dispatched their own ship, and it is not even
certain that they had discovered the plot. In theory, all should
still have been well; but it was not. On December 6, before he
reached the island, Van Dam wrote to William telling him that,
as promised, he had sent £2,000 to France but had as yet
received no word that the powder had been dispatched or even
that the money had arrived. He explained that if the powder
could not be forwarded, he had instructed that the money should
be sent to a friend in Holland, who would ship out its value in
dry goods, as there might be no other means of getting the
money safely back. If this should be necessary, Van Dam would
then refund the £2,000 in cash from his own funds. That was
the situation as it stood when William returned to St. Eustatius:
no word from France, and all the bills sold and committed to
that purchase, except two to the value of £400. Van Dam, of
course, was not going to refund the money until he knew that
the powder had not been forthcoming and had received his dry
goods from Holland. Goodrich realized that he might have to
wait for months to get the money back, by which time Van Dam
would undoubtedly have learned that he was not there to return

4 Dunmore to Secretary of State, Jan. 4, 1776; ibid.

it to the patriot treasury. There was nothing to be done except to take the remaining two bills and leave while the going was good —and that was what he did.

Colonial commerce had always functioned on this extraordinary mechanism, powered by promissory notes and held together with faith and hope—faith that the notes would be honoured, and hope that they and the cargoes would survive the journey. The gentlemen's agreement and the belief that a man's word was his bond were the very foundation stones of the colonies' economy. Lord Dunmore now found it necessary to venture into those same waters to seek funds to buy essential supplies, since the Crown had lost its income from Virginia taxes.

If anyone had forgotten that the King's money had ceased to flow, they were reminded of it by Receiver General Corbin's melancholy statement in the *Virginia Gazette*[5] that the two-shilling tax on every hogshead of tobacco would no longer be obtainable during "the Continuance of the present Troubles," and informing "such Officers and others, who have been usually paid out of that Fund, that the whole of the Revenue to the 25th of October last will be exhausted by the Payment of such Salaries, as are authorized by his Majesty's immediate Warrants."

The governor's concern over salaries was less than his fear that he would not be able to feed and equip his supporters, and it was with this in mind that he invited the wealthy Norfolk merchant Neil Jamieson to dinner. The loyalist Scot was doubtless canny enough to realize that it was unlikely to be a purely social visit, but it is improbable that he realized the size of the service that was required of him. Dunmore wanted Jamieson to accept a £5,000 draft, which the governor was certain would be honored by General Howe, who was reportedly the new British commander in chief. He had not yet consulted Howe, but he assured Jamieson that the cost of his military efforts in Virginia were just as much a part of the King's work

[5] Dixon & Hunter, Nov. 25.

as were the expenditures in the North, and therefore they could and should be charged to the same account. It was perfectly logical; but £5,000 was a lot of money, and Jamieson was far from excited by this opportunity to display his loyalty. The next day he wrote to his Glasgow associates saying: "Lord Dunmore has applied to me to negotiate some money matters. I am not fond of this business; but if he urges it, and gives the necessary security, I suppose I must comply." [6]

When November began, the patriots were still buoyant over their success at Hampton, and as men continued to assemble at Williamsburg from every corner of the colony, expectations of a speedy, exhilarating, and decisive action mounted daily. But on November 3 there arrived melancholy news from Philadelphia that was instantly sobering; the foremost statesman of Virginia, Peyton Randolph, was dead. He had been attorney general, speaker of the House of Burgesses, grand master of the Williamsburg Lodge, chairman of the Virginia Convention, and finally president of the General Congress. It was he who, on returning from Philadelphia at the end of May, had been cheered into Williamsburg and hailed as the father of his country—and so he might have been, had he lived beyond his fifty-fourth year.

Of the Virginia leaders Randolph was undoubtedly the most respected; Jefferson was young and relatively inexperienced, Henry erratic and too radical for most, and Washington was no politician, while the others were little known beyond the walls of the Williamsburg Capitol. Peyton Randolph was a man of whom it could truly be said that his "distinguished virtues, in every station of life, gained him the affection and confidence of his country." [7] There could be no question that his support of the patriot cause was motivated by anything but the most noble and selfless of considerations. His counsel would be most sorely missed.

[6] Neil Jamieson to Glassford, Gordon and Co., Nov. 17; *American Archives*, 4th ser., IV, 344.

[7] *Virginia Gazette* (Purdie), Nov. 10.

Randolph had died of an apoplectic stroke on Sunday, October 22; the funeral was held at Christ Church in Philadelphia on the following Tuesday afternoon, and the coffin escorted to the burial ground with the dignity and honor befitting the man and his office. Purdie's *Virginia Gazette*,[8] its entire issue black-edged, printed a Philadelphia report of the processional order: "The three battalions, artillery companies, and rifle-men of this city. The clergy. The body, with the pall supported by six magistrates. Hon. John Hancock, Esq. The members of the Congress. Physicians. The members of the Assembly Committee of Safety. Mayor the [sic] and corporation. Committee of city and liberties. Vestry of Christ and St. Peter's churches. Citizens." The *Gazette*'s first report suggested that the body had been permanently buried in Philadelphia, but it was later made clear that it was only temporarily interred in an existing vault until such time as it could be brought home to Virginia. This was eventually done, and the coffin still lies today in a vault beneath the chapel of the College of William and Mary in Williamsburg.

On Sunday, November 5 (the traditional day for letting fly at King and parliament), a hundred minutemen from Chesterfield County arrived to swell the ranks of the patriot army assembling at Williamsburg, as also did seventy more riflemen. Additional companies came in on succeeding days, all, as historian Burk colorfully put it, "fired with patriotic and holy enthusiasm" and courting "the toils and dangers of the tented field." [9] By midweek there were enough to make it worth moving part of the army across the James; and once again, hearing that something was afoot, Dunmore sent his flotilla up the river. This time it was a more formidable array, comprising three large tenders (a schooner and two sloops) as well as the man-of-war *Kingfisher*, all under the command of Captain Montagu. Unfortunately they were a little late. A letter written aboard the *Kingfisher* confessed with considerable exaggeration

[8] Ibid.
[9] *History of Virginia*, IV, 65.

that: "The day before our arrival in the river, about a thousand rebels, from Williamsburg, got over opposite to Jamestown, where they are now encamped, in order to march down to Norfolk, to attack our few troops there, and to punish the Norfolk people for declaring for Government." [1]

Montagu arrived off Burwell's Ferry on November 9, a point six miles below Jamestown, in spyglass range of the island but not of the settlement itself. It was far too far away for the British ships to prevent any crossing between Jamestown and the newly established camp on the Surry shore at Cobham Landing. Just why Montagu decided to halt at Burwell's Ferry when the enemy troops were at Jamestown is hard to explain, but it is possible that he was attracted by the presence at Burwell's of a small Virginia boat, which he thought he could annex without much opposition. Montagu duly hailed the vessel in what Burk called "a haughty and peremptory tone," [2] ordering it to come alongside the *Kingfisher*. While the skipper was debating whether or not to comply, he was shouted at from the shore by a party of Virginia riflemen, who told him to stay where he was. At this point the American vessel was said to have been some 300 yards from the landing and about a mile from the *Kingfisher*, making voice communication with either a little hard on the larynx.

When the patriot boat failed to move, Montagu lowered a barge and sent it off with a boarding party, which was promptly fired on by the riflemen—who later claimed to have killed three, having seen them fall down. It would seem that some key factor is missing from the various accounts, for if the American boat remained where it was, 300 yards from shore, the boarding party would almost certainly have made its approach from the lee side and should have been protected from the marksmen on the bank. Besides, the very same issue of the *Virginia Gazette* [3]

[1] W. Griffin to George Gifferina (sec. to Admiral Graves), Nov. 14; *American Archives*, 4th ser., IV, 343.

[2] Burk, *History of Virginia*, IV, 65.

[3] Purdie, Nov. 17.

that gives the fullest account of the affair lauds the prowess of patriot riflemen, saying that "they can hit a man if within 250 yards, and his head if within 150." Yet here (as at Hampton), at considerably more than 300 yards, they were able to kill three. In all fairness, however, it must be admitted that the *Gazette* said only that the British *lost* three men; it was historian Burk who stated that they were killed. But no matter how, or if, this was true, there was no doubt that the rifle fire from the shore caused the barge to turn about and row back to its parent ship.

The *Kingfisher* and its companions, in line of battle, now drew abreast of the landing and proceeded to give it the benefit of their broadsides. One six-pound ball went through both sides of a storehouse by the water's edge, while another crashed into the more substantial ferry house, fortunately missing the members of a large family which was sheltering there. Other balls thudded into the clay banks below the positions held by the riflemen, but none was hurt. As only two hits were reported by any source we can assume that a great many shots fell short or went badly wide. Having, as they supposed, softened up the enemy with their cannon fire, the British again sent their barge off, only to have it meet with the same smart reception, and once again its repulsion was followed by cannonading from the four ships.

Captain Montagu had achieved nothing by his digression at Burwell's Ferry, beyond perhaps giving the patriots further encouragement and the troops near Jamestown plenty of time to withdraw to a safe distance. There is some disagreement regarding the dates of the various phases of the Montagu expedition; Purdie's *Gazette* [4] puts the ferry incident at "last Thursday," which was November 9; Burk attributes it to November 10 and adds that the next night the flotilla moved on up to Jamestown Island; Purdie reports the moving as having occurred on the night of November 13/14. But no matter which were the correct dates, Purdie was certainly right in boasting that "by the bravery of a mere handful of men, the ferry-boats

[4] Ibid.

have been preserved from destruction; and the boat in dispute still remains where it was, and where our people ordered it should stay." He went on to say that the ferry's defenders claimed that they needed no reinforcements, and, providing Montagu did not land at too many points on their flanks at once, they were quite capable of repelling any attempted assault. The next night was to show that their ten or twenty men was vastly more than was needed to do the job.

The troops camped on or near Jamestown Island awaiting their turn to cross the river were commanded by Captain Green, who mounted pairs of sentries along the beaches to keep watch on the King's ships (now augmented by an additional tender) strung out abreast of the island. In the course of Tuesday night a boatload of men slipped away from the darkened ships and pulled toward the shore at a point about half a mile downstream from Green and his camp. The boat reached within fifty yards of the beach before it was challenged, and when it failed to respond two sentries opened fire. While one ran off to get help, the other calmly reloaded his musket and shot again; the boat still kept coming and was within twenty yards when the lone sentry fired a third shot, "upon which he heard a terrible shrieking on board," [5] and the boat turned about and headed back into the darkness. By the time Captain Green arrived, it was all over; one sentry had been enough to rout "a boat crowded with men." It has not been determined exactly what Montagu's men (if, indeed, they were Montagu's men) had in mind; but we can only suppose that they were trying to land scouts to discover the size of the forces that were waiting to cross into Surry.

It is not certain which troops, or how many, were encamped on Jamestown Island that night, but they were probably part of the five companies of minutemen who, along with the second regiment of regulars, made up the bulk of the army with which Colonel William Woodford was to threaten Norfolk. They would make the attempt while their commander in chief,

[5] Ibid.

Patrick Henry, remained behind in Williamsburg, unable to instruct them or even, as it turned out, to receive direct reports of their progress. To see how this extraordinary state of affairs came about, it is necessary to go back to August and the meetings of the Richmond convention, at which the patriots' political and military structure was established.

There were originally to be three regiments, each to be commanded by an officer appointed by the convention, the colonel of the first regiment to be commander in chief of them all. No one was more anxious to obtain this job than Patrick Henry, who, after his march to Doncastle's Ordinary during the affair of the powder, considered himself to be as inspired in the field as he was in the debating chamber. There was no denying that he had vast public support, but it was not necessarily negotiable into delegates' votes. Four names were put forward as possible commanders of the first regiment: Henry's, and those of Thomas Nelson, William Woodford, and Hugh Mercer. The last was far and away the most experienced, and all the delegates knew it. Mercer was a Scot who had fought in the Jacobite Rebellion of 1745 and had been with Braddock in the French and Indian War. Both Nelson and Woodford announced that they would feel privileged to serve under him and so declared for Mercer on the first ballot, and he won by the breadth of a digit, capturing forty-one votes against Henry's forty, Nelson getting eight and Woodford one. But at the second ballot Henry won, in part because of his popular backing, but perhaps as much because Mercer was a "Scotchman" and, unlike the other candidates, did not have a seat in the convention. With Henry as commander in chief and colonel of the first regiment, Nelson was chosen to lead the second, and Woodford the third. However, when Nelson was elected to be a Virginia delegate to the congress, he declined to accept the military command, and Woodford was named in his stead, the latter's third regiment being abandoned before it was raised.

Ten days after the election of officers for the Virginia regiments, the Richmond convention appointed a Committee of

Safety to administer the affairs of the colony on a day-to-day basis, from the end of this to the assembling of the next convention. It was an eleven-man committee comprising the best of the Virginia leaders still without roles on the national stage, among them John Page, Richard Bland, George Mason, Thomas Ludwell Lee, Carter Braxton, and, as chairman, the respected Edmund Pendleton. The mandate of the committee was virtually all-embracing; giving it power to appoint officers, raise money for munitions, call militia and minute units into service, and order the movement of any Virginia forces throughout and even beyond the boundaries of the colony. Furthermore, the committee was free to meet when and where it liked; and in October and November it chose to do so in Williamsburg, making the town the command center for the entire campaign against Lord Dunmore.

It so happened that Edmund Pendleton was a firm friend of William Woodford and an avowed admirer of the latter's own Caroline Independent Company. He had even presented it with a "STAND of COLOURS, a DRUM, and two FIFES," [6] a complete ceremonial kit. At the same time Pendleton's opinion of Henry's military potential was low, and he even went so far as to say so in a letter to Woodford. He was not alone in that view, and the writings of both Washington and Jefferson support it. Consequently when the Committee of Safety was ready to launch its offensive, Pendleton and his friends balked at handing the command to Henry. Now Patrick Henry's commission, given him by the convention, made him colonel of the first regiment and commander in chief of "all such other forces as may, by order of the convention, or committee of safety, be directed to act in conjunction with them. . . ." [7] But supposing the second regiment and other militia and minute forces were not ordered to act in conjunction with Henry's own regiment? Suppose, instead, the Committee of Safety gave them orders of their own,

[6] *Virginia Gazette* (Purdie), Oct. 13.

[7] Mays, *Pendleton*, II, 62; quoting W. W. Henry, *Patrick Henry*, I, 338.

omitting the first regiment altogether: what then? Surely Patrick Henry could not be construed as their field commander? Such was the rationale that enabled Pendleton to bypass Henry and give the command to Woodford.

Woodford's orders from the committee told him: "With your regiment, and the 5 companies of minute-men, from the Culpeper battalion, you are to march towards Norfolk; and when you have informed yourself of all necessary circumstances, by enquiry of Colonel Hutchings and other gentlemen in whom you can place confidence, you will fix an encampment, having regard among other things, to the convenience of winter-quarters, which the approaching season makes necessary. . . ." The instructions were not to engage the British in a decisive battle, but to move closer to them and to put the fear of God into the inhabitants of the lower counties to discourage them from joining the loyalists. "You are to use your best endeavours," Woodford was told, "for protecting and defending the persons and properties of all friends to the cause of America, and to this end, to attack, kill, or captivate all such as you shall discover to be in arms for the annoying of those persons, as far as you shall judge it prudent to engage them." He was to prevent all traffic in and out of Norfolk and Portsmouth, to detain anyone who looked in the least "inimical," and to seize any and all traveling slaves. The committee noted that there might still be people in and around the towns who were intimidated by the presence of the King's navy and so had not declared their real sentiments. "We think, therefore, that all those who will continue peaceable, giving no assistance or intelligence to our enemies, nor attempting to annoy your troops, or injure our friends, may for the present remain unmolested; those Tories and others who take an active part against us, must be considered as enemies; your own humanity and discretion will, however, prevent the wanton damage or destruction of any person's property whatsoever." [8]

The orders concluded by telling Woodford that he was to

[8] Burk, *History of Virginia*, IV, Appendix 3.

use his own good judgment and discretion, "to be attentive to the force and motions of the enemy, and act offensively or defensively, as your prudence may direct for the good of the common cause we are engaged in, giving intelligence by express, from time to time, to the Committee of Safety and the Commanding Officer here, of such things as you shall appear necessary to be communicated." Here, in this last sentence, lay the key to Woodford's authority; he was free to map his own strategy, to use his forces as he thought fit, and simply to report the results of his actions to the Committee and to the commander in chief—again, only as fully or as frequently as he thought necessary. It was hardly surprising that Patrick Henry took a very dim view of the seven members of the committee who signed the orders.

While Woodford's troops were assembling and drilling in and around Williamsburg and while Montagu was being abortive in the James, Lord Dunmore kept himself busy counting his troops and trying to devise methods of raising more. In a later letter to the Secretary of State he noted that the total detachment of the Fourteenth Regiment that he had received amounted to 134 privates, "Sixty of which Arrived here the 31st of July the remainder the 7th of November." [9] The latter 74 were presumably "all the Grenadiers, and as many men from the battalion as made up a detachment of sixty, including non-commissions" [1] whom Captain Fordyce brought from St. Augustine on October 7 and who, according to Fordyce, reached Norfolk on the twentieth of the same month. That they did so is supported by the Fourteenth Regiment's commanding officer in Virginia, Captain Leslie, who listed 134 privates in his monthy return for November 1. It would seem, therefore, that Lord Dunmore (as well as those writers who have believed him) was mistaken in stating that he was reinforced in November.

[9] Jan. 4, 1776; PRO,CO 5/1353.
[1] Fordyce to Captain Urquhart, Dec. 1; *American Archives*, 4th ser., IV, 350.

Although Dunmore did not actually receive more men, he did have prospects. Major John Connolly had returned from his meeting with General Gage, having obtained approval of the governor's plan to raise a regiment from among the loyalists of the "back woods" and another from the friendly Indians of the frontier. Connolly was appointed Lieutenant Colonel of the Queen's Royal Rangers and was to proceed to Detroit. General Gage had also authorized Dunmore "to send for another small Detachment from the Illinois," [2] and this also was to be part of Connolly's force, which when assembled would move down to seize Alexandria and there await the arrival of his Lordship. It was a plan just as exciting and full of promise as it had been in August, when they first thought it up, and when Dunmore saw Connolly off on his mission early in November they both considered it the stroke that would sever America and save the parts for Britain. Whether it would actually have done so is an academic point, for the scheme came to grief only ten days after it was launched. No sooner had he crossed the Virginia–Maryland border than Connolly was recognized, and on November 23 he was hauled before the Frederick-Town Committee of Safety. This body quickly realized that it had caught a very large fish and so sent him on under heavy guard to Philadelphia to be interrogated by the congress.

Fortunately for Lord Dunmore's immediate peace of mind, news of this catastrophe did not reach him for some weeks. In the meantime he could derive considerable encouragement from small successes. The remaining inhabitants of Norfolk and its environs were seeming a little more staunch in their loyalty, and he may even have heard the same rumor that Nicholas Cresswell picked up, to the effect that "300 people on the Eastern shore in Maryland had gone over to Lord Dunmore." [3] Of much more consequence, however, was an actual test of strength on land, between the King's soldiers and the rebels, and fought as toe to toe as the latter would permit. The result was a genuine and

[2] Dunmore to Secretary of State, Jan. 4, 1776; PRO,CO 5/1353.
[3] *Cresswell*, 128; Nov. 1.

unmistakable British victory, which did much to remove the
rank flavor of Hampton from the governor's palate.

On November 14 Dunmore discovered that 120 or more
rebels from North Carolina had crossed the border and were
encamped at Great Bridge on the Elizabeth river, about twelve
miles south of Norfolk. They were there, so Dunmore was
informed, to be of service to the Virginia patriots. "This,"
declared the governor, "I was determined not to suffer, I
accordingly embarked in the Night in boats, with all of the 14th
Regiment that was able to do Duty, to the amount of 109 Rank
and file, with 22 Volunteers from Norfolk," [4] There is no
knowing whether the North Carolinians got wind of Dunmore's
intended assault before it was launched or whether they simply
decided that they were too far out in front for comfort, but the
fact remains that when his Lordship reached Great Bridge he
found that "the Carolina people had fled the Evening before. . . ." [5] However his effort was not entirely wasted, for
while at the Bridge Dunmore learned that "there were between
three and four hundred of our Rebels" [6] assembled at the village
of Kemp's Landing (now Kempsville), the same place he had
previously raided in search of patriot arms, which lay some ten
miles to the northeast. After ordering Lieutenant Batut to erect
a rudimentary defensework at the north end of the causeway
leading from Great Bridge, Dunmore and his military commander, Captain Leslie, moved out at the head of the British
force in search of the rebel militia.

About a mile outside Kemp's Landing a straggly volley of
musketry bloomed like cotton from the thick woods on the left
side of the road. It was aimed at the British advance guard and
did no damage, but it did serve to alert the main body of the
troops, who were following at a safe distance. The British had
been ordered to hold their fire until attacked "and even then to

[4] Dunmore to Dartmouth, from aboard the ship *Dunmore* off Norfolk,
Dec. 6; PRO,CO 5/1353.
[5] Ibid.
[6] Ibid.

march close up to their enemies with fixed bayonets, before they should discharge their muskets." [7] The patriots hidden in the bushes fired again, without any better effect; meanwhile the body of Dunmore's troops broke column and rushed into the woods in an effort to outflank them. This was not at all the way the militia had expected the game to be played, and they promptly ran for their lives. Leslie's men pursued them for about a mile, killing five, two of whom were drowned in attempting to cross a creek; several others were wounded, and seven were captured, including the fiery and loquacious Colonel Joseph Hutchings, who had scared so many in October by his threats to burn Norfolk. According to young Helen Maxwell, who happened to be staying at Kemp's Landing, the colonel was "full of Dutch courage" and was found lying flat on his back in a field, dead drunk. [8] None of the British reports mentioned this unseemly exhibition, but Leslie did note that he had been told that some of the enemy ran away even before the firing began. Mrs. Maxwell, who was no Tory, supported him, saying that "when they saw the British coming, with colors flying, arms shining, and drums beating, they all took to their heels and ran away as fast as their horses and legs could carry them, without staying to fire a single shot. I saw them myself," she said, "racing off at a fine rate through Kempsville and Mathews among them, whipping up his horse and crying out as loud as he could bawl take care of the powder, take care of the powder." [9]

Mrs. Maxwell was an elderly lady when she recorded her memories of the Revolution, and it is obvious that she was sometimes confused, not only as to the chronology of events but also as to their elements. Her reference to the fleeing Mathews and to his concern over the powder shows that she was confusing the November engagement with the pursuit of the ammunition in October, for it was then that Mathews was captured. As for Colonel Hutchings, James Parker, you will

[7] *Virginia Gazette* (Dunmore), Nov. 25.
[8] Maxwell, "My Mother," *LNCVA*, II, 132–3.
[9] Ibid., 132.

remember, had reported his being drunk on that occasion and his escape after being found in a ditch by the town butcher. All in all, Mrs. Maxwell's testimony must be treated with caution. However the commander of the November effort, Colonel Lawson, also fled; but he was captured the next day along with eight other militiamen. The British losses, as reported by Captain Leslie, amounted to one grenadier, wounded in the knee. Neil Jamieson wrote that the wounded man was a sailor, but Captain Leslie's report is obviously the more authoritative. However Jamieson's personal comment on Lord Dunmore's part in the affair is notable, if only because he is one of the few Virginians who have gone down in history as having had a good word to say for him. Wrote Jamieson: "His Excellency's humanity appeared in a conspicuous light, as he could easily have surrounded and cut off the most of these people; but he was satisfied with taking some prisoners." Later in the same letter he added: "His Lordship is a humane, good man, and will use as much lenity as in prudence may be necessary for the unfortunate." [1]

Captain Leslie's report to General Howe did not quite tally with Jamieson's portrait of a humane governor sportingly calling off the chase when a fair bag of prisoners had been taken. Instead he confessed that "Their very precipitate flight, and the closeness of the woods, prevented our giving a much better account of them." [2] The American view of the entire matter differed considerably from that of the British, the newspapers reporting that there were only about two hundred militiamen and that they were hideously outnumbered by Dunmore's troops. Purdie added that not only were the patriots in a minority, but they were also hemmed in by a fence, which presumably prevented them from maneuvering. Declared Purdie: "Our people fought a considerable time, and it is thought

[1] Jamieson to Glassford, Gordon and Co., Nov. 17; *American Archives*, 4th ser., IV, 334–5.

[2] Leslie to General Howe, Nov. 26; *American Archives*, 4th ser., III, 1717.

did great execution; but were at last overpowered and forced to retreat." [3]

Although the papers did their best to minimize the loss by making much of the very few patriot casualties, American leaders were fully aware that the Princess Anne militia had departed the field in unseemly haste, and they were both embarrassed and irate. Lord Dunmore, for his part, was jubilant and looked upon the skirmish as a demonstration of British superiority. It was just what he needed, and it prompted him to take the step that had been scratching at the door of his conscience for months. At Kemp's Landing he hoisted the royal standard (actually a "pair of Colours" as he had nothing better) and read a proclamation declaring martial law and calling on all good men to come to the aid of their King. But there was more to it than that, enough, in fact, to make Dunmore's name a dirty word in the South for years to come: "I do further declare all indentured servants, negroes, or others (appertaining to rebels) free, that are able and willing to bear arms, they joining his Majesty's troops as soon as may be, for the more speedily reducing this colony to a proper sense of their duty to his Majesty's crown and dignity." [4]

This, Lord Dunmore's so-called "Emancipation Proclamation," had probably been discussed with Governor Martin as long ago as the beginning of January. He had hinted at it when the Williamsburg patriots had been peevish over the powder in April, and he had mentioned it more than once in his letters to Lord Dartmouth, who, in turn, had written approving the use of Indians and Negroes in the loyalist defense of the colony. Dunmore knew full well that this move was the one most feared by the colonists. He had hatched a nest of potential vipers in the home of every slaveowner in Virginia, and, regardless of whether or not the slaves accepted their freedom, few Virginians could be expected ever to forgive him. The proclamation had been written aboard the *William* on November 7 and had

[3] *Virginia Gazette* (Purdie), Nov. 17.
[4] Burk, *History of Virginia*, IV, 68.

been printed there using the equipment recently seized from Mr. Holt. It was a good workmanlike job, well set out, though with no fancy blocks or ornament, and the governor must have been well pleased with it. That he retained it unissued for ten days can be explained not by last-minute doubts but by the necessity to find an opportunity to successfully show the flag on land. The rout at Kemp's Landing was precisely that.

Patriot reaction was immediate and vociferous, and his Lordship was called everything from "King of the blacks" [5] to simple obscenities. But the principal and presumably official response appeared in all three *Virginia Gazettes*,[6] though no one cared to acknowledge authorship. The proclamation had opened by repeating Lord Dunmore's often-voiced hope that an accommodation might have been effected between Britain and her Virginia colony. The patriot reply was aimed, it said, at "two sorts of people," those colonists who might be drawn to the royal standard because they feared to be dubbed rebels, and those to whom Dunmore offered the bait of freedom. It began by reviewing the events of the year: the affair of the powder, Dunmore's setting of traps at the magazine, his flight, and his subsequent attacks on the property of law-abiding colonists, all refuting his contention that he desired a settlement. The writer declared that Virginians had been forced to take up arms in the defense of right and honor and that they did so, not against a lawful authority but to oppose "usurped and arbitrary power." He argued that "To preserve the rights they have reserved is the duty of every member of society, and to deprive a people of these is *treason*, is rebellion against the *state*." Therefore the patriots were "the dutiful members of society," and Lord Dunmore the rebel. It was an argument that sounded pretty convincing if said loudly and often enough, and not looked at too closely. But the pitch to the second sort of people contained such extraordinary reasoning that it must have caused liberal friends in England to spill their port. So clearly does it display the slaveowner's

[5] *Virginia Gazette* (Pinkney), Nov. 16.
[6] Purdie, Nov. 24; Pinkney, Nov. 23; Dixon & Hunter, Nov. 25.

approach to the Negro that it must be allowed to speak for itself
—even if does so at some length:

> They have been flattered with their freedom, if they be able to
> bear arms, and will speedily join Lord Dunmore's troops. To
> none, then, is freedom promised but to such as are able to do
> Lord Dunmore service. The aged, the infirm, the women and
> children, are still to remain the property of their masters, of
> masters who will be provoked to severity, should part of their
> slaves desert them. Lord Dunmore's declaration, therefore, is
> a cruel declaration to the negroes. He does not pretend to
> make it out of any tenderness to them, but solely upon his
> own account; and should it meet with success, it leaves by far
> the greater number at the mercy of an enraged and injured
> people. But should there be any amongst the negroes weak
> enough to believe that Lord Dunmore intends to do them a
> kindness, and wicked enough to provoke the fury of the
> Americans against their defenceless fathers and mothers,
> their wives, their women, and children, let them only consider
> the difficulty of effecting their escape, and what they must
> expect to suffer at the hands of the Americans.

Having thus described how the seekers after American
freedom could be expected to revenge themselves on blameless
Negro women and children, the writer went on to explain that it
was the British who favored a continuance of the slave trade and
the Virginians who opposed it. "Can it then be supposed," he
asked, "that the negroes will be better used by the English, who
have always encouraged and upheld this slavery, than by their
present masters, who pity their condition, who wish, in general,
to make it as easy and comfortable as possible, and who would,
were it in their power, or were they permitted, not only prevent
any more negroes from losing their freedom, but restore it to
such as have already unhappily lost it?" As a final argument, the
anonymous writer went on to insist that when the British had
been served by the slaves and they were no longer needed, the
Negroes could expect to be turned back to their owners or
shipped to the West Indies, "where every year they sell many
thousands of their miserable brethren, to perish, either by the

inclemency of weather, or the cruelty of barbarous masters."
Having thus threatened, cajoled, and dissembled, the literary
peroration ended with a smart crack of the whip: "Whether you
will profit by my advice I cannot tell, but this I know, that
whether we suffer or not, if *you* desert us *you* most certainly
will."

It is doubtful whether very many Negroes were able to read
the *Virginia Gazette*, but it is likely that thoughtful masters
may have read it to them. Nevertheless there were some who
could do so for themselves, among them Robert Brent's house
servant Charles, who was described as "a very shrewd sensible
fellow, who can both read and write." The notice offering a
reward for his capture appeared in the same issue of Pinkney's
Gazette [7] that contained the previously quoted argument on why
Negroes should remain slaves. Mr. Brent admitted that "From
many circumstances, there is reason to believe he intends to get
to Lord Dunmore," and he added somewhat plaintively: "His
elopement was from no cause of complaint, or dread of a
whipping (for he has always been remarkably indulged,
indeed too much so) but from a determined resolution to get
liberty. . . ." It was not prompted, however, by Lord Dunmore's proclamation, for the notice of Charles's "elopement"
was dated November 3, four days before he wrote it.

Having erected the King's standard at Kemp's Landing,
Dunmore set up his headquarters in the home of Mrs. George
Logan, one of the principal inhabitants. Earlier in the year her
late husband's dry goods store had been acquired by the newly
established township as a courthouse, while his wet goods store
had been transformed into its prison. The widow Logan was
therefore, in the truest sense of the word, one of the first citizens
of Kemp's Landing—and it would appear that she was not
particularly averse to the presence of Lord Dunmore in her
home. As night drew on, candles began to light the windows of
the town, and, according to Helen Maxwell, the Logan house

[7] Nov. 23.

"appeared almost illuminated." [8] She went there, she explained, only in the hope of complaining to Lord Dunmore of the treatment she had received at the hands of one of his heroes.

Earlier in the day Mrs. Maxwell and her sister had left Kemp's Landing, for with the place full of soldiers and their raggle-taggle adherents, they feared for their safety. The two women had hardly arrived at the home of Charles Sayer, a short distance from town, "when an ugly looking negro man, dressed up in a full suit of British regimentals, and armed with a gun, came in upon [them], and asked with a saucy tone—Have you got any dirty shirts here? (this is the name by which our soldiers were known) I want your dirty shirts." [9] The Negro pushed past the frightened women and proceeded to search the house. When he found nothing he went off, warning that he intended to return. The sisters were so unnerved by this incident that they decided they would be safer in town than in the country, and so back they went to Kemp's Landing.

Lord Dunmore listened to Mrs. Maxwell's complaint and then told her: "Why, madam, this is a provoking piece of insolence indeed, but there is no keeping these black rascals within bounds. It was but the other day that one of them undertook to personate Capt. Squire, and actually extorted a sum of money from a lady in his name. But we must expect such things whilst this horrid rebellion lasts." [1] The governor then asked after her husband and told her that he expected him to rally to the standard. Mrs. Maxwell did not spoil the meeting by telling Dunmore that she was sure that her husband had no intention of doing any such thing. To her astonishment, the governor was in such good humor that he even offered to escort her to her lodgings, and although she tried to talk him out of it, pointing out that he might be shot at by rebels from the darkness, Dunmore insisted, claiming that his sentries were all

[8] Maxwell, "My Mother," *LNCVA*, II, 134.
[9] Ibid.
[1] Ibid., 134–5.

around and there was no possible danger. Mrs. Maxwell
recalled that "the truth is, I was only afraid that they might
miss their mark and shoot me." [2]

Mr. Maxwell had been in hiding all day, and late that night
he came to his wife and assured her that he would not join the
loyalists. In the small hours a pair of Captain Leslie's grenadiers
broke into the room, obviously unaware that Mrs. Maxwell
already had company. Her husband leapt out of bed and loudly
ordered the men out, and after a brief scuffle in the darkness
they fled, leaving him with a bayonet rip in his shirt and a
slightly grazed chest. Early next morning Maxwell slipped
away and was not seen for several days. Meanwhile Lord
Dunmore moved out and returned to Norfolk on the afternoon of
November 16, planning to repeat the standard-raising ceremo-
nies there on the following day. The format at Kemp's Landing
had called for the reading of the Proclamation, after which the
inhabitants were collectively required to declare under oath that
they renounced the "Committees, Conventions and Congresses," [3] which had violently usurped the powers of government and that they did, instead, bear true allegiance to his
sacred Majesty, George III. Furthermore (and it was quite a
furthermore) in discharge of their duty, they pledged themselves to defend the entries into the county to the last drop of
their blood. In a slightly ironic confirmation of this resolve all
good men were to be identified by a strip of red cloth sewn or
pinned to their chests.

When Mr. Maxwell finally reappeared his wife was astonished and mortified to see the strip of red on his breast. "Believe
me," she cried, "I would rather have seen you dead than to have
seen you with this red badge."

To which he replied, "Phast! do you think it has changed
my mind? Don't you see how Dunmore is carrying all before
him, and if I can save my property by this step, ought I not in

[2] Ibid., 135.

[3] Burk, *History of Virginia*, IV, Appendix 2.

common prudence to wear it, for your sake and the children?" [4]

There were plenty like Maxwell who sported the red cloth but who had no intention of fighting for King George—and some who had no idea of fighting for America either if they could get out of it. But the governor was not deceived by the large numbers who turned out to take the oath. The first issue of the new *Virginia Gazette* to emanate from his floating printing-office told how the mayor, aldermen, and citizens of Norfolk had flocked to the standard and how they had been quickly followed by the inhabitants of Portsmouth and the surrounding area, until there were "now upwards of 3000, men determined to defend this part of the country against the inroads of the enemies to our King and constitution." [5] Lord Dunmore enclosed a copy of this issue (which is now the only surviving copy) with his December 6 letter to the Secretary of State, in which he wrote: "Your Lordship may observe that about three thousand have taken that Oath, but of this number not above three or four hundred at most are in any degree capable of bearing Arms, and the greatest part of these hardly ever made use of the Gun, but I hope a Short time (if they are willing) will make them as good if not better than those who come down to oppose them." [6] Four hundred doubtful assets was a very different tally to the publicized three thousand ready and willing to shed the last drop. But the standard was up, and his Lordship's bridges were burned; it was imperative that it should generate popular support, even if that only amounted to three thousand paper soldiers. Wars had been won with less. "I am now endeavouring," wrote Dunmore, "to raise two Regiments, one of white People (Called the Queen's own Loyal Virginia Regiment) the other of Negroes Called Lord Dunmore's Ethiopan Regiment." The latter title did not pass unnoticed in the taprooms of Virginia; but public laughter could not entirely

[4] Maxwell, "My Mother," *LNCVA*, II, 136.
[5] *Virginia Gazette* (Dunmore), Nov. 25.
[6] Dunmore to Dartmouth, Dec. 6; PRO,CO 5/1353.

drown private fears. Negroes were disappearing, and if one
wanted proof of it a visit to the Williamsburg public jail would
reveal eleven who had been caught attempting to get away
together in boats. It was said that the prisoners were to be made
examples of in the hope of deterring others. But there was little
doubt that many had already reached Lord Dunmore's protection or that, regardless of examples, more would try to follow.

It is unlikely that the governor really expected to make
anything very reliable out of his Ethiopian Regiment, but he
knew that its terror value could be considerable. Mrs. Maxwell
had encountered her Ethiopian in full British uniform, but this
was probably before the regiment was formed. It is highly
unlikely that Dunmore thought it worth while, or was able, to
supply all his Negro recruits with such formal attire. We do
know, however, that they were to wear across their chests the
slogan LIBERTY TO SLAVES, possibly an intentional parody of
the shirtmen's "Liberty or death."

Hair-raising reports of Dunmore's Negroes being used to
raid and loot isolated farms and homesteads had been rife for
months, and some of them no doubt were true. On November
30, Pinkney published a rather curious variation whose very
oddity would suggest that at least part of it was factual. "One of
Dunmore's tenders," the *Gazette* reported, "lately went to a
place called Mulberry Island, in Warwick County, and landed
her men, who went to Mr. Benjamin Wells's house, with their
faces blacked like negroes, whose *dear* companions they are, and
robbed from thence all his household furniture, four negroes, a
watch, and stock buckle. The inhuman wretches even took the
bed on which several sick infants were reposing." The inference
is, of course, that the raiders came from one of Captain
Montagu's tenders then patrolling the James, for Mulberry
Island lies more or less midway between Jamestown and
Norfolk. But why would they carry off household furniture;
negroes and provisions one can readily understand, but beds and
tables are peculiar booty for men living aboard small ships.
However, the watch and the stock buckle are such small things,

though valuable, that their inclusion in the list of losses gives the story a ring of authenticity. But perhaps that was intentional. More extraordinary than the nature of the loot was the claim that the robbers had blacked their faces. Why? Was it to help them move unseen in the dark—a precaution hardly necessary on the thinly populated island. Was it a device to spread fear of the Negro—if so, why not use real Negroes, as had reportedly been done so many times before? Then again, was it done to conceal the identities of the men—a pointless piece of coyness, now that the active loyalists had been brought into the open. Besides it is unlikely that Wells would have known any of Montagu's men, and if he had, it would have made no difference. But recognition might have made a very considerable difference if the raiders had been seen to be neighbors who had nothing whatever to do with the British tenders. Perhaps this is no better an explanation that Pinkney's; nevertheless, one cannot help thinking that there was more to the affair than met the eye of Mr. Benjamin Wells.

Throughout the eventful days of mid-November Captain Montagu sat in the middle of the James, sending his tenders scurrying up and down trying to bar the patriots' progress. The companies who had crossed the river before the *Kingfisher's* arrival were encamped about five miles from Cobham, while their commander, Lieutenant Colonel Scott, waited for Woodford and the main body of his troops to catch up. It was Scott who spotted a flatboat loaded with oysters heading for the British ships and who sent out a couple of small boats to head it off. The tenders opened fire without success and Scott's men managed to drive the heavy flat past the ships and so close to the Jamestown shore that it came within range of Captain Green's riflemen. The latter then forced it to come in, whereupon he seized its cargo, and his men ate the oysters "and skimmed the shells in contempt at the Kingfisher and her tenders." [7]

Nothing had turned out well for Montagu; he had arrived too late to prevent Colonel Scott's men from crossing, he had

[7] *Virginia Gazette* (Purdie), *Supplement*, Nov. 24.

failed to seize the boat at Burwell's Ferry, had been driven from Jamestown Island by a single sentry, and could not even provide adequate cover for a provision boat to reach him. In addition he had suffered the mortifying experience of watching one of the tenders being fired on by Captain Green at a range of a full 400 yards, and seeing it so disconcerted that it stood away and ran aground on the Surry shore.

On or about November 24 Colonel Woodford assembled his forces at Sandy Point, some eight and a half miles above Jamestown, in the hope of crossing the river while Captain Green kept the British ships busy and out of sight. But just as the troops were embarking, a large sloop tender came abreast to block them. Now Woodford was in a hurry; he had received a dispatch telling him that Lord Dunmore was marching on Suffolk and was expected there late on November 21 or early on the twenty-second. He knew too that Scott had taken 215 of his best men and had set out on a forced march to try to reach the town first and to defend it against the Crown's rumored 2,000; there was no more time to lose. The British tenders might stay in the river for weeks. So Woodford decided to continue embarking and to head the first boatloads straight for the sloop in an audacious attempt to capture it. The British skipper had seen the boats gathered at Sandy Point, but he complacently supposed that his presence would put a stop to any rebel nonsense. He was astonished, therefore, to see the boats putting out and then coming in his direction. Astonishment quickly turned to alarm as he realized that he was now the hunted and that he was a long way from the protection of the rest of the squadron. There was a very real possibility that a single sailing ship with light guns might be no match for half a dozen small boats loaded with Virginia riflemen. The sloop decided that she would not stay to find out, and regardless of the need to prevent Woodford from crossing the James, she tacked about and ran down river to the safety of her sister ships. By the time she reached the *Kingfisher* and her master had reported to Captain

Montagu, it was too late to do anything but to fire impotent broadsides at Jamestown. So that was what they did.

Colonel Woodford did not have the satisfaction of capturing a sizable British ship, but he did get his entire force across the river without interference, and that was much more important. It may or may not be a coincidence that his landing place is known today as "Sloop Point."

The next day Captain Montagu and his tenders abandoned their now useless vigil at Jamestown and withdrew to Gosport. Exactly how they explained their poor showing when they got there is anyone's guess. Montagu presumably reported first to Captain Squire as senior naval commander. The latter had been virtually absent from the records throughout November, perhaps lending some credence to the story of his lost ear. If this was so, one might suppose that he would have been in no humor to hear that the best of his fleet had been away for two weeks and had nothing to show for it but depleted stores and a multitude of failures.

Colonel Woodford reached Suffolk on November 25 and was relieved to find that the report of Lord Dunmore's impending attack was false, deriving perhaps from his warlike preparations at Great Bridge, where a small British garrison under Lieutenant Hill Wallace was busily strengthening the newly established fort. Contrary to popular belief, these preparations were not to provide a springboard for further British expansion, but only a necessary and, one would have thought, obvious measure to guard the only landward approach to Norfolk. According to a contemporary map the outpost had been named Fort Murray, but the patriots derisively called it the "hogpen," it being built only of timber, not out of choice but because it stood on a marshy promontory, where there was no deep and dry soil into which to dig a ditch and throw up the usual rampart. Frail though the structure undoubtedly was, it would have to be taken before Norfolk could be reached, and the only way to do so was by way of a frontal attack across a wooden bridge whose flooring timbers Lieutenant Wallace had thoughtfully removed.

Before Woodford reached Suffolk, Colonel Scott had already arrived and, finding that the British were not coming, had moved on to the village of Deep Creek, seven miles from Great Bridge. He sent back a jubilant report that most of the British regulars had gone and that the fort was guarded only "by Tories & Blacks" [8] and asked for permission to launch an immediate attack. Woodford told Scott to wait until he arrived, and added that this was not imminent, as he found it impossible to leave Suffolk " 'till a number of Ball is run, cartirages made, arms Repair'd, powder Horns &c &c." [9] Scott might well have asked, as may we, why Woodford should be delayed by such problems at this late stage, and what in the world his armorers had been doing throughout their long stay in Williamsburg? Nevertheless the fact remains that Colonel Woodford was not ready, and he said so without prevarication in his first report to Edmund Pendleton written from Suffolk on November 26.

The colonel's dispatch stated that informants had told him that Lord Dunmore had pulled his troops out of Gosport and Portsmouth and was massing his entire force in and around Norfolk. A quantity of planking had been seen on its way to the distillery, which, so it was said, the governor was converting into a barracks. All this was probably true, for on Thursday, November 23, Dunmore formally accepted the citizens of Norfolk's request to direct the defense of the town. Woodford also reported that "Several of the princable Scotch Tories in Norfolk I'm told command Black Companys, & speak with great confidence of beating us with the odds of five to one." The whole of Princess Anne County, he added, had rallied to the standard and had been armed by Lord Dunmore. "But I'm told," he said, "they are falling off upon our arrival & few or none of them it is expected will Fight." [1]

Reviewing his own position, Colonel Woodford stated that

[8] Woodford to Pendleton, Suffolk, Nov. 26; *RCHP*, I, 104.
[9] Ibid.
[1] Ibid.

he understood that several hundred militiamen from North Carolina had been offered by that colony's Committee of Safety to aid in the destruction of the British at Norfolk, and that they were even now moving toward the village of Currituck, which would put them within a day's march of Great Bridge. However, Woodford thought that he could handle Lord Dunmore's force himself, but added that he would be guided by further intelligence as it came in. It was possible, he wrote, that the enemy might decide to quit Norfolk and cross the Elizabeth river to Portsmouth. It might therefore be wise to send an additional column to secure that town. If he did this, his existing forces could be seriously depleted. He was worried too by friends who urged him to issue some sort of proclamation to offset Lord Dunmore's. "But," he said, "as my instructions warrent no such thing, I was apprehensive it might be consider'd as presumption in me to take such a step unadvised, & should suppose it would have more waite from the Convention, or other Executive power, if they instruct me to do this or any other thing, I am by no means afraid to put my name to anything they please to recommend." [2]

Woodford concluded by saying that he understood that Patrick Henry had gone home, and so had not written to him, "which," he added, "I should have consider'd it my Duty to have done, had he been at Williamsburg. . . ."

With the small patriot army spread from Suffolk to Great Bridge the loyalist-inclined inhabitants of the lower counties began to screech and flutter like chickens with a fox in their coop. The sound of British drums and the sight of the well-disciplined redcoats had given them sufficient confidence to declare themselves. But now the martial show was over, and in its place came the ill-disciplined but equally persuasive army of their peers, and they feared for their property and their lives— probably in that order. Woodford was anxious to avoid allowing fear to swell Lord Dunmore's ranks, and he let it be known that citizens who would join him now, regardless of having taken

[2] Ibid., 105.

Dunmore's oath, would have nothing taken from them but their weapons, "as these," he said, "are articles I think such Folks should not be trusted with." [3]

Woodford's reassuring statement followed quickly on the heels of another issued by the Committee of Safety aimed at scotching rumors that the patriots were planning to destroy the homes of the inhabitants of Norfolk and Princess Anne County. Over the signature of Edmund Pendleton, the committee solemnly declared that the rumors were false and that the army had been instructed "particularly to support and protect the persons and properties of all friends to *America,* and not wantonly to damage or destroy the property of any person whatsoever." This appeared in the supplement to Purdie's *Virginia Gazette* of November 24, and, although it may have satisfied those who had refused to wear Dunmore's red badge, it can only have heightened the apprehension of those who had not. It was probably for this reason that Colonel Woodford issued his own amnesty and ordered it to be broadcast by Colonel Scott, who, as commander of the vanguard, was deep in the red-rag country.

Scott had moved on from Deep Creek to Great Bridge and had started to build breastworks across the northern end of the single village street to protect his men from enfilade fire from the fort. He had found the British position to be somewhat better built and better manned than he had expected, having a stout stockade and armed with two four-pound cannon, as well as swivels and other light guns mounted both on the walls and seated within the pointed corner bastions. Although ordered not to attack, Scott very properly sent out patrols and mounted a heavy guard over a wide stretch of the river frontage. One of these guard details of twenty men, returning cold and wet from duty, requested permission not to remove the charge from their damp guns and so waste powder, but instead to fire them at the fort. Colonel Scott commended the men and gave his permission, thus commencing the first exchanges at Great Bridge.

[3] Ibid.

The patriot riflemen moved out onto the causeway leading to the dismantled wooden bridge and approached to within seventy yards of the fort before opening fire. Lieutenant Wallace returned their rifle shots with cannon balls, killing one man, Corporal Davis, and injuring another. The exchanges went on for two hours in an encounter reminiscent of the Hampton affair almost exactly a month before. The British had their cannon in a wooden fort rather than aboard wooden ships, but they had the same advantage: enfilade fire down the causeway as they had up the main street of Hampton. The Virginians took cover in the houses and fenced yards on the "island" at the head of the causeway and were able to demonstrate the same accuracy of fire as before, constantly forcing the British gunners to keep their heads down. What had started as an amusing way of emptying one's rifle prior to cleaning it, had developed into a prolonged test of fire power and a considerable waste of precious powder on both sides. The *Virginia Gazette* [4] account says only that after two hours "our men then retreated, and brought off their dead man with them." But it is likely that Colonel Scott's satisfaction at the zealous conduct of his men turned to anger when he realized that they had committed him to a fight he had been instructed to avoid, and it was probably at his direct command that they withdrew.

There the matter ended, the patriots claiming that a great many of the fort's defenders had been killed, and the British declining to admit it. In Norfolk Lord Dunmore was busily putting all available hands to work to erect earthworks around the town to create an effective second line of defense—in case anything unfortunate should happen at Great Bridge. There was no reason to expect that anything would, at least not until the rebels could muster artillery, but it would be rash not to prepare for the worst. For their part, the patriots seized on the ditch-digging as an opportunity to pump more propaganda at the Negroes. The escaped slaves, said Pinkney, were deserting the British in droves; many of them had been shipped to the

[4] Pinkney, Nov. 30.

West Indies to be sold to defray Lord Dunmore's expenses, while others that he did not like were sent back to their owners. As for the rest, "these were kept constantly employed in digging entrenchments in wet ground, till at length the severity of their labour forced many of them to fly." If that was not discouragement enough, the *Gazette* concluded by adding: "such is the barbarous policy of this cruel man, he keeps these unhappy creatures not only against their will, but intends to place them in the front of the battle, to prevent their flying, in case of an engagement, which, from their utter ignorance of fire arms, he knows they will do." [5]

The end of the month found Colonel Woodford still equipping in Suffolk and Colonel Scott maintaining the status quo at Great Bridge. The latter had been reinforced by two companies from Woodford's Second Regiment, commanded by Major Spotswood, and the road between Suffolk and the Bridge was being patrolled by volunteers to keep communications open and to prevent any attempt by the British to divide them. It was estimated that the patriot army now threatening Norfolk amounted to about 900 men, nearly all of whom could be relied on to the last. However, some of the local volunteers quickly tired of their patrolling and went home without saying a word to Woodford.

Lord Dunmore's situation was worse, in that more than half his force was made up of slaves and reluctant volunteers, and he could expect a much higher desertion rate than the patriots. On November 30 he wrote to General Howe in Boston asking for the rest of the Fourteenth Regiment and for the loan of the Sixty-fourth. "Had I but a few more men here," he declared, "I would march immediately to Williamsburg . . . by which I would soon compel the whole colony to submit." [6] There were still loyalists who believed that this was yet possible—as, indeed, it might have been in November. Wrote one of them: "It

[5] Ibid.
[6] Dunmore to General Howe, Nov. 30; *American Archives*, 4th ser., III, 1714.

is a great misfortune his lordship has not a sufficient force to go
against the vast numbers of rebels assembled in different parts;
for he is a brave man, it is a wonder some assistance is not sent
him." [7]

But General Howe had problems of his own, and it was
natural that his own shortages should seem infinitely more
important than those of a Southern colony where no battles were
being fought and where a civilian governor was only playing at
soldiering. On November 26 Howe wrote to the Secretary of
State asking for more men and complaining about the quality of
recruits being rounded up in Ireland for American service. The
Roman Catholic Irish, he said, were "certain to desert if put to
hard work; and, for their ignorance of arms, not entitled to the
smallest confidence as soldiers." If good Englishmen could not
be found, he proposed hiring from the Hanoverian and Hessian
armies and incorporating them, without officers, into the twenty-
seven battalions of foot. In addition, he added, "I would . . .
humbly propose a re-enforcement of four thousand Russians, of
which fifteen hundred to join General Clinton, and two thousand
five hundred the corps to act at New-York." [8] The idea of hiring
Russians was not merely a happy idea conceived by Howe; as
long ago as September 5 Lord Dartmouth had sent him a secret
letter informing him that the Ministry's confidence of having a
large army in America by the spring of 1776 rested on an
assurance from the Empress of Russia that she was ready to
supply all the infantry that England might need. Taking the
Empress at her word, the British government had promptly
asked for twenty thousand. The degree of reliance placed on
these Russian troops by the Ministry may, indeed, have been a
well kept secret, but the fact that their services had been offered
had been known in Virginia for months. In his issue of July 28,
Purdie had published extracts from letters written in London

---

[7] Extract from an intercepted letter from George Rae, of Norfolk, to
his brother in London, Nov. 7; *Virginia Gazette* (Purdie), Dec. 29.

[8] Howe to Germaine, Nov. 26; *American Archives*, 4th ser., III,
1673.

early in May, one of which had reported that in gratitude for the "friendly part they the British government took in her recent quarrel with the Turks" the Empress had granted Britain exclusive trade in her dominion. She had also "promised the ministry her assistance to reduce (what they call) the rebellious Americans, for which purpose she has 40,000 *Russian bears* at their service, to tear us in pieces." Purdie commented that, if true, this was dreadful news, but he suspected that it was "a mere ministerial trick, and only calculated to deceive and frighten a few timid misery souls . . ."

True though the offer undoubtedly had been, forty or even twenty thousand Russians next year was of no help to Lord Dunmore now, nor was the fact (still unknown to him) that troops had already been authorized to prepare for a Southern campaign. His principal hope lay in the weather. It had been a wet and stormy autumn, and now it looked as though it was to be a cold winter. Reviewing the situation in his report to Admiral Graves, Captain Squire observed: "I have great reason to suppose, and hope from their being such cowards, and cold weather coming on, that they [the patriots] will return to their respective homes. and we shall be quiet for the remainder of the winter." [9] It was a reasonable assumption, for it was obvious that though Woodford's army may have been eager to fight it was not ready for war; it was short of tents, bedding, victuals, and ammunition—and that was no way to start a wet winter's siege. Lord Dunmore, on the other hand, was not the hibernating type, and he was not looking for Squire's quiet winter. On the contrary, he dreamed of: "A winter campaign which would reduce . . . the whole of this Southern Continent to a perfect state of obedience." [1] It was a stirring, satisfying vision, enough to make his Lordship smile in his sleep.

Meanwhile, Colonel Scott's sentries huddled beneath dripping blankets, watching the British stockade across the black river as the marsh fog opened and closed around it. From

[9] Squire to Graves, Dec. 2; *American Archives*, 4th ser., IV, 352.
[1] Dunmore to General Howe, Dec. 2; ibid., 357.

within, Wallace's men warily eyed the darkened houses on the
"island" and across the causeway, listening to the rain dripping
from the muzzles of their cannon and wondering whether what
they thought was the splash of a water rat slipping from the
bank might have been something more. Both sides were glumly
watching, listening, and waiting for something to happen.

[*XII*]

DECEMBER

Lord *Dunmore did not mention it, the loyal-*
ists did not write about it, and the patriots apparently were not
interested, but the fact remains that on or about December 1 his
Lordship changed ships. The only evidence of it is to be found
in the headings of two letters written to General Howe, one on
November 30 and the other on December 2, the first written
aboard the ship *William* and the second from "On board the
Dunmore, off Norfolk."[1] The latter vessel appears not to have
been a newly seized prize bearing a fortunate name, but rather
an old captive long in preparation and now newly fitted and
freshly christened. The large and unrigged ship *Eilbeck* commandeered from Messrs. Eilbeck, Ross and Company, in August would seem to have become the governor's new abode. The
patriot sources, however, did not refer to the *Dunmore* when
listing the ships at the Crown's disposal, though they did
mention the *Eilbeck*, describing it as being pierced for twenty-
two guns but having "only seven, three and four pounders,
badly mounted."[2] Nevertheless one must deduce either that the
patriots did not know that the ship's name had been changed
(which is unlikely) or that they were just being difficult. That
the *Dunmore* was the *Eilbeck* under new management is
revealed by a petition submitted to the British government a
year later by the firm of Eilbeck, Chambré, Ross and Company

[1] *American Archives*, 4th ser., III, 1713; ibid., IV, 357.
[2] Report of the Virginia Committee of Safety to Mathew Tilghman
and others, in turn reporting to the congress, Dec. 29; ibid., IV, 576.

for the chartering of the ship *Dunmore*, which they claimed had
been impressed on August 22, 1775—the same day the *Eilbeck*
had been seized.

So, while Lieutenant Wallace sat in his wet and chilled
"hogpen" and the patriot army shivered under canvas at Suffolk
and Great Bridge, his Lordship moved to the greater comfort of
his new, large, and dry quarters. There was time for social
visiting between the ships, convivial conversation between
gentlemen, the flow and ebb of wine, even trips ashore to enjoy
the hospitality of Tory friends in Norfolk. Helen Maxwell and
her husband (who claimed not to be Tory sympathizers)
entertained Captain Fordyce at their home, and while Mr.
Maxwell played on some unspecified instrument the captain
turned the music and hummed the tunes. "He was not handsome," said Mrs. Maxwell, "but very genteel" [3] and very fond
of music. Much time, of course, was spent in writing home to
relatives, friends, and business associates and, for the gentlemen
of the army and navy, in preparing reports to their superiors.
Then, too, there were the private diaries to be kept, and the
sketchbooks to be filled in pencil, ink, and water color—a
priceless documentation of history, nearly all of it now lost.

The official documents fared best, for even if they did not
reach their intended destination, they were nevertheless carefully preserved as incriminating evidence. Lord Dunmore's quill
was constantly a-scratching during these first days of December, first to Howe and then to Lord Dartmouth, whom Dunmore
still believed to be holding the reins of the American Department in Whitehall. He could not know that on November 10
Dartmouth had been made Keeper of the Privy Seal and that
Lord George Germaine (who had disgraced himself at the battle
of Minden) was the new Secretary of State for American affairs.
Indeed, Dunmore had only recently discovered that General
Gage had been replaced, and he opened his letter of November
30 to General Howe saying that "the report here is, that
General Gage is gone home, and that you are appointed to

[3] Maxwell, "My Mother," *LNCVA*, II, 136.

succeed him; if so, from my heart I wish you joy, and am well persuaded you will soon evince to the world that you are well deserving the honour conferred on you by your Sovereign." [4] He then went on to summarize his recent successes, declaring: "I think we have done wonders," but adding that he could do much more if only he could be supplied with more small arms, a couple of field guns, and a consignment of cartridge paper, "of which not a sheet is to be got here, and all our cartridges are expended."

Being without cartridges was not as dire a situation as one might suppose, for it did not mean that his Lordship's muskets could no longer be fired. The loading of a musket normally involved the use of a cylindrical paper cartridge, containing at one end the lead ball and on top of it the correct quantity of powder for the charge. The soldier was required to bite off the end of the cartridge, tip the rest down the muzzle, the powder being followed by the ball. The empty paper sleeve was then pushed down after them and thrust home with a few deft prods of the ramrod. It was an operation that could be accomplished in less than fifteen seconds, but only when all the priming and loading components came in a kit. The gun could also be loaded by taking the powder from a horn, the ball from a box, and, if pushed, tearing a wad off the tail of one's shirt; but it took considerably longer. It was for this reason that Lord Dunmore was concerned over his shortage of cartridge paper.

He was also deeply worried, or so he claimed, about the correctness of his actions and how his ladder of military escalation would be viewed by the King and his ministers. In his letter to General Howe, Dunmore declared that since May he had not received a word from anyone in the administration, "though," he said, "I have wrote volumes to them, in each of which I have prayed to be instructed, but to no purpose." [5] Less than a week later he wrote in the same vein to Lord Dartmouth,

[4] Dunmore to General Howe, Nov. 30, *American Archives*, 4th ser., III, 1713.
[5] Ibid.

speaking of his "anxiety of mind, not knowing how to act in innumerable instances that occurred every day. . . ." Later in the same letter he outlined with some pride his efforts to assemble a fleet and to raise an army, "all this without any order from your Lordship, or any other person, but if I have done wrong," he added, "the blame must not be laid at my door, I have prayed and entreated your Lordship over and over again for Instructions, but not one Syllable from your Lordship for these Six Months past." [6] It is a somewhat futile exercise to attempt to read a man's mind from a distance of some two centuries, for there is no way in the world of determining whether or not you are right. Nevertheless, there may at least be reason to suggest that Lord Dunmore had very few doubts that his activities in the fall of 1775 would be received in Whitehall with anything less than loud applause. It is possible, then, that his harping on this lack of communication was more an attempt to put Lord Dartmouth on the defensive and so to minimize any reprimand that might be due him as a result of his ignominious flight from Williamsburg in the spring.

Apart from this oft-repeated request for approval and from his entirely valid calls for arms, men, and ships, the governor's letters bore overriding notes of satisfaction at a difficult job being well done. No less than three thousand had taken the oath, Negroes were flocking in from all quarters, the merchants were ready to equip him (if General Howe would supply the funds), the trenches were almost finished, and the new regiments were taking shape. On top of that, as Captain Squire had observed, the singularly inclement weather was likely to send the rebels shivering homeward without ever entering the lists in earnest.

General Howe might or might not be more inclined to recognize the importance of Virginia than had his predecessor. In any case, Dunmore was not going to miss an opportunity to do as good a public relations job as was humanly possible. He was sending his letters to Howe aboard the sloop *Betsey*, whose principal cargo was to be potatoes, Indian corn, and oats—a

[6] Dunmore to Dartmouth, Dec. 6; PRO,CO 5/1353.

Virginia food parcel for the army in Boston. If only his colony could be secured, explained the governor, "I could supply your army and navy with every necessary of life, and that in the greatest abundance, which is more than any other colony on the Continent could do." [7]

There was more than a little substance to Lord Dunmore's claim, and even the control of Norfolk and its approaches represented a pearl of considerable price—as the patriots were the first to acknowledge. Later in the month Colonel Robert Howe, of North Carolina, wrote to Edmund Pendleton admitting that the British could not want for a better base. Norfolk is, he wrote, "so well calculated for defence, situated between two Colonies, so that the same Troops could execute their purposes upon both, & from which their Shiping could convey their men to any part of this Colony to which they may choose to detach them; added to this its being in the neighbourhood of your Norfolk, Princess Ann & Nansemond Counties & our Perquemonds, Parquetank & Currituck, the three latter living by the Grain and pork they produce, consequently able to supply Norfolk with great quantities of provision." [8] Furthermore this town, which Dunmore called a "little dirty Borough," provided an excellent harbor in a highly strategic location. It lay, as Colonel Howe reminded Pendleton, "within five or six leagues of the Capes, commanding the navigation of two Colonies [making] it perhaps the most noble place of arms for *them that* the world ever produce[d]." [9] On the other hand, Howe added that the town and harbor were of little value to the patriots unless they also had control of the sea; and that did not seem to be within reach. Congress was aware of the need to match Dunmore's fleet, and on December 2 it authorized for that purpose the assembling of a small squadron in the Chesapeake

[7] Dunmore to General Howe, Dec. 2; *American Archives*, 4th ser., IV, 357.

[8] Robert Howe to Pendleton, Dec. 22; *RCHP*, I, 138.

[9] Ibid.

Bay. However, before it was ready two British warships arrived on station there, and the project was quietly dropped.

It is one of the ironies of history that although his own superiors failed to appreciate and adequately support Lord Dunmore's contributions, the patriot leadership took him extremely seriously. In the course of December, George Washington showed his concern in four different letters. On December 14 he urged the congress to take every possible measure "to disposses Lord Dunmore of his hold in Virginia," [1] adding that the sooner steps were taken the better chance they would have of succeeding. The next day, in a letter to Joseph Reed in Philadelphia, he called Dunmore "that arch traitor to the rights of humanity" and asserted that if the Virginians were wise he should be "instantly crushed," even if it took the whole colony to do it. [2] On December 18 Washington again wrote to the president of the congress, urging that punitive action be taken against the governor. "I do not mean to dictate," he said, "I am sure they [the Congress] will pardon me for freely giving them my Opinion, which is, that the fate of America a good deal depends on his being obliged to evacuate Norfolk this winter." [3] Later, in writing to Richard Henry Lee, Washington made his point even more forcefully: "If, my dear Sir, that man is not crushed before spring, he will become the most formidable enemy America has; his strength will increase as a snow ball by rolling; and faster, if some expedient cannot be hit upon to convince the slaves and servants of the impotency of his designs. . . . I do not think that forcing his Lordship on shipboard is sufficient; nothing less than depriving him of life or liberty will secure peace to Virginia." [4] Had Dunmore been able to read those letters, any doubts about the value of his endeavors would quickly have been dispelled. It seems almost unsporting

[1] Washington to president of congress, Dec. 14; *Writings*, IV, 161.
[2] Ibid., 167.
[3] Ibid., 172.
[4] Ibid., 186; Dec. 26.

that his Lordship was denied that pleasure, particularly when his letters to General Howe were to provide George Washington with such informative reading.

The sloop *Betsey* sailed from Norfolk on about December 4 under the command of John Atkinson, a petty officer from the *Otter*. In addition to her hold full of foodstuffs, the ship carried four specimen prisoners: Virginia convention delegate Robinson and minute captain Mathews, both of whom had been captured after the first Kemp's Landing affair; and two Boston ships' captains, Oliver Porter and Simeon Dean, who had been seized while running supplies to the patriots. "I have sent them," Dunmore explained to Howe, "more with a view of intimidating others than to punish them, as they expect here that so sure as they are sent to Boston they are to be hanged." [5] Also aboard were Colonel Moses Kirkland, a South Carolina loyalist for whom Dunmore supplied the most glowing recommendations, and John Eustace, the governor's own ward. Of the latter, Dunmore wrote: "I have had the charge of him for these three years past, and have given him the best education this country could afford. He is a very good Latin scholar; of exceeding good spirit and quick parts; of excellent temper and disposition; has conceived a great desire to go into the army." [6] Whether or not there were other passengers on board remains in doubt, but we do know that Dunmore informed Captain Leslie that there was no room for the noncommissioned officers of the Fourteenth Regiment, who had come with him from St. Augustine en route to join the rest of the regiment at Boston. It is possible, of course, that the governor's statement that the *Betsey* was "already too much crowded" [7] was only an excuse to prevent these valuable men from leaving. His Lordship hoped that their staying would "be attended with no inconveniency," adding that in any case he expected General Howe would shortly be sending

[5] Dunmore to General Howe, Nov. 30; *American Archives*, 4th ser., III, 1713.

[6] Dunmore to General Howe, Dec. 2; ibid., IV, 357.

[7] Dunmore to Captain Leslie, Dec. 2; ibid., IV, 349.

the remaining part of the regiment to Virginia. Besides the food and people, the sloop carried a quantity of highly important correspondence, including the governor's letters to General Howe; reports from Governor Tonyn regarding the defenses of St. Augustine; a letter from Captain Leslie to General Gage and another much longer report to Howe; a long letter from Captain Fordyce to Captain Urquhart with the Fourteenth at Boston; and a dispatch from Captain Squire to Admiral Graves. All together, the letters of these officers provided a full account of the accomplishments, strength, and weaknesses of the King's forces in Virginia and Florida.

At about the same time the *Betsey* sailed from Norfolk, the *Lee*, a privateer armed schooner commanded by Captain John Manley, left its home port of Beverly, Massachusetts, to make a nuisance of itself in the shipping lanes leading to Boston. The *Lee*'s efforts in this direction had previously been astonishingly successful, and her master was credited with having brought home to Beverly in the course of a fortnight "two large brigs, of two hundred and twenty tons each, laden with military stores and provisions, and two ships of three hundred tons each, laden with English goods, porter, live hogs, &c., to the amount of forty thousand pounds sterling the whole." [8] As a result of these lucrative exploits Captain Manley had become a celebrity, and, as one proud Beverly citizen put it, "as many towns contend for the honour of his birth as they did for that of Homer's." [9] This may have been less than fair to the shades of Homer, but there was no doubt that Captain Manley was the last person in the world young John Atkinson would want to find across his bow. Nevertheless, fourteen days out from Norfolk the *Betsey* and the *Lee* crossed each other's paths, giving the latter another prize, one that Washington termed "but little inferior to any . . . our famous Manley has taken." [1]

[8] Extract from a letter, author unidentified, written from Beverly, Dec. 18; *ibid.*, IV, 313.

[9] Ibid.

[1] Washington to president of congress, Dec. 18; *Writings*, IV, 173.

Every British ship's captain was aware that official papers should never be allowed to fall into enemy hands, and Lord Dunmore's instructions, given to him at the time of his appointment in 1771, specifically stated: "you are to give Directions to all Masters of Ships, or other Persons, to whom you may intrust your letters, that they put such letters into a Bag with sufficient weight to sink the same immediately, in case of imminent Danger from the Enemy." [2] Why John Atkinson failed in this duty is hard to understand. We can only suppose that this being his first command, he became unnerved by the sight of the enemy bearing down on him and by the prospect of losing his ship. However, he was not alone in his failure to preserve Lord Dunmore's secrets, for his own ward, John Eustace, of whom Dunmore had written so glowingly, readily revealed on questioning that before John Connolly had set out on his ill-fated mission to build a western army, he had hidden his commission and his most important documents inside the mail pillion of his portmanteau saddle. This same young man who was so anxious to serve his King by joining the army, readily described how he saw the secret compartment built into the saddle, "the papers put in, and first covered with Tin and over that with a waxed canvas Cloth." In his report to congress, Washington observed that Eustace "is so exceedingly pointed and clear in his Information, that I have no doubt of it being true." As for the papers themselves, he added, "I could wish 'em to be discovered, as I think they contain some curious and extraordinary plans." [3] However, they were never found, for, although Connolly's own saddle had been taken apart by his captors, his servant, who had been released by the patriots, found the second saddle hanging in a shed, managed to extract the papers, and burned all of them except his master's commission. It was an act

[2] "Aspinwall Papers," MHS *Collections*, 4th ser., X, 663, instruction No. 84.

[3] Washington to president of congress, Jan. 30, 1776; *Writings*, IV, 291.

of loyalty and courage in marked contrast to the conduct of Master John Eustace.

Although the capture of the *Betsey* provided the patriot leadership with its best packages of mail to date, the letters of lesser fry fell into Virginian hands from time to time. They were rarely of much intelligence value, but they did give the patriots an opportunity to see who was on which side, and the *Gazettes* delighted to print succulent extracts for the embarrassment of their authors. Robert Shedden, of Portsmouth, whose quillmanship had previously landed himself and the Goodrich family in Lord Dunmore's frying pan, followed this up with another that dropped him neatly into the patriots' fire. Writing to John Shedden in Glasgow he recounted the stirring events of November, describing the victory at Kemp's Landing, the standard-raising, and the people of the counties of Norfolk and Princess Anne "to a man" flocking in to take the oath of allegiance. "Before Saturday night," he wrote, "I think government will have such a party here as the shirtmen dare not face." It was a sight to gladden a Scotsman's heart. "Depend upon it, you will never have such another opportunity to make money by drygoods in this country. Osnabrugs, canvas, &c. bring as many as you can get credit for. If Gibson's sloop is at Glasgow, I would wish him loaded also. If you bring 20,000£. in goods, they will sell to advantage." [4] It was clear that Mr. Shedden knew a winner when he saw one. Furthermore he was prepared to back his judgment with an enormous investment.

John Brown of Norfolk wrote home in a similar vein describing the honor he felt at having been one of the volunteers who had marched with Lord Dunmore to Kemp's Landing. "I can assure you," he declared, "lord Dunmore is so much admired, in this part of the country, that he might have 500 *vollunteers* to march with him to any part of Virginia." Brown too was prepared to invest in the future—though to a more modest extent than Mr. Shedden. "You are hereby ordered to

[4] *Virginia Gazette* (Purdie), Dec. 22.

ship," he added, "by the first opportunity, 1000£. sterling value
in Linen goods." [5]

Andrew Sprowle of Gosport, who had been in trouble
earlier for having allowed British troops to be billeted in his
house, was now in it again for having advised an associate in
Scotland that "I would have no fear in bringing in a vessel with
osnabrugs, Irish linens, and other sortable goods," adding that
it would be well protected by the men-of-war. Purdie's *Virginia
Gazette* reminded its readers that Sprowle had been "chairman
of the Committee of Trade, who, at the head of all the
merchants (most of them his countrymen) voluntarily signed
the continental association in November 1774, at a General
Assembly of the representatives of this colony, then convened at
Williamsburg." [6] He and his money-grubbing Scotch Tory
friends would doubtless be spoken to quite sharply if and when
the patriots of Virginia could lay hands on them.

Although the patriots obviously had more to gain by
intercepting enemy mail than did the British, Captain Squire
and his minions were not ones to leave a seal unbroken. Lord
Dunmore made it his business to read everything that came to
hand, and though he rarely found anything of military value, he
did obtain a fair idea of his standing in the eyes of influential
Virginians; not that any of this would have been news to him.

On December 9 John Hatley Norton wrote to his father in
London discussing the current status of the confrontation in
Virginia, saying that at heart the colonies were "as Loyal as any
of his Majesty's Subjects, & wou'd go to great lengths in Support
of his Crown & Dignity," but once wounded by tyrants they
could do no less than defend themselves. This letter was one
that fell into British hands, and, although part of it is now
missing, it seems to have begun in sober and considered words
that even the governor could have read with respect if not with
concurrence. The end, however, was enough to set his scalp
burning beneath his wig.

[5] Ibid., Dec. 29.
[6] Ibid., Dec. 22.

I have hitherto been silent about our Governor's Operations, [wrote Norton] but I cannot help saying something of them, as they are marked with almost every Species of Cruelty that a wicked Mind cou'd Suggest; After pillag:g the Plantations on the Rivers for some Months past, taking Negroes, burning Houses, & the like Depredations he hoisted his Standard & issued a Damned, infernal, Diabolical proclamation declaring Freedom to all our Slaves who will join him, & obliged great Numbers to take an Oath that they will arm themselves & assist him with their Lives & Fortunes. Most of the Scotch have joined him & a great Number of Negroes: he is now entrenched with a Body of Men at the Great Bridge to prevent our Men from geting to Norfolk. he has tis said 500 Whites & as many Blacks. our Men in number about 700 under Colo. Woodford are entrenched within a few hundred Yards of his Party. . . . Colo. Howe from Carolina wth. abt. 600 Men & a good Train of Artillery are daily expected to join Woodford, when a general Engagement may probably happen.[7]

John H. Norton's summary of the current situation was reasonably accurate, though he put the patriot numbers a little low and the British somewhat high. But it was true that the North Carolinians' offer of assistance had been accepted and that they were expected to bring with them an undetermined quantity of much-needed artillery. Woodford had reached Great Bridge with the main body of his army on December 2 and found Colonel Scott well in control and with substantial breastworks erected across the north end of the village street facing the causeway and the British fort. It required no great tactician to deduce that a frontal assault across the causeway and dismantled bridge could only result in the useless spilling of much blood. Two courses seemed open: to wait for Colonel Howe's artillery, or to cross the river and marshland downstream and to outflank the fort. Woodford wisely decided to prepare for both. He ordered the raising of batteries adjacent to the village from which the guns could be brought to bear on

[7] PRO,CO 5/40, *Intercepted Letters;* quoted in *Norton Papers,* 391-2, date incorrectly given as Oct. 16.

the British stockade, and he sent out a nocturnal skirmishing party to see whether a flanking attack was feasible.

The only likely crossing place lay about five miles down the branch and was defended by a small British outpost largely manned by Negroes. Woodford ordered sixty men under Captain Taliaferro to move there and remain hidden near the south bank, and then to attempt a crossing after dark. It was a large enough force not only to probe the enemy defenses but also, if conditions seemed favorable, to establish permanent positions from which to hold the fort in a cross fire. However, Captain Taliaferro did not get over that night, as the boat he intended to use could not be floated until morning—which tended to defeat the purpose of the exercise.

As it turned out, it was Lieutenant Wallace's men who undertook a sortie that night, taking the patriots quite by surprise. Lieutenant Colonel Scott was sitting quietly in his quarters at Great Bridge, writing by candlelight to a friend in Williamsburg: "The Carolina forces are joining us," he wrote. "One company came in yesterday, and we expect 8 or 900 of them by to-morrow, or next day at farthest, with several pieces of artillery, and plenty of ammunition and other warlike stores." Then suddenly: "A gun fired—I must stop." [8]

The sound of the shot brought the patriot companies tumbling out of their blankets and propelled their officers half dressed into the street. They found the houses on the "island" at the far end of the causeway burning briskly. As the men struggled into parade order, a fusillade of small-arms fire crashed out from the British stockade, the volleys mixed with the occasional roar of cannon fire. The barrage, coupled with the glare from the burning houses, prevented the patriots from doing anything to save the buildings. The four sentries posted on the causeway realized that they were sitting ducks and wisely took flight. Colonel Scott stated that they could give no account of how the fire started, but Woodford reported that it had been

[8] *Virginia Gazette* (Pinkney), Dec. 6. This newspaper was now reduced in page size and was being issued twice weekly.

set by "some blacks" [9] from the fort and that one of them had
been shot. In all, five properties were destroyed, some of them of
considerable value. Patriot sources seem to have been surprised
by this exploit, but from the British point of view it was an
obvious step, depriving the rebels of the cover which their
snipers had found so useful in their first exchanges.

So far, the British regulars had never met the shirtmen toe
to toe, fighting the same kind of battle with the same kind of
weapon. The closest they had come to it had been the second
encounter at Kemp's Landing, from which the Virginians had
fled in unseemly haste. At Hampton and at Great Bridge the
accuracy and range of rebel rifles had easily outgunned the
British muskets. The latter's shorter range and inferior accuracy had to be offset by volley firing, and for this reason the
regulars needed to fight in the open. The riflemen, on the other
hand, took a full minute to load (as against the musket's fifteen
seconds), and they had no desire to do it in full view of the
enemy.

Colonel Woodford was well aware that the British had
nothing to gain by coming to him. The fort controlled the
approach to Norfolk, and its defenders had only to wait for the
patriots to rush it. When they did, the Brown Bess musket
would come into its own. Captain Taliaferro's landward ploy
might work, providing he was not cut to pieces by Dunmore's
main force, which was waiting in Norfolk and reportedly
growing ever larger and stronger. All in all, the Carolinian
artillery seemed to be Woodford's best bet. But waiting for it to
arrive was bad for morale and the Taliaferro mission would at
least keep some of the men busy. Suppose the Carolinian men
and supplies did not turn out to be all that was promised, what
then? In his December 4 dispatch to Pendleton, Woodford
reported that he had written to Colonel Howe urging him "to
bring no men but what are well provided with arms &c.," and to
Pendleton he admitted that "it is very uncertain how these
Carolina Troops may be arm'd & what sort of men & officers

[9] Woodford to Pendleton, Dec. 4; *RCHP*, I, 107.

they are." [1] Woodford begged the Committee of Safety to authorize the sending of part of Patrick Henry's First Regiment to reinforce him and also to send ammunition and extra blankets for the men, many of whom were forced to sleep on the wet ground, there being no straw for bedding.

Woodford's position was far from attractive; though militarily he was playing a difficult game as best he could, the politicians at home were becoming restive. Even to some of the Committee of Safety members it seemed ridiculous that the patriot army should have been halted by a heap of sticks and a handful of Tories and Negroes. It is almost superfluous to add that the complainers had never seen the fort and probably had never been to Great Bridge in their lives. The political unrest was not helped by the fact that the fourth Virginia convention was now in session, having convened in Richmond on December 1. This it had done in response to the directive of the previous session, at which time there had been no knowing whether, come December, Williamsburg would be still in patriot hands. Now, with Dunmore well contained at the mouth of the James, the convention elected to move its deliberations to the capital, where it would be closer (though not too close) to the action. Thus on December 5 the delegates assembled in Williamsburg and formed themselves into a committee to review the state of the colony. Fortunately for Colonel Woodford, Edmund Pendleton had been elected president of the convention and therefore the policies of the Committee of Safety were continued—including the side-stepping of Patrick Henry's authority. The convention was apparently satisfied that Woodford was in sole command and that he was reporting directly to it, rather than through its appointed commander in chief. The latter, however, was not at all satisfied, and on December 6 Henry wrote to Woodford chiding him for not keeping him fully informed. "I wish to know your situation particularly, with that of the enemy, that the whole may be laid before the convention now here. The number and designs of the enemy, as you collect it,

[1] Ibid., 109.

might open some prospects to us, that might enable us to form some diversion in your favor." [2]

To this Woodford sharply replied that he was constantly in touch with the convention and that no doubt Henry, "as commanding officer of the troops at Williamsburg" would be supplied with that information. He went on to add that if and when Henry was sent down to join him, he, Henry, would be in command. In the meantime, when "sent to command a separate and distinct body of troops, under the immediate instruction of the committee of safety—whenever that body or the honourable convention is sitting," declared Woodford, "I look upon it as my indispensable duty to address my intelligence to them, as the supreme power in this colony." [3] Henry was not at all entertained by this letter, and he duly laid it before the convention, demanding to know whether it really expected its commander in chief to put up with such insubordination from a junior commander. It was all very embarrassing, and the gentlemen of the convention were agreed that they should look into the matter very carefully—and very slowly. Pendleton's supporters were anxious not to aggravate Henry's adherents, but at the same time they were just as anxious not to rock Woodford's boat. If he resigned, Henry would undoubtedly leap into the saddle, and heaven knows where that would land them. The more Pendleton and his friends saw of Henry the more strongly they shared the opinion that George Washington would later voice, saying: "I think my countrymen made a capital mistake, when they took Henry out of the senate to place him in the field." [4]

While the politicians fussed and wrangled in Williamsburg, Colonel Woodford was endeavoring to advance the cause at Great Bridge. Having received Captain Taliaferro's report that he could not launch his boat, Woodford sent Captain Nicholas down with an additional forty-two men to help him on his way.

[2] Mays, *Pendleton*, II, 79; quoting W. W. Henry, *Patrick Henry*, I, 335.

[3] Ibid.

[4] Washington to Joseph Reed, March 7, 1776; *Writings*, IV, 381.

Nicholas had the advantage of knowing the terrain and of having fought a British boat guard there on the day after his arrival at the Bridge. In addition, Woodford put both parties under the command of Colonel Adam Stephen of the minute battalion. Around midnight on December 4, the force of about a hundred men successfully crossed the branch and reached the British guard-post before they were spotted. A sentry challenged them, and when he received no answer, fired. According to Scott, "Our people being too eager, began the fire immediately, without orders, and kept it up very hot for about 15 minutes." [5] The element of surprise, so essential to the plan, was therefore lost, and most of the post's defenders ("26 Blacks & 9 Whites" [6]) escaped into the night. Reported Woodford: "an over Eagerness at first, & rather a backwardness afterwards, occation'd some confusion, & prevented the Colos. plan from being so well executed as he intended." However, Stephen was able to set fire to the defenses and to the house, in which one Negro was burned; another was shot "dead upon the spott," [7] and two others were taken prisoner. Portable booty amounted to "4 exceeding fine muskets." [8] Nevertheless, it was not for four muskets and as many Negroes that Woodford had risked a hundred of his best men.

He was no happier when he received a report from Carolina that his worst fears were likely to be realized—the promised cannon were not mounted, and there was no powder for them except 300 pounds, to be picked up on the way; furthermore, the men's arms were described as "Indifferent," [9] and there was no furniture, such as swabs, worms and rammers, for the cannon. On top of this Woodford learned that Batchelor's mill dam over Deep Creek (across which supplies came from Suffolk) had been either washed away or knocked out by local

[5] *Virginia Gazette* (Pinkney), Dec. 6.
[6] Woodford to Pendleton, Dec. 5; *RCHP*, I, 110.
[7] Ibid.
[8] *Virginia Gazette* (Pinkney), Dec. 6.
[9] Woodford to Pendleton, Dec. 5; *RCHP*, I, 111.

Tories. The messenger who brought the news reported that he had heard that Lord Dunmore was planning to establish a post there. There was no alternative but to send a large enough party back to the dam to repair and protect it, and an officer and twenty-five doubtless reluctant men were sent on their way.

Along with this doleful report, Colonel Woodford sent the convention a specimen musket ball taken from cartridges captured by Colonel Stephen. It was presumably a slit bullet intended to expand on contact, and, as the cartridges were extremely well made, Woodford thought them to be the handiwork of noncomissioned officers from the British regulars. "I have never suffer'd a soldier of mine to do a thing of this kind," Woodford declared, "nor will I allow it to be done for the future, notwithstanding this provocation." [1] Also included with Woodford's December 5 dispatch were statements taken from the two captured Negroes, George and Ned. Both said that they had been sent down from Norfolk on December 4, but one thought he had been accompanied by 55 Negroes and two white men, while the other claimed to have been in a group of "twenty odd Blacks & three whites." [2] They both said that a ship and a snow had recently arrived at Norfolk carrying soldiers, and George volunteered that he had been told that they comprised four or five hundred men expected from St. Augustine. He also revealed that the fort was now manned by thirty whites and ninety Negroes, and that they had six cannon mounted on carriages and goodly supplies of ammunition.

On December 6 Woodford reported that during the previous night the fort had been reinforced with about ninety men, all of whom seemed "very Busey at Worke." [3] He had also discovered that the soldiers from St. Augustine were nothing of the sort; they were merely a boatload of servants (Scots emigrants bound for North Carolina), whose ship had been commandeered by Lord Dunmore. There was still no sign of the

[1] Ibid., 112.
[2] Ibid., 113.
[3] Ibid.

cannon from Carolina, and the British had returned to their outpost previously visited by Colonel Stephen—which left everyone just where they had been before.

That night Colonel Scott set out with 150 men to see if he could not do a little better than Stephen had. Again the shirtmen crossed the branch without trouble, but again the alarm was raised too soon. This time the colonel's force bumped into a cart traveling from Norfolk and guarded by four men. These promptly opened fire and so warned the post before it could be attacked, allowing the garrison of seventy men to escape. The score this time was one white man and four Negroes killed, three Negroes captured, and six muskets and three bayonets seized; for which Scott paid the price of one man grazed on the thumb. It was a better tally than the first try, but it still could hardly have been said to be worth the effort.

In Williamsburg the convention pored over Woodford's reports and agreed to send him anything he asked (if it could be found) in the hope of seeing some quick action. On December 7, three companies of the First Regiment (mercifully without their colonel) were ordered to Great Bridge—where the 500 pounds of powder and the 1,500 pounds of lead they brought with them were received with much more enthusiasm than they were. Their disgruntled senior officer, Captain Ballard, reported back that "Our reception at the Great Bridge was to the last cool, and absolutely disagreeable. We arrived there fatigued, dry and hungry, we were neither welcomed, invited to eat or drink, or shown a place to rest our wearied bones. . . ."[4] Six further companies of minutemen, from Southampton and Amelia counties, were also ordered to proceed to Woodford's aid with all possible dispatch. Thus, even if the Carolina men failed to appear at all or declined "to remain any longer than is agreeable to their own Inclinations,"[5] the Virginia patriots should be numerous enough to finish the job themselves.

[4] Captain Ballard to Henry, Dec. 20; W. W. Henry, *Patrick Henry*, I, 337, footnote 1.

[5] Woodford to Pendleton, Dec. 4; *RCHP*, I, 109.

Nevertheless, when Woodford went to bed on the night of December 8, neither his Virginian nor Carolinian reinforcements had arrived, and there was every reason to suppose that the present stalemate would continue until they did. As dawn broke and the reveille drums called the men to duty, the sound of gunfire came from the direction of the fort; but the patriots gave it little attention, thinking it no more than a "morning salute." However, a few moments later Woodford's adjutant was heard calling "Boys, stand to your arms," [6] a cry that sent Woodford himself running down the road to the breastwork. To his astonishment he found that the British had laid planks across the dismantled bridge and were pouring out of the fort onto the "island" at the head of the causeway in an array that looked for all the world like Dunmore's entire combined force of regulars, Tories, and Negroes—which was precisely what it was, plus a few gentlemen of the navy and a couple of Captain Squire's gun crews thrown in to make weight. Woodford blinked and wondered whether he was awake. As far as he knew there were no more than about 140 men in the fort at most, and now suddenly it was disgorging five hundred. Besides, every rule in the book and every ounce of common sense told him that *he* was supposed to be the attacker, and no one in his right mind would launch an assault just after reveille, when the enemy was up, armed, and ready for parade. Nevertheless, that was precisely what was happening.

From that day to this, historians have debated the reasoning behind this extraordinary decision, and some have even suggested that Dunmore was out of his mind. Woodford later claimed that the governor had been tricked by a servant who had "deserted" from Colonel Scott's raiding party and who had told him that "there were not more than three hundred shirtmen" at the Bridge. According to Woodford, the man had "completely taken his Lordship in . . . . and that imprudent

[6] Major Spotswood to a friend in Williamsburg, Dec. 9; *Virginia Gazette* (Purdie), Dec. 15.

man caught at the bait" [7] and so resolved to hazard all in one wild throw. This was a clever story, and it made Woodford appear satisfyingly shrewd; but if the servant did give the British the wrong figures, there is little doubt that neither Woodford nor any of his officers knew the first thing about it.

Lord Dunmore's own report of his decision makes no mention of any devious servant (though one would hardly expect it to); instead, he claimed that it was the news of impending rebel reinforcements that prompted him to act as he did. "Being informed," he wrote, "that the Rebels had procured some Cannon from North Carolina, and that they were also to be reinforced from Williamsburg, and knowing that our little Fort was not in a condition to withstand any thing heavier than Musquet shot, I thought it advisable to risque something to save the Fort." [8] This was an understatement indeed; but there was both truth in his information and logic in his reasoning. If the fort could not hold out against an enlarged rebel force armed with artillery, the only courses open to him were to attack before they arrived or to pull back. The latter was a very poor alternative, for both sides knew that the bridge was the gateway to Norfolk; once past it, "we must expect to be cut off," wrote Dunmore, "from every supply of Provisions from this Colony." [9]

After dark, on Friday, December 8, Captain Leslie marched out of Norfolk at the head of his full detachment of the Fourteenth Regiment. Most of the names of the men who set out that night are long since forgotten, but a few survive: Captain Charles Fordyce commanding the grenadiers, Captain David Cooper with the light company, lieutenants Napier, Lawrie, and Leslie (nephew of Captain Leslie); ensigns Wools, Boys, Ogle, and Lindsay. Lieutenant Wallace was already at the fort and so perhaps was John Batut, although it is possible that the latter had been withdrawn earlier and was now making the twelve-

[7] Woodford to the Virginia Convention, Dec. 10; *RCHP*, I, 119.
[8] Dunmore to Dartmouth, Dec. 13; PRO,CO 5/1353.
[9] Ibid.

mile march again. Lord Dunmore's white hopes reached the fort at 3:30 A.M. and after a brief rest began to prepare themselves for action.

The governor later stated that his orders to Captain Leslie were that if on arrival he found the status quo much as it was supposed to be, he was to order two companies of Negroes to leave the fort under cover of darkness, to make a detour across the branch, and at dawn to launch a diversionary attack on the enemy rear. This, it was hoped, would draw the rebels away from their breastwork and allow Leslie to mount a frontal assault across the causeway. But when he arrived, Leslie found that the Negro companies were out guarding the twice-attacked outpost near the river, too far away to be reached with new orders and to get into position before dawn. So, for some reason which will never be explained, "Captain Leslie not finding the Negroes there, imprudently sallied out of the Fort at break of Day in the morning," only to find, as Dunmore stated, that "the Rebels . . . having got intelligence of his design were prepared to receive him from behind their trenches." [1] But this, as we have seen, was not the case at all.

First out of the fort was Lieutenant Batut with an advance party to give covering fire to two field guns, which were quickly hauled across the bridge and set up on the "island" end of the causeway, from which they were able to bring their fire to bear on the rebel breastwork. This step was accomplished without a hitch, for there were only two or three patriot sentries on the island. Each of these fired at least three rounds before retreating, and one, stationed behind a pile of new shingles, stayed to load and fire eight times before being driven out by the fire of a full platoon. This sentry, who is believed to have been a Negro named Billy Flora, had to cross a plank to reach the breastwork, and, in a hail of bullets, he was seen to stop and pull up the board behind him before taking cover.

Lieutenant Batut's men now set fire to the remaining houses on the "island," as well as to the pile of shingles. Then, from

[1] Ibid.

out of the swirling gray smoke, came Captain Fordyce at the head of his grenadiers. Resplendent in their red-fronted bear-skin caps, buff-laced red coats, buff breeches, and thigh-length black gaiters over gleaming-buckled shoes, they strode out onto the causeway, six abreast and in perfect parade order, marching proudly through the mud. They were a sight to make English-men cheer, and to provoke in an enemy what Dr. Benjamin Rush described as a "supersitious fear of the valor and disci-pline of the British Army." [2]

John Batut's advance platoon provided flanking fire, and the two cannon were well enough placed to rake the village street, throwing chain shot as far as the church at its opposite end. Backing up the grenadiers were the remainder of the regulars under Captain Leslie, with a goodly number of Negroes and volunteers, about 230 in all. But these came no further than the "island," and some said they stopped at the bridge, waiting for the breastwork to be stormed and the causeway secured before venturing further. On the American side no more than twenty-five men under Lieutenant Travis were ready at the breastwork; the rest were frantically trying to assemble their gear and to muster out of range of Captain Squire's gunners.

The last stretch of the causeway, about 160 yards in length, offered not so much as a single tree's protection and dropped off into low and oozing swamp on either side. Out into the open came the grenadiers, bayonets fixed, pacing to the thud of their drums, along a road which, for some, stretched to eternity. After an initial ragged volley of musketry the breastwork was silent; Travis was holding his fire. For the unseasoned Virgin-ians, the waiting and the watching, as the red wall moved inexorably toward them, would be remembered for the rest of their lives. Twenty-five muskets were aimed at Captain Fordyce and the six men of his front rank, and at fifty yards Travis gave the order to fire. At that first volley Fordyce went down with a

[2] Benjamin Rush, *The Autobiography of Benjamin Rush; his "Trav-els through life" together with his Commonplace Book for 1789–1813*, George W. Corner, ed. (Princeton, 1948), 156.

bullet in his knee, and for a moment the grenadiers faltered. But plucking a handkerchief from his wrist and wrapping it round his wound Fordyce stood up, urging his men onward and shouting that the day was theirs. With blood and mud staining his gaiters he staggered forward to regain his place at the head of the column. Another volley thundered out from the breastwork, and although their targets were now obscured by smoke, the range was short enough for even the most nervous of marksmen to strike with every ball. Shot after shot tore into Fordyce and toppled the men behind him like a reaper in a field of corn; but still they came on. It was said that Fordyce had his hand on the breastwork before he was finally stopped. When he fell the mutilated column broke and reeled back across the causeway, taking with it as many of its dead and wounded as it could carry or could find amid the pall of sulfur-laden smoke that blanketed the road.

By this time Colonel Woodford had reinforced the breastwork and poured a fierce fire into the retreating grenadiers, while Colonel Stephen and his Culpeper riflemen had moved round to westward into previously prepared entrenchments to bring an equally murderous fire to bear on the British flank. The battle was now fifteen minutes old. Captain Leslie did what he could to consolidate his bleeding forces, but penned in on the "island" they could only move forward to certain slaughter or retreat back over the bridge to the fort. It was not much of a choice, and after holding his ground for a further costly quarter of an hour, Leslie pulled back, dragging his cannon with him. Colonel Woodford, not wishing to play the British at their own rash game, decided not to follow up his advantage and refused to let his men pursue their enemy.

The battle was over. It was time for both sides to count the cost. For the Virginians, the price was one man (possibly Captain Thomas Nash, of Gosport) wounded in the hand, but for the British it was disastrous. Captain Fordyce still lay in front of the breastwork, shot, it was said, by as many as eighteen bullets. More dead and wounded were scattered along the causeway, some lying like grotesque robins half in and half out of the swamp. Wrote one Virginian: "I then saw the horrors of war in perfection, worse than can be imagin'd; 10 and 12 bullets thro' many; limbs broke in 2 or 3 places; brains turned out. Good God, what a sight!" [3] As soon as it became evident that the British had had enough, Colonel Woodford sent an officer out under a flag of truce, offering to bring in the casualties if Captain Leslie would hold his fire. This he readily agreed to do, and he came out of the fort to bow his thanks to Woodford.

Twelve dead were brought in by the patriots as well as seventeen wounded, the latter including Lieutenant Batut shot through the leg. The list of the grenadiers' wounds is, perhaps, the most eloquent testimony to what it must have been like to have marched in their forward ranks:

1. Wm. Chalmers—in the Leg & Knee—Ball lodged in the Leg—no Fracture
2. Saml. Windsor—in ye Thigh—no Ball lodged—nor Fracture
3. Wm. Stokes—in ye Thigh—Ball passed thro without Fracture
4. Thomas Brisson—in ye Leg & Knee, passed thro' Bone much shattered
5. Stephen Chislet—in the Thigh—pass'd thro'—Bone Fractured
6. Richard Abbot—in both Thighs—one with Ball lodged & bone shattered—the other passed thro, & no fracture
7. Edwd Villis—in the Thigh, arm & Belly—Ball lodged in his Bowels—judged mortal [4]

and so on through the sixteen names.

According to one account the wounded were terrified that

---

[3] Richard Kidder Meade to Richard Bland from "Norfolk Town Camp," Dec. 18; *Bland Papers*, 39.

[4] List of wounded prisoners compiled by Dr. W. Browne, enclosed with Woodford to Pendleton, December 10; *RCHP*, I, pp. 117–18.

they were about to be scalped "and called out, FOR GOD'S SAKE, DO NOT MURDER US." [5] Lord Dunmore had supposedly warned them that this would be their fate if they should fall into the hands of the shirtmen. But if they really did expect to lose their hair (which is doubtful) they soon found that their captors "shewed the greatest humanity and tenderness." [6] Their treatment was the best that could be managed under the circumstances—considering that the American surgeon's baggage and medicines were still in Williamsburg. The twelve dead grenadiers were interred with suitable reverence, while Captain Fordyce was given a burial with full military honors. There was not a patriot present who did not gladly and loudly attest to his bravery. It was agreed that he and his men had deserved a better fate: "they fought, bled, and died, like Englishmen," [7] and had they done so in a different cause they would have been considered heroes. Helen Maxwell stated years later that prior to the battle, Fordyce had given "his watch to his friend [Mr. Maxwell?], with a message for his wife, for he knew, as he said, that he was going to his death." [8]

From the equipment left behind on the causeway, the patriots guessed that at least two more commissioned officers had been killed, for among the arms recovered were three officers' light muskets and three silver-mounted cartridge boxes. Their deduction proved to be right, for in addition to Captain Fordyce, whose body could not be reached, those of Lieutenants William Napier and Peter Leslie were carried back to the fort. In his first short report, written only hours after the engagement, Woodford estimated that the British losses "must be upwards of 50." [9]

No more firing was heard that day, though the patriots remained under arms expecting another attack, possibly by "a

---

[5] *Virginia Gazette* (Pinkney), December 23.
[6] Ibid.
[7] Meade to Bland, Dec. 18; *Bland Papers*, 39.
[8] Maxwell, "My Mother," *LNCVA*, II, 137.
[9] Woodford to Pendleton, Dec. 9; *RCHP*, I, 115.

Reinforcement of Highlanders," [1] which, according to prisoners, had just been added to Lord Dunmore's forces. These were, as it turned out, just another manifestation of the fictitious aid which was supposed to have reached him aboard the two newly arrived ships. Perhaps, if Colonel Woodford had known that the Highlanders were largely emigrant servants rather than soldiers, he might have been tempted to send Colonel Scott across the branch once again to prevent the British from retreating to their Norfolk entrenchments. Instead he did nothing, and, as the early December night slowly curtained the British fort, he believed that the stalemate would be resumed until his cannon arrived from Carolina. But once again Woodford was in for a surprise, for when morning came it looked as though the British had slipped away as wholly undetected as they had arrived.

Cautiously Woodford's advance party moved out across the causeway onto the still smoldering "island," but not a single shot came their way. The planks thrown across the bridge trestles were still there, but there was no smoke from the familiar cooking fires inside the fort, not the sound of a voice or so much as the jingle of a harness. The scouts crossed the bridge and circled the fort. There was no trick, no Trojan horse; the regulars, Tories, Negroes, all had gone. Six cannon had been left behind, each with a spike driven through its touchhole. Other abandoned stores comprised "7 guns, 4 of which indifferent; 1 bayonet; 29 spades; 2 shovels; . . . a few shot; some bedding; part of a hogshead of rum; 2 or more barrels, contents unknown, supposed to be rum; 2 barrels of bread; about 20 quarters of beef; about a box and a half of candles; 4 or 5 dozen quart bottles; 4 or 5 iron pots; a few axes; some old lumber." [2]

It seemed that the enemy had been hurt far more grievously than Woodford had initially supposed. "From the vast effusion of blood on ye bridge & in the Fort," he now wrote, "from the Accounts of the Centries who saw many bodies carried out of ye

[1] Ibid.
[2] Burk, *History of Virginia*, IV, Appendix 9.

Fort to be inter'd, & other circumstances I conceived their loss
to be much greater than I thought it yesterday, & the victory to
be complete." [3] In his report to the convention, written on the
same day, Woodford declared: "This was a second *Bunker's
Hill* affair, in miniature, with this difference that we kept our
post and had only one man wounded in the hand." [4] The
analogy was a fair one, and for the Virginians, who had been
asking for some achievement comparable to the Battle of
Lexington to start them off on the right foot, the victory at
Great Bridge was all and more than they could have hoped it to
be.

Besides the stores found in the fort, the loot picked up along
the causeway and stripped from the British dead included (in
addition to the officers' guns already mentioned) "24 well fixed
muskets with bayonets; 28 cartouch boxes and pouches; 3 silver
mounted cartouch boxes; 2 common ditto; 2 bayonet-belts; 27
caps; 2 hats; 1 barrel with powder and cartridges; one silk
handkerchief with linnen in it; 2 watches; cash 12s. 6d; 1 pair
of gloves; 4 stocks and buckles; 1 pair of silver shoe buckles; 3
pair ditto knee ditto; 2 snuff boxes; 10 knives; 1 barrel with ball
and oakum; 12 coats; 12 waistcoats; 11 pair of shoes; 12 pair of
garters, 1 pair of breeches; 1 shirt; 1 pair of stockings; a parcel
of old knee buckles; 1 black handkerchief." [5] This poignant list
is filled with information, though we, unfortunately, are incapable of accurately interpreting it. It might seem that Captain
Fordyce was buried in his uniform, but it is likely that his
corpse first suffered the indignity of having its pockets rifled,
and his snuff box, handkerchief, and silver buckles taken from
it. The twelve grenadiers were stripped of their coats and
waistcoats, but all save one were interred in their shirts and
breeches. The fact that one shirt and one pair of breeches were
among the prizes might suggest that it was not consideration for
the dead that left eleven bodies partially clothed, but rather

[3] Woodford to Pendleton, Dec. 10; *RCHP*, I, 116.
[4] Ibid., 120.
[5] Burk, *History of Virginia*, IV, Appendix 9.

that the clothes were badly bloodstained. The same reason may
have left one man with his shoes, for it is hard to imagine that
any other reason would have prevented the patriots from taking
them. Only four days before, Colonel Woodford had written to
Pendleton asking for shoes for his men, saying that some were
already in dire need and that before long the entire army would
find itself inadequately shod.

Enclosed with Colonel Woodford's reports and lists of
British losses was the Virginians' full tally of sick and wounded,
seven men in all: one shot in the thigh, another in the wrist, and
all the rest struck down, not by the British but by nature—one
with a cyst on his hand, and the remainder hospitalized in the
church at Great Bridge with colds. One of the latter deserves to
be remembered; he was listed as "in ye church—this day—has a
cold a slight Pleuratic complaint." [6] His name was Adam
Cough.

A report reaching Colonel Woodford from Norfolk on
December 11 put the British losses at 102 killed and wounded.
Assuming that only the regulars fought at Great Bridge, it
sounded as though the Virginia contingent of the Fourteenth
Foot had virtually been destroyed. This was a distinct exaggeration; the actual losses being three officers killed, one wounded,
three sergeants and two drummers wounded, and fourteen
privates killed and forty-three wounded. Nevertheless, it was a
stunning blow to Lord Dunmore's aspirations. But worse still
was the loss of the fort, for the road was now open to Norfolk.

Captain Leslie had only waited for darkness before pulling
out, having made up his mind to withdraw almost as soon as the
battle was over. Dunmore's explanation of this decision suggested that Captain Leslie's judgment was impaired by his grief
at the death of his nephew, adding that Leslie expected that the
enemy would be "so elated at this little advantage they had
gained over us" that they would "force their way a cross the
branch, either above or below, and by that means cut off the

<hr>

[6] "List of Sick and wounded Provincials" prepared by Dr. W. Browne
and enclosed with Woodford to Pendleton, Dec. 10; *RCHP*, I, 119.

communication between us." [7] Grieving or not, there was logic in this possibility, perhaps more than there was in Woodford's rejection of it.

Had there really been a shipload of eager Highlanders ready for the fray, Captain Leslie might have been expected to have stood his ground, but he knew very well that virtually all Lord Dunmore's eggs were in this frail wooden basket. The only reasonable course would be to withdraw to the recently dug defenses of Norfolk and there ensure that the newly recruited loyalists were given the leadership they needed to keep them steadfast.

At about seven on December 9 the British withdrew from Great Bridge, the wounded piled groaning on the baggage wagons. Shortly before midnight they reached Norfolk, the news of their approach and their defeat having run ahead of them. Helen Maxwell watched the wagons and carts go by "with the poor creatures in them, crying water, water,—and I and the young women," she recalled, "moved with pity went out and carried them pitchers of water, which they drank with a rabid thirst which it seemed impossible to satisfy." [8]

The effect of this melancholy progress on the Tories of Norfolk and Princess Anne counties was immediate and predictable: they took to their heels. The realization that they had backed the wrong side was made the more unequivocal by the fact that the British regulars, instead of taking up defensive positions around Norfolk, immediately "embarked on board ships prepared for that purpose." [9] The seemingly abandoned loyalists were in despair, each embowelled upon his own visions of his impending fate at the hands of the patriots. Those who could, took to the water in every merchant vessel available, seeking protection behind the guns of Captain Squire's warships; the rest did their best to melt into the landscape, tearing

[7] Dunmore to Dartmouth, Dec. 13; PRO,CO 5/1353.

[8] Maxwell, "My Mother," *LNCVA*, II, 138.

[9] Extract from a letter by a midshipman aboard the *Otter*, Jan. 9, 1776; *American Archives*, 4th ser., IV, 540.

off their red badges and pretending that they were really the
truest and bluest of patriots. Lord Dunmore consoled himself by
trying to believe that if help should even now arrive from Boston
or St. Augustine, his Loyal Virginians "possibly may be
induced to return to their Trenches." [1] But one doubts whether
even he would have been prepared to wager the smallest bet on
it.

By some curious accident, the mantle of Macbeth seems to
have hovered throughout the year around the shoulders of Lord
Dunmore. It began with the witches' opening lines of Act I,
Scene i, scrawled on a pillar of the Capitol, followed him
through the tragic ferment of rebellion, and now forced him into
a parody of Act V, Scene v, when, according to an informer who
was there when Dunmore received news of the battle, "he
Raved like the madman he is, & swore to Hang the Boy that
gave the Information this Day." [2]

The few Norfolk inhabitants still in the town by morning
expected every minute to hear that the head of Woodford's
column was in sight. But they did not, and it was not. It had
taken a while for the shirtmen to realize that the fort was theirs,
and even longer to decide what to do next. Woodford's decision
was still to do nothing, and two days after the battle he rather
nonchalantly wrote to Edmund Pendleton saying: "I forgot in
my letter of yesterday to inform the Honble the Convention that
my small stock of Provisions had induced me to dispatch most
of my waggons to Suffolk & Cabbin point for Flour &c, & not
foreseeing this Luckey attempt of the Enemy (which fortune
has thrown in my way) render'd it impossible to march with any
stores & Baggage." [3] So he stayed where he was. Later in the
same letter, Woodford seemingly contradicted himself, saying
that his men had now so nearly finished repairing the causeway
and bridge that they would be passable by nightfall. If reports
that the Norfolk Tories had fled were true, he would imme-

---

[1] Dunmore to Dartmouth, Dec. 13, PRO,CO 5/1353.
[2] Woodford to Pendleton, Dec. 11; *RCHP*, I, 121.
[3] Ibid.

diately advance and "leave our Baggage to come up." It seems curious that the British could advance and retreat across the causeway and bridge and yet Woodford could not, and odder still that in one breath he declared that he could not move without his baggage wagons and in the next that he could. It is true that Woodford was the custodian of patriot hopes, a responsibility as heavy as that of being a military commander; but nonetheless, at this crucial moment, a mite more initiative could have served Virginia well.

The first major Carolina reinforcement reached Great Bridge on December 10, and they proved to be as rag, tag, and bobtail a lot as Colonel Woodford had feared. There were 250 of them, "compos'd of Regulars, Minute Men, Militia & Volunteers, badly armed, with only 15 rounds of cartridge pr man. their large quantity of powder turn'd out to be only 30 lbs. They brought 6 honeycomb'd Cannon, almost useless, and most of them rather inferior to the horrizontal pointed pieces planted in the streets of Wmsburg." [4] There was still no sign of Colonel Howe and his main Carolinian force, though the letters that Woodford had received from him left no doubt that he was on his way and that if his commission should be of earlier date than Woodford's he would expect to take command of the combined army. Seemingly without rancor, Woodford wrote that his regard for his "unhappy Country" was such that before it should be injured by any squabble over seniority, he would relinquish the command to Howe "or any other Gentleman of merit." [5] Two days later Howe arrived, complete with 340 poorly armed but "tolerable good men" [6]—and seniority.

In the meantime Colonel Woodford kept busy writing letters, receiving doubtful intelligence from dubious informants, and listening to the pleas of neighboring inhabitants. On December 11 he had issued a proclamation calling on the people of Princess Anne and Norfolk counties to come out of the

[4] Woodford to Pendleton, Dec. 10; ibid., 116.
[5] Ibid., 117.
[6] Woodford to Pendleton, Dec. 12; ibid., 122.

woodwork and to give aid to the patriot forces; in exchange Woodford assured them of his protection. This produced an almost nauseating petition from the inhabitants of Norfolk, who, with cap in hand, "humbly sheweth That your poor unfortunate petitioners have at all times wished for Liberty and have upholded the same as far as their ability lay and now & at all times ever ready to comply with the same to the utmost of our endeavours. . . . Therefore your poor petitioners humbly craveth your protection & advice so that we may remain in safety as true Sons of Liberty. . . ." [7]

On the same day Woodford also received an equally humble petition from the Scots emigrants whom Dunmore had turned off their ship, the *Lord Donluce*, and had left to their fate in Norfolk. It was the petition, they claimed, "of upwards of 250 Neutrals," who "not being acquainted with the art of warr are all now lying in a deplorable Condition and must all certainly suffer unless relieved By your Honourable Protection." [8] They asked to be allowed to continue their journey overland to Cape Fear, where they were to settle. This and all the other requests were duly sent back to Williamsburg for the convention to approve or reject. Meanwhile Woodford detained the individuals who had brought them. He did not, however, hold Lord Dunmore's emissary, Lieutenant Wallace, who came under a flag of truce, carrying a proposal for the exchange of prisoners. But this, too, was referred to the convention.

Colonel Woodford's first punitive move had been to send Colonel Stephen forward to Kemp's Landing with a force of six companies to secure the village and round up "every person in that neighbourhood that had left Norfolk since the Battle of the great Bridge." [9] The project proved rewarding and yielded a

[7] Petition addressed: "To the Right Honourable Army Intitled the Sons of Liberty & property in & over the Colony & Dominion of Virginia &c.," enclosed with Woodford to Pendleton, Dec. 12; ibid., 123.

[8] Petition enclosed with the same letter and addressed as above though with spelling variations; ibid., 124.

[9] Woodford to Pendleton, Dec. 12; *RCHP*, I, 121.

motley array of onetime loyalists. Each of those proved to have been active on Lord Dunmore's behalf was handcuffed to one of his "Black Brothers," which, Woodford declared, "is the Resolution I have taken, shall be the fate of all those Cattle" [1] until the convention should instruct him what to do with them.

On the evening of December 14, still led by Woodford (and still without its baggage), the patriot army of about 1,275 men, moved unopposed into Norfolk. Colonel Scott called it "the most horrid place I ever beheld," [2] and Howe regretted that they had met with no resistance and so could not treat it as it deserved. "Had I not pass'd thro' Princess Anne & Norfolk counties I could not have believed," he wrote, "that a colony so truly Respectable as this in every other Part, could have belonging to it, so contemptible a lot of wretches. We were receiv'd," he went on, "with a servility disgraceful to Humanity, and worthy only of those who lost to every sense of publick virtue or private Honour . . . become willing Instruments in the hands of government to anihilate the liberty of their country." [3]

Earlier in the day Woodford and Howe had sent a joint message to the mayor and inhabitants of Norfolk, telling them of their impending arrival and saying that the people's property would be respected providing that the patriots were not opposed. They were furious when they later discovered that the message had been immediately taken to Lord Dunmore to see what he thought of it. Although the patriots got their assurance of compliance, there was shooting during the night that wounded three shirtmen. No one was sure who did it or where it came from, though some said from the houses, causing Woodford to write to the convention, saying that it "may be assured the Town of Norfolk deserves no favour." [4] On December 16 Howe

---

[1] Ibid., 122.

[2] Scott to Captain Southall, from Norfolk, Dec. 17; *American Archives*, 4th ser., IV, 292.

[3] Howe to Pendleton, from Norfolk, apparently incorrectly dated Dec. 13; *RCHP*, I, 125.

[4] Woodford to Pendleton, from Norfolk, Dec. 14; ibid., 128.

and Woodford wrote jointly, asking that the convention should make up its mind whether to fortify Norfolk as an American base or whether it should be "Totally distroy'd to prevent its furnishing the Enemy with good Barracks for six or seven Thousand Troops." [5]

It will be noticed that it was now "Howe and Woodford" who signed the dispatches rather than the other way round. The day after their arrival in Norfolk the two men examined their commissions and, to no one's surprise, found that Howe's was of longer standing. He therefore was now in command of Virginia's army, and Woodford wrote to Pendleton as president of the convention, asking for leave of absence to see his family and to attend to his personal affairs. Earlier, on December 12, the convention had unanimously resolved that it approved of Woodford's conduct as well as of the prowess of the Virginians who had fought at the bridge.

Unfortunately applause warms the clapper more than it does the recipient, and the patriot army in Norfolk was chilled to its bones. Its baggage seemed incapable of traveling the twelve miles from Great Bridge, the weather was not only bitterly cold but snow was beginning to fall, and there was not nearly enough food to go around. The Tories who had escaped to the ships were safe but equally unhappy. "It is a melancholy sight," wrote Lord Dunmore, "to see the numbers of Gentlemen of very large property with their Ladies and whole families obliged to betake themselves on board of Ships, at this Season of the year, hardly with the common necessary of Life, and great numbers of poor people without even these, who must have perished had I not been able to supply them with some flour, which I had purchased for His Majesty's service some time ago." [6] The distribution of a few of the Tory families is known, but the majority are as anonymous as the wretched river craft and packet boats on which they found themselves. The prosper-

[5] Howe and Woodford to Pendleton, Dec. 16; ibid., 131.
[6] Dunmore to Dartmouth, Dec. 13; PRO,CO 5/1353.

ous Andrew Sprowle of Gosport shared the brigantine *Hammond* with John Hunter; Jonathon Eilbeck, whose best ship now housed Lord Dunmore, put his family aboard the sloop *Peace and Plenty;* John Goodrich and Robert Shedden and their relatives were scattered through three small sloops; John Brown and his family shared two schooners; while Neil Jamieson was ensconced on his brigantine the *Fincastle*, presumably named after the noble father of his misfortune, the Viscount Fincastle and fourth Earl of Dunmore. Those Tories who did not have ships of their own, but who were on close and good terms with the officers of the navy, managed to obtain berths aboard the warships. Among these was our old and loquacious friend James Parker, who found safety on the *Kingfisher*.

While, on the night of December 14, the patriots were complaining that they had been fired on in the town, Captain Squire was enraged to see a number of balls shot at the *Otter*. Next morning he sent a midshipman ashore to warn Woodford or Howe (or whoever might be in command) that their men had only to loose off one more round at the King's ships and "they must expect the town to be knocked about their ears." [7] Colonels Howe and Woodford returned their compliments to Captain Squire, assuring him that they had given no such order and that they supposed that the shots must have come from their guard, "who fired by mistake upon one of our own parties." [8] It was apparent, as is so often the case, that there was a shortage of discipline among the victors. Later, Dunmore, in one of his more purple passages, would speak of the patriots' "many excesses such as Robbing, plundering and Ravishing young Women before their Parents." [9] This was, perhaps, an attempt to match the Virginians' accusations of his treatment of the girl from the Norfolk poorhouse, as well as for Pinkney's statement

[7] Extract from the midshipman's letter, Jan. 9, 1776, *American Archives*, 4th ser., IV, 540.

[8] *Virginia Gazette* (Pinkney), Dec. 20.

[9] Dunmore to Secretary of State, Feb. 13, 1776; PRO,CO 5/1353.

that all the emigrant Highlanders had been able to escape from Dunmore's clutches save for "two maidens, who were detained as bedmakers to his Lordship." [1]

Three days after it had arrived in Norfolk the patriot army was still in disarray, in part because of its changed command, but more because it was uncertain about what it was supposed to be doing. Wrote Colonel Scott: "Duty is harder than ever I saw before. Our guard has not been relieved for forty-eight hours." [2] The North Carolinians had marched all this way only to find that they were too late to participate in the Battle of Great Bridge and that now they were expected to sit around in Norfolk doing nothing, watching the enemy bobbing about in their boats in easy range of their rifles. A steady stream of small craft pulled back and forth between Dunmore's motley fleet and the harbor. "Flags are continually passing," wrote Scott, "asking water, provision, or to exchange prisoners." [3] Captain Squire demanded to know whether it was the Americans' intention to deny the King's ships essential food and water, to which Howe replied that it was his purpose to prevent any relationship between the port and the ships. Attempts to work out an exchange of prisoners fared no better. Dunmore proposed a straight swap, officer for officer, private for private, but Howe would have none of it, pointing out that he "could by no means submit to place the officers and soldiers of the army, who have been taken in battle, upon a footing with those officers of militia and the peasants that you have thought proper to deprive of their liberty." [4] Instead, he offered to exchange these lesser warriors for Tories of similar station who had been picked up at Kemp's Landing and elsewhere since the Battle of Great Bridge. This was not at all what his Lordship had in mind, and the negotiations thereupon collapsed.

[1] *Virginia Gazette*, Dec. 30.

[2] Scott to Captain Southall, Dec. 17; *American Archives*, 4th ser., IV, 292.

[3] Ibid.

[4] *Virginia Gazette* (Dixon & Hunter), Jan. 6, 1776.

It was apparent that there was going to be very little rapport between Howe and Dunmore, the former having demonstrated from the outset that he had come to Virginia to fight a war and not as a diplomat intent on healing the rift between the colony and its governor. Even before Howe had taken command he had written to the Virginia convention informing it that his scouts had reported that a British man-of-war and a large brig had been spotted in the Chesapeake Bay. "This may probably give us something to do," he wrote with obvious relish, "and I hope we may execute it properly." [5]

On the afternoon of December 17 Howe had his first opportunity to score off the British. It came about not through any carefully laid scheme but as a result of another of those unfortunate errors to which Lord Dunmore's forces were currently prone. Watched by idle patriots on the Norfolk wharves, the two men-of-war, *Otter* and *Kingfisher*, had hoisted sail and set out for the distillery, where supplies of water could be obtained. Their guns had hitherto protected a recently seized prize, a snow laden with 4,000 bushels of salt, and when the warships moved off they ordered the snow to follow. She, however, was slow off the mark and quickly found herself parted from her captors and a sitting duck for patriot marksmen. The shore guard ordered her to remain where she was, and the *Kingfisher* sent back a boat loaded with fifteen men to make sure that she moved. The officer of the guard called on the British boat to turn back or be fired on, and, having played this game before at Burwell's Ferry on the James, the boat returned to the man-of-war, leaving the snow and its precious cargo in patriot hands. The ship was subsequently moored alongside one of the wharves, and Colonel Howe ordered that the cargo should be bagged up and removed to a warehouse out of range of British guns. This was hard to accomplish as there were neither bags nor warehouse immediately available; consequently the salt was left on board. A more readily portable bonus

[5] Howe to Virginia convention, Dec. 13; *RCHP*, I, 126.

prize was found on the ship in the shape of Mr. Cary Mitchell, the Lower James River customs collector, who had escaped from Hampton in October to join Lord Dunmore. He was extracted, along with his official papers, loudly declaring that his involvement with the governor was all a ghastly mistake.

The next day Captain Squire sent a message to colonels Howe and Woodford claiming that the snow (now described as a brig) was a prize belonging to the King and that it was to be instantly released. He added that he would be sending a boat over to bring the ship off and that if anyone shot at it he would "most assuredly fire on the town." [6] Once again Howe and Woodford presented their compliments to Captain Squire and said that they would "give orders to fire upon any boat that attempts to take her away." [7] If Squire was bluffing, he had been called, and it seemed that he was, for no further attempt was made to retrieve the salt ship. There is reason to believe that neither Howe nor Woodford cared whether he was or was not bluffing and that they were anxious to push the British into a fight. Wrote Woodford in tones much more aggressive now that Howe was in command: "My observation about the Salt Vessell is likely to bring on the dispute I expected." [8]

As we have seen, the patriot army did not relish this period of cold inactivity, and if Dunmore could be provoked into firing on Norfolk the shirtmen would have an opportunity to let off steam, and, if anything dire should happen to the town in the process, no one would be to blame but his Lordship. The problems of keeping the men in line had not been resolved as easily as Colonel Woodford had hoped. The various companies still thought of themselves as independent units rather than parts of one army, an impression that was not helped by the presence of the Carolinians or by the contingent from Patrick Henry's First Regiment. Matters were made worse by the fact that the officers were more difficult to control than their men.

---

[6] *Virginia Gazette* (Purdie), Dec. 22.
[7] Ibid.
[8] Woodford to Pendleton, Dec. 19; *RCHP*, I, 134.

Wrote Woodford: "I am extreemly sorry to think it my Duty to inform the Convention that the service begins to be very Irksome to some of the Officers, & I have several applications to Day for leave of absence, which I thought inconsistant with the good of the service to grant—upon which they desired leave to Resign—this I likewise thought it my Duty to refuse—I have done every thing in my power to keep all easy, & have had great Reason to complain before. . . . one Gentleman thinks himself Ill used if he is not allow'd to do this, another chuses to Judge for himself in other Instances, the men I fear will follow this bad example & where it will end is hard for me to say." [9]

While Woodford was finding himself in a somewhat unhappy position at Norfolk, Patrick Henry was faring better at Hampton. He had gone there simply to inspect the militia's preparedness, but shortly after he left, a rash of successes followed, and these he could claim as the product of his visit. On the evening of December 22 an express reached Henry informing him that a Hampton armed pilot boat had captured two vessels laden with 4,600 bushels of salt, as well as another empty craft bound for the Eastern Shore region in search of provisions, aboard which was seized a crew of fifteen Negroes. The busy pilot boat commanded by Captain Barron was even now out again, in appalling weather, in pursuit of a British tender, which had been seen at anchor between the lighthouse point and the mouth of the York river. A party of twelve riflemen under Captain Alexander of Henry's regiment set out overland, and once again, without their stirring, the prey fell into the Virginians' laps. In the course of the night, "which was exceedingly tempestuous" [1] and snowing hard, the tender was forced to cut her cable and subsequently drifted ashore. The crew of fourteen whites and two Negroes, thankful to be alive, promptly fled but were pursued by Alexander's men and eventually rounded up. The tender remained stuck fast on the beach, but as the storm continued into the morning, the waves

[9] Ibid., 135.

[1] *Virginia Gazette* (Pinkney), Dec. 30.

were constantly breaking over her and she was in danger of going to pieces. The Virginia riflemen therefore waded out to her and, after being several times swept off their feet into the icy water, managed to clamber aboard. There they found twenty-four stand of arms as well as some new British uniforms. A few days later, on December 27, another prize was brought into Hampton: "a sloop (in ballast) capt. Bartlett Goodrich, who has been 20 days only from St. Eustatius." [2] While the content of his hold may have been disappointing, it was expected that he himself would be brim full of fascinating family secrets.

That Henry had some news of his own to report to the convention must have given him considerable satisfaction, as also must Colonel Woodford's discomfiture and loss of command at Norfolk. On the same night that Henry heard of Captain Barron's successes at Hampton the convention finally made up its mind about Henry's complaint that he had been bypassed by Woodford. It unanimously agreed that Woodford, though "acting under a separate and detached command, ought to correspond with Colonel Henry" [3] and make returns to him regarding the activities and state of his forces. Furthermore Woodford was to be subject to Henry's orders whenever the convention or the Committee of Safety was not in session. The delegates assured themselves that they had created a statesman-like resolution that would keep Henry happy. One is almost forced to suppose, therefore, that they thought him an idiot (which he assuredly was not), for everyone knew that when the convention was not in session, the Committee of Safety was—it had been specifically set up for that purpose. Thus the resolution continued to deny Commander in Chief Henry the authority to command, but it did so in such equivocal terms that its framers seemed to be mocking him.

The two British ships that Colonel Howe had reported as being sighted in the Bay on December 13 finally joined Lord

[2] *Virginia Gazette* (Purdie), *Supplement*, Dec. 29.

[3] Mays, *Pendleton*, II, 80; quoting W. W. Henry, *Patrick Henry*, I, 343.

Dunmore's fleet on the twenty-first. The larger of them proved to be the *Liverpool* man-of-war commanded by Captain Henry Bellew, whose seniority gave him precedence over Captain Squire. The second vessel was a store ship loaded with arms and ammunition, and between them they carried some four hundred men. Colonel Howe's initial report had declared them to be crowded with men, and it was at once assumed that they were soldiers. But they were not—except for the usual complement of marines. Nevertheless, there was cause for considerable jubilation aboard the Dunmore fleet. "Norfolk, Hampton, and all the river settlements, are threatened with fire and sword," announced Purdie's *Virginia Gazette*. [4]

Lord Dunmore was advised of the *Liverpool*'s impending arrival on December 19, and the next day he went out to meet it aboard a pilot boat. It was then that the governor received his first official dispatches since May 30. Among them were the letters from Lord Dartmouth telling him of the arms delivery (July 22) and giving him leave to return to England if his position should become untenable. This last (August 2) was the most recent, and there was no denying that they were very old letters. Nevertheless, they did give Dunmore the words of approval that his ego and his conscience so ardently desired. He informed Captain Bellew of some of their contents, confessing to what Bellew already knew, that part of the arms shipment was to be made available to Governor Martin to help him in his pacification of North Carolina. Shortly after the *Liverpool*'s arrival a tender came from Martin asking for 3,000 stand of arms and ammunition in proportion. This was precisely the sum of the entire shipment, and it is probably just as well that no one has recorded Lord Dunmore's comments upon receiving the request. He later wrote to Lord Dartmouth (whom he still supposed to be at the head of American affairs): "I have sent him one third, which I do assure your Lordship goes to my heart for was I even now to receive reinforcement I am sure I could

[4] Dec. 22.

get men enough for double the Number of Arms left me." [5]

Lord Dunmore's almost pathological conviction that all would eventually be well was, in a way, his most valuable asset, for he had the resilience to spring back after suffering blows that would have felled more experienced commanders. Even now, after being driven from his last foothold in Virginia, Dunmore was still able to envisage a successful popular rising in support of the Crown—if only a few more troops could be spared him. He still imagined that Connolly's mission would somehow be carried out and that an army would come marching down from the Ohio to carry out the Dunmore plan to split the colonies in half. In the meantime, as he must have explained to Captain Bellew, there was satisfaction to be derived from the knowledge that his blockade was making the people of Virginia both poor and hungry. It was just too bad that it affected rebel, neutral, and loyalist alike. The price of sugar had risen from sixpence a pound to 4 or 5 shillings, and a bushel of salt, which a few months ago sold for 1 shilling, now sold for 15. His Lordship delightedly explained that the dearth of salt distressed the populace beyond measure "as they cannot without it either preserve the Cattle in the upper part of the Country that are alive, nor can they in the lower part of the Country cure the Meat they live upon during the whole of the Summer." Rum, too, had rocketed in price from a half crown a gallon to 12 and even 14 shillings. "I think the want of Rum," Dunmore observed, "will damp their Courage more ways than one." [6] We do not know what Captain Bellew thought of all this; but he was a loyal British officer who knew where his duty lay and could doubtless have been relied on to listen politely and even to throw in nods and knowing smiles at appropriate moments. There would be time for sober reflection after his spirited and loquacious visitor had departed.

The *Liverpool* and her attendant brig had first dropped anchor in sight of a popular landmark known as the "Pleasure

[5] Dunmore to Secretary of State, Jan. 4, 1776; PRO,CO 5/1353.
[6] Ibid.

House," near what is now Virginia Beach; on December 21 Bellew brought the ships through Hampton Roads into a broadside anchorage opposite the central section of Norfolk's wharves. He ordered the *Kingfisher* to station herself at the southern end of the town with the *Otter* between them. The *Dunmore* was to anchor off the northern extremity and thus complete a formidable array that left little doubt that it could serve the city of Norfolk most uncivilly should the occasion demand. For those rebels with an eye for such details, the threat was implicit in the fact that all four ships were riding with springs on their cables, a necessary step preparatory to opening fire while at anchor. Nevertheless, regardless of this show of force, as Dunmore himself noted, Captain Bellew was "unwilling to shed the blood of any of his Majesty's Subjects, and much more so that of the innocent." [7] He therefore sent a message ashore to Colonel Howe reminding him that "the Power which sent me hither only can recall me"; [8] in the meantime his men would have to be provisioned. He trusted, therefore, that Howe would not see fit to prevent his obtaining the supplies he needed. That note was written on Christmas Eve, and on the same day he received a stalling reply saying that Howe would have to discuss the request with his fellow officers and that Bellew could expect a formal answer by ten o'clock the next morning.

Colonel Howe's inclination was to let Bellew have what he needed; after all he was at the end of a long voyage and had had no part in any of Lord Dunmore's exploits, nor for that matter had he been involved in any of the colonies' disputes. Nevertheless, Howe decided that the decision should be made by the convention and not by him. The answer he eventually got back (not by ten the next morning) was equivocal in the extreme. It spoke of the colony's long-standing hospitality toward the gentlemen of the navy and how it had recently been sadly interrupted by the conduct of some elements of it toward the good people of Virginia. Bellew, the delegates noted, had said

[7] Ibid.

[8] Copy of Bellew to Howe enclosed with the above; ibid.

that "the effusion of the Blood of the Innocent and Helpless" was most distant from his desires. This sounded very much like a threat. Who, they wanted to know, "were the innocent and helpless whose blood this officer would not wish to shed?" In short, the convention was no more anxious to commit itself than was Howe. It ended up by saying that if Bellew would give his assurance that "he had come to Virginia on a friendly errand, he might depend on proper respect and attention; if, on the contrary, his design was to aid schemes and efforts inimical to the Colony, he must not blame the inhabitants of Virginia for totally declining to contribute towards their own destruction." [9]

Sea captains, particularly navy sea captains, have never been renowned for their command of the more delicate aspects of semantics. Captain Bellew knew, and the convention knew, that he had no alternative but to support the Crown's interests, and both were equally aware that they were not compatible with friendship toward the rebels. If Norfolk would not sell provisions to the *Liverpool* then Bellew would "be obliged by marauding parties to snatch from the indigent farmers of this colony those provisions they were so willing to purchase." [1] Howe, Woodford, and the gentlemen of the convention all waited for the bombarding of Norfolk to begin. So sure were they of the outcome that when Pendleton received a letter from Hampton dated December 29 saying that, the previous evening, heavy cannonading had been heard from the direction of Norfolk, it was at once deduced that the firing had been prompted by the convention's reply. There was a general sense of disappointment (officially concealed) when it was discovered that the gunfire had been nothing more than "a Christmas frolic between Lord Dunmore and the captains of the navy, upon visiting each other on board their ships." [2]

No one expected the stalemate to last very much longer; the question was simply how long could Henry Bellew keep his

[9] Burk, *History of Virginia*, IV, 100.
[1] Howe to Pendleton, Dec. 25; *RCHP*, I, 140.
[2] *Virginia Gazette* (Purdie), *Supplement*, Dec. 29.

temper. Reinforcements in the shape of 180 minutemen had reached Norfolk on Christmas Eve, and during the same week 350 had reported for duty at Hampton. They were more than enough to prevent Lord Dunmore from attempting a landing anywhere at the mouth of the James. Inflated with success, the shirtmen paraded around Norfolk and made an exaggerated performance of guarding the wharves abreast of the men-of-war. On December 30 Captain Bellew wrote the following short letter to Howe:

> As I hold it incompatable with the Honor of my Commission to suffer Men in Arms against their Sovereign and the Laws, to appear before His Majesty's Ships I desire you will cause your Centinals in the Town of Norfolk to avoid being seen, that Women and Children may not feel the effects of their Audacity, and it will not be imprudent if both were to leave the Town.
>
> I am, Sir, your most hble Servt
> Henry Bellew [3]

The same day, Colonel Howe replied with studied courtesy, saying: "Sir, I am too much an Officer to wish you to do anything incompatable with the Honor of your Commission, or to recede my self from any point which I conceive to be my duty. Under the force of reciprocal feelings consequences may ensue which each of us perhaps may wish to avoid." The sentries would not be withdrawn, and Howe asked only that the civilians be given time to remove themselves and their effects, "which to Night they have not." [4] This passing reference to the lateness of the hour suggests that Bellew did not receive his answer until New Year's Eve. It was a Sunday, hardly the moment to begin so distasteful a task as the destruction of a port which had taken nearly a century to build.

Nicholas Cresswell ended his year in Leesburg, having spent 1775 doing nothing "but wore out my clothes and

[3] Enclosed with Dunmore to Secretary of State, Jan. 4, 1776; PRO,CO 5/1353.
[4] Ibid.

constitution." For him, he wrote, "according to the present prospect of affairs, the New Year bears a forbidding aspect." [5] He planned to go home as soon as an opportunity presented itself, but it would not do so until eighteen months later. For John Harrower the year closed as it had begun, quietly working out his indenture and looking forward to the day when he could bring over his family and build a plantation of his own. It would never come; he died, still in servitude, in the spring of 1777.

On the broad stage of American hopes, December ended in disaster. The splendidly successful thrust into Canada that had followed the capture of Ticonderoga came to icy grief on the night of December 31 below the heights of Quebec. With General Montgomery killed and Arnold wounded, the American army, which had come so far and achieved so much, was put to rout and saw its dream of a Canadian conquest wafted away in the driving snow.

In London, on another stage, another aspiration was sorely wounded, not by a musket ball but by a dramatic critic's Parthian shot for 1775. A new production of the *Merchant of Venice* had opened on December 29 in the freshly remodeled Drury Lane and with a new young actress in the role of Portia. After admitting that the part was such that all an actress could do with it was to learn the lines and speak them clearly, the critic of the *Middlesex Journal* [6] decided that the young lady's performance "left no room to expect anything beyond mediocrity. Her figure and face," he informed his readers, "though agreeable, have nothing striking, her voice (that great requisite of all public speakers) is far from being favorable to her progress as an actress. It is feared she possesses a monotony not to be got rid of; there is also vulgarity in her tones. . . ." The name of the critic has long been forgotten; the young actress was Sarah Siddons.

As the star of Virginia's version of *Macbeth*, Lord Dunmore had at least two more scenes to play. His guns would fire on

[5] *Cresswell*, 134; Dec. 31.

[6] Dec. 30; quoted in Hampden, *Journal*, 238.

Norfolk at 3:15 P.M. on January 1; his shore party would set fire to the wharves, believing that the wind would confine the flames to that section of the town, but the shirtmen would seize the excuse to set a torch to the rest of it. Later in the year Dunmore would again grasp a precarious footing on Virginia soil, and again he would be pushed off it. Throughout the rest of the war, apparently driven by a self-tormenting need to prove himself, he would beg for the chance of a "come back." He would still be trying in the spring of 1782, six months after the last flourish and the final exeunt at Yorktown.

BIBLIOGRAPHY

(Books cited in full in the footnotes are not listed here.)

American Archives. 4th series. Vols. II, III, and IV. Washington, 1839, 1840, and 1843, respectively.

Annual Register or a View of the History, Politics, and Literature of the Year, 1774. London, 1775. Also, *Annual Register, 1775.* London, 1776.

"Aspinwall Papers." *Collections of the Massachusetts Historical Society,* edited by Thomas Aspinwall. 4th series, Vol. X. Cambridge, Mass., 1871.

BAILEY, N.: *An Universal Etymological Dictionary.* 3rd edition, London, 1737, and 13th edition, 1749.

BERWICK, KEITH BENNET: "Loyalties in Crisis: A Study of the Attitudes of Virginians in the Revolution." Unpublished Ph.D. dissertation, University of Chicago, 1959.

BEVERLEY, ROBERT: *History and Present State of Virginia, 1725,* edited by Louis B. Wright. Chapel Hill, N.C., 1947.

BLAND, THEODORICK: *The Bland Papers: Being a Selection from the Manuscripts of Colonel Theodorick Bland, Jr., of Prince George County, Virginia.* Petersburg, Va., 1840.

BRAND, JOHN: *Observations on the Popular Antiquities of Great Britain.* 3 vols. London, 1849.

BRUCE, PHILIP ALEXANDER: *The Virginia Plutarch.* 2 vols. Chapel Hill, N.C., 1929.

BURK, JOHN: *The History of Virginia from Its First Settlement to the Present Day.* 4 vols. Petersburg, Va., 1805.

CALEY, PERCY BURDELLE: "Dunmore: Colonial Governor of New York and Virginia, 1770–1782." Unpublished Ph.D. dissertation, University of Pittsburgh, 1939.

CAPPON, LESTER J., and STELLA F. DUFF: *Virginia Gazette Index, 1736–1780.* 2 vols. Williamsburg, Va., 1950.

CARSON, JANE: *Colonial Virginians at Play.* Colonial Williamsburg research department report, 1958.

———: *Lady Dunmore in Virginia.* Colonial Williamsburg
research department report, n.d.

CARTER, COLONEL LANDON: *The Diary of Colonel Landon
Carter of Sabine Hall, 1752–1778,* edited by Jack P.
Greene. 2 vols. Published for the Virginia Historical
Society. Charlottesville, 1965.

CHAMBERS, E.: *Cyclopaedia: or, an Universal Dictionary of
Arts and Sciences.* 2 vols. London, 1738.

CHAPELLE, HOWARD I.: *The History of American Sailing
Ships.* New York, 1935.

———: *The History of the American Sailing Navy, the Ships
and Their Development.* New York, 1949.

CHASTELLUX, FRANÇOIS-JEAN, MARQUIS DE: *Travels in North
America in the Years 1780, 1781 and 1782,* edited by
Howard C. Rice, Jr. 2 vols. Chapel Hill, N.C., 1963.

COLDEN, CADWALLADER: "The Colden Letter Books." *Collections of the New-York Historical Society.* Vol. X. New
York, 1878.

CRESSWELL, NICHOLAS: *Journal of Nicholas Cresswell, 1774–
1777.* New York, 1924. Also London, 1928, same pagina-
tion. MS now owned by Colonial Williamsburg, Inc.

FITHIAN, PHILIP VICKERS: *The Journal and Letters of Philip
Vickers Fithian, 1773–1774,* edited by Hunter Dickinson
Farish. Williamsburg, 1957.

FORCE, PETER: *Tracts and Other Papers, Relating Principally
to the Origin, Settlement, and Progress of the Colonies in
North America, from the Discovery of the Country to the
Year 1776.* Vol. II. Washington, 1838.

FORD, WORTHINGTON CHAUNCEY: *British Officers Serving in
the American Revolution, 1774–1783.* Brooklyn, N.Y.,
1897.

GAGE, GENERAL THOMAS: *The Correspondence of General
Thomas Gage with the Secretaries of State, 1763–1775,*
edited by Clarence Edwin Carter. 2 vols. New Haven,
Conn., 1931.

*The Gentleman's Magazine and Historical Chronicle for the
Year M.DCCLXXV* (London) Vol. XLV (1776).

GOODWIN, RUTHERFOORD: *A Brief & True Report Concerning Williamsburg in Virginia.* Williamsburg, Va., 1941.

GRAY, ARTHUR P.: "Washington's Burgess Route," *Virginia*

Magazine of History and Biography (Richmond), Vol. XLVI, No. 4 (October 1938), pp. 299–315.

GRIFFITHS, ARTHUR: *The Chronicles of Newgate.* London, 1884.

HAMPDEN, JOHN: *An Eighteenth-Century Journal, 1774–1776.* London, 1940.

HARROWER, JOHN: *The Journal of John Harrower, 1773–1776,* edited by Edward Miles Riley. Williamsburg, Va., 1963.

HENRY, WILLIAM WIRT: *Patrick Henry, Life, Correspondence and Speeches.* 3 vols. New York, 1891.

Historical Records of the 14th Regiment, from its Formation in 1685 to 1892, edited by Captain H. O'Donnell. Devonport, England, 1892.

HONE, WILLIAM: *The Year Book of Daily Recreation and Information.* London, 1832.

JOHNSON, SIR WILLIAM: *The Papers of Sir William Johnson,* edited by Alexander C. Flick. Vols. VII and VIII. Albany, N.Y., 1931 and 1933.

JONES, JOHN SEAWELL: *Defence of the Revolutionary History of the State of North Carolina from the Aspersions of Mr. Jefferson.* Boston and Raleigh, N.C., 1834.

Journal of the House of Burgesses, 1773–1776, edited by John Pendleton Kennedy. Richmond, 1905.

LAWSON, CECIL P.: *A History of the Uniforms of the British Army.* 3 vols. New York, 1962.

Legislative Journals of the Council of Colonial Virginia, edited by H. R. McIlwaine. 3 vols. Richmond, Va., 1919.

MANUCY, ALBERT: *Artillery Through the Ages.* (National Park Service Interpretive Series, History No. 3.) Washington, 1955.

MARKS, ALFRED: *Tyburn Tree, Its History and Annals.* London, n.d.

MAXWELL, HELEN: "My Mother," *Lower Norfolk County Virginia Antiquary* (Baltimore), Vols. I and II (1897 and 1899). As dictated to her son, William Maxwell.

MAYO, CHARLES: *A Compendious View of Universal History from the Year 1753 to the Treaty of Amiens in 1802.* 4 vols. Bath, England, 1804.

MAYS, DAVID JOHN: *Edmund Pendleton, 1721–1803.* 2 vols. Cambridge, Mass., 1952.

MAZZEI, PHILIP: "Memoirs of the Life and Voyages of Doctor

Philip Mazzei," translated by E. C. Branchi, *William and Mary College Quarterly Historical Magazine* (Williamsburg), 2nd series, Vol. IX, No. 3 (July 1929) and No. 4 (October 1929).

NAMIER, SIR LEWIS: *Crossroads of Power*. New York, 1962.

Naval Documents of the American Revolution, edited by William Bell Clark. Vol. I (December 1, 1774, to September 2, 1775). Washington, 1964.

NEWMAN, ERIC P.: *Coinage for Colonial America*. New York: American Numismatic Society, 1956.

NORTON, JOHN, and others: *John Norton & Sons, Merchants of London and Virginia, 1750–1797*, edited by Frances Norton Mason. Richmond, 1937.

PARKER, JAMES: Letters to Charles Steuart, "Charles Steuart Papers, 1775–1776." MS. No. 5029 in the collection of the National Library of Scotland, Edinburgh.

PETERSON, HAROLD L.: *Arms and Armor in Colonial America, 1526–1783*. Harrisburg, Penna., 1956.

PHILLIPS, E.: *The New World of Words: Or a General English Dictionary*. London, 1671.

POWNALL, THOMAS: *A Topographical Description of the Dominions of the United States (1784)*, edited by Lois Mulkearn. Pittsburgh, 1949.

PREVOST, AUGUSTINE: Journal of Augustine Prevost, 1774. MS in London Library, London, England.

RANKIN, HUGH FRANKLIN: *The Theater in Colonial America*. Chapel Hill, N.C., 1965.

Report on the American Manuscripts in the Royal Institution of Great Britain. Vol. I. London: Historical Manuscripts Commission, 1904.

RIEDESEL, BARONESS VON: *Baroness von Riedesel and the American Revolution, Journal and Correspondence of a Tour of Duty, 1776–1783*, translated by Marvin L. Brown. Williamsburg, Va., 1965.

SCHLESINGER, ARTHUR M.: *Prelude to Independence, The Newspaper War on Britain, 1764–1776*. New York, 1958.

SHURTLEFF, HAROLD R.: "Research Report on the Governor's Palace." Colonial Williamsburg MS research report, 1930.

SMITH, ABBOT EMERSON: *Colonists in Bondage: White Servi-*

tude and Convict Labor in America, 1607–1776. Chapel Hill, N.C., 1947.

SMYTH, JOHN FERDINAND DALZIEL: "Smyth's Travels in Virginia, in 1773," *Virginia Historical Register and Literary Companion* (Richmond) Vol. VI, Nos. 1, 2 and 3 (1853); condensed from Smyth, *Tour in the United States of America.* London, 1784.

STONE, WILLIAM L.: *History of New York City from the Discovery to the Present Day.* New York, 1872.

SWEM, EARL G.: *Virginia Historical Index.* 2 vols. Roanoke, Va., 1934–36.

TATE, THAD W.: *The Negro in Eighteenth-Century Williamsburg.* Colonial Williamsburg research department report, 1957.

WASHINGTON, GEORGE: *The Diaries of George Washington, 1749–1799,* edited by John C. Fitzpatrick. 4 vols. Boston and New York, 1925.

———: *Writings of George Washington from the Original Manuscript Sources, 1745–1799,* edited by John C. Fitzpatrick. 39 vols. Washington, 1931.

WATERMAN, THOMAS TILESTON: *The Mansions of Virginia, 1706–1776.* Chapel Hill, N.C., 1946.

WERTENBAKER, THOMAS J.: *Norfolk, Historic Southern Port.* Durham, N.C., 1931.

WILSON, J. G.: *Memorial History of New York.* 4 vols. New York, 1892–93.

WIRT, WILLIAM: *Sketch of the Life and Character of Patrick Henry.* Philadelphia, 1817.

WORMELEY, RALPH: Wormeley Family Papers. Original MSS in the University of Virginia Library, Charlottesville, Virginia.

WRIGHT, LOUIS B.: *The Cultural Life of the American Colonies, 1607–1763.* New York, 1957.

INDEX

All place names are located in Virginia unless otherwise stated. Names of persons and places cited in the bibliographic footnotes are omitted.

A NOTE ABOUT THE AUTHOR

Ivor Noël Hume was born in London and studied at Framlingham College and St. Lawrence College in England. He served in the Indian Army during World War II. In 1949 Noël Hume joined the staff of the Guildhall Museum in London as an archaeologist. During the time he was at Guildhall, he was responsible for the recovery and recording of antiquities revealed as a result of wartime bombings in London. In February 1957 Noël Hume became chief archaeologist and in 1965 director of the Department of Archaeology of Colonial Williamsburg, Inc. In 1959 he became an honorary research associate of the Smithsonian Institution, a position he still holds. He is the author of *Here Lies Virginia*, published by Alfred A. Knopf in 1963, in which he tells the archaeological story of colonial Virginia by describing the excavations at Roanoke Island, N.C., and Jamestown, Yorktown, and Williamsburg, Va. He is also the author of three other books on archaeology and is presently engaged in writing a book on the techniques of historical archaeology.

A NOTE ON THE TYPE

The text of this book is set in Monticello, a Linotype revival of the original Binny & Ronaldson Roman No. 1, cut by Archibald Binny and cast in 1796 by that Philadelphia type foundry. The face was named Monticello in honor of its use in the monumental fifty-volume *Papers of Thomas Jefferson*, published by Princeton University Press. Monticello is a transitional type design, embodying certain features of Bulmer and Baskerville, but it is a distinguished face in its own right.

Typography and binding by
GUY FLEMING